the
challenge
of german
literature

the challenge of german literature

Edited by

Horst S. Daemmrich WAYNE STATE UNIVERSITY

&

Diether H. Haenicke WAYNE STATE UNIVERSITY

Wayne State University Press

Detroit, 1971

Published simultaneously in Canada
by The Copp Clark Publishing Company
517 Wellington Street, West
Toronto 2B, Canada.
Library of Congress Catalog Card Number 75-131425
International Standard Book Number 0-8143-1435x

This publication is in part supported by funds contributed
in honor of Harold A. Basilius, Director of the Wayne State
University Press, who retired July 1, 1970.

to Harold A. Basilius
humanist, teacher, scholar

Contents 🍃

Preface 🍃

The present volume is primarily intended for the American reader and for students of the humanities. In tracing the main currents in German literature it seeks to show a continuum of specific themes and forms which affected Germany as well as the Western world. The contributors have tried to incorporate in their presentations the conclusions reached by the best authorities in the field. They never hesitated, however, to express original opinions. Consequently the book also contains many fresh insights for the student of German literature.

One consideration which guided each contributor in his approach was to look for the truly significant ideas and expressions of the past. Indeed, we hoped to attain a measure of the same appreciation which characterized Goethe's attitude toward his cultural heritage: The past will reveal its treasures and speak to us when it is approached with an open mind and the honest desire to comprehend it. It is our hope that we have been able to transmit a feeling for the qualities of the masterpieces of German literature. We trust that the reader will share our own excitement stimulated by the realization that repeatedly German poets, dramatists and novelists have issued a challenge to the public by raising questions and frequently proposing original solutions which may hold answers to the problems confronting us today.

H.S.D.
D.H.H.

1. Courtly Literature of the High Middle Ages 🍂

George F. Jones

I

The sudden efflorescence of courtly literature in Germany at the turn of the thirteenth century was unprecedented in the history of letters, unprecedented not only because of the high quality achieved, but also because of the speed with which it was developed, disseminated, and critically evaluated. It often takes years, sometimes even generations, for new literary trends to be appreciated and properly appraised; yet the German courts accepted and appreciated this new literature without delay or hesitation.[1]

One of the earliest critiques of the new literature, and still one of the best, was made by Gottfried of Strassburg in his *Tristan*.[2] About a fourth of the way through his epos Gottfried reaches the point where his young hero is to be knighted, a welcome occasion for a courtly poet to indulge in lavish descriptions of costumes, trappings, and hospitality. Having had previous opportunity to prove his virtuosity in such description, Gottfried reneges on the grounds that, even if he had twelve times his own talent and twelve tongues with which to sing, he could not possibly depict such splendor as well as others have already done. Therefore, instead of presenting the dubbing scene, he discusses the authors of his day, beginning with the narrator, who could have described the knighting ceremony much better than he.

> Hartman of Aue, ah, how he colors and adorns his tales both inside and out with words and with meaning! How he establishes the meaning of his story with his words. How clear and lucid are his crystalline words, and may they ever remain so! They approach you with decorum and they ingratiate and endear themselves to good minds. If anyone can value good words properly and justly, he must leave the man of Aue his wreath and laurel branch.

After thus praising Hartman, Gottfried vents a tirade against a certain "friend of the hare" who makes high jumps on the word-heath and invents wild tales yet aspires to wear the wreath. This passage is almost unintelligible, but purposely so; for it is ridiculing Gottfried's chief rival, Wolfram of Eschenbach, who often affected an obscure style and took liberties with his language as well as with his sources. As we shall see, most modern critics, particularly German ones, entirely reject Gottfried's strictures against Wolfram, who is usually presented as Germany's greatest medieval narrative poet.

Gottfried next praises a certain Bligger of Steinach, whose chief epic work, the *Umbehanc* (*Curtain*) is unfortunately lost; and here again we see that he is less concerned with plot and motivation than with rhetorical devices, verbal ingenuity, and speech melody. Next Gottfried eulogizes Henric of Veldeken,[3] a poet from Maastricht in the Netherlands, who introduced the new French literary styles into Germany. To use Gottfried's metaphor, Henric grafted the first shoot onto the tree of German poetry, a shoot which has sprouted branches from which poets pluck many blossoms.

Having discussed Hartman, Bligger, and Wolfram, who were primarily raconteurs, and Henric, who was both raconteur and lyric poet, Gottfried next treated the lyric poets or minnesingers, who were the heirs of the Provençal troubadours and French trouvères. These he lauds as singers and composers rather than as poets; for it is the melody he praises rather than the meaning of their songs. Now, after the death of Reinmar, the Nightingale of Hagenau, the natural leader of the nightingales is Walther of the Vogelweide, who sings so skillfully and "modulates his voice in the melody commanded by Venus at Cythera."

Before pursuing these courtly poets further, it might be well to note that this outburst of courtly song and story did not occur in a vacuum; for there had been a long preparation, both linguistic and literary, before the new styles were imported from across the Rhine. Ever since the Roman legions reached the Rhine and recruited German mercenaries, Latin exerted a steady influence on the German language. The Germans first borrowed concrete words from the fields of warfare, government, commerce, agriculture, and manufacture; then, after the arrival of Christian missionaries, they borrowed the terms necessary for the Christian faith, including its creeds, liturgy, administration, and physical establishments. This religious influence completely remolded the language, changing it from a barbaric pagan to a civilized Christian idiom capable of expressing all ideas common to Western Christendom. In the process the native language absorbed and assimilated many Latin words; but far more important were the many new compounds formed of native roots to render abstract concepts. In addition, many German words received a new secondary meaning that gradually displaced the original meaning. For example, *taufen* acquired the meaning of "to baptize" rather than just to dip, and *Heilig Geist* came to mean the Holy Ghost rather than "prosperity-bringing spook." The influence of Latin concepts can be measured by the Old High German glosses, or word-for-word translations written on the margins or between the lines of Latin manuscripts as memory aids for learners of Latin.[4]

During the Middle High German Period (c. 1100–1400) the area of present-day France enjoyed the leading military, economic, and cultural position in Europe; and consequently the French language (*lingua franca*) became the common language (*lingua franca!*) of all Western Europe. Many German knights acquired French culture either by serving on French crusades or by being fostered at French courts. German princes took French brides, and these brought with them their retinues of French squires, tutors, musicians, and clerics. By the beginning of the thirteenth century French was a second language at many German courts, and many French words entered the German language, particularly terms relating to knighthood and courtly culture.

This linguistic preparation was accompanied by a literary one. Like most primitive peoples, the ancient Germans had recorded their history in songs. In his *Germania*, the Roman historian Tacitus tells us that they celebrated their gods in songs, which were their only form of recorded history; and they also chanted the praise of great heroes on their way into battle.[5] Although almost nothing survives of this mythological and heroic poetry in Germany, some has survived in the closely related Scandinavian languages; and fleeting references to it are made in some Latin chronicles, which often record, as historical fact, certain plots that had obviously been taken from oral literature.

In addition to their mythological and heroic ballads, we can assume that the ancient Germans sang other songs at work and play as well as at their religious observances, particularly as accompaniment for dances performed as a part of their springtime fertility rites. None of these songs survive, and we can only guess at their nature. On the other hand we are more familiar with the songs that arose during the great tribal migrations, since these can be partially reconstructed from surviving monuments, especially when these are compared with the early songs of other Germanic peoples, such as the Anglo-Saxons and Icelanders. The only German song to survive from the vast body of oral heroic literature is the fragmentary *Song of Hildebrand,* a short alliterative ballad treating the widespread theme of the father-son conflict.[6] Although badly recorded and badly preserved, this short song reveals the dramatic power and emotional intensity of which the ancient poets were capable. Also surviving from ancient native tradition are a few magic charms or chants against sickness, capture, and other evils. The almost total loss of pre-Christian oral literature does not mean that the Church succeeded in stamping it out; it only means that, with very few exceptions, churchmen considered such secular works unworthy of being perpetuated on parchment. Many of these ancient themes must have maintained a subliterary existence, since they emerged again in the late Middle Ages as ballads and as constituent parts of longer narratives, to say nothing of the many popular dance songs that echo ancient and long-forgotten pagan rites.

Being a monopoly of the Church, written literature at first served the task of conversion; therefore it produced a large body of catechisms and confessions as well as translations and paraphrases of Scripture and of the writings of the Church Fathers. Most Old High German works were strictly functional and are therefore not true literature, even though they are valuable cultural monuments. There are, however, some exceptions that have a certain degree of literary merit. Among these are two Bavarian poems of the ninth century, now known as the *Wessobrunn Prayer* and the *Muspilli,* which describe the creation and the day of judgment respectively. Although based entirely on Christian Scripture, these songs would well have appealed to the fantasies of people newly converted from their Germanic gods, who did not even enjoy immortality, being doomed, as they were, to die in the *Götterdämmerung* or "Twilight of the Gods."

Of some charm is a short song about Christ and the Woman of Samaria, as is also a hymn to St. George. Much skill and diligence, with occasional flashes of talent, are revealed in a long gospel harmony composed by an Alsatian monk named Otfried, who is the first German poet known to us by name and who is usually credited with having introduced end rhyme into German verse. In a similar meter is a short panegyric in praise of the West Frankish King Louis III, who won a victory against the Vikings at Saucourt in 881. Without question the most fascinating work of this period is the anonymous *Heliand (Savior),* a life of Jesus written in the Old Saxon language of Northern Germany.[7] Although composed in the alliterative formulas common to Old Germanic heroic songs like *Beowulf*, this song is completely Christian in sentiment, despite what some of our earlier literary historians said to the contrary.

With regard to written literature of the Middle Ages, one must remember that Latin works were far more important than vernacular ones, their importance being indicated by their far greater number of surviving manuscripts. Since all literates could read Latin and preferred to do so, vernacular literature was written almost exclusively to be read or sung to illiterates. As a tool of the Church, Latin literature was concerned chiefly with theology, church history, saints' lives, and other ecclesiastical subjects. Nevertheless, some churchmen did see fit to compose secular works, with the result that several interesting profane works in Latin have survived, including the *Waltharius*, a heroic epic based on Old Germanic materials; the *Ruodlieb*, a forerunner of the courtly romance; the *Ecbasis captivi*, an allegorical beast epic; and some dramas by Hrotswitha, a nun of Gandersheim.[8]

Neither these Latin narratives nor Hrotswitha's dramas seem to have influenced later German literature, for all were consigned to oblivion. The contrary was true, however, of a large body of Latin lyric verse from the twelfth and thirteenth centuries, much of it amatory, that is generally attributed to the "vagabond poets," a race of wayward students and defrocked monks who wandered from university to university singing the praises of wine, women, and song. Whether we wish to accept this romantic conception of wandering scholars, or whether we prefer to think that these songs were written by otherwise respectable clerics in carefree moments, we must marvel at the virtuosity of their verse and meter, their witty turn of phrase, and their brilliant and often blasphemous satire.

While written literature remained in the service of the Church, the old oral traditions, both lyric and narrative, continued their underground existence. New themes were steadily added, many of them brought back from the fabulous Orient by pilgrims, crusaders, and merchants, either directly or via French literature. Some of these international motifs found their way into the long Biblical paraphrases and saints' lives then in vogue and thus made these pious works attractive even to secular audiences. Others blended with native narrative elements and thus gave birth to a popular genre of secular tale that is known as *Spielmannsdichtung* (minstrel poetry). These unpolished adventure stories were formerly attributed to unlettered minstrels, but scholars now suspect that they were composed, or at least recorded, by learned clerics. A good example of such entertaining literature is the story of *King Rother*, a tale of the abduction and recovery of a bride.[9]

Although love played only a minor role in such narratives, it did inspire lovely lyric verse in Austria and the surrounding Danubian region in the second half of the twelfth century. These songs, some of which were composed in a melody ascribed to a certain Kürenberger, present a sincere and reciprocal love. They were usually duets or dialogue songs; and it is often the woman who expresses the greater passion. The poet was, to be sure, a man. Whereas chauvinistic critics of the nineteenth century claimed that these lyrics were of native origin, as opposed to the courtly lyrics later imported from France, it is now evident that they too were part of a general Western tradition, for songs of similar content also appeared in Portugal and elsewhere. These Danubian songs were composed, however, in strict accord with the genius of the German language; and their long verses still echoed much of the rhythm and melody of the ancient Germanic alliterative verse, even though they employed the more recently imported end rhyme.

All these native literary developments were quickly forgotten, at least by the nobility, when the new courtly culture was introduced from France during the Hohenstaufen era (1152–1250).[10] For reasons still disputed by scholars, the French-speaking courts of the West had produced a new literature, both lyric and narrative, that appealed chiefly to feminine tastes. Many conflicting theories have been advanced concerning the origin of the courtly love lyrics, which has been found in Latin panegyrics, Arabic love songs, Ovid, or a secularization of Mariology or of mystical writings such as those of Bernard of Clairvaux or even of the liturgy of heretical sects like the Albigensians. No doubt some, if not all, of these precedents contributed to the new language of love, but that is a problem for Romance scholars to ponder. As far as the minnesingers, or German love poets, are concerned, suffice it to say that they found models for their structural forms, melodies, and subject matter ready-made in the poems of the Provençal troubadours. This does not imply that the minnesingers, as individuals, were any less original or creative than the Provençal poets, for the latter also closely followed carefully circumscribed traditions and expressed themselves only within certain accepted norms. Neither group aimed to say anything new, but just to say it better than anyone else. The merit of the minnesingers lay not only in introducing the French matter, but also in adapting it to German tastes and sensibilities.[11]

This French courtly literature, both lyric and narrative, was the shoot that Henric of Veldeken grafted so fruitfully on the tree of German poetry. Henric's love lyrics successfully reproduce the meters, rhyme schemes, and flavor of the best French verse; and his romance about Aeneas closely renders the ideas and sentiments of the Old French *Roman d'Eneas*. Whereas Henric composed his lyric poems in his native Limburg dialect, he composed his *Eneide* in a Middle German dialect for the benefit of his patron, the Landgrave of Thuringia; and for this reason it could serve as a model for all High German authors.[12] And for the same reason he is usually known today as Heinrich von Veldeke, rather than as Henric van Veldeken. The new French trends naturally influenced the nearest German poets first, many of whom lived near the French language frontier: Henric came from Limburg, Frederick of Hausen from the upper Rhineland, Reinmar from Alsace, and Rudolf of Fenis from western Switzerland. Perhaps it is significant that both Henric and Reinmar carried their art from the west toward the east, namely to Thuringia and Austria.

The spiritual basis of all minnesong is the adoration and service of women, or rather of ladies, since such poems were written only for and about ladies of high birth. Just as a vassal served his lord by fighting on his campaigns, so he could serve his lady by singing her praises; and therefore much of the terminology of feudalism was transferred from the service of one's lord to the service of one's lady. The knight was her vassal (*dienstman*), and she was his lady (*frouwe*). She rewarded his fealty (*triuwe*) with her grace (*genâde*) and favor (*huld*); but, if she were ungracious (*ungenaedec*), she might refuse him his reward (*lôn*), even though he only expected a greeting (*gruoz*). This selfless veneration of womankind became a kind of cult, in which the idealized woman acquired most of the traditional attributes of the Virgin Mary. Such exalted and sublimated love service was termed *hôhiu minne* (lofty love).

It is to be remembered, of course, that all this adoration and veneration was but a fiction, a parlor game and social gallantry, and that the emotions were more feigned than felt. In reality, the poet was usually either a professional singer praising his patroness or a vassal praising the wife of his liege. Even a happy marriage and a large brood of children were no barrier to his declaring his undying devotion to his lady, who was for him but the impersonal embodiment of exalted womanhood. Courtly ladies welcomed this romantic make-believe as an escape from their own dreary lives, during which they were carefully chaperoned until being married off for strictly dynastic reasons.

The languishing lover realizes that his yearning is futile and that he will never consummate his love, not only because the lady is inaccessible, but also because, were she accessible, she would have to come from her pedestal and thus cease to be the idol he has been worshipping. Nevertheless, he follows the tradition, probably of Arabic origin, of deploring the spies (*merkaere*) who keep surveillance (*huote*) over his lady-love. Despairing of consummating this love or even having it requited, he would be satisfied if only his lady would accept his service and acknowledge it with a single glance or nod. Yet the poet's service is not in vain: he is exalted, and his worth is enhanced, by his selfless devotion and by his lady's ennobling influence.

Modern critics often use the term "courtly love," but this term, which did not exist in the Middle Ages, is quite misleading because it is sometimes used to characterize the spiritualized love discussed above (*fin amor* in Provençal, *hôhiu minne* in German) and sometimes to designate the adulterous love found in *Tristan* and *Lancelot*.[13] Although devoted primarily to sublimated love, the minnesingers could extol carnal and adulterous love, too, for example in the dawn song (*alba, morgenliet*), a genre of dialogue song sung by lovers who must part when morning comes. Dawn songs were composed by many German poets, some of the best by Wolfram. In addition to the dawn song there were other forms of dialogue song, for example, the *wechsel* and the *botenliet*. The *wechsel* (exchange) was a duet, the strophes of which were sung alternately by two lovers who were separated in actuality but faced each other in their imagination. The *botenliet* (messenger's song) is sung by a lady and a messenger who has just brought greetings from her lover or is being told what message to take to him. Another popular genre among the minnesingers is the *kriuzliet* (crusade song), which is both religious and amorous, because the poet must decide whether to cross the sea to serve God or to stay at home to serve his lady. The song may take the form of a dispute between the body and the heart, the former of which wishes to serve God. Some

of the best crusade songs were written by Hartman, whom Gottfried mentioned only as a narrator.

Great virtuosity is shown in the songs of Frederick of Hausen, who seems to have first imported the Provençal tripartite or
canzon strophe. Of superior formal artistry and gifted with even
greater imagery was Henry of Morungen, who presents *minne* as an
uncanny and demonic force. The most stylized of all these poets
was Reinmar of Hagenau, whom Gottfried praised as the leader of
the nightingales. The editor of Reinmar's works rejected as spurious
nearly all songs that do not express melancholy resignation to
unrequited love; but Gottfried's praise might well persuade us to
accept some of the other less-restricted songs as genuine.[14] The
most universal of all the minnesingers was, of course, Walther of
the Vogelweide, whom Gottfried so rightfully nominated as Reinmar's successor; but we shall discuss him later as the culmination of
the whole literary movement.

Many minnesongs are almost entirely subjective. The singer
analyzes his own emotions, and we learn very little about the object
of his affections, except that she is an ideal that probably has no
counterpart in the real world. In discussing similar Provençal songs,
a French scholar once said that he would not swear that all
troubadour songs were sung by the same man, yet he was sure they
were all sung to the same woman. The lack of true individuality in
the ideas and attitudes expressed in these lyrics can be explained by
the conformist nature of courtly society, which was exclusive and
thoroughly integrated. To be accepted into this closed group, a lord
or lady had to conform to its dictates, and any deviation in behavior
was not only ridiculous but also suspect.

Despite six or more centuries of Christianity, the aristocracy
still lived in a "shame culture" in which the greatest incentive to
virtue and the greatest deterrent from vice was a regard for the
opinions of one's peers. Disgrace (*schande*) was equated with sin
(*sünde*), except that it was far more feared in courtly circles. With
the exception of Parzival, the heroes of the romances exert themselves almost solely to win the acclaim and applause of their courtly
colleagues, particularly of the ladies. To be sure, the heroes and
heroines are punctilious in their external religious observances and
glib with their pious invocations; but time and time again it appears
that religious observances are merely a part of genteel behavior
patterns, for example, when a damsel goes to a mass "as a well-bred
young lady should."

The goal of every knight is honor (*êre*), or the admiration of his fellows. To enjoy *êre* he must have not only courage (*muot*), but also wealth (*guot*), which is the outward and visible manifestation of his inner worth. To prove his wealth he must not only be exquisitely attired and accoutered but also practice largess (*milde*). As a feudal lord he must also show loyalty (*triuwe*) both to his lord and to his lady and to his peers. A few romances and legends also demand that a hero enjoy God's grace or favor (*gotes hulde*), but this factor hardly appears in most of the Arthurian romances, which were the most popular during the Hohenstaufen era. Since man creates God in his own image, the courtly poets naturally created a "courtly" God (*höfischer got*), as their works clearly attest. Good works had little value unless witnessed, preferably by many people, especially by women. Although many of these attitudes and values are only vaguely suggested in the lyrics, they are immediately evident in the courtly romances, which appealed to the same audience and were in part written by the same poets.

II

At the turn of the thirteenth century the French poet Jean Bodel aptly described the subject matter of contemporary narrative literature as the Matter of Rome, the Matter of France, and the Matter of Britain. By the Matter of France he meant the *chansons de geste* or heroic epics based on French history, which were already known in Germany through Priest Conrad's paraphrase of the *Song of Roland*. The Matter of Rome designated the reworkings of stories from classical antiquity, such as the *Trojan War*, the *Aeneid*, and the *Thebans*; and the Matter of Britain comprised all tales told about King Arthur and his fabulous round table.

To satisfy the new courtly taste, the Matter of Rome and Matter of Britain suffered a sea change, having been imbued with the amorous values and themes of the troubadour love songs. Like its French source, the *Roman d'Eneas*, Henric of Veldeken's *Eneide* is more concerned with Aeneas' passion for Lavinia than with the founding of Rome; and the various fairy-tale motifs borrowed from Celtic countries, when joined by Chrétien of Troyes and other courtly poets, became great love stories.

As Gottfried so astutely saw, the greatest of Henric's imitators was Hartman of Aue, a Swabian knight who likewise turned to

France for the subject matter of most of his stories. Hartman, who seems to have been a *ministerialis* (*dienstman*) or unpropertied knightly servitor, was born about 1165, possibly at Eglisau in what is now northern Switzerland. Like most of his literary contemporaries, Hartman also composed love songs and crusade songs; but he was most successful as a narrator and is best known for two Arthurian romances, *Erec* and *Iwein,* which were based on two similarly named romances by Chrétien.[15] Hartman had previously composed a *Klage* (complaint), or an allegorical disputation between a lover's heart and his body. In this didactic dialogue the heart instructs the body in the rules and ethics of love and thus formulates a rational and systematic program for pleasing both God and man in matters of love service. Although the awkward effort of a beginner, this work clearly foreshadows all of Hartman's later productions.

Nineteenth-century scholars tried to deduce Hartman's biography from his writings, ascribing his turning from secular to religious themes to his sorrow at his liege-lord's death; but now we know that medieval poets seldom wrote from firsthand experience or from the need to express their inner feelings. Hartman, in fact, frankly states that he wrote what people wished to hear, so we have reason to believe that his choice of subjects was sometimes determined by his patron. *Erec* and *Iwein* follow their sources quite closely, the second even more closely than the first, but this did not prevent Hartman from interjecting his own personality and values into them.

Erec and *Iwein* complement each other well, since both treat the conflict between love and honor, though from different points of view. Erec is so in love with his young bride that he devotes all his time and thought to her and thereby neglects his knightly fame. Overhearing Enid lament his loss of reputation, he realizes his fault and sets out, taking her along with him as a sort of ragged patient Griselda, to redeem himself by winning honor through deeds of prowess. Iwein does the reverse. After winning and wedding a lovely widow, he is so obsessed with winning acclaim in tournaments that he forgets to return to her at the stipulated time. Then, being publicly denounced at Arthur's court as a troth-breaker, he loses all self-esteem and lives like a wild beast. Cured of his madness, he eventually regains his reputation through a series of difficult trials and thus gains his wife's forgiveness.

Hartman seems to have deviated from Chrétien's Erec largely because he had not yet mastered his medium; for his *Iwein* renders

19

its source much more closely. Because the style of *Iwein* changes abruptly after the first thousand verses, it has been conjectured that he began the story soon after *Erec* but then dropped it until sometime after completing his two religious legends, by which time he had perfected his style. Although it is true that Hartman often interjected himself into *Erec* and *Iwein* and often expressed his own moral judgments, it is wrong to claim, as some critics do, that he first gave them ethical values, for Chrétien's stories were already *romans à thèse* teaching the golden mean between amorous love and pursuit of glory. Hartman may sometimes whitewash or justify his heroes' and heroines' behavior; but his values are not necessarily deeper than Chrétien's, even if his didacticism is a bit heavier.

Hartman's two shorter works, *Gregorius* and *Poor Henry* (*Der arme Heinrich*), are religious in theme;[16] yet they too are written in the language and the style of the courtly romances. The first of these, a medieval version of the Oedipus story, concerns a knight who is the child of a brother and sister and who unknowingly commits incest with his mother. Discovering his sin, he expiates it by having himself tied to a rock in the sea for seventeen years, at which time he is elected pope and is able to intercede for his mother.

The second of these stories concerns a wealthy nobleman named Henry, who enjoys all the goods of this world but fails to recognize them as gifts of God. Afflicted with leprosy as punishment for his pride, Henry gives away all his wealth and retires to a small property in a forest clearing, where he is cared for by a faithful peasant and his little daughter. Advised by the doctors of Salerno that he can be cured only by the heart-blood of a maiden who is ready to die for him, he desponds of ever being cured; but the peasant's daughter insists upon sacrificing herself and argues so eloquently that her parents finally agree to let her do so. However, after she and Henry have journeyed all the way to Salerno and the doctor is about to cut out her heart, Henry, who has peeked through a hole in the wall, thinks better of it and forbids the cure, at last realizing that he deserves his punishment and has no right to accept her sacrifice. Having resigned himself to the divine will, he is miraculously healed on the way home; and he subsequently marries the little girl who was ready to die for him.

It will be seen that the two romances present a man's loss of honor through failure to observe the golden mean between conflicting duties, while the two legends show a man's fall through sin and his eventual penitence, expiation, and forgiveness. The first two heroes achieve society's approval by performing feats of valor, and the other two achieve God's grace by overcoming pride.

Because of his crystal-clear style, which Gottfried so rightly praised, Hartman was the classic of the Hohenstaufen period and served as a model for many writers. Hartman was a consummate storyteller, whose stories we should enjoy as skillfully wrought entertainment rather than as disguised theology. Just because Erec rescues some captives from a fairy world, we need not think that Hartman intended him to be a Christ image; nor do we have to find spiritual symbolism in the many numbers that appear in his works. It is easy to note certain relationships in minnesongs between the number of stresses in a verse, the number of verses in the strophe, and the number of strophes in the song; but these number relationships probably have aesthetic rather than symbolic function. The same is no doubt true of the ratios that are sometimes observed in the number of verses assigned to each of the sections of a romance. It will be noted, for example, that Gottfried's literary excursion mentioned above is exactly 200 verses in length, but we have no reason to assume that Gottfried had some secret symbolism in mind when he composed it. The same is true of Biblical exegesis as applied to courtly romances. To be sure, theological writers did sometimes write on various levels, but we have no proof that the secular writers did so. In any case, no two modern scholars have come up with the same solution; and it is highly improbable that the unlearned lords and ladies of the courts would have been any more astute or would have devoted any more time in trying to dissect the stories that were told for their amusement. This is particularly the case of those who heard but did not see the romances.

The greatest of Hartman's admirers was Gottfried, who so well appreciated his clarity of style and the technical skill with which he adorned his stories.[17] Like Hartman, Gottfried selected a French source and followed it closely, at least for the plot. This was the *Tristan* of Thomas of Britain, who appears to have been Anglo-Norman. Whereas many of the proper names and motifs of his story were ultimately Celtic, Thomas seems to have followed an anonymous Old French archetype written near the middle of the twelfth century, which, for all we know, could have been the story of King Mark and Iseult the Blonde composed by Chrétien and mentioned in his *Cligès*. The *Tristan* story had made its way to Germany by 1175, when it appeared in the *Tristrant* of the North

German poet Eilhart of Oberg, yet Gottfried ignored this poet in his literary review.

Instead, Gottfried insists that he has followed Thomas; his claim is confirmed by comparing his *Tristan* with the Old Norse *Tristramsaga*, which closely rendered the plot of Thomas' work. By happy chance Thomas and Gottfried almost exactly complement each other; for the sole surviving part of Thomas' work (only about a sixth of the whole) covers the missing end of Gottfried's unfinished work. Even though the two authors cannot be directly compared, there is reason to believe that Gottfried surpassed his source in artistic skill. In any case, many of his best passages, such as his literary review and the description and allegorical interpretation of the love grotto, are clearly his own work. To understand Gottfried's artistic purpose we merely have to read his praise of Hartman and Bligger of Steinach, for we may be sure that he was aiming at the same clarity, adornment, verbal ingenuity, and use of rhetorical devices that he praised in their works.

Tristan, whose birth has caused the death of his recently widowed mother, is brought up incognito to protect him from his father's enemies. Knighted at the court of his uncle, King Mark of Cornwall, he frees Cornwall from having to send an annual tribute of young people to Ireland by defeating the Irish champion Morold in a trial by combat. Because the poisoned wound he has received in the combat can be healed only by Morold's sister, the Irish queen, he sets out in disguise for Ireland, where he is healed by the queen in return for instructing her daughter in music and other accomplishments. Mark wishes to remain single so that Tristan can be his heir, but his jealous barons insist that he marry; and Tristan is commissioned to fetch Isolde, the daughter of the Irish queen. This he does, after slaying a dragon; but on the way back to Cornwall he and she inadvertently drink a love potion destined for Isolde and Mark. Overwhelmed by the potion, Tristan struggles to remain loyal to his uncle and liege; but he finally succumbs to its magic power, and he and Isolde confess and consummate their love while still on shipboard. Feeling responsible for having left the fatal potion unguarded, Isolde's confidante, Brangaene, saves her mistress' reputation by taking her place on the wedding night; and from then on she protects the lovers and carries messages between them.

Despite much incriminating evidence, Mark wavers and can

take no action against the two people whom he loves so dearly. Love makes Isolde astute in evasion and persuasion, and she even clears herself in an ordeal by fire through a cleverly worded oath. Discovered together again, the lovers are banished and spend some time in a love grotto, where they are sustained by their passion. Finding them lying together, but separated by a sword, Mark forgives them once again and allows them to return to court; but it is not long before they are caught *flagrante delicto* and Tristan must flee. Finally, believing that Isolde has reconciled herself to his absence and being intrigued by the name of his companion's sister, Isolde of the White Hands, Tristan lets himself be married to the latter, without, however, being able to consummate the marriage. At this point Gottfried's story breaks off; and we must turn to Thomas' fragment to learn of Tristan's and Isolde's love death.

This is without doubt the most controversial medieval work, especially in regard to the author's intention. Some critics view Gottfried as a deeply religious man, while others consider him a blasphemous atheist. Some see him as an art-loving hedonist, others as a heretic who is trying to create an anti-Christian cult of demonic love. One thing is generally accepted, that his language closely echoes that of St. Bernard of Clairvaux, especially the language he used in his sermons on the Song of Songs. Just as medieval churchmen used that erotic Hebrew song for religious purpose, namely to illustrate the mystic union of the soul with Christ, Gottfried used their interpretation of it for purely secular purpose. It is even possible that Gottfried was influenced by Catharism or other heresies popular in Strassburg in his day; and it is conceivable that fear of the Inquisition, which began there in 1212, may have been one reason that he did not finish his questionable work. Perhaps no one explanation is satisfying for Gottfried's masterpiece because he brought all the philosophical and theological trends of his time to bear upon it.

We know little about Gottfried but what his work tells us. Later poets called him Master (*meister*), as opposed to Sir (*her*); so we may assume that he was a burgher. His great erudition attests that he was a Master (*magister*) of Arts; and we can suppose that he had as rigorous a training in the liberal arts as he attributed to his hero Tristan. His familiarity with Latin, French, theology, and the classics suggests that he may have been an advocate at the episcopal court in Strassburg. His refined and moderate language indicates

23

that he was a member of the patriciate, or at least that he associated with its members, and this might explain his familiarity with hunting and court protocol.

Whereas Gottfried is assumed to have been a burgher, Wolfram was a knight, as he himself proudly asserts on several occasions and as his romance clearly confirms. Early in his story he states that women would be foolish to love him for his singing, since he should earn their love with shield and spear; and elsewhere he boasts that he was born to the knightly profession (*schildes ambet ist mîn art*). Unlike Gottfried, and even Hartman, he gives evidence of having actually been in combat. To be sure, he sometimes follows literary tradition in describing battles as a series of individual and fairly fought jousts between chivalrous gentlemen; but on other occasions he describes war more realistically, with blockade and starvation, siege engines, baggage trains, mercenaries, and camp followers, to say nothing of well-planned strategy. Also, he uses many metaphors from the art of warfare. Nevertheless, even though he was a knight, he often complained of his poverty; and he must have been of very minor social and political significance to have left not a single legal document with his signature as principal or even as witness. Wolfram is believed to have come from East Franconia, from a town now named Wolframs-Eschenbach, not far from Ansbach. While his dates are unknown, numerous allusions in his works to current events and personalities indicate that he composed between 1200 and 1220; and it is unlikely that he lived very long afterwards.

In addition to his dawn songs, Wolfram composed three epic works: *Parzival, Willehalm,* and *Titurel.*[18] Of these *Parzival* is the longest and by far the most famous. Like Hartman, Wolfram chose a work by Chrétien for his model, namely *Le Conte del Graal;* but, unlike Hartman, he denied his source. To justify his deviation from Chrétien, he claimed to have followed a certain Kyot of Provence, who found the story in an Arabic document written by a heathen named Flegetanis. Despite this fantastic tongue-in-cheek explanation, generations of humorless scholars have laboriously searched for Kyot with the result that we have our choice of numerous learned theories and conjectures about him. However, most scholars now suspect that Kyot was only a hoax, perhaps fabricated to justify Wolfram's originality, or perhaps as a comical retort to Gottfried's accusation that he was an inventor of wild tales (*vindære wilder mære, der mære wildenære*). That Kyot was fictitious would accord with Wolfram's usual independence of his source, which is easily revealed by comparing his *Willehalm* with its source, the Old French *Battle of Aliscans.*

Before returning to *Parzival*, it might be well to mention that *Willehalm* is also an excellent work, one which is now receiving considerable scholarly attention, but one that does not tell us as much about Wolfram as we learn in his longer and more original *Parzival.* His other narrative, *Titurel*, survives in only two fragments totalling some 170 verses, which may be all that the author completed. The editor's title, *Titurel*, was badly chosen, that being merely the name of the Grail king who is fleetingly mentioned in the opening verse; for the plot concerns Sigune and Schionatulander, two characters whose ill-starred love is outlined in *Parzival.* This work is composed in an unusual lyric strophe, which has a strange and haunting melody.

Whatever the merits of *Willehalm* and *Titurel*, *Parzival* has always been the most appreciated of Wolfram's works, both by his contemporaries and by modern readers. Stated briefly, the plot is as follows. Reared in a solitary forest by his mother Herzeloyde to keep him from learning the knight's trade that has killed his father, Parzival is irresistibly attracted to Arthur's court the first time he beholds some knights. Unable to dissuade him from leaving, his mother dresses him in fool's clothing, gives him some bits of wisdom for his journey, and drops dead as soon as he has departed. Misapplying his mother's advice about accepting ladies' kisses and rings, the inexperienced youth unwittingly causes a lady named Jeschute to be suspected and maltreated by her husband. Next he meets Sigune, a damsel who is mourning her recently slain lover; from her he learns his identity. Reaching Arthur's court, he sees Sir Kay chastise a damsel and a mute knight for predicting that he will become the greatest member of the Round Table. Arthur grants him the arms of a Red Knight, who is waiting outside the castle with a claim to the realm; and Parzival kills the knight by ungentlemanly means and takes his armor.

Parzival visits an old knight named Gurnemanz, from whom he learns the rules of courtly conduct and knightly warfare; and, thus prepared, he is able to rescue and marry Condwiramurs, a queen besieged by a jilted suitor. Leaving her to visit his mother, he chances upon the Grail Castle, where he witnesses the ceremony of the Grail and sees the ailing king but fails to ask the redeeming question which would cure him of his affliction. From Sigune, whom he finds with her now embalmed lover, he learns about the Grail and about the sin he has committed in not asking the question. He next reconciles Jeschute with her husband by defeating him and swearing her innocence. Reminded of Condwiramurs by the sight of three drops of blood on the white snow, he falls in a trance; but his rapt contemplation is interrupted long enough for him to unhorse Sir Kay and break his arm and leg, thus avenging his mistreatment of the damsel and the mute knight at Arthur's court. Parzival's friend Gawan leads him back to Arthur's court, where both are highly honored until a Grail messenger arrives and denounces Parzival for failing to ask the fateful question.

Chagrined at his disgrace, Parzival feuds with God, whom he considers a faithless liege-lord for having rewarded his service so poorly; and he sets out to regain the Grail by force of arms. At the same time Gawan, who has been falsely accused of treachery, sets out to vindicate his honor; and most of the remainder of the story concerns their respective adventures, which cross from time to time. Parzival eventually meets a hermit named Trevrizent, who teaches him humility and reconciles him with God. Having acknowledged his guilt, Parzival is ready to see the Grail and release the suffering king, thus becoming Grail king in his stead as he has been destined from birth. He is joined by Condwiramurs and their two sons, one of whom will one day succeed him while the other will journey to the Orient and become the father of Prester John.

From Chrétien's fragment of 9,234 verses Wolfram made a romance of 24,812 verses. Keeping most of Chrétien's plot, which reached through the encounter with Trevrizent and Gawan's following adventures, Wolfram added the happy ending and also expanded nearly all Chrétien's actions and situations by adding a host of new characters and subplots. He also added a prehistory explaining the birth of Parzival and of his piebald brother Feirefîz, the son of Parzival's father Gahmuret by a black princess. Feirefîz later enters the story, has an almost fatal combat with Parzival, accepts conversion, and marries Repanse de Schoye, the guardian of the Grail.

Critics are amazed at Wolfram's skill in organizing the vast amount of material he has fitted into his story. Despite the huge cast and many subplots, it is all systematically integrated; and almost all the actions are in some way interlocked. The main characters are interrelated, all of them belonging to either the family of King Arthur or the family of the Grail king, and Parzival is descended from both families. The major protagonists, Herzeloyde, Trevrizent, the Grail king Anfortas, Sigune's mother Schoysiane, and Repanse de Schoye, are brothers and sisters; and these close family ties contribute to the literary unity of the work. Unity is also achieved by having certain people, such as Sigune, appear periodically at important stages of Parzival's career. When Parzival wishes to swear to Jeschute's innocence, he does so not at any shrine, but at that of the hermit Trevrizent, who later plays such a key role. There are also many reminiscences of past occurrences, as well as predictions of coming events; and Wolfram never fails to pick up loose threads and wind them together again. Typical are the intricate correspondences and parallels between the concurrent quests of Parzival and Gawan.

Because of Wolfram's uncommon ability in organizing his material, some scholars are unwilling to concede that he was illiterate, even though he boasts of the fact (*ichne kan deheinen buochstap*). It would seem that he would have had to have before him a list of characters, a genealogical table, and even a chronological check list in order to keep track of all the interrelated plots and personages, to say nothing of the precise dating of many events. Therefore some scholars insist that he must have exaggerated his illiteracy, perhaps as a snide dig at Hartman, who gloried in his ability to read books. Oral improvisation is suggested by Wolfram's style, which employs all the techniques and tricks common to tellers of tales. The syntax is often loose. For example, a sentence can begin not with a subject or an object, but rather with a topic. Wolfram mentions, in the nominative case, the person or thing he wishes to talk about; and only then does he decide whether it will be the grammatical subject or object: "The King of Kukumerlant, he was . . .," or "The King of Kukumerlant, we saw him . . . ."[19] Like a storyteller, Wolfram participates directly in the story, addressing remarks to his characters and to the audience too, as well as to personified abstractions like Lady Love or Lady Adventure. As a result of these tricks, he achieves a marked degree of sympathy for his characters. Made with the proper gestures and voice modulations, his performance must have served as a surrogate for drama.

There are indications that Wolfram's story grew by accretion; scholars have been able to demonstrate on stylistic grounds that the first two books were added after the completion of books three through six. Even such organizational complexity would, however, be possible in an orally composed work, provided it were created

27

gradually, with the various threads elaborated in successive retellings and corrected when, perhaps with the help of the audience, they were found to conflict or fall apart. Perhaps the work was not dictated to a scribe until after the myriad of persons and events had gradually found their proper places; and probably the first written version suffered changes and corrections before our earliest surviving manuscript was copied.

Whereas Erec and Iwein had set out to regain the worldly honor they had lost through their lack of moderation or balance, Parzival sets out to reconcile the demands of the world with those of God. Once instructed by Gurnemanz, he is as good as any Arthurian knight, as good as his father Gahmuret and equal to Gawan, the ideal Round Table knight. But worldly honor is not enough for Parzival. Through his mother Herzeloyde, who is of the Grail family, he is destined to better things and must attain God's grace as well as human adulation. Wolfram sums up the matter at the close of the work by stating that it is a useful travail if anyone can so live that he can win the world's favor without God's losing his soul through the guilt of his body. Unfortunately, in order to achieve these contradictory ends, Wolfram had to take recourse to the never-never land of the Grail.

Because Wolfram's message is so vaguely stated, scholars have been able to propose as many solutions as there are meanings of the word *zwîfel*, which Wolfram discusses in his opening verse and which is variously translated as doubt, despair, inconstancy, and alienation from God. Most scholars realize that Parzival can win the Grail only after acknowledging his sinfulness, but they cannot agree on the precise nature of his sin. In any case, it is generally accepted that Wolfram was influenced by St. Augustine's ideas on sin and expiation. Similarly, there have been innumerable explanations for Wolfram's concept of the Grail and its ceremony, which have been attributed to Celtic, classical, ecclesiastical, and even Hermetic origins, rather than to Wolfram's unbridled fantasy and misunderstanding of Chrétien's account. For Wolfram, the Grail was not a dish or a chalice, but a stone called *lapsit exillis*, for which numerous etymologies have been proposed. In this and many other ways Wolfram's Grail differs sharply from that in all other versions of the story.

In contrast to their divergent views on Trevrizent's theology and the question of grace versus free will, all scholars note that Wolfram has greatly altered the significance of the fatal question.

Instead of the purely fairy-tale nature of the question in other versions, Wolfram makes it into a *Mitleidsfrage* or sympathetic inquiry. Thus Parzival is guilty not only of having abandoned his mother, caused Jeschute's suffering, and killed his kinsman, the Red Knight, but also of having been too self-centered to feel compassion for the ailing king. This explanation is not entirely satisfying to the twentieth-century reader, because Parzival sinned unwittingly and had refrained from asking the question because Gurnemanz had advised him not to ask too many questions; but we must remember that medieval man had other views about sin and guilt.

Parzival was formerly cited as an early example of the *Bildungs-* or *Entwicklungsroman*, a developmental novel like Rousseau's *Confessions* or Goethe's *Wilhelm Meister*. This is incorrect, if the word "development" implies that the hero begins as a raw material on which his experiences stamp a character; for Parzival's eventual character was determined the day he was begotten. As the child of Gahmuret and Herzeloyde, that is to say of the Arthurian and Grail families, he had to develop as he did. Upon leaving his silvan seclusion, he was like a chrysalis emerging fully formed from the cocoon. To be sure, he had to stretch and dry his wings before flying off, but that was done quickly with the help of Gurnemanz and Trevrizent. All Gurnemanz has to do is to give a few pointers, and Parzival is immediately the world's best knight. Once Trevrizent explains Parzival's sin of pride, it takes little time for that Grail descendant to acknowledge his guilt and be cured of his sin, for his character is inborn.

The Trevrizent scene is clearly the high-point of Parzival's spiritual progress and of the romance as a whole. Whereas Herzeloyde gives Parzival the rudiments of his religion and Gurnemanz gives him his social graces and knightly skills, it is his uncle, the hermit Trevrizent, who teaches him his true purpose and raises him above the more worldly-minded knights of the Round Table. As Parzival rises in the world, he sinks into sin; and it is precisely at the peak of his glory at Arthur's court that Cundrîe, the Grail messenger, denounces his sinfulness.

Parzival remains the most admired of medieval German romances, yet an increasing number of scholars prefer Gottfried's clarity and sophistication. Though they do not share Gottfried's disapproval of Wolfram's invention of wild tales, they do object to his jumping around on the "word-heath." Among the counsels Herzeloyde gives her son is the advice not to cross dark fords. Soon

29

thereafter Parzival comes to a brook so narrow that a rooster could step across it; but, because he cannot see the bottom, he assumes it is deep and therefore follows it all day to its source before crossing it. Wolfram too sometimes seems to confuse obscurity with profundity; and the obvious reason that scholars cannot find a satisfactory and systematic solution to the many mysteries of the work is that Wolfram was not a consistent thinker. We must, therefore, accept the story for what it is, a deeply moving story of sin, remorse, and reconciliation with God; and we must not demand a logically or theologically consistent explanation.

III

Walther of the Vogelweide also devoted much thought to the question of life's ultimate meaning, even though he was best known for his love lyrics. After Reinmar's death Gottfried proclaimed Walther the leader of the nightingales; like most of his contemporaries, he appreciated Walther more as a minnesinger than as a seer or as a composer of religious and political songs. As is the case with his fellow singers, Walther has left us no vital statistics.[20] Since his last political songs refer to events of the year 1229, we can assume that he did not long survive that time, since he was not the man to hold back his political views. In one song he claimed to have sung of love for forty years (*wol vierzic jâr habe ich gesungen oder mê*); and, even though forty was a proverbial number, we have no reason to doubt that Walther flourished from about 1190 to 1230 and that he had been born a score of years earlier. Nor is anything definite known about his birthplace, except that it must have been somewhere within the present Austrian Republic or in South Tyrol. His art of minstrelsy he claimed to have learned in Austria (*in Osterrîche lernte ich singen unde sagen*); and it is to be remembered that the term *Osterrîche* then designated only Lower Austria, or the region immediately surrounding Vienna. All his life Walther yearned for the court of Vienna, which was his earthly paradise.

It is often said that Walther "studied under" Reinmar at Vienna; yet there is no evidence for this, even if it is likely that the younger artist did learn something from the older one. Their similarities, at least as far as *hôhiu minne* is concerned, probably resulted from their following common literary traditions. Walther

quickly mastered the art of composing courtly songs; and his songs of *hôhiu minne* are second to none. Nevertheless, despite his success with songs of lofty love, he seems to have found the highly stylized constraints of this genre too restrictive; and he eventually rebelled from the convention that the singer must love without hope of having his love requited. He therefore sang the praises of simple unmarried girls who could and would return his love, as the highborn married ladies of the court could or would not. Such requited love he called *nideriu minne* or "low love" in contrast to *hôhiu* or "high" love; but we might well call it natural love, since it represented a more normal relationship between the sexes, one in which the affection was shared by both parties. Thus, in this regard, Walther reverted to the attitudes expressed in the so-called "Danubian" lyrics that were popular at the time of his birth, such as those attributed to Kürenberger. Perhaps the best known and most loved of his songs of natural love is the girl's confession beginning "Under the linden, on the heath," in which a country lass joyfully recalls an amatory assignation. Although this song followed in the tradition of the French pastourelles, in which a courtier seduces a country wench, Walther's song makes no suggestion of class lines or of social exploitation. All we have is an ingenuous confession of a girl who has found happiness in love; besides, the song appears so natural that we hardly recognize that it is artfully contrived and based on literary motifs and techniques of the vagabond Latin poets as well as of the troubadours and trouvères.

Walther's treatment of nature is also misleading. At first sight his nature descriptions appear almost modern; but further scrutiny reveals that they seldom go beyond the traditional *locus amœnus* or ideal landscape, which is restricted to a small number of conventional stage properties such as spring, brook, linden, birds, flowers, and grass. And this ideal landscape is only a setting for a rendezvous or a dream; or else it serves as a foil to be compared to the superior beauty of one's lady love. Walther's nature descriptions are best in his summer songs, a genre of rollicking dance-song with which people welcomed the May after their long cold winter. Critics used to assume that Walther first followed the convention of lofty love, which he later abandoned in favor of songs of natural love; but stylistic studies indicate that he never deserted the former completely; and it is probable that the choice between the two was determined by the patron.

In singing the praises of natural love Walther discovered something new, or at least something not then acknowledged at the courts, namely that there was more virtue in being a woman (*wîp*) than in being a lady (*frouwe*). By that he meant that true womanhood was superior to the external qualities of birth, wealth, and social position; and in one song he even claims that he would rather receive a plain glass ring from his sweetheart than a golden ring from a queen. Walther's championship of simple girls as opposed to wellborn ladies brought him into conflict with Reinmar, who continued to favor wellborn ones; enough of their songs on the subject survive for us to reconstruct their contest. This singing contest is usually called a feud; but it is more likely that the two singers were collaborating in entertaining the court with a sort of lyric disputation. Nevertheless it is true, as Walther frankly admits in an elegy on Reinmar, that he cared little for the man even though he greatly admired his songs.

While declaring *wîp* a more honorable title than *frouwe*, Walther was no less eloquent than Reinmar and other minnesingers in extolling the ennobling influence of womanhood; for he saw that this quality was found not only in aristocratic ladies but also, and possibly even more, in simple and unspoiled women and girls. Perhaps the creed of this cult was best expressed in Walther's words: *swer guotes wîbes minne hât, der schamt sich aller missetât* (Whoever has the love of a good woman will be ashamed of any misdeed). This adoration of the feminine principle survived in German literature down to Goethe, whose concept of *das Ewig-Weibliche* may (through intermediaries like Walter Scott) have influenced our antebellum ideal of Southern womanhood.

In bursting the bonds of conventional minnesong by singing the praises of simple country maids, Walther paved the way for new lyrics and melodies of a popular nature; and soon the courts were flooded with rustic melodies, including those of Neidhart of Reuental, a knight who sang summer songs and songs in the pastourelle tradition. Such songs are now called *höfische Dorfpoesie* (courtly village poetry); but they should be called rustic court poetry, since they were composed for the courts and not for the peasants. In fact they should not be called *Poesie* at all, just as the words *Gedicht* and *Dichter* should not be used in connection with the minnesingers, who composed songs, not poems. Walther was one of the first to realize Gresham's law of music, that bad music drives out good music; and it was not long before he wrote bitter diatribes against the new boorish melodies, which he likened to the noise of frogs in a pond or of grindstones in a mill that discourage even the nightingale from singing.

Whether singing of high love or low, Walther always advocated courtly behavior. His songs consistently praised *vuoge*, or propriety, that is to say conduct "befitting" courtly culture; and he, as a seer and singer, posed as final arbiter in all matters of decorum. Scholars have always assumed that Walther was a *ministerialis*, or unfree knight; but his songs do not bear this out. He himself complained bitterly of his poverty and mendicancy; and he never once boasted of bearing a sword, a prerequisite for knighthood. His humble social station is revealed in an apparently humorous, but actually virulent, song against a certain Gerhard Atze who shot Walther's horse but refused to pay any indemnity. Walther referred the matter to the judgment of their common overlord, the Landgrave of Thuringia; this indicates that he was not socially entitled to demand satisfaction by challenging Atze. In addition, Walther's song contrasts Atze's steed (*ross*) with his own palfrey (*pferit*), which was the kind of horse ridden by women, clerics, and other unarmed people.

Whereas Walther's contemporaries appreciated him chiefly as a minnesinger, we today are more moved by his political poetry, which appears to have begun in the year 1198. The chief event of this fatal year for Walther was the death of his patron, Frederick of Austria, on a crusade; because Frederick's successor, Leopold, did not continue his patronage. For most other Germans three other events were of even direr consequence: the coronations of both Otto and Philip as emperor and the election of Innocent III as pope. When Frederick Barbarossa died on the Third Crusade in 1190, he left the Empire to his son Henry VI, a strong-willed and astute ruler who kept some semblance of order in the realm; but after Henry's death in 1197 the Empire fared less well. Henry's son, Frederick II, was still an infant and therefore unable to control the turbulent territorial princes, especially after the Guelph candidate, Otto of Brunswick, was crowned emperor with the support of King Richard of England and also of the new pope, who opposed the Ghibelline or Hohenstaufen claims upon Sicily. Realizing that the infant king could not compete successfully, Henry's brother Philip agreed to become interim king instead of merely regent; and he was crowned with the proper insignia but in the wrong place (Frankfurt), whereas Otto had been crowned in the right place (Aachen) but without the imperial insignia.

It was during this period of confusion that Walther composed his best known song, the one that inspired our only picture of him. The miniature of Walther in the Great Heidelberg Manuscript shows the singer sitting on a large rock, chin in hand and elbow on knee, in the traditional posture of one deep in sorrowful meditation; and this is the way Walther depicts himself as he contemplates his troubled world. Knowing it impossible to reconcile wealth and honor with God's grace in such violent times, he calls upon the German people to crown Philip and to force the lesser kings and territorial lords to obey him. Walther continued composing songs in support of Philip until the latter was assassinated and succeeded by Otto, to whom Walther seems to have given reluctant support.

Although never fond of the new emperor, Walther did support him in his struggle against Pope Innocent, whom he accused of wilfully playing one candidate against the other in order to prolong the civil war and thus reduce German pressure on Papal properties in Italy. Because Otto continued the Italian policies of the Hohenstaufens, Innocent excommunicated him as he had previously excommunicated Philip; and this gave Walther occasion to damn either the Pope's logic or his integrity. Walther thereupon began a long series of bitter lampoons against the Pope, which continued even after Frederick II came of age and ousted Otto as emperor. These scathing denunciations are brilliant examples of vituperation at its best and worst, for they accused the Pope not only of simony, but also of theft, greed, and mendacity.

Walther has sometimes been considered a forerunner of Luther, but this is entirely unjustified. It is true that both objected to Papal abuses, but Walther never attacked the dogma of the Church. In fact he was not even anti-clerical. Our only historical document concerning Walther is a travel account of a bishop of Passau who gave him five pieces of silver for a fur coat in the year 1203; and we know that many other clergymen were among Walther's patrons. A song praising Archbishop Engelbert of Cologne, who acted as regent to Frederick II's son Henry VII, was followed by a bitter execration of his murderer and an appeal for suitable divine punishment.

Whereas Walther's political songs are very convincing, it is not easy for us to judge the emotional depth of his religious songs, which comprise a large part of his entire opus. These songs all follow definite conventions and echo concepts and beliefs long current in Latin liturgy and literature. It is often supposed that he wrote most of these songs in his old age after losing faith in the life of this world, but stylistic studies hardly bear this out. Since medieval composers were craftsmen who produced the goods their public demanded, it is more likely that, throughout his career, Walther composed either sacred or profane songs, according to the wishes of his secular or spiritual patrons.

In addition to his amorous, political, and sacred songs, Walther also produced many didactic works for the moral betterment of lords and ladies, children, or the world at large. Many of these songs were based on popular wisdom, much of it ultimately derived from the Old Testament, particularly from the books then ascribed to Solomon. Although Walther considered himself primarily a courtier, the morality taught in these songs strikes us as thoroughly bourgeois and modern; and he, perhaps more than anyone else of his time, seems to speak to future generations even more than to his own. The basic attitude of Walther's ethos is what later scholars have termed *Weltfrömmigkeit,* or secular piety. To be sure, Walther did compose a few songs denouncing the vanity of this world, one of which describes Dame World as beautiful when seen from the front but loathsome and devoured by worms when seen from behind; but these were exceptional, and most of his songs praise life in this world, provided, of course, that one live with moderation and in accord with the dictates of religion and propriety.

One of Walther's most ambitious and impressive works is his so-called *Elegie,* beginning *Ouwê war sint verswunden alliu miniu jâr* (Alas, whither have all my years vanished?). This song, composed as a recruitment song for a crusade, regrets the passing of the good old days and laments the singer's failure to utilize his time in preparing for his eternal salvation; it calls upon the knights to assure their own salvation by fighting in the Holy Land. Because of Walther's apparent pessimism about the world, this song is often called a "palinode," or song of retraction, in which he takes back all the good things he has said about life in this world. A careful reading, however, shows that this is not entirely the case. To be sure, the last of the three strophes does follow convention in saying that, although the world is externally beautiful and colorful, it is as black as death inside and that the knights should therefore avail themselves of the chance to win salvation by fighting in the Holy Land. Here, probably for propagandistic purpose, he does compare life in this world unfavorably with life in the world to come; but the first two strophes do not support this otherworldly view; one feels that the poet is really complaining that the world is no longer as he once knew it and that society is no longer so courtly as it was in the good old days. He does not seem to regret having lived a worldly life, but rather having outlived it. But even if this and several other songs do express a dualistic view of life, it is easily seen that most of his songs expressed a gradualistic view, the view that all God's creation is good, not only trees, flowers, and birds, but also lords, ladies, and simple people, and that, through good behavior, we can reconcile the demands of the world with those of God.

IV

In his criticism of contemporary literature, Gottfried disdained to mention a work which impresses many modern critics as the greatest, or at least one of the greatest, of its age. This was the *Song of the Nibelungs*,[21] a compilation of oral materials, mostly of ancient and native origin, which had been written down shortly before Gottfried composed his *Tristan*. Although this ancient tale of murder and revenge was composed in courtly love strophes similar to those of the previously mentioned Kürenberger, its author neglected to reveal his own identity. Nevertheless, Wolfram saw fit to allude to it in his *Parzival*, and this shows that it was known to his courtly audience.

Much has been conjectured, but nothing definite is known, about the author. As long as critics followed romantic tradition in believing the song a haphazard coalescence of ancient ballads, they put little importance upon the "last poet" and concerned themselves more with his postulated sources. Now that recent scholars have shown that the song was an individual literary creation, it is no more justifiable to speak of the "last poet" of the *Nibelungenlied* than to speak of the "last poet" of Shakespeare's *Hamlet* or of Goethe's *Faust*. It is now evident that the *Nibelungenlied* author used not only ancient oral traditions but also written literature both German and French. Such literary influence is, however, very unobtrusive, it being the nature of the so-called "popular" or "national" epics to dispense with scholarly pedantry. In fact Rüdiger, the most exemplary character in the song, seems to have been inspired by Ogier, the hero of *Renaus de Montauban*, a French *chanson de geste*.

The author does not appear to have been a nobleman, and his intense interest in courtly life suggests the outsider looking in with all the fascination of a self-made society columnist sent to cover the doings of high society. Also, his descriptions of hunting and fighting are far from convincing. In view of his apparent, albeit largely suppressed, learning, it would seem that the author had enjoyed some education and was therefore a "cleric," even if he probably never took his vows.

The geography of the first half of the song, which deals with the Rhineland and vague areas northward, is inaccurate and sometimes outright fanciful; yet the journey in the second half is geographically accurate, especially regarding the route along the Danube in the vicinity of Passau. This, along with the introduction of a former bishop of Passau as a gracious host and brother of the Burgundian queen, suggests that the song may have been composed for the current bishop of that diocese, who was none other than Wolfger of Ellenbrechtskirchen, the donor of Walther's fur coat. It is probable that the song was composed by an Austrian, but there is no absolute proof that it was not composed by Walther himself.

The *Nibelungenlied* consists of two somewhat distinct yet causally connected plots: the murder of Siegfried and the subsequent destruction of his murderers. The core of the second part can be easily traced to an historical event, the annihilation of the Burgundians by the Huns in 437; and the first part seems to owe something, surely more than just a few names, to events in early Frankish history. Scholars have argued at great length about these origins and have postulated older versions, which they then used as facts on which to base further conjectures. But all this expenditure of ink and intellect has served to draw people away from the song rather than to it, and it is only in recent years that critics have seriously tried to appreciate the song for what it is and not for what it must have been before being corrupted by later redactors.

Siegfried, a prince of Netherland, journeys to Worms on the Rhine to woo Kriemhild, the sister of the Burgundian kings Gunther, Gernot, and Giselher; and he earns her hand by helping Gunther win Brunhild, a remote and semi-mythological princess who will marry only him who defeats her in three physical contests. Posing as Gunther's vassal, Siegfried helps him win the games and the bride by using his cape of invisibility which he must use soon again to subdue Brunhild for Gunther on their wedding night. After feeling uneasy about her marriage for some years, Brunhild persuades Gunther to invite Siegfried and Kriemhild to visit them at Worms; for she wishes to know whether Siegfried is really their vassal. The visit provides an occasion for the two queens to fight over social precedence, and Kriemhild angrily reveals that it was Siegfried rather than Gunther who overpowered Brunhild on her wedding night. To avenge this insult to his liege-lady, as well as to protect the realm, Gunther's faithful vassal Hagen determines to murder Siegfried; and he does so after tricking Kriemhild into disclosing her husband's one vulnerable spot. After Siegfried's death Hagen also deprives Kriemhild of the Nibelungen hoard, the treasure that Siegfried had given her as a nuptial gift, and had it sunk somewhere in the Rhine.

Some years later Kriemhild, now the wife of the mighty Etzel (the Hunnish King Attila), invites her brothers to visit her. Despite Hagen's warnings they insist upon making the trip to Etzel's land to avoid the appearance of cowardice, but they go well armed. On the way they enjoy hospitality at the castle of their guide, the "good" Rüdiger, who exchanges gifts with them and betroths his daughter to Giselher. As soon as they reach Etzel's land, Kriemhild incites a battle between them and Etzel's men and sets fire to the hall in which they are quartered. Despite his ties of friendship, kinship, and hospitality, Rüdiger must fulfill his fealty to Etzel and his personal vows to Kriemhild by fighting against the Burgundians, and he does so after great moral anguish and with the loss of his life. Unwilling to surrender Hagen to Kriemhild, the Burgundians are all killed except Gunther and Hagen, who are brought bound to Kriemhild. When she demands the hoard from Hagen, he replies that he cannot reveal its location as long as any of his lords are still alive. She thereupon has Gunther beheaded. When Hagen still refuses, Kriemhild decapitates him too, whereupon she in turn is decapitated by one of Etzel's angry vassals.

In comparison with the courtly romances, the *Nibelungenlied* has many narrative faults. Its medium was ill chosen, it being written in quatrains of long-lines rhyming *aabb*, which do not lend themselves to epic action: the author sometimes completes his idea or scene before completing his strophe, with the result that he must pad the last verse. There is much repetition, not only of phrases but even of almost entire verses; and there are also numerous contradictions. Some discrepancies result from the superimposition of courtly elegance and splendor on a much simpler story with resulting friction between the two levels of narration. For example, the author follows his ancient sources in letting Hagen row all the Burgundians across the Danube, even though his new notions of splendor have increased their forces to eleven thousand men and horses.

Such discrepancies also appear in personal behavior, especially between the two sometimes badly joined halves of the song. Siegfried alternately blanches and blushes while wooing Kriemhild, yet after their marriage he thrashes her soundly for betraying his secret to Brunhild. Gunther is a coward in the first half of the song but a hero at its end; Kriemhild is a modest maid and meek wife until Siegfried is killed, whereupon she is suddenly a she-devil. Critics used to attribute such changes to psychological development; but now they realize that the author was using the common technique of episodic characterization: a character was tailored to fit a certain role even though this role differed sharply from other roles assigned to the same person elsewhere in the song.

Likewise, the apparent discrepancies in time are of no significance, since the author makes use of epic time. The actions and dialogue are dramatic, one might say cinematographic; for the individual scenes, which often take not much longer to tell than they would last in real life, are separated by long intervals. If these intervals were reckoned seriously, then Kriemhild would be a middle-aged woman before her brothers visit her in Etzel's land. Like Goethe's mythological woman she never gets old and never gets grey, and she is still wooed at an advanced age.

To appreciate the epic correctly, we must accept it as it has been passed down to us, and not the way it may have been in its earlier stages. For example, the author never explicitly states, or even implies, that Siegfried and Brunhild were once betrothed, or even acquainted. Nor should we assume that Siegfried deflowered her for Gunther, since this would have gone against Siegfried's role as Kriemhild's perfect courtly lover. We must also accept both the heroic Germanic ethos and the courtly elegance as integral elements of the epic; for the author saw no clash between the two ingredients. In his opening two verses he promises to tell not only of famous heroes but also of festivities; and we must remember that his audience enjoyed hearing his detailed descriptions of the latter even though we might find them rather tedious. The lavish and protracted descriptions of costly clothing not only gave vicarious pleasure to the lords and ladies of the court, who had probably never seen such luxury, but also enhanced the status of the heroes of the story, whose clothes were an outward and visible sign of their inner worth.

Christianity and Christian solace play almost no part in the epic. With the possible exception of Rüdiger, no one seems concerned with immortality; and even he seems unable to distinguish between it and his posthumous fame. Going to mass is but a social convention; pious invocations are but polite speech, practiced, incidentally, by the pagan Etzel as often as by any of the Christians. A church is introduced, but as a place for the two queens to wrangle over social precedence; and a chaplain accompanies the Burgundians to Etzel's land so that Hagen can throw him overboard to test the prophesy of a nix who has predicted the Burgundians' approaching doom.

Yet, despite his high praise of courtly culture and heroic deeds and his almost total neglect of Christian ethos and mythos, one gets the impression that the author was a deeply religious, or at least deeply committed, person. In fact, rather than a genuine courtly romance or heroic epic, his masterpiece resembles a sermon against worldly vanity. This pessimistic mood is struck in the very first canto when Kriemhild has a dream which her mother interprets as an omen of impending tragedy. We are constantly reminded that all joy must turn to sorrow, and we are never allowed to hope for a happy ending; because the otherwise unfilled fourth verse of many a strophe contains a foreboding of coming ruin. In fact, the few brief moments of unmitigated joy, such as the hunt and the visit at Pöchlarn, seem included only to contrast with and thus stress the following misery.

The suspense of the work is not one of what, but only of how and when; for we know from the outset that our brave heroes are proceeding to inevitable destruction, to a destruction caused by their own arrogance and pride. At the end of the catastrophe, with the ground covered with gore and corpses, the only consolation is a heroic one, the assurance that brave men have vindicated their past deeds by facing death defiantly. But such consolation could at best satisfy the heroes themselves, not their loved ones at home who face a meaningless future. This existentialist outcome far better suited the war-weary and disintegrating Hohenstaufen era than did the "happy ending" of Wolfram's fanciful Grail romance.

V

With the death of Walther the high tide of Middle High German literature began to ebb. Later poets made up in quantity what they lacked in quality; few could do more than follow in the footsteps of their revered masters. Some of these imitators showed occasional spurts of skill and even of talent, but seldom attained the excellence of their models. Despite the turmoil of the Hohenstaufen era, the cities had prospered at the expense of the nobility; and wealthy burghers gradually displaced the landed nobility as the chief patrons of the arts. In their drive towards social betterment the burghers attempted to ape the dress, manners, and graces of the nobles and to promote their literature; yet they seemed unable to comprehend the aesthetic and cultural values of the literature they had inherited. Even when they reproduced the same subjects, situations, genres, and even literary idiom, the courtly spirit was somehow lost; and the longer romances often lost all ideal vision, as well as literary unity, and degenerated into disconnected episodes.

Many classical masterpieces were reworked: for example, Wolfram's *Willehalm, Titurel,* and *Parzival* all inspired considerably longer continuations or imitations. New themes, often borrowed from Latin and French literature, also became popular, especially when put into the courtly diction of the great masters by Rudolf of Ems, Conrad of Würzburg, and other talented narrators. While poets still extolled the good old days, they began to question their own age and to deplore the discrepancy between courtly ideals and current conduct. A literary result of this critical attitude is Wernher the Gardener's charming little tale, *Helmbrecht,* which relates the downfall of a young peasant lad who aspires to rise above his order.[22] This story, which claims to be an eyewitness account, is so cleverly told that the reader hardly observes that it is actually a disguised sermon against social ambition. Following in the tradition of Neidhart of Reuental, the author achieved considerable humor by putting courtly speech in the mouths of his rustic cast.

Another unusual work of this period of decline is Ulrich of Lichtenstein's *Frauendienst,* a fantastic biographical account of a knight's adventures in the service of his lady, in which the narrative is interspersed with elaborate minnesongs. The most popular genre during all this period were the many farces and verse tales which, although often based on foreign models, were adapted to the tastes of the general public and enjoyed a sub-literary existence until eventually written down by various collectors.

Simultaneously with the various genres of secular verse, the older clerical literature continued unabated; and the saints' lives, Biblical paraphrases, hymns to the Virgin Mary, and other devout works were produced in ever-increasing numbers. Also popular were collections of homely aphoristic wisdom such as Freidank's *Bescheidenheit* and anthologies of long and elaborate love allegories. Usually devoid of literary form or unity, many of these compilations strike the modern reader as too diffuse and destitute of feeling. Exceptions are found in the introspective writings of some of the mystic writers such as Eckhart, Tauler, and Seuse, who coined new words to fit their needs. Some of them, like Eckhart, sharpened their language into a keen tool for precise intellectual argument; others, like Seuse and many female enthusiasts, found it necessary to create a whole new emotive vocabulary in their effort to "eff" the ineffable and "ut" the unutterable in describing the mystic union of their souls with Jesus. To these mystics the German language owes much of its *Innerlichkeit.*

The increased use of prose during this period freed poets from the shackles of rhyme and meter and thus enabled them to increase the range and precision of their language. This was true not only of the emotional outpourings of the mystics, but also of the extensive treatises devoted to legal codes, the liberal arts, and the natural sciences, which could now be written in German as well as in Latin. Perhaps the greatest innovation of the age was the development of exact technical languages which brought theoretical and practical knowledge to the reach of the non-Latinist.[23]

A new literary genre had meanwhile developed in the liturgical plays which appeared throughout Western Europe, especially in those celebrating Easter.[24] These had evolved from the Easter service, being first performed in the church and sung in Latin. Later, as more characters were added, the performance sought the open; and, to make the plays more intelligible and entertaining for the populace, German was substituted for Latin and comical scenes were interpolated between the serious ones. The most striking characteristic of these plays, and of late medieval literature in general, is the crass juxtaposition of the sacred and the profane, of the sublime and the ridiculous. Such contradiction, which was expressed philosophically in the *coincidentia oppositorum* of Nicholas of Cues, permeated all life and literature; writers no longer tried to reconcile the conflicts in their works as the Hohenstaufen poets had tried to do, since life, as they experienced it, was full of unresolved contradictions. A favorite genre throughout the waning Middle Ages was the *disputatio* or *Streitgedicht,* a debate in which the two sides of an argument were both illuminated with no real attempt to come to any conclusion.

The disharmony of the times is evident in contradictory attitudes towards life and death, which fluctuated between morbid obsession with death and desperate craving for the fleeting pleasures of this life. Gone was the old optimism of the Hohenstaufen era. No longer did men believe in the ideal of one happy and united Christendom ruled in spiritual matters by the Pope in Rome and in secular matters by the Emperor in Germany; for both of these had lost much prestige and authority. Indeed, at times there were two, even three, popes, and sometimes a like number of emperors, none of whom could furnish leadership for church or state. The breakdown of imperial authority permitted constant strife between the territorial lords, and the realm was afflicted with wars and the rumors of wars. In addition, frequent plagues, the greatest of which was the Black Death of 1349, sometimes left scarcely enough survivors to bury the dead, and the stench of death was everywhere. Popular preachers fulminated about the Day of Judgment, and men lived in constant fear of fire and brimstone. Swarms of flagellants crossed the land confessing their sins and calling all men to penitence before sudden death should take them away in their sins; and the dance of death became a favorite theme in art, literature, and popular spectacles. Yet, despite, or perhaps because of these ascetic extremes, man in his despair also sought solace in sensual pleasures, knowing that any gluttony or sexual indulgence might be his last.

Despite the many negative aspects of the times, the early fifteenth century did produce three truly gifted authors, authors who reached the first magnitude despite the age in which they lived. The best known of these was Johann of Tepl, formerly known as Johannes of Saaz, who wrote a short *disputatio* entitled *Death and the Plowman (Der Ackermann aus Böhmen)* in the first year of the new century.[25] In thirty-two paragraphs of rhetorical prose the author accuses Death of having stolen his bride, while Death answers that it was meet and right for him to do so. Here, as so often in late medieval literature, we find the glaring contrast of man praised as God's own image and at the same time reviled as a stinking heap of manure. Both the Plowman and Death argue well; and in chapter 33 God gives the honor to the former but the victory to the latter.

The greatest lyric poet of the age, and one of the most dynamic of all time, was the South Tyrolian composer Oswald of Wolkenstein (1377–1445).[26] Unlike most of his literary predecessors, Oswald was a man of political importance whose life is fully documented; and his opus is well preserved in two handsome manuscripts compiled under his own supervision and adorned with realistic portraits of the author himself. His songs, which are often biographical and cover the whole gamut of late medieval themes, might well serve as a mirror of the age, for they abundantly illustrate the juxtaposition of sacred and profane, of serious and frivolous. Sometimes it is hard to decide whether a certain song is an erotic song to his mistress, or a devout one to the Virgin Mary, and it is significant that the same melody can be used for songs either pious or pornographic.

The only poet able to bridge the gap between the serious and the frivolous was the Swiss poet Henry Wittenwiler, who wrote an incredible comic-didactic mock epic called the *Ring*.[27] The plot of this work is based on the *Peasant Wedding* (*Bauernhochzeit*), a popular peasant satire in the Neidhart tradition; but Wittenwiler stretched the 400 odd verses of the original to almost 10,000 by expanding its motifs and adding a myriad of new ones, especially didactic matter often inappropriate for the peasant characters in the epic. In his preface Wittenwiler claims that his work is serious in purpose and that he has included the peasant humor merely to make the work more palatable for a world that cannot accept serious matter alone; he even distinguishes the serious from the jocular matter by running a green line through the former and a red one through the latter. Amazingly enough the author accomplished his two conflicting goals, to instruct and to entertain, and achieved unity in both endeavors. Despite a fanciful chronology, the action is unified; and the encyclopaedic knowledge he wished to impart, even though extensive and complete in itself, is unobtrusively incorporated into the story, mostly in debates and discourses spoken by the peasant protagonists themselves.

The triumvirate Johann of Tepl, Oswald of Wolkenstein, and Henry Wittenwiler found no worthy successor until near the end of the century, when German literature at last produced an international best seller in Sebastian Brant's *Ship of Fools* (*Nar-*

renschiff), which was immediately done into Latin and then translated from Latin into most Western languages.[28] This somewhat
formless accumulation of human foibles, which assembled popular
motifs of medieval fool's literature together with themes and ideas
from the new age of humanism, set the style for a number of
literary works denouncing or praising folly. Whereas the late medieval era produced little first-rate literature, it did serve as a period of
consolidation and preparation. The learning that had once been the
monopoly of clerical Latinists trickled down to a far larger number
of bourgeois laymen, whose increased reading gradually prepared
them both spiritually and intellectually to play a role in the coming
Reformation.

2. Literature of the Sixteenth and Seventeenth Centuries ✍

Ingrid Merkel

I

During the fifteenth and sixteenth centuries Europe underwent a tumultuous process of transformation. With the decline of the social and spiritual powers of the Middle Ages, movements which had originated in previous centuries began to unleash their previously subdued energies. In Italy a national ideal arose which eventually produced a genuine rebirth of the Roman past. In Germany the former aristocratic culture was adapted to a more popular taste, theology began to free itself from its scholastic tradition, and the arts developed greater realism. Such developments can rightfully be called "renaissance" or rebirth.[1] But in order to avoid any ambiguity *Renaissance* is to be understood solely as the revival of classical heritage in Italy. This somewhat restrictive definition still allows us to see the Renaissance as a phenomenon with wide range, encompassing all spheres of life: arts and politics, social life, and religion. In due time Italian painting, architecture, and music would set the pace in European art. The new concept of man which the Renaissance projected and which is best defined as *Humanism,* soon outgrew its Italian sources and developed into a common European concept with a lasting effect.[2] Humanism represented both a distinct philosophy and a new style inspired by classical models. Its philosophy praised the dignity of man's worldly existence, extolled human reason, and advocated the freedom of the individual. Its style emulated the ideals of classical writings and influenced for centuries the language of European men of letters.

In Germany, the innovations of the changing times focused on the reform of man's spiritual life and culminated in a great religious upheaval. In fact, Luther's *Reformation* was as symptomatic for Germany as the Renaissance was for Italy. Still, Reformation as a phenomenon is not exclusively German, since it embraced not only many specifically German but also humanistic impulses. Consequently, Renaissance, Humanism, and Reformation, as divisions of the age, should be considered only as guidelines. They do not exclude, but rather complement one another. Likewise, the study of German literature of that time must take its European context into consideration, that is, its Latin and Italian models.

Italy's rebirth of the Roman past was initiated by men of letters. Petrarch (1304–1374), though in many aspects still a medieval man, admired the ancients and saw them as catalysts for a national consciousness. Extraordinary economic and social progress had strengthened the self-confidence of the Italian burgher who wished to free his city-state from foreign, "barbaric" dominance. These city-states, favored by their trade with the Orient, had accumulated enough wealth to turn the splendor of the past into the adornment of their own age. While Petrarch deplored the discord of his nation and yearned for its unification, the art of the Renaissance evolved through the very competition of the Italian states for cultural excellence. The ruins of Rome rose from ignominy. Their solemn simplicity inspired buildings and monuments all over the country, if only for the glory of princes and governments. Ancient beauty began to produce a new vision of life.

Some authors drew new inspiration from their careful study of the ancient texts. Petrarch and Boccaccio (1313–1375) were enthusiastically engaged in the search for manuscripts. Princes spent fortunes on their acquisition and editing. Amidst such activities a new science arose: *Studii Humaniores,* the critical study, editing, and interpretation of rediscovered ancient texts with the aim of restoring them to their original status. The *humanisti* developed new standards for philological accuracy and a notion of truth very different from that of the Middle Ages. Medieval man had found evidence about himself and the world in the sanctified Christian revelation; the new generation, though deeply immersed in Christian thought, ventured into the pagan past. They formulated their own concept of humanity, one which enabled them to appreciate human reason, objective understanding, and independent judgment of the world. Thus the classical writings shaped the intellectual and artistic ideals of generations of humanists who sought to duplicate the formal elegance and clarity of the Latin models. These ideals had the widest effect on literature and education.

Dante (1265–1321) had raised the vernacular to literary standards. Now Petrarch in the *Canzoniere* (1348) molded the language in accordance with the refined style of the Latin classicists. The popular language maintained its newly acquired standards even when the learned poets preferred the universal Latin. In Germany, however, the abyss between learned (i.e. Latin) language and the vernacular could never be bridged. Latin remained, in spite of the growing importance and refinement of the vernacular, the preferred language of learned men as it had been in medieval Europe. Greek and Hebrew also developed into flourishing disciplines of humanistic endeavors. Cosimo Medici (1389–1464) founded the Platonic Academy in Florence (1459) at which illustrious contemporaries such as Pico della Mirandola (1463–1494) and Marsilio Ficino (1433–1499) explicated the Platonic heritage. The academy furnished a home to Greek scholars who had been expatriated by the seizure of Constantinople (1453). They familiarized their disciples with the riches of the Greek language. Reuchlin (1455–1522) embraced Greek at the Platonic Academy; he also took up the study of Hebrew, which he then introduced into Germany.

The new ideal of eloquence reached Germany in the late fourteenth century. Cola di Rienzo (1313–1354) had found protection at the court in Prague and there acquainted his friends with his rhetorical style. Petrarch arrived in Prague five years later. An early humanistic literature began to bloom at the Prague court, furthered by Charles IV and his chancellor, Johann von Neumarkt (1310–1380), who cultivated the new eloquence imported by Rienzo and Petrarch. Neumarkt's writings, both in Latin and German, were indebted to the ideal of Ciceronian rhetorical forms. Bohemian humanism produced its first masterpiece around 1400. Mourning his wife's untimely death, Johann von Tepl (1350–1414), rector of the Latin school in Saaz, wrote *Der Ackermann aus Böhmen* (*Death and the Plowman*), commonly considered the first representative work of "modern" German literature. A plowman defends the dignity of human life in a passionate dialogue with Death. His attitude clearly reflects humanistic aspirations while the rejection of life by Death expresses medieval thought. In this unique way the *Plowman* exemplifies vanishing and emerging tendencies of its time. The *Plowman* is also unique in its form, which incorporates for the first time the principles of classical and Italian rhetoric. This combination constitutes a singular achievement in the early fifteenth century.[3]

The German mind, unlike the Italian, could not of course as easily identify with the Roman heritage. The Germans imitated the Latin or Italian models, because they considered them superior to the fading ideals of their own medieval culture. Still certain developments in Germany resemble the Italian events. The decline of the spiritual balance of power between Church and Empire greatly affected the elaborate social system of the Middle Ages. Clergy and knights, the classes which had profited from the feudal caste-structure and whose culture had mirrored lofty spirituality and exclusiveness, lost their position in a growing middle-class society. German cities prospered through the expansion of trade and their burghers became increasingly aware of social and cultural issues. Education broke with its religious and courtly ties and reoriented itself toward the new world and its problems. A substantial part of the population formerly barred from education became interested in culture. A new awareness of reality resulted in activities which concentrated on worldly problems and their understanding. The middle class had truly become the cultural standard bearer when the classical heritage made its first appearance in Germany. Indeed German humanism was shaped by the fusion of foreign tradition and middle-class mentality. To understand the always ambiguous, sometimes tumultuous progress of German literature of the time, one has to consider the affinities, tensions, and antagonisms between the German middle-class tradition and the classical tradition, since these currents were to determine the literary landscape of the following centuries. This point is perhaps best illustrated by the development of the literary genres.

Many popular books were published during the fifteenth and sixteenth centuries. Their theological or scientific content satisfied the needs of the middle class for moral guidance and instruction. The writings of Mysticism combined the expression of a personalized religious experience with high ethical norms; it helped to popularize theology and thus introduced the masses, still deeply entangled in the practice of magic, to a more profound understanding of Christianity. The refinement of religious experience strengthened the feeling for personal relevance and also affected man's assessment of his worldly existence. These tendencies finally culminated in the Reformation, which provided one answer to the challenges of the new time.

The literary documents of the early fifteenth century show a similar popularization and transformation of medieval poetic standards. The courtly epic and lyric verse declined as burghers and peasants emulated these literary forms. The courtly epic dissolved into broad and heterogeneous prose novels as is evidenced by Johann Hartlieb's treatment of the medieval *Alexander* and Elisabeth of Nassau's *Huge Scheppel*. In poetry the stylized veneration of the courtly *frouwe* (lady) was transformed into the happy experience of fulfilled love, into "affairs" with young burgher or peasant girls. Such poems continued the low *minne* themes of Walther of the Vogelweide and Neidhart of Reuental. Oswald of Wolkenstein, a great lyrical talent, succeeded in fusing *minne* tradition and popular aspirations. Both the lyrical and epic genres produced a wealth of popular literature. The narrative technique of the prose novel influenced the style of the *Volksbücher* (chapbooks) whereas minnesong survived in the various forms of the folksong.

As early as the fourteenth century the craftsmen guilds of cities such as Augsburg, Nürnberg, and Mainz engaged in the competitive practice of poetic composition known as *Meistersang*. The tradition of minnesong was copied in a very formal manner. Topics and melodies were fixed, and the *Meister* had to "invent" his composition along the line of a preset *tabula*. In the process the stylized fervor of the minnesong had to give way to a mechanical, somewhat sterile reproduction of verses. Yet the usually denigrated *Meistersang* deserves more attention than it has been accorded; for the combined effort of its numerous authors assisted greatly in the shaping of the artistic language of the sixteenth century. The heavy tongues of cobblers and tailors became more pliable and receptive to refined expression.

The folksong transformed minnesong differently from the *Meistersang*: Rather than preserving rules and topics in a regulative manner and elaborating on them in artisan fashion, the folksingers infused the traditional songs with their personal experience. While the original text and melody were *zersungen* (garbled), typical forms arose with simple rhyme, a refrain, plain language, and repetitive imagery. They conveyed typical experiences like the joys and sorrow of love. Or they dealt with the life of hunters, horsemen, and peasants. Variations of the folksong were the popular ballad and the historical folksong which sometimes treated political events and heroes in a factious spirit. The *Liederbuch der Clara Hätzerlin* (*Songbook of Clara Hätzerlin*, 1471) and the *Rostocker Liederbuch* (*Rostock Songbook*, 1478) represent many forms and show various transformations of *minne* elements in the anonymous process of their popularization.

The fifteenth century was still able to produce Wittenwiler's *Ring*, an epic of European stature. The work transformed a motif of the Neidhartiana (a peasant wedding) into a moral allegory, treated with superb irony and blunt objectivity. But like the *Plowman*, it constituted a singular artistic achievement in a time which favored prose. Satires, jokes, and pranks (e.g. *Der Pfarrer von Kahlenberg; Stories about the Pastor of Kahlenberg* by a Philipp Frankfürter around 1450) centered around a person of popular origin. Neidhart of Reuental's depictions of peasant life had established a tradition which made the peasant the scapegoat and laughingstock of the other classes. He demonstrated the reversion of values, the distortion of the social perspective. This pattern of satire and prank continued the long tradition of moral teaching applied to the social circumstances prevailing then. Still the leading figure presented more than a moral or social issue. The very vitality of his depiction, along with his somewhat crude directness in approach and outlook, mirrored the attitude of the contemporaries, their candid and new awareness of life. The writers seem to be almost obsessed by such realism. Plain and without perspective they string the scenes, events, and problems of their surrounding world like a bead on the cord of their stories.

Such realism took different forms in the various genres. The simpleness which we admire in the folksong and which contrasted sharply with the artistry of courtly poetry expressed an inner reality, an emotion or mood, whereas the tale reflected exterior life. This inner reality emerged in the mystical writings as a personal religious experience. In the mystery plays it developed as an external dramatic event.

The mystery play, which originally centered around the Easter and Christmas liturgy, took up themes of a general religious content. The Biblical stories of the *Prodigal Son*, of *Susanna*, and *Josef* were used as plots. German translations were partly substituted for the Latin text. Burghers took part in the performances and made inroads into the former domain of the priests. Mundane and hilarious scenes, crudely designed to convey the "moral" to the simple audience, became part of the plays. One such scene depicted Christ chasing the merchants from the temple. Eventually the performances were banned from the interior of the church. People who saw themselves surrounded everywhere by manifestations of the Christian faith in painting and music, who lived and entertained themselves with the stories from the Bible, could see the supernatural in the play. They viewed the play like a story comprising a series of pictures in a picturebook. The plays lacked a genuine plot and structure and the characterization of heroes did not evince great psychological depth. The performances, however, appealed to the eye; and the visual reality of the spiritual event produced a spontaneous involvement of the spectator, who felt that his world was inextricably tied to the world beyond.

Despite great diversity, the popular literature of the early fifteenth century displays certain common denominators. It was a literature of great vitality and immediacy produced by skilled craftsmen. And though their literary expression lacked the elegance of the Italian *Rinascitá*, they brought forth the idea of a true *uomo universale*. Nicholas of Cues (1401–1464) was perhaps the most outstanding representative of the new renaissance man north of the Alps. In *De docta ignorantia* (*Of Learned Ignorance*, 1440), he combined the rationalism of Scholastic thinking with the spirituality of the *Devotio moderna*.[4] He also served as a diplomat for several popes and enjoyed political involvement as much as the study of classical writers. Most importantly, he envisioned a reform of Christianity within the old Church, though his vision proved premature.

At the end of the fifteenth century popular German literature found itself faced with Italian classicism. Its promoters swarmed to the universities, especially the recently founded University of Basel, but also to Heidelberg, Erfurt, Leipzig, Vienna, and Prague, the first German university, founded by Charles IV in 1348. They changed these revered institutions not only through a new philosophy, but also through a new style of life. They introduced poetry as an important science among the traditional disciplines. The study of classical languages began to attract men from all social strata. In fact the *humanioria* brought to the traditional structure of the learned classes an addition, the *literati*. The *literatus*, intimately familiar with classical texts and writers, tended to apply the restrictive rules of eloquence to his own expression. As Albrecht of Eyb stated in the *Margarita poetica* (1459), a collection of excerpts from classical writings, "For what does beautiful knowledge serve, if one cannot speak about it in a dignified manner and if one only writes about ludicrous things." Linguistic elegance and the mastery of oratory frequently established a man's reputation in the educated world. The study of Cicero, Lucian, and Terence and the reading of anthologies like the *Margarita poetica* familiarized the young humanists with the new style. Meticulous translations of Italian and Latin masterpieces, of Plautus, Boccaccio, and Enea Silvio (1405–1464) served the same end. The young men who undertook these translations were convinced that beauty and form of the Latin rhetoric could also be applied to the German language. Niklas of Wyle (1410–1478) in his *Translationes* (1461) had set his mind on the art of eloquence and poetry, on the *oratoria*, and did not care whether people "unable to speak" would understand him or not. His translation of Enea Silvio's novella *Euriolus and Lucretia* was an outstanding achievement not only in the German language but also in regard to its tectonic structure. Another master of classical writings, Rudolf Agricola (1443–1485), had acquired his knowledge in Italy and became one of the first teachers of Greek in Germany. His principal work *De inventione dialectica (Of Dialectical Invention*, 1521), an eclectic compilation of philosophy and quotations from classical texts, wanted to introduce its reader to the vital art of "expressing oneself clearly and understandably on every subject." The same concern for style led Konrad Celtis (1459–1508) to establish poetic rules in *Ars versificandi (The Art of Poetry*, 1486). He explained the structure of poetry and the classical meter with examples from Horace. *Ars versificandi* can be regarded as the first attempt to conceive of poetry as an aesthetic phenomenon. It started in Germany the long tradition of systematic expositions of norms for poetical expression in Germany. The *Libri amorum (Books of Love*, 1502) demonstrate Celtis's rhetorical skills. This elaborate allegorical system will probably appeal less to the modern reader than the lyrical tone of Celtis's odes.

The favorite genre of the early fifteenth century, the satire, improved greatly under the influence of Latin models. In fact it developed into the most effective literary form of expression. As artists began to look at the world with a critical eye, they discovered a fearful human condition. This sobering awareness prodded some writers to satirize the existing conditions. Both the critical and reformatory impulses were humanistic in the proper sense, yet man's world was still measured by the standards of Christian ontology and morality. A person who permitted the fictitious reality of mere appearance to govern his body and soul was a fool bound to be excluded from salvation. The fool of the sixteenth-century satire nevertheless differed from his medieval ancestor because his follies had become more worldly.

Sebastian Brant (1457–1521), an ardent humanist, wrote his famous *Ship of Fools* (1494) in the tradition of moral teaching. But the more than a hundred forms of follies depicted in verse and woodcuts are primarily social vices. Brant focused on reality, mostly on the life of the burgher, and wanted a change in man's imminent relations rather than in his transcendental ones. The *Ship of Fools*, medieval as it may appear in its moral teachings, was popular and humanistic in its concern for man's immediate state. The grotesquery of folly arises from imminent distortions, as Rabelais's giants expressed them by their exaggerated physical size. To rearrange the distorted proportions, the humanist applied wit and laughter, which were very much of popular origin. It was also picturesque. For that reason the woodcut constituted an essential part of the message. Word and picture worked to the same effect. The *Ship of Fools* enjoyed enormous popularity and became a model to many writers in the popular tradition or with humanistic intentions. Thomas Murner (1475–1537) displayed skillful artistry in the satire *Von dem großen Lutherischen Narren* (*Of the Great Lutheran Fool*, 1522), a piece of venomous religious polemic. He had followed Brant's example in two earlier works. The *Schelmenzunft* (*The Rogues' Guild*) and *Die Narrenbeschwörung* (*The Exorcism of Fools*), both in 1512, condemned, in the Brant manner, abuses of the time such as drunkenness, craze for fashion, and the vanity of all strata of society, including his own class of clergymen. Murner's humor shows structural similarity with Brant's, the same image-orientation, though the *Great Lutheran Fool* developed a new style. Apart from exaggerations and crudity, Murner injected classical erudition into the satire. Wit became an intellectual game that required clear reasoning and perfection in the language (both classical ideals). The jests aimed to persuade by amusing and simultaneously challenging man's mind through the "pointed" combination of true and false statements.

Johann Fischart (1546–1590), a generation later, went even further to intellectualize wit. *Flöhhatz* (*The Flea-hunt*, 1573) was a delightful piece of social caricature written with rhetorical pathos (a flea, having just escaped death, complains to Jupiter about the persecution its species suffers from women). In his *Geschichtsklitterung, von Taten und Raten der Helden Gargantua und Pantagruel* (*Historical Sketch of the Acts and Counsels of the Heroes Gargantua and Pantagruel*, 1575) he surpassed his French model in sheer verbosity. However, it is precisely the playful and skillful use of language that deserves attention. Fischart's command of German was admirable. The supply of new comical word formations was almost inexhaustible and he delighted in the witty exploitation of *figurae, tropi,* and quotations. Some of Fischart's sound-combinations prefigure those later found in the poems of the Nürnberg poets. If Celtis's *Ars versificandi* established literary art as a sovereign field of human activity, Fischart emancipated language within such literary art. He obviously disregarded classical elegance, which had aimed at the proper balance between the object and its literary presentation.

The satire reached its artistic perfection in a Latin work. *The Praise of Folly* (1509) by Erasmus of Rotterdam (1466–1536), marked by intellectual sobriety, proved an unsurpassed masterpiece. Sparing no one, the book criticizes the whole social fabric of the time. In a lengthy self-eulogy Folly boasts of the grip it has on countries, people, and classes. But soon wit changes into irony. Folly emerges as the vital principle of life. "What kind of God, so enraged would force man to be born into such misery, I dare not explain here . . . But I help in this misery with ignorance. . . . forgetfulness. . . . hope for the better." Such lines are not only a triumph of intellect but also convey a deeply felt skepticism and resignation which only the sovereign mind of the writer is able to conquer.

Latin eloquence of the time produced still another masterpiece of satirical writing. When Johann Reuchlin (1455–1522) defended the collection and preservation of Hebrew texts, he aroused the enmity of Pfefferkorn, a baptized Jew, and other Scholastics. Humanists from all over Europe supported Reuchlin; in 1514 he published the famous *Clarorum virorum epistolae* (*Letters of Famous Men*) in his defense. In 1515 the even more famous *Epistolae obscurorum virorum* (*Letters of Obscure Men*) began to appear, completed in 1517 with seven additional letters. These letters of obscure men were purportedly addressed to Ortvinus Gratius, the Dominican leader of the conspiracy against Reuchlin. A parodistic *contrafactura* of the letters of famous men, they revealed and denounced the obscure attitude of the Scholastics. The letters' barbaric and ignorant Latin became the laughingstock of educated Europe. Their first part, composed by Crotus Rubeanus, amusing in tone, discriminated smilingly and with pleasure. The second part, however, conveyed a different mood. Ulrich von Hutten (1488–1523) provided his contribution with a much grimmer pathos and a new aggressiveness not only intended to ridicule but to destroy.

This tone was to prevail when the satire was used in religious disputes and became the favorite weapon for denouncing and pursuing an ideological enemy. Murner's *Great Lutheran Fool* is but one example for the spreading literary activism in and through which the old and new Church attacked each other. *Der Barfüßermönche Eulenspiegel und Alkoran* (*Master Owlglass and Alcoran of the Franciscan Monks,* 1542) by Erasmus Alberus (1500–1553), a sarcastic caricature of Saint Francis, may serve as an example for vitriolic Protestant criticism. The ferocious battle of faiths eventually corrupted the literary genre, which had evinced much of the time's mentality: its critical attitude, its morality and artistic aspirations. Humanism, essentially supra-denominational, had to abandon aesthetic detachment for the sake of ideological indoctrination.

Erasmus and Reuchlin, heirs to the classical tradition, clung to a cosmopolitan humanism which refrained from the exclusive profession of faith. Reuchlin promoted the study of Hebrew and furthered the exegesis of the Old Testament in its original text. He thus prepared Luther's translation of the Bible, but he himself was much more attracted to Plotinus's speculation and to the secret sciences of the Judaeo-Hellenistic tradition. Erasmus was accused by Luther of having betrayed the Reformation.[5] His Greek edition of the New Testament (1516), with a Latin translation and commentary, nevertheless furnished Luther with the basic text for his translation. In spite of his critical views on the Church, Erasmus stayed within its universal realm. Much has been said about the enigma of his personality. His genius transcended the factious spirit of his contemporaries, fusing the classical and Catholic tradition into a very personal vision of a purified Christian and humanized man. Such qualities he found in the pre-Christian philosophers, in the life and word of Christ, and in the church fathers: "The primary authority always belongs to the Biblical texts, but at times I find with the old authors and in pagan writings words of such purity, holiness . . . (that) perhaps the spirit of Christ works and spreads further than we assume."[6] His *Colloquia familiaria* (*The Colloquies* or *Familiar Discourses,* 1522) attest to his exemplary tolerance, to his serene mood, wit and skepticism. Erasmus adopted the dialogue from Lucian, whom he had translated into Latin (1512). The *Colloquia* are with all their structural perfection and delightful eloquence an educational manual for the teaching of Latin and for the improvement of urbane manners. They are the earliest masterpiece of a tradition which developed a century later and give rise to such works as Harsdörffer's *Conversational Plays for Ladies.*

Hutten's *Dialogi novi* (*Book of Conversations*, 1521), modeled on Lucian like those of Erasmus, reveal a different literary temperament. A scion of Franconian knights, he mobilized nationalistic impulses present in the reform movement. In Italy they had been directed against the "barbaric" North, in Germany they turned against the Roman Church. Symptomatically the national concern of the German humanists had been aroused by Italian nationalism. A new field of humanistic interest developed in the study of German history and geography. Indeed the *Germania* of Jakob Wimpfeling (1450–1528) and Celtis's fragmentary *Germania illustrata* (1500) fascinated the succeeding generation. Hutten's national interest quickly turned into passion and moral indignation. He saw Germany as prey to the Roman lust for power and attacked violently the vileness and corruption of the Holy See. The *Clag und vormanung gegen dem gewalt des Bapst* (*Complaint about and Warning against the Power of the Pope*, 1520) is as vitriolic and inciting as any of his many pamphlets. It ends with the famous "I have dared!" which was to unite nobleman and burgher in the fight for truth and justice. "We want to extinguish the lies/So truth may come to light." Yet his national idea was, as things stood, only anachronistic. Germany could not be reformed by a class of noblemen which had long lost all influence. And Arminius, the "freest, most German" liberator from the Roman yoke, whom Hutten made a national hero, only inspired romantic dreams.

At the dawn of the Reformation the literary situation showed a variety of tendencies without true focus. Literature of artistic value was created by the humanists and in Latin. The classical heritage had never merged into the popular German tradition. It had brought forth an occasional work of popular appeal in the German language (Brant's *Ship of Fools*), but for the most, its aesthetic ideals remained restricted to the small group of *literati*. Most popular literature was utilitarian and without great artistic impact. With Hutten, though, an orator and humanist broke with the tradition and appealed directly to the popular movement. His use of the German language was a sign of changing times.

The Reformation absorbed and assimilated most of those divergent tendencies. Its effect on the spirit and the literature of the age and future times was incommensurable. The focal point and catalyst of the time was Martin Luther (1483–1546). When in 1515 this Augustinian monk, since 1508 professor of theology at the University of Wittenberg, posted his ninety-five theses for public discussion, he continued a well-established tradition of criticism directed against the "worldliness" of the Church. Scores of humanists had expressed their dismay over the superstitious misuse of the sacraments, over indulgences, over the idolization of saints. A large part of literature dealt with the corruption of the clergy. True, Luther had seen the luxury and abundance of Renaissance Rome with his own eyes. The pomp of the art-loving Pope Leo X, who had just engaged Michelangelo for the decoration of the Sistine Chapel, offended his austere and religious sensitivity. But this experience does not account for the dynamic impulse of his reform. The galvanizing effect which Luther had on his contemporaries springs from the radically different morality of his teaching, the integrity of his conviction, and above all from his unique talent as a writer. His morality had perhaps its origin in Occam's (1290–1349) philosophy, in the spirituality of the *Devotio moderna,* or in the teachings of Wycliffe (1325–1384) and Hus (1369–1415). The fact is that it became effective only through Luther.

Focal points of Luther's faith were the inner experience of the divine and the "justification of man." Man in the state of nature is a totally corrupt sinner who can only rise and be saved by the grace of a merciful God. Good deeds, pilgrimages, and charity which were encouraged by the old Church to attain salvation are dangerous temptations. Man can only be saved through his faith and not through his deeds. Faith in God's mercy bridges the eternal gap between the perfection of the Creator and man's corruption. The true Christian rejoices in that faith. It excludes the necessity of a visible church since mercy is attained individually and without mediation. The faithful form an invisible community, united in love and spirit.

The Protestant Church did not realize the spiritual vision of its founder. Luther himself had to yield to the pressure of the Counter-Reformation and had to curb the scurrilous use of his ideas by fanatics. He denounced the peasant uprising which had been inspired by his sermons and appeals, as for instance in *Von der Freiheit eines Christenmenschen (On the Liberty of a Christian Man,* 1520). Confronted with such political realities Luther decided that in all worldly matters Christians owed their allegiance to the state. This decision had far-reaching political and cultural consequences. It shaped German thinking for centuries to come. German *Innerlichkeit,* a circumlocution for an emotive spirituality, is a direct offspring of Luther's attitude. His concept is basically medieval in allowing a dualism of spiritual and worldly existence and trusting that the inner conviction would eventually shape political and social conditions. All worldly matters were left to the state, a decisive factor in its ultimate secularization. As the political situation developed the princes finally decided on the fate of religion in their states. The "Augsburg Confession" rallied all Protestant principalities against those which remained Catholic, events which a century later led to the Thirty Years' War and the cultural and political devastation of the country. Thus the Reformation, in spite of its strong national overtones, did not prompt the unification and rebirth of Germany as the Renaissance had done in France, Spain, and England, which had integrated the classical heritage of Italy's past into their national substances. These countries developed a cultural homogeneity of Christian and Latin elements which produced their remarkable efflorescence in art and literature during the sixteenth and seventeenth centuries.

Luther integrated the literary tendencies of the time into a vivid, personal style which as a result of his translation of the New Testament left an indelible mark on the German mind. Translators before him had used the Latin Vulgate, as had the unknown author of the first complete German Bible, printed by Mentel in 1466. Luther profited from the groundwork laid by humanistic endeavors: Erasmus had shown the way with his Greek edition of the New Testament and Reuchlin's studies of Hebrew furthered Luther's translation of the Old Testament which was completed in 1534. It is Luther's unique merit, however, to have used humanistic philology for his religious message. Classical and popular tendencies merged into a national aggregate, for the Reformation was not only a religious but also a national movement, as Calvinism, Gallicanism, and the Anglican Church show best. To turn against Rome almost required the creation of a unique, national vision of man. As a humanist, Luther was aware of the importance of the vernacular for such a purpose. The supranational Latin which served the universality of the Church had to be replaced by the idiom of the people he wished to reach. Luther broke with the tradition of looking upon Latin as a model language; he used idiomatic German expressions and wrote his translation in the chancery language of Saxony which contained East Middle German and Upper German elements. This idiom had an enormous impact on the development of a standard German language.

The translation of the New Testament, a monumental work,

was completed in the year of enforced exile at the Wartburg (1522). The difficulties of the task and the painstaking thoroughness it required are best illustrated by Luther's remark that he and his collaborators at times pondered for days over the translation of one word or one phrase. As the *Sendbrief vom Dolmetschen (Epistle on Translating,* 1530) states: "Should I describe the causes and thoughts of all my words, I would have to spend a year just doing that. I have experienced what art and work translating is." The same *Epistle* also explains the method which Luther applied in order to popularize the Biblical text. One must "ask the mother in her home, the children in the street, the common man in the marketplace . . . and translate accordingly; then they understand and realize that one speaks German with them." Luther's Bible spread with remarkable speed and left its mark even on Catholic translations which were put together to counter the Protestant influence. Johann Gutenberg's new printing device (invented in 1453), which made books cheaper and available to more people, brought the Bible to every German home.

Luther's translation, his hymns, and his many treatises—*An den christlichen Adel deutscher Nation: von des christlichen Standes Besserung (To the Christian Nobles of the German Nation), Von der babylonischen Gefangenschaft der Kirche (Concerning the Babylonian Captivity of the Church), Von der Freiheit eines Christenmenchen (On the Liberty of a Christian Man),* all in 1520 —reveal a great poetic talent. He gave the hymns an important place in the liturgy of his church and thus initiated a tradition which inspired poets throughout the following centuries. He composed about forty songs of ardent faith, power, and sonority of language. Some of them were patterned after Latin hymns and psalms as the "battle hymn" of the Reformation, "A Mighty Fortress Is Our God," or "Out of the Depths I Cry to Thee." Others were original creations like "Vom Himmel hoch da komm' ich her" ("From Heaven Above to Earth I Come").

All appeared singly or in small collections from 1524 on and were suited for use by large congregations. In contrast to Protestant songs of the seventeenth century, these hymns live and celebrate the collective experience of new confidence and of new joy arisen from common faith.

As Luther's spirituality was gradually absorbed by the world, it underwent decisive changes. Philip Melanchthon (1497–1560), a scholar of Erasmian erudition and the closest collaborator of

Luther, undertook to determine a "Protestant morality," which has ever since influenced German intellectual life.[7] It was based on the needs of the citizen, oriented toward the social demands of a small principality and demanded that all moral decisions be founded on the obedience to religious and secular laws. Man's allegiance to this morality left his freedom to cultivate his soul unimpaired. Historically, Protestantism has realized both tendencies: extreme orthodoxy and speculative or emotive spirituality. Large areas in seventeenth-century literature center on mystic speculation and the pietistic cultivation of a personalized religion. Melanchthon's reform of higher learning has earned him the title of *Praeceptor Germaniae*. His system provided a balanced program of classical studies (readings in Terence, Quintilian, Cicero, and Plautus) and the study of the *realia* (mathematics, geography, and physics). Rigid discipline on the secondary school level prepared the student for obedience and social duties and provided the knowledge for his success in the world. The familiarity with classical eloquence was to civilize him. The Protestant reform brought forth famous centers of learning, such as the *gymnasium* at Strassburg under Johann Sturm (1507–1589). Soon the Jesuit Order (founded in 1539) also established schools with a similar curriculum.

Protestant and Jesuit schools preserved the classical tradition. They produced a new drama, the so-called "school drama." It differed from the preceding mystery play in its refined tectonic structure and developed perspective: truly human characters instead of types or allegorical figures appeared on stage. While the earlier miracle play had merged man's natural and supra-natural existence, the school drama focused on his human interests. The plays were performed in Latin (later German plays with Biblical themes followed) to provide the students with practice in eloquence. They also taught their middle-class audiences the Protestant way of life. Among the most productive authors were Burkard Waldis (1490–1556) with a drama *Prodigal Son* (1527), Paul Rebhuhn (1505–1546) with a play *Susanna* (1535), and Nikodemus Frischlin (1547–1590) with a *Joseph* play. The activity of Protestant playwrights was equalled by Jesuit dramatists. They retained the Latin language, chose their themes from the Bible and legends, and developed from the beginning a very distinct technique. This technique was to evolve with greatest effect only in the seventeenth century when the Jesuit drama reached its artistic climax. But the early dramas already appealed to the eye and the other senses.

The astounding dramatic abundance of the time culminated in its greatest talent, Hans Sachs (1494–1576). A cobbler in Nürnberg, he practised poetic writing in the fashion of the *Meistersinger*. His 4275 master-songs are now forgotten, but some of his many farces are still read and enjoyed, e.g., *Die ungleichen Kinder Evä* (*The Unlike Children of Eve*). Sachs regenerated a long-standing popular tradition: the Shrovetide play, short humorous scenes, performed during the Shrovetide procession. His *Der fahrend Schüler im Paradeis* (*The Vagabond Student in Paradise*, 1550) and *Das Narrenschneiden* (*Excision of Follies*, 1536) show simple structure, lively dialogue, and realistic characterization, prerequisites which could have established a German comedy. But he had no successor. Sachs's humor is saturated with common sense and he ridicules with great moderation, a rare attitude in sixteenth-century German letters.

By the middle of the sixteenth century new and different plays began to be performed in the market places of German towns. Traveling English troupes brought Shakespeare's drama to the continent, though in a popularized and much distorted form. First performing in English they relied on exaggerated dramatic action, visual effect, and naturalistic directness. Later when they put on plays in German they had already developed a very distinct style of their own which delighted in pomp, in the depiction of bloody cruelties, in melodrama mixed with farce and grotesquery. Up to the middle of the seventeenth century broad audiences were attracted to their jigs and clowneries.

The favorite genre of the sixteenth century, however, was the chapbook, into which the pranks and funny tales of the fifteenth century had developed. There was the famous *Till Eulenspiegel* (*Master Tyll Owlglass*) with a peasant hero who outwits all classes of burghers, *Fortunatus und seine Söhne* (*Fortunatus and His Sons*, 1509), the curious tales of the citizens of Schilda *Die Schildbürger* (*The Residents of Schilda*, 1597), and best known of all, the *Historia von Dr. Johann Fausten, dem weitbeschreyten Zauberer und Schwarzkünstler* (*The History of Doctor Faustus, the Widely Known Sorcerer and Necromancer*, 1587). Christopher Marlowe's tragedy *Doctor Faustus* (1588) demonstrates perhaps best the deep gulf separating the world of Elizabethan England and that of a provincial Germany, still deeply entangled in religious disputes and harrowed by moral scruples. Marlowe's hero is driven by thirst for knowledge to the demonic expansion of the self beyond all human limits. The German chapbook centers around the historical Georg Faust, a magician and astrologer of the early sixteenth century, and alludes to such aspirations, only with great moral reservation, indeed frequently with Christian indignation. Through the example of the arrogant Faust all "proud, curious and Godless people" are warned to "obey the Lord, and resist the Devil, that he will flee from you." This moralistic tendency is symptomatic for most of the prose productions of a century which wavered between the temptations of new human horizons and the values of former times. Still the *History of Dr. Faustus* is told with unusual verve and ease equalled only by the narrative talent of Jörg Wickram (d. 1562). Breaking away from an earlier preoccupation with courtly prose, Wickram achieved a first mature prose novel which presented the daily life of the middle class, its temptations, conventions and morality with vigor and artistic appeal. The story of *Der jungen Knaben Spiegel* (*The Mirror for Young Boys*, 1554) is basically didactic. But this intention is for the first time subordinated to aesthetic considerations. *The Mirror*, Wickram's *Rollwagenbüchlein* (*Coach Book*, 1555), and the comedies by Sachs mark the zenith of popular literature. The literary taste of the following decades, however, was shaped by a translation of *Amadis of Gaule* into German in 1569.

II

The reception accorded to *Amadis of Gaule* points to the direction which literary interests were to take at the end of the sixteenth century. This "treasure of beautiful, gracious orations, letters, conversations, lectures" came to Germany from Spain and France, which had assumed political leadership on the continent during the sixteenth century. Under their influence German principalities consolidated their bureaucratic structure into strong autocracies and the courts became once more centers for cultural life. The adventures of Amadis suited the taste of the nobility whose courtly ideals left their trace in the literature of the time. The cultural efflorescence in Spain and France exerted an overwhelming influence on seventeenth-century Germany with its political and cultural schisms, its discord of faiths and the ferocious Thirty Years' War (1618–1648). In fact all German cultural activities of that time must be seen in the light of the French and Spanish predominance. Within its realm German literary men established a small domain for their art. Their achievements cannot compete with the masterpieces of French classicism, nor with those of Calderón and Shakespeare, who exerted an enormous influence on the age.

Literary historians classify the heterogeneous literary phenomena of the century as "Baroque." This term, originally coined to describe the style of seventeenth-century architecture and painting, has caused confusion in the field of literature and led to a lively discussion of its merit.[8] It has validity if we see in Baroque art the manifestation of the ideas of the time, an expression of the spirit of the Counter-Reformation and its profound impact on the Protestant cultural sphere, and keep in mind that Baroque art expressed an all-pervasive conflict between reason and emotion in a manneristic style.[9] Tension is the most outstanding characteristic of the period. It is evident in the distortion of the art, in the internal contradictions between excessive formalism and emotionalism, and in the antagonism in the cultural landscape of the German seventeenth century, between the Catholic lands of imperial Hapsburg and the Protestant principalities. The art of the Counter-Reformation was the last manifestation of unity within Western civilization. Superseding the Renaissance, the Baroque is more fraught with inner contradictions than the preceding periods, yet it presents a unique and powerful blend of classical tradition and Christian elements. Though the spirit of the age was nationalistic, Baroque art linked Germany to the great artistic achievements of Catholic Europe. Furthermore the classical heritage reached Germany through the works of French and Dutch writers. This stream of predominantly Protestant origin merged with the ever-flourishing Neo-Latin literature, with courtly ideas, and with powerful middle-class aspirations to form the colorful, paradoxical and lively scene of seventeenth-century German literature.

The first decades of the seventeenth century saw continuous efforts to lay the foundation for a standardized German literary language and the attempt to formulate a comprehensive aesthetic theory. Noteworthy are the poems and various translations of Paulus Melissus Schede (1539–1602), Jacob Regnart (1540–1599), and Johann Hermann Schein (1586–1630), who perfected such tendencies in *Venuskränzlein* (*Wreath of Venus*, 1609) and *Musica boscareccia oder Waldliederlein* (*Songs of the Woods*, 1621). Convinced that literary perfection was possible in the German language, Martin Opitz (1597–1639) published in 1624 a short but enormously influential treatise *Buch von der deutschen Poeterei* (*On German Poetics*) which set the poetic standards for his time.

On German Poetics is a treatise in the classical and humanistic tradition, relying on the authority of Horace, Quintilian, Scaliger, and Ronsard. It explains the "invention and division of things," the "preparation and ornamentation of words," and "the meter of syllables, verses, and rhymes." It considers the traditional genres (elegy, hymn, eulogy, epigram, and heroic poem) and treats drama in the conventional manner: "tragedy . . . deals only with princely matters," leaving the comedy to "things which occur among common men." Such a definition had been reiterated in the standard works on poetics since Aristotle.

Opitz's greatest concern was the purity of German poetry. As for meter he recommended the iambus and the trochee; among the iambic verses he preferred the French Alexandrine, which from then on dominated German poetry till the eighteenth century. The language of Rudolf Weckherlin (1584–1653) and the pre-Opitz poets had not been free of dialectical influence. Opitz now required a purified literary language and standardized versification. The most revolutionary innovation was his new law of stress and intonation which followed the regularly alternating sequence of accented and unaccented syllables in the German language. Opitz thus offered rational laws for poetry. These were broadened by August Buchner (1591–1661) who added the dactylus to the iambus and trochee in his *August Buchners kurzer Weg-Weiser zur Deutschen Dichtkunst* (*Short Guide to German Poetry*, 1665). Generally the new poetry was highly rhetorical, stressed rational organization, and developed standardized figures of speech which were adopted from classical rhetoric (*figurae* and *topoi*). This poetry dazzled its readers through the artistic display of language.

Opitz's own poems are perfect illustrations for his theory. In fact it is difficult to judge whether his work was prompted by artistic or theoretical considerations. He represented a new type of poet: the *virtuoso*, an artist who had acquired great skills through the painstaking study of classical writings. His scholarly and artistic ambitions induced Opitz to offer an almost indiscriminate variety of lyrical forms. The *Deutsche Poemata* (*German Poems*, 1624) betrayed him as an eager disciple of Dutch, French, Italian, and Neo-Latin poets on whose achievements he capitalized. For the most he proved himself as a skilled young litterateur who gathered laurels from an educated society. His diction was never personal but

65

delighted in intellectual versatility and subtle wit. It was detached and restrained, combined rationality with elegant form, and almost always brought about an ironical "twist."

German Poems strove even harder for formal elegance. All irregularities yielded to grammatical correctness. Convention and logic determined the flow of thought and organized expression and rhythm. The meter evolved as a rational and repetitive scheme. But Opitz had matured beyond mere playfulness. His greatest work, *Trostgedichte in Widerwärtigkeit des Krieges* (*Poems of Consolation amid the Adversities of War*, 1633) showed him as a moral preceptor to society. With elegant loquaciousness and numerous illustrations of a sorrowful life he administered the moral guidance of a somewhat Christianized stoicism to the citizen of war-torn Germany. Beyond the apparent whims of history, he was to recognize a rational principle. The *Consolation* represented a first document of a German thinking which combined eloquence and a Christian-Classical ideal of life. Opitz's Christianity, symptomatically, lacked religious fervor and did not relate to any particular faith. It was secularized, enlightened, and close in spirit to eighteenth-century rationality. It offered man a civilized humanism and enlightened morality.

Opitz also set an example for the drama through a translation of Seneca's *The Women of Troy* (1625) and a free rendering of Sophocles' *Antigone* (1636). Seneca's tragedies provided examples of the stoic acceptance of life's unavoidable suffering and of human superiority in the face of an unpredictable fortune. They were to strengthen man in his tragic existence. Opitz's translations bore the signs of a rationalist: Seneca's passionate pathos was reduced to aphoristic and generalizing reflections, and actions were transformed into contemplation. Such tendencies are even more evident in the free translation of *Antigone*. Here Opitz changed heroism into stoicism; all personal greatness diminished in the broader context of general norms. These translations, however, paved the way for a secular German drama, especially since Opitz fused in them the Greek, Roman, and Christian traditions.[10]

Translations, like imitations, were legitimate artistic endeavors at the time. To some degree all art was imitation of established models. It was regulated by pre-established standards, by the requirements of the genre, and by the apparatus of the classical tradition. Poetic genius was therefore limited to the gift of combination, to the ability to express a given fact in new and witty ways, or to use a quotation, a metaphor or rhetorical figure effectively and with finesse. It was an intellectual art which relied for its effectiveness on a refined, sophisticated society which could enjoy the subtle allusions and understand the elegant play of words.

Opitz analyzed the genre of "heroic poems" in his *On German Poetics* and also furthered the translation of two influential English novels: Sir Philip Sidney's (1554–1586) heroic, adventurous novel *Arcadia*, translated from a French version in 1629 by Valentin Theocritus von Hirschberg, revised and published by Opitz in 1638, and John Barclay's (1582–1621) *Argenis*. *Arcadia* laid the groundwork for a German pastoral and introduced its readers to the world of courtly elegance and graces. Opitz's *Schäferei von der Nymphe Hercynie* (*Pastoral Play about the Nymph Hercynia*, 1630), an elegant but also instructive play which combined a pastoral atmosphere with political reasoning, served the same end. *Argenis*, on the other hand, championed the rising power of absolutism but was nevertheless read as a manual of courtly instruction.

Opitz succeeded in Germanizing humanism a century after its arrival in this country and at a time when it had been entirely integrated into the national cultures of the other Western nations. He also made the eloquent poet acceptable to the Germans. In Germany, where form and elegant speech never had been in great demand, humanists had been respected for their erudition, less so for their gift of speech. They had served as teachers in the rectories, as clerks at the courts or chancellories; they had excelled as orators at the festivities of the noble society and frequently become theologians. Opitz did not succeed in changing the social status of the German man of letters, but his example created a growing esteem for the artist.

Opitz's attempts to establish standards for a refined German language paralleled the efforts of the many flourishing language associations which carried out these aims on a larger scale. These societies, such as the Fruit-bearing Society or Palm-order, the Company of German Patriots, the Shepherd- and Flower-order, had literary as well as social ambitions. Especially the Palm-order furnished the princes with a sophisticated circle of friends whose presence graced their festivities. In most cases the activities of the language associations were rather pedantic. Princes dabbled in literature and literary men wrote poems in honor of princes. However, the associations greatly furthered the translation of Italian and French literature; they helped in refining the language and initiated many new word-formations in modern German.

The rules espoused by Opitz, especially his formalism, left a deep mark on both the secular and religious poetry of the epoch. Paul Fleming (1609–1640), one of the foremost poets, combined the new ideals with a strong popular background (as is seen in his student and drinking songs). He owed much to Neo-Latin poetry, to Heinsius, Johannes Secundus, and Petrarchism. Petrarchism represented one of the strongest traditions in European poetry since the songs of the troubadours. It had been inspired by Petrarch's *Canzoniere*, a collection of sonnets to Laura. His imitators had codified the motifs, expressions, and situations. This highly stylized poetry had been introduced into German art by Opitz, and Fleming had been indebted to the tradition in his early Latin poems. His German sonnets still displayed a rare formal perfection derived from the tradition. But Fleming transformed the conventional situation into a personal, intimate tone. Breaking with tradition, he produced a new style in love poetry which culminated in the passionate expressiveness of Johann Christian Günther (1695–1723) at the end of the epoch.

Intimacy and sincerity were outstanding qualities of poems of Simon Dach (1605–1659). He was the most eminent of the so-called Königsberg poets, a group of writers which honored Opitz as their master. Though most of them wrote verses for special occasions, they surpassed their contemporaries in simple expressions of genuine feeling. In a unique way, Dach imbued the style of Opitz with the older tradition of song, which gradually led to a more personal expression than the laws of the *On German Poetics* permitted. Whereas Opitz postulated impersonal generalization, Dach expressed individual, personal emotions. Describing an experience he succeeded in evoking a mood or an atmosphere. Minutely observed objects gave greater realism to the poems which presented a humane world. He refrained from highly stylized forms such as the ode, the sonnet, and the epigram and rather favored popular genres which common people also could enjoy. His best known songs communicated a feeling of brotherhood and friendship: "Man has no more human trait,/nothing befits him better,/than that he can show good faith and keep friendship." In a secularized manner Dach's poems reflected the communal spirit found in the Protestant song of the sixteenth century. They already contained many of the concepts elaborated in the *Freundschafts-lieder* (*Songs of Friendship*) of the eighteenth century.

Andreas Gryphius (1616–1664) developed as a poet in much the same way as Fleming. He set out with studies in Latin genres (*Olivetum* in 1646, a description of Christ's suffering at the Mount of Olives) and with translations of Latin poetry (the odes of Jakob Balde). At first he was apparently unwilling to create poetry in German. Indeed he found his style comparatively late, but then it transcended by far the standards set by Opitz, though it should be remembered that when Gryphius began writing, the poetic language had become flexible, and was capable of expressing every imaginable content.

Gryphius, like Opitz and Fleming, was a *virtuoso* who cherished technique. Like Fleming and Dach, however, he transcended his formalism. Gryphius did not expand the traditional forms through individual expressions. Quite the contrary, he refrained entirely from manifestations of personal feeling. His poetry involved a striking paradox: its formalism embraced a philosophy which is opposed to form. Thus content and form clashed in a constant struggle which affected language, rhyme, and structure. Such poetry, highly stylized and with verbal pomp, expressed the existential torment of the seventeenth century, which was grounded in the negation of and disdain for all worldly existence. Gryphius and his generation had experienced great suffering. They grew up in a raging war which exhausted virtues and hopes and left the nation in decay and discouragement. "What is worse than death I do not mention/Harder than plague, fire, and famine:/Many lost their souls." History seemed to be ruled by chance and man appeared to be left at the mercy of an unpredictable fortune. In such adversities Gryphius, as much a humanist as Opitz, stoically accepted the suffering (*constantia*). His inner disposition, however, was non-humanistic. It was deeply and radically medieval, Lutheran. Gryphius violently rejected ephemeral existence in the search for eternal life. "Nothing is eternal, neither metal nor marble . . ./Everything we cherish and esteem/is but worthless nothingness." Thus *vanitas* and *fortuna* function as leitmotifs in a poetry which also excelled in formal perfection and a variety of verse; odes, epigrams, hymns, and sonnets were his favorite forms. In 1637 he published a volume of *Sonette*, which was followed in 1639 by *Sonn- und Feiertagssonette* (*Sonnets for Sundays and Holidays*). His *Deutsche Reimgedichte* (*German Poems*, 1643 and 1657) contained, among sonnets and odes, two lyrical cycles on the "Tränen über das Leiden des Herrn" ("Tears over the Lord's Passion") and "Kirchhofsgedanken" ("Thoughts at the Cemetery"). Their medieval *danse macabre* and cruelty evoked a longing for eternal peace.

Gryphius fused, like the contemporary Jesuit writers, a metaphysical pathos with a paradoxical need for representation. With Opitz he shared the conviction that form can organize the shattered and accidental matter of reality into a work. His poems thus exploded with the tension of competing metaphysical, worldly, and intellectual tendencies; the struggle is also reflected in tortured rhythm, piled-on metaphors, and hyperboles. Passionately, the poems tried to master the conflicts of life through rational organization, yet aimed at the final axiom "All is vain."

Although Gryphius' "negative" pathos remained a singular event in seventeenth-century poetry, his contemporary Christian Hofmann von Hofmannswaldau (1617–1679) equalled or even surpassed his formal perfection. Profiting from the achievements of his predecessors, Hofmannswaldau soon became the most elegant and versatile poet of the time. He excelled in all forms and all meters, though the alexandrine and the sonnet were his favorites which he polished to perfection. Besides a hundred epigrams *Sterbens-Gedanken* (*Thoughts on Death*) he composed heroic letters in the style of Ovid. The *Lustgedichte* (*Poems on Pleasure*) were not intended for publication. Edited by Benjamin Neukirch (1665–1729), they were responsible for Hofmannswaldau's reputation as a frivolous poet ever since.

His art seems witty, gracious, and amorous. Like other poetry of the time, it draws on the themes of *vanitas*, *constantia*, and religious topics. But though the themes are set in an erotic context the many ironical twists soon unmask the futility of pleasure. To achieve this effect, Hofmannswaldau searched for the surprising, exquisite term and the rare, artificial epithet. His style owes much to the technique of European mannerism which had spread from Italy and Spain to the North.[11] In literature the movement had perfected a style offering clever, exaggerated *figurae* and *topoi*, elaborate antitheses, and luxurious metaphors spun into paradoxes. Mannerism was almost a way of life which blossomed in the conventional atmosphere of the great absolutistic courts and constituted a last refinement of Renaissance art.

Despite the profound ontological differences between Catholic and Protestant poetry, they shared in the growing spirituality in the second half of the sixteenth century. The new spirituality responded to the increasing demands of the people for a deepened and relevant religious experience. The new Church had sacrificed its spiritual fervor to a new form of scholasticism and not brought about the envisioned total reform of life. A revival of medieval mysticism seemed to hold the promise of satisfying man's spiritual needs. It offered speculative, emotional, and practical impulses, and a *unio mystica* through contemplation and visionary inspiration. Both impulses had served to transform and improve religious practice already in the Middle Ages. Ascetic writings and the *Devotio moderna* had sought to prepare the Christian for a more intense and personal devotion, for a spiritual rebirth of human existence. Such sources were revived in the seventeenth century. The treatises of the nun Mechthildis (1212–1283) and of Master Eckhart (1260–1327) were rediscovered as was the entire speculative tradition of Pansophia.[12] The Counter-Reformation had stressed the ecstatic writings of Teresa of Avila (1515–1582) and of Saint John of the Cross (1542–1591), both Spanish mystics. The concept of a rebirth and a total regeneration had also survived in individual enthusiasts (Kaspar von Schwenckfeld, 1489–1561 and Valentin Weigel, 1533–1588). At the end of the sixteenth century secret associations were formed which nourished the hope for a general reform of life. They modeled their communities on early Christian ideals. The Rosecrucians strove beyond that for a reform of philosophy and theology through the impact of pansophical wisdom and the secret sciences. Such efforts had lasting effect in the works of early Pietism. Johann Arndt (1555–1621) and Johann Valentin Andreae (1586–1654) were the fathers of this Protestant movement which decisively influenced the spiritual growth of future generations by keeping alive the hope for the ultimate establishment of the true realm of Christ.

Johann Arndt's main concern was a correct Christian life. His treatise *Vom wahren Christentum* (*Of True Christianity,* 1606–1609) inspired by the *Imitatio Christi* of Thomas à Kempis (1380–1471) aimed at reviving Lutheran faith by the spark of inner experience and profound conviction. Middle-class complacency was to be transformed by truly moral actions and an intimate relation of man with God. Johann Valentin Andreae broadened Arndt's ideals into the Utopian vision of a totally Christianized society. His *Reipublicae Christianopolitanae descriptio* (*Christianopolis, an Ideal State,* 1619) forms part of the long tradition of political and

Christian utopias ranging from Thomas More's *Utopia* to the communist society envisioned by Karl Marx. Andreae, like most utopian writers, combined ideals of early Christianity with humanistic and democratic visions. In *Christianopolis,* unlike in later socialist dreams, the citizens were devoted to the imitation of Christ. All institutions served Christian principles and all education prepared for the community with God. Arndt and Andreae both turned their ideals into practice. Their exemplary lives influenced their communities and awakened a new Christian morality in them.

Visionary mysticism flourished especially in Silesia. Kaspar von Schwenckfeld's enthusiasm had attracted a great number of followers. Polish enthusiasts believed in a concealed "true church" and the Bohemian Brethren hoped for the final realization of the community of Christ. The region also brought forth Jakob Böhme (1575–1624), the greatest mystic of the seventeenth century. He lacked formal education (he was a cobbler in Görlitz), studied on his own, and was profoundly touched by the Neoplatonic tradition. In a tortuous, obscure language which never seems to appropriate his visions he tried to articulate his innermost experience of the divine. Intellect and emotion grappled with the existence of God and His relation to man in a world of conflicting forces. How does God allow the existence of good and evil, light and darkness? Böhme arrived at a dialectical principle which explained the paradoxical structure of existence in a meaningful plan. The "eternal essence" brings forth the visible world in which good and evil materialize as opposing forces. Human history provides the eternal battleground for the antagonistic energies of the Divine paradox but through Christ also their ultimate integration. Christ, the son of God and man, reconciles the adverse forces through his life and passion and thus gives mankind hope for reconciliation and peace. Böhme strove for unity in discord, for the conciliation of existential antagonisms. He firmly believed that history would bring the revelation of the Divine *mysterium.* All adversities would vanish in the glory of the ultimate *visio mystica* of God.

Böhme's vision inspired not only his disciples but also much later the young Goethe and the German Romantics. Since he was denied the right to publish, his works and ideas spread through manuscripts and by word of mouth. *Morgenröte im Aufgang (The Aurora)* appeared in 1612, followed by *Beschreibung der drei Prinzipien göttlichen Wesens (The Three Principles,* 1618) and *Von der Menschwerdung Jesu Christi (Of the Incarnation of Christ,*

1620). His disciples started editing his works, but this difficult task has only recently been completed.

Among the Catholic poets Friedrich Spee von Langenfeld (1591–1635) was a mystic who sought to articulate religious enthusiasm and the yearning of his soul for the *unio mystica*. His language vibrated with religious ecstasy. It was feverish, extreme, and often thrived on Petrarchist attitudes. A nervous sensuality prevailed resulting from an insoluble antagonism of spiritual and sensual intentions: to grasp the Divine in human words. Such conflict dominated the literary fashions of the time. Many of Spee's poems were *contra-facturae* of love poetry; in others the poet disguised as a shepherd searched for a spiritual idyll. Thus his poems were rich in *topoi amoeni*. His *Trutz-Nachtigall* (*Defiant Nightingale*, 1649), extolling the "beautiful" Christ and the *Güldnes Tugendbüchlein* (*Golden Book of Virtue*, 1649) served religious edification. In contrast to Jakob Balde (1604–1668), another Jesuit poet who wrote poems in Latin for moral instruction, Spee composed his poetry in the German language. The best testimony for his humanistic views, however, is a courageous pamphlet against the trials for witchcraft, the *Cautio Criminalis* (*Legal Considerations on the Trials for Witchcraft*, 1631). In a century obsessed with superstition and fanaticism, this pamphlet advocated justice and attested to a profound belief in the sacrosanct nature of man.

Ecstatic poetry drew primarily upon two distinct traditions. Spee's *Defiant Nightingale* was inspired by the *seraphic* tradition, the lyrics of Bernard of Clairvaux (1090–1153) and the "Song of Solomon." Such poetry portrayed either the author's experience of the Lord's passion or the joys in the union with the divine bridegroom. Seraphic poems were replete with erotic metaphors from mundane love poetry and with allegories which were to convey religious emotion. The *cherubic* tradition, on the other hand, integrated mystical speculation and was more intellectual. Cherubic writers heeded the advice of Opitz in an effort to rationalize and formalize the mystical paradox.

Religious poetry had reached its peak by the middle of the seventeenth century. Mysticism produced one work of art which delicately fused mystical inspiration with the new Opitzian aestheticism and achieved a unique and precarious balance between spirituality and rationalism: *Der Cherubinische Wandersmann* (*The Heavenly Wanderer*, 1675) by Johann Scheffler (Angelus Silesius, 1624–1677). This work was produced by an artist who was basically detached from experience and essentially concerned with an intellectual challenge. Scheffler was no visionary; none of his epigrams reveal any personal inspiration. Indeed the *Wanderer* was a collection as eclectic as any of the much favored contemporary encyclopedias, which contained quotations from medieval mysticism, from the Spanish ecstatics, from Böhme and Weigel, from theosophical and Neoplatonic wisdom. It was a collection of paradoxical religious epigrams, a genre that lends itself best not only for brief and serious but also for witty and satirical reflections.

Friedrich von Logau (1604–1655) had perfected the art of the epigram after the satirical poems of Martial and of John Owens (1560–1632) had been translated into German. Logau, acclaimed as theirs by the defenders of middle-class ethos, was in fact a perfect courtier who combined sobriety and political genius with intellectual elegance. Most of his *Erstes Hundert Teutscher Reimensprüche (First Hundred German Epigrams,* 1638) and *Deutscher Sinngedichte drei Tausend (Three Thousand German Epigrams,* 1654) depicted the courtly world with satirical wit, though he basically adhered to the virtues of nobility. "The diplomat: How to be a politician. Lie hidden in the bushes./Walk graciously and deceive politely." His many religious epigrams showed that he was a rather tolerant Protestant.

Scheffler appreciated Logau's epigrams as much as he admired the *monodisticha* of Daniel Czepko von Reigersfeld (1605–1660). Czepko was a follower of Böhme and had tried to inject poetic notions into his mystical inspirations. *Sexcenta Monodisticha Sapientium (Six hundred Monodisticha of Wisdom,* 1647) depicted in "pointed," precise and concise style the religious paradox, the mystery of the *unio mystica.* The arrangement of the *monodisticha* showed little planning. Each poem existed as a single unit and was not connected with the other poems. They all centered, however, around a spontaneous visionary experience. Scheffler's five books of *Geistreiche Sinn- und Schlussreime (Spiritual Epigrams),* later (with a sixth book added) published as *The Heavenly Wanderer,* appeared four years after his conversion to Catholicism (1653). Much discussion has surrounded the influence of this conversion on the content and style of the *Wanderer,* all the more since the sixth book seemed to reveal distinct Catholic thought. But such tendencies became evident only in his later years when he engaged in Counter-Reformation activities, and when he had joined the Jesuit order (*Sinnliche Beschreibung der vier letzten Dinge—*

Physical Depiction of the Last Four Things, 1675). The epigrams of the *Wanderer*, concise, witty, reflective, attested primarily to a supradenominational mysticism and to the practice of an elegant art. They try to capture an unfathomable event sharply and with the "pointed" wit of courtly poetry. Thus Scheffler's collection represented the zenith in the evolution of German mysticism. Inner vision had entered the realm of intellect and inward-directed spirituality took the form of the intellectual exclusiveness of conceptual poetry. *Heilige Seelenlust* (*Holy Joy for the Soul*, 1657) had a greater impact on Scheffler's contemporaries. These songs were rooted in the seraphic tradition and expressed an emotional rather than an intellectual experience. Like other seraphic poems, it abounded with *contra-fracturae* of erotic poems in gallant style. If the epigrams presented the divine mystery as a paradox of thought, *Holy Joy* expressed the same *mysterium* as a paradox of emotion. Both attempts were exemplary manifestations of seventeenth-century mentality.

The years in which mystical poetry reached its zenith also witnessed some of the greatest achievements in the realm of Protestant poetry. Following the lead of Luther's hymns, writers of the Protestant church song made use of Opitz's innovations. The older hymns were intended to be sung by the congregation and were, for the most part, sober expressions of universal Protestant faith. Seventeenth-century hymns, however, began to express a personal relationship with God. They were more subjective and were more varied. Poetically they were more attractive and more tender than the older hymns. Paul Gerhardt (1607–1676) emerged as the most gifted religious poet after Luther. Although he had learned from Opitz, his poetry was deeply rooted in the congregational song of the sixteenth century. His diction flows with perfectly natural rhythm, and its simplicity sounds as if it has never been touched by a poetical convention. Eighteen songs appeared in 1647, followed by sixty-three church songs in 1663. Both collections reveal a new personal intuition, an immediacy of faith. But their subjective tone is not personal in a biographical sense; they do not immediately reflect the horrors of the war which overshadowed Gerhardt's life.

Indeed all of Gerhardt's songs were a celebration of faith and worship. He took a new, more realistic look at God's creation and described its marvels with great natural ease, often with minutely observed details and genuine delight. Yet the poet did not indulge in realistic art for the sake of reality. If he turned to God's creation, he truly approached Him as the only end of his art. Gerhardt's songs initiated the long tradition of intimate devotion practiced by Pietism in the eighteenth century. One of his best known creations is "An das leidende Angesicht Jesu Christi" ("The Suffering Countenance of Jesus Christ"), a major song of the *Matthäus-Passion* by Johann Sebastian Bach.

The Protestant hymns and the many poems that found their way into prayer books and hymnals undoubtedly had the most decisive and lasting influence on the German mind. But it is also necessary to remember that Protestant art had cut the ties with the rest of Catholic Europe and that it was the art of the Counter-Reformation which retained a European perspective. The Council of Trent (1545–1563) had restored the confidence of the old Church and strengthened its religious and political impact. But Catholic Restoration owed its sweeping success mostly to the foundation of the Society of Jesus (1539) by Ignatius of Loyola (1491–1556). Loyola's order applied the spirit of political absolutism, of military regulations and discipline in order to attain its goal: the reconquest of the faithful. This goal significantly paralleled the political interest of the Empire. The German Imperial Court was intellectually and emotionally attached to the tradition of the Holy Roman Empire; its universal mission envisioned the establishment of a Christian Commonwealth of nations. Thus the Catholic Restoration in Germany represented ecclesiastical as well as imperial (Hapsburg) interests.

The Restoration succeeded once more in rallying the intellectual, social, artistic, and literary forces around an ideological center. Baroque style was the manifestation of a unique spirit. Forceful and aggressive, it blended spirituality and sensuality. Its emotions and formal values embraced the ecstasy of Spanish mysticism, the exuberance of ecclesiastical and secular architecture and sculpture of Spain, Italy, and Austria. It produced the austere dramas of Calderón de la Barca (1600–1681) as well as a dazzling new stagecraft. Stern religious asceticism paralleled the festive splendor which united Church and State in a powerful display of propaganda.

Although rooted in Spanish spirituality, Baroque art has its artistic home in Rome, for the popes were the chief patrons of the new style. There Michelangelo (1475–1564) and Bernini (1598–1680) created the St. Peter's Cathedral, a resplendent symbol of

Catholic Christianity. With Spain ranking foremost as political power, the family relations between the courts in Madrid and Vienna made the house of Hapsburg the European center of gravity. This accounts for the Spanish influence in style and literary expression of the German Jesuit art. It was an art that recognized its indebtedness to the artistic achievements of the Renaissance, but rejected the latter's pagan elements.

The Jesuits employed the arts for religious and political propaganda; they encouraged splendor and pomp in order to attain their goal, namely the abnegation of the world. The alluring appearance of art was to lead to the sobering conclusion: the world has to be conquered in order to be overcome. The Jesuits chose artistic forms which promised the widest effect on prospective converts. Around 1570 huge processions and shows, customary in Italy and Spain, became popular in southern Germany. Colorful, monumental and passionately devout, they were to prove the triumph of the Church and to exert a soul-stirring effect. Amid such mass festivities a new collective feeling assured the impact of Catholicism.

The educated classes were won over by a new, very effective form of drama. The order had been working on a dramatical theory since the middle of the sixteenth century. Jakob Pontanus (1542–1626) and Jakob Masen (1606–1681) established a code for the structure of the plays. Four representative types of plays developed: the Eucharistical Play, which emerged from the liturgy; the imperial plays (*Ludi Caesarei*) aimed particularly at a courtly audience; the tragedy, which treated the spectator to Biblical stories, pious legends, and historical events; the comedy, which served a similar end by satirical means. The intended moral effect of this variety of plays was always to induce contrition and repentance which would ultimately lead to conversion. Their allegorical and illusionistic character necessitated revolutionary innovations in the art of stage-craft. Complicated devices were invented to create theatrical effects. Wings with painted perspective gave the scenery new depth and allowed for changing vistas and extended horizons. The stage was divided into distinct units which could be closed off by curtains: front (street scenes, processions), center (rooms, palace), left (heaven), right (hell). The goal of Jesuit dramaturgy was nothing less than a total work of art which combined music, dance, pantomime, word, and decoration in a phantasmagory of visual and acoustic effects.

Udo (1598) by Jakob Gretser (1562–1625), one of the early Jesuit dramas, revealed, with striking effect, man's situation between life and eternity. Udo, a prince of the Church, enjoys a luxurious life amid pleasure and sin until, at the end of the play, he has to face judgment and is damned. The catharsis was induced by Udo's ultimate fate. The spectator realized then the fortuitousness of mundane life and experienced the true tragedy. The alluring charm of comfortable life was pushed rudely aside by the metaphysical weight of the final judgment which left the onlooker shocked and ready for conversion.

The most talented playwright among the Jesuit authors was the Swabian Jakob Bidermann (1578–1639), whose drama showed man in every moment of his earthly existence at the crossroads of good and evil, forced to choose either time or eternity. *Cenodoxus: Der Doctor von Paris* (1602) impresses the audience with the fate of a vain physician who only lives to satisfy his ambition, yearns for praise and fame, and rejects all admonitions by his guardian angel to think of his soul. The action culminates in the impressive fifth act in which Jesus sits in judgment. Rejecting the soul's plea for mercy, He condemns Cenodoxus to eternal damnation. The play shows the eternal consequence of man's action. Contemporary reports indicate that the first performance of *Cenodoxus* so deeply moved several high-ranking courtiers that they changed their entire way of living.

With the following generation of authors the structure of the plays became more intricate and antithetical, presentations on the stage ever more drastic, and the religious cosmos was transformed into the world of actual politics. A good example is the play *Pietas victrix sive Flavius Constantinus Magnus de Maxento tyranno victor* (*Triumphant Religion or Flavius Constantinus Magnus Conqueror of the Tyrant Maxentus*, 1659) by Nikolaus Avancini (1612–1686) which extolled the strength of triumphant faith but also the power of the reigning Hapsburg monarchy. The world of this play was divided into natural and supra-natural spheres, but every event bore a direct political reference. In the second half of the seventeenth century the Jesuit drama had finally exhausted its power and deteriorated into frequently schematic combinations of abstract notions and political realities, which actually represented a positivistic rather than metaphysical view of the human situation.

It has been argued that the Jesuit drama exerted great influence on the work of two outstanding dramatists of the time, Andreas Gryphius and Daniel Casper von Lohenstein (1635–1683).

Perhaps it is equally true that their tragedies reflect the same conflict between world and eternity which dominates the Jesuit plays. Gryphius, the greatest German dramatist of the century, fused cultural impulses from Holland (Jost von Vondel), England, and France, Lutheran piety, mystical spirituality, and humanism into a uniquely personal work of art. His outstanding achievement is the careful development of scenes and action in his plays. He also succeeds in portraying more convincingly than his contemporaries man's existential dilemma, his fear (*Weltangst*), and his suffering in the face of a fate which he could only master through the complete renunciation of the world. Gryphius's characters suffered defeat in the world but triumphed in the realm of eternal morality. The subject matter of his tragedies *Leo Arminius* (1652), *Carolus Stuardus* (1649), *Dying Aemilius Papinianus* (1659), and of his martyr play *Catherine of Georgia* (printed in 1657) was drawn from the political arena. The one play that had a conciliatory outcome, *Cardenio and Celinde* (printed in 1658), introduced for the first time middle-class characters on the German stage. His comedies (*Absurda Comica oder Herr Peter Squentz*, 1658, and *Horribilicribrifax*, 1663), generally praised for their humorous, individual scenes, demonstrate his ability to portray almost realistically individual characters.

This is especially noteworthy since Gryphius did not develop his characters in the tragedies in the modern sense of the word. They are exponents of an idea. In *Catherine* he extols one virtue, a stoic, steadfast faith in Christ; in *Papinianus* he praises justice. And the antagonists, raging and vile tyrants who are driven by their primitive emotions, are prototypes of evil. Thus these tragedies represent a world of absolute contrasts between sin (the abandonment to instincts) and virtue (the adherence to the ideal). The frequently drastic action (Carolus is decapitated on stage; Julia tears out Laetus' heart; Catherine is tortured) and the use of antitheses, hyperboles, and exaggerated metaphors enforce this basic conflict. As a consequence the structure of the plays resembles that of a disputation which seeks to convince the spectator.

The radical, ideological position of his tragedies found few followers; Gryphius also failed to lay the foundation for a national drama. But his stylized diction, his pathos, and the grand decorations had an immediate imitator in Casper von Lohenstein. Lohenstein's tragedies were held disreputable for a long time because of their sadism, exaggerated passions, and erotical bombast. "Lohenstein-pomp," as the following generation classified his stilted style, was not only a diction but also a mental attitude. It presented the antagonism of virtue and pleasure without a metaphysical super-structure. As in Gryphius's tragedies prolific vitalism clashed with stern rationality. But the metaphysical antinomy between natural life and supranatural determination of man had been reduced to a worldly conflict. Despite their fiery ardor the heroes appear cold. In Lohenstein's dramas *Cleopatra* (1661), *Agrippina* (1665), and *Sophonisbe* (1669), the universal norms have given way to individual judgments of right and wrong. The "psychology" of Baroque voluntarism and the schematic "reality" of Baroque rationalism are basically altered in these works. In other plays, reality had been envisioned in a very distinct manner. Each phenomenon or person in the drama stood for a concept. These signs were in themselves arbitrary. What mattered was the relation between them and the concepts; for the ultimate "truth" revealed itself only in and through such relationships. Thus the drama mirrored a system of correspondences. The "actual historical" situation on which the play was based was viewed as a chain of events for right or wrong decisions. Since the hero was but a sign within a constellation he lacked individuality no matter how psychologically interesting he might have been depicted. Free to decide within a realm of changing correspondences, his decision could result in a new con-stellation. These tragedies represented therefore a vast and com-plicated network of correspondences between accidental facts or signs (*exempla*) and morality. They were highly rationalized and of almost mathematical structure. Gryphius's heroes struggled to create a constellation in accordance with divine Providence, with absolute morality. Lohenstein's Agrippina or Cleopatra, on the other hand, thrown into a world of chance without Providence and subjected to ever-accelerating changes of fortune, can no longer escape this compulsion. With the decline of the Baroque plays to mere pomp and formalism their importance yielded to the growing influence of the French masters. And with the rise of the philosophy of the Enlightenment the basic conceptual framework of the plays was swept away. It was not until the twentieth century that affinities to Baroque art were rediscovered.

This is especially true of the Baroque novel, a genre recog-nized for its potential by Opitz and several artists who gave the language a new elegance and flexibility. The three principal forms were: the pastoral, the heroic, and the picaresque novel.

The pastoral and heroic novel was inspired by French models. *Argenis* by Barclay, d'Urfé's *Astrée,* and *Amadis* had set the gracious and courtly atmosphere of the pastoral novel. This genre provided from its beginnings not only for entertainment but also for instruction in social manners. Mlle. de Scudéry (1607–1701) had broadened the French pastoral novel with observations on morality and minute depictions of society. The German translations of her works enhanced the tradition of the German pastoral novel. It presented the courtier in his urbane world, searching refuge from stern rules and conventions in a bucolic dream. The idyllic scenes of simple country-life, however, were as precious and artificial as the *milieu* which the courtier wanted to flee. In *Adriatische Rosemund* (1645) by Philip von Zesen (1619–1689), young Rosemund, waiting for her distant lover, retired into a precious blue shepherd-cottage, dressed in a light summer robe of blue satin "as the shepherdesses used to wear." Such artificiality expressed the illusionary character of the pastoral set. The courtier (and the middle-class man who tried to imitate him) took his shepherd's role as one of the many he played on the stage of life. But he performed this role with charm and poise.

Philip von Zesen changed the courtly set to middle-class surroundings but with a courtly atmosphere in accordance with the purpose of the pastoral novel to introduce the middle class to gallant style and fashion. In fact, the adoption of such fashion had been slow and the resulting literary productions pedantic and stilted, as in the fifteenth century, when the burghers had imitated the fashions of the knights. Still the middle-class writer eventually succeeded in adding amorous style to middle-class spirituality of mostly Protestant origin. A peculiar fusion occurred. Courtly style refined the expression of the middle class. Middle-class mentality, on the other hand, transformed the gallant diction into a tool for its own expression of individuality. Though Baroque in diction, Zesen's *Rosemund* depicted an entirely different reality. It revealed private experiences of individual people, the love of a middle-class Protestant poet for the daughter of a Catholic Venetian nobleman, touching two immediate contemporary problems: the conflicts between religions and between classes. The plot renounced the intricate structure of the Baroque novel, although Zesen adopted its code in *Assenat, das ist derselben und des Josefs heilige Staats-, Lieb- und Lebensgeschicht (Assenat, that is the Holy Story of the Life, Love, and Politics of Her and Josef,* 1670). *Rosemund* started with the departure of the poet Markhold from Holland, related the previous events by way of conversation, and, in the loquacious manner of contemporary elegant manuals such as Philip Harsdörffer's, 1607–1658, *Frauenzimmer-Gesprechspiele* (*Conversational Plays for Ladies*, from 1641 on) discoursed expansively on travel-experiences, events in the life of lonely Rosemund, letters, secret and public meetings, final separation of the lovers, and Rosemund's fatal disease. *Rosemund* for the first time depicted the emotional disposition of the heroes in great detail and with much sensitivity. It mirrored the intimate life of a class which had grown consistently in refinement and would eventually take the cultural lead. Zesen articulated the individual and private interests of a politically still-subordinated class; he also developed an individual style while experimenting with a socially and intellectually alien idiom.

The Baroque style is fully manifest in the heroic novel. *Argenis* and *Astrée* had developed intricate plots with numerous characters and portrayed the political world in chivalric or pastoral disguise. German novelists wrote in a similar vein. Anton Ulrich von Braunschweig (1633–1714), created two novels, *Die Durcheuchtige Syrerin Aramena* (*The Illustrious Syrian Aramena*, 1669–1673) and *Römische Octavia* (*Roman Octavia*, 1677–1679), of enormous political and historical dimensions. *Aramena* depicted Asia Minor and the Occident. A complex scheme of events and occasions involved thirty-four leading characters, not counting minor persons, and the main figures Aramena and Cimber, whose mettle was tested in an elaborate system of conflicts, abductions, battles until they were finally united. Their wedding occasioned seventeen more princely weddings. *Roman Octavia*, an even more colorful novel, shows that though the author certainly tried to entertain his readers he also hoped to mirror a divine order in the perfection of the absolutistic state. A person acted truly heroically when he subordinated his desires to the law of the state. Lohenstein produced an epic of teutonic background *Arminius and Thusnelda* (1689), eighteen volumes of historical events, adventures, and heroic qualities. Anselm von Ziegler und Klipphausen (1663–1697) wrote in the same year *Die Asiatische Banise oder blutiges, doch mutiges Pegu* (*The Asian Banise or Bloody, yet Courageous Pegu*). This work displayed great rhetorical splendor and its language was charged with bombastic imagery. But the structure of the novel was already much simpler. The conflicts of the heroes developed in scenes of gruesome splendor, mostly on the battlefield. Also an "unrepresentative" person, the servant Scandor, attracted more attention than was "proper" in a heroic set. In *Asiatische Banise* adventure, exoticism, mere pomp, and a great display of factual knowledge finally constituted the main interest. Consequently, it reads like an encyclopedia of contemporary knowledge.

While the heroic novel expressed the political and moral views of the absolutistic courts and the reigning classes, the emerging middle class had refined a traditionally popular genre: the moral satire with its realism and concern for reform. The middle-class satirist was much more concerned with the social reality at hand than with metaphysical problems. He attacked the pretentious system of upper-class morality and especially its adoption by the non-courtly classes. Hans Michael Moscherosch (1601–1669), of Spanish descent, translated a French adoption of *Los Sueños* (1606–1627) by Francisco de Quevedo (1580–1645), the leading representative of Spanish *conceptismo*. In *Wunderliche und wahrhaftige Gesichte Philanders von Sittewald* (*Curious and True Visions of Philander von Sittewald*, 1640 ff.), Quevedo's dreams were transformed into a parade of follies in the tradition of the sixteenth century. Moscherosch's satire was social rather than religious. It unmasked the pretentious ascetic ideals of the upper classes. Instead of the unrealistic demands of the courtly life Moscherosch postulated a strongly personal morality and individual responsibility, as the Protestant faith and the humanistic tradition had established them.

The best known literary works of the period were written by Hans Jakob Christoffel von Grimmelshausen (1621/22–1676). His cycle of novels *Der Abenteuerliche Simplicissimus* (*The Adventurous Simplicissimus*, 1669), *Die Landstörtzerin Courasche* (*Courage, the Adventuress*, 1670), *Der seltsame Springinsfeld* (*The Strange Springinsfeld*, 1670), and *Das wunderbarliche Vogelnest* (*The Magic Bird's Nest*, 1672–1675) fused Baroque idealism with middle-class individuality and a new realism. His novels throbbed with vitality. Grimmelshausen emancipated the spirit of the people. He spoke their language, depicted their world, and bemoaned their destiny. Neither Simplicissimus nor Courasche were political types. They were common people—though Simplicissimus eventually discovered his aristocratic descent—caught in the events of their time and threatened by the changes of *Fortuna* which befell soldiers, peasants, and low-class people. Nevertheless, their experiences were exemplary. Simplicissimus rushed through life as the *picaro*, the sinner and fool who could not resist the charms of the world (*Frau*

83

Welt), although he was convinced of their futility. *Simplicissimus* might seem remote in tone and life from the heroic novel; nevertheless it presented the Baroque concepts in a popular milieu with great religious pathos and a strong dualism of nature and grace. The realism of the novel cannot therefore be equated with the realism of nineteenth-century prose. Rather, Grimmelshausen's realism filled the abstract notions of Baroque concepts with human relevance. Time and space became essential qualities for a novelist who created a fictional matrix in which people lived and suffered. Simplicissimus is not only the *picaro* type but a true person who grew and matured. Experiencing danger and failure, winning fame and riches, then losing both, he recognizes how deceptive the pleasures of the world really are. And though his intellectual and moral development leads to greater self-insight, it also gives rise to the feeling of resignation; his quest ends in ascetic withdrawal: "Oh world, impure world! therefore I entreat you, I beg you and request . . . you should no longer be part of me . . . Posui finem curis, spes et fortuna, valete! (I put an end to my sorrows, hope and fortune, farewell!)"

Later generations saw in Grimmelshausen's novels an accurate portrait of his time and praised his sober characterization of man's behavior. However, neither his diction nor the aims of his novels completely break with the Baroque tradition. His style is still rhetorical and man's actions are measured in terms of a possible eternal salvation or condemnation. A similar fusion of realism and rhetorical finesse characterizes the sermons of Abraham a Sancta Clara (Ulrich Megerle, 1644–1709), a renowned preacher at the Vienna Court.

From a European perspective, German literature of the seventeenth century represents a transitional phase. Foreign influences in themes and forms shaped the emerging literature which freed itself only slowly from this yoke. By the end of the century the ever-present conflict between the world and eternity had shifted to new conflicts arising from the growing middle-class culture (Johann Christian Günther) and to the question of man's ability to assert himself in the world.

3. *The Establishment of Standard Modern Literary German* 🖉

Stanley N. Werbow

All of us use language for a variety of purposes and can upon reflection recognize that our language varies greatly with its function. Familiar talk, formal speech, personal letter writing all are somehow different. The nature and status of a language then is a function of the status of its users and the purposes it serves.

With this truism as a basis, we can imagine that when the Germanic tribes hunted, fought, and tended their flocks and primitive farms untouched by Roman civilization or Judaeo-Christian culture they used a language which was suitably simple in syntax and word structure. Unfortunately we have no direct knowledge of this stage in the development of German since the essentially illiterate tribesmen of the period from 1,000 to 100 B.C. left no written records. Historical linguistics does provide the information that Germanic word inflection was of the synthetic and, from the point of view of analytical English grammar, complicated type which we know from Indo-European grammar as seen in, say, Greek or Latin. Early syntax is more difficult to know, but we imagine the sentences as essentially single, one-clause structures with little sophisticated logical interconnection.

In order to focus our attention better on the Germanic languages that were in closest contact, that interacted most in the post-Roman period and, most importantly, which came to make up the dialects and finally the language of Germany, we exclude North Germanic, that is Scandinavian and Gothic, and look at the South Germanic, or more specifically the continental South Germanic languages without those South Germanic groups which migrated to the British Isles. For convenience, let us use "German" for the moment as a short reference term for any speaker of a continental South Germanic language whether his tribal dialect eventually ended up as the language of the Flemish minority in modern Belgium, the Standard Dutch of both North and South Netherlands, the Saxon dialect of Northeastern Netherlands, that separate and equal language of the Netherlands province of Friesland called

Frisian, a variety of the *Plattdeutsch* (Low German) of Northern Germany, or one of the dialects of Central or Southern Germany known variously as Franconian, Hessian, Thuringian, Silesian, Swabian, Alemannic or Bavarian-Austrian, to name most of them. At the same time we remember that we make no claim of political-cultural unity or dependence.

Strictly speaking, none of these geographical dialects is a dialect of Modern Standard German, but rather a variety of continental South Germanic from whose predecessors at various times more or less standard languages have emerged and of which Modern Standard German is one. The other extant standard languages of this origin are Netherlandic (*Algemeen beschaafd Nederlands* or 'general cultured Dutch' of Belgium and Holland), Afrikaans in South Africa, literary Yiddish, and in a sense also Zwitzerdütsch.[1]

For full understanding of the early stages in the development of the literary norm in Germany proper we need to learn more about the political-cultural relationship of the emerging standard language in medieval and early modern times to the tribal dialects and the regional or territorial languages.

We must also understand not only that languages change but something about how they change, both genetically, according to the tree-branching theory (*Stammbaumtheorie*), and environmentally, as languages in contact[2] according to the wave theory (*Wellentheorie*). That is to say that some changes in language come about within the linguistic tradition of a given language or dialect by innovation within the group of its speakers while other changes are the result of interaction with other groups speaking different but related dialects or even wholly different languages. For example, the weakening of full quality unaccented vowels in case and personal endings to the indefinite central schwa sound, usually cited as the main difference between Old High German and Middle High German (OHG *gebun* 'we give' becoming MHG *gebən*), is probably a genetic change resulting as a late effect from the shift from musical and free accentuation of Indo-European to the dynamic and later fixed accent of Germanic. On the other hand, the very shift in accentuation may have been the result of contact with another language. A more recent and obvious example of wave-like change is the acceptance in Standard German of the plural marker -*s* in words like *Jungens, Autos*. This came clearly from contact with Low German, perhaps reinforced by French and more recently English.

The history of the High German literary language is then the complex story of how tribal languages became the vehicle of social intercourse at the Frankish court in the eighth century and of religious expression in the ninth century, how they largely faded from our view in the Ottonian tenth and in the eleventh century in favor of a revival of Latin as the literary language, how they emerged to view in the twelfth and thirteenth centuries serving first ecclesiastical authors and then lay poets and how they broke through in the late thirteenth century as the accepted language of legal documents and court correspondence in a progression interrupted only by a second revival of Latin in the Renaissance although Latin dominated the written and the printed page on into the late seventeenth century.

Germany did not have the continuity of a prestige dialect as had been assured to the language of the Île de France and of Paris since the twelfth century. In Old High German, no claim can be made for a single, standard language, and almost every major document is written in a different dialect. While a better case can be made for Swabian Alemannic as the linguistic ideal of the late twelfth and early thirteenth centuries, the political hegemony of the Hohenstaufen lasted only about a hundred years, from approximately 1150 until soon after the death of Frederick II in 1250. This was too short a time to assure southwestern German a strong position in the competition for linguistic prestige, and the emerging New High German was not a continuation of southwestern or even of Upper German but blended East Middle German and southeastern German or Bavarian-Austrian in a fascinating way which, as we shall see later, only most recent scholarship has amply demonstrated.

In a real sense, the history of written or cultured German is the history of the interaction of a variety of German and a language with which it is in contact, either another variety of German or importantly and pervasively Latin, later French, and now English. From the *Germania* of Tacitus, the Edicts of Rothar, from schoolboys' and scholars' Old High German interlinear glosses in textbooks, from scribal emendations in legal, scholarly, and literary documents, from the proofreaders' changes in successive editions of Luther's Bible and Wieland's works (to name only two) on up to the pages of *Der Spiegel* and *Konkret* we read the signs of the continuing struggle of German speakers, of necessity at least bilingual, in a world dominated or strongly influenced by a different variety of German or by Latin, French, English or Russian. The phoneme *uo* of "standard" Old High German is a Franconian development from Germanic *ô* to which Bavarian *oa* and *ua* gradually conformed. The triumphal march of the thirteenth-century southeastern innovation *au* for Middle High German *û* (*mûs* to *maus*) spreading first to various Upper German and Middle German literary dialects and finally into Standard German could result only from the prestige of the East Upper German lands which developed or adopted the change.

While these phonological changes claim the most space in the research of the last 150 years and hence in our handbooks, it is in fact a relatively trivial hindrance to understanding whether a speaker says *guot* or *gût*, *wîp* or *waip* (*Weib*) compared to whether his word for "trinity" is *drînessi* or *Dreivaltigkeit* or whether his simple clauses are strung together endlessly with "and then, and then, and then" (OHG *dô*) or whether, as in the *Bohemian Plowman* his "clauses, sentences, and periods run along after the latest fashion," learned from Cicero.[3]

For the purposes of this book, it will not be useful to rehearse systematically the phonological changes which differentiate early stages of German, but we should note those major ones that are usually supposed to separate modern German from medieval German or more properly New High German from Middle High German. While these phonological changes—Middle German monophthongs in place of the older Upper German diphthongs in *bruoder* (now *brüder* 'brother'), *liəb* (now *lîb* 'love'), *brüeder* (now *brüder* 'brothers') and diphthongs for the old monophthongs in *mûs* (now *maus* 'mouse'), *mîn* (now *main* 'my') and *miuse* (now *mɔize* 'mice')—were observed as early as the twelfth and eleventh centuries respectively, their combination in a single dialect along with other features of New High German is the product of the fourteenth and fifteenth centuries and their spread and eventual canonization in Modern Standard German the intriguing story of the sixteenth to nineteenth centuries.

Yet these changes in sounds alone do not give modern German its distinguishing stamp. Of greater distinguishing force is, for example, the new reduced inventory of forms of the strong verb or the altogether new, so-called "mixed" declension of feminine nouns. Luther still uses the old Middle High German past tense forms distinguishing singular and plural by the stem vowel *ich bleib/ wir bliben; ich sang/wir sungen*, etc. The Old and Middle High German weak noun declension had nominative singular ending in *-e* while all other cases singular and plural had *-en*. Late Middle High German began the change by having the accusative singular agree with the nominative while dative and genitive kept *-en*, and Early New High German vacillated on into the eighteenth century accounting for poetic and frozen forms like *auf Erden*. Ultimately, however, *-en* like *-er* long before it and like umlaut, with or without final *-e*, began to be thought of as plural markers; and a new declension was born, strong in the singular, weak in the plural: *die Frau/ die Frauen* (cf. MHG Nom. Sg. *diu vrouwe*, Acc. Sg. *die vrouwen*). Only those feminine nouns with the powerful plural markers, umlaut and *-e*, could hold out against inclusion in this new class: *die Hände, die Nächte, die Städte*.[4]

Unfortunately, while tremendous energy has gone into the study of the spread of NHG phonology to the various High and Low German chanceries and scriptoria of the fifteenth to seventeenth centuries, the grammatical unification is less well documented though by no means as unknown as the handbooks would make it seem. Another feature that adds to the unstable picture of the transitional period is the split from the old weak masculine nouns of the inanimate ones by the extension of the *-n* of the other cases to the nominative singular with inflection like the strong masculines:

MHG	*der garte*	*des garten*
NHG	*der garten*	*des gartens*

Even Modern Standard German is, however, not free from vacillation as we learn from any detailed study of a large corpus such as that on the nominal inflection by Ljungerud.[5]

While detailed knowledge of German dialect geography is not required for our sketch of the emerging German literary language, a schematic geographical orientation will be helpful:

LOW GERMAN

WEST MIDDLE GERMAN	EAST MIDDLE GERMAN
Ripuarian	
Mosel Franconian	Thuringian Upper Saxon Silesian
Rhine Franconian	

WEST UPPER GERMAN	EAST UPPER GERMAN
Alemannic-Swabian	East Franconian	Bavarian-Austrian

While Low German is significant in the spoken modern standard language because some of its phonetic features such as aspirated voiceless stops contrasting with voiced stops (e.g., *p-* vs *b-*) mark the German standard *Hochsprache* apart from Middle German and Upper German dialects which use a fortis versus lenis contrast, the active contribution of Low German to the standardization process is negligible otherwise, and we shall leave it aside.

In Old High German times, only Upper German and West Middle German were significant, and the main cultural-religious centers from which documents have come down were Reichenau and St. Gall; Straßburg, Weißenburg, Lorsch, and Fulda; Freising, Tegernsee, and Monsee. The only force operating toward standardization was the Carolingian dynasty which was too multilingual and too short-lived to have much effect.

For the monastery culture of the eighth to the eleventh century, Latin was the significant language, and by and large it mattered little which dialect of German performed the ancillary function of glossing and literal translation for school or church purposes. Even Charlemagne's famous capitulary of 789 which urges making the liturgy comprehensible to the people, presumably in the vernacular, can have had no effect on standardizing German. The Latin *pater noster* or *Credo* was the only one effective as ritual, after all, and Notker Labeo's ambitious renderings of the Psalms, of Boethius, and Martianus Capella into Alemannic were for local consumption. Only Otfried's gospel poem, the *Evangelienbuch* in the new end-rhymes (about 865) and the Old Saxon alliterative treatment of the life of the Savior (*Heliand*, German *Heiland*) were intended as major independent literary works, and in them there is no evidence of standardization though, as in any written document, one can trace social and geographical dialects in contact. The main dialects of this early period were Upper German ones.

In Middle High German times (ca. 1050–1350) the number and geographical spread of religious, literary, and technical documents were larger and broader including in fact everything from Veldeke's Limburgish, a Low Franconian dialect, to Morungen's Thuringian, from the Middle Franconian of *King Rother* to the many works of Bavarian-Austrian authors including Reinmar the Elder, the *Nibelungenlied* author, Ulrich of Lichtenstein, Stricker among many others. Yet the main literary blossoming took place in and under the influence of the West Upper German (Alemannic) courtly culture surrounding the Hohenstaufens. Here we can speak of a literary and probably a social norm which is palpable in the sounds, inflection, and word choice of courtly verse.

While the existence of a Middle High German literary norm has been argued endlessly, the latest consensus is once again in favor[6] and the best evidence is still the fact that between the West Upper German Hartman and the East Upper German Walther only one dialect rhyme betrays its author's dialect origin, Walther's Bavarian-Austrian *a* for *o* in the rhyme *verwarren: pfarren* and Hartman's Alemannic *sh* for *s* in *laschte* (NHG *löschte*): *glaste* (NHG *glänzte*); cf. A. Bach, *Geschichte*, p. 211. Even with the recognition[7] that Upper German documents of the eleventh and twelfth centuries cannot be localized further by their language, not even Swabian against Alemannic, there were certainly gross dialect differences which all written documents would tend to play down. The desire to have their songs sung from one end of the German-speaking part of the empire to the other, from Vienna to Mainz or even perhaps to Utrecht, caused poets to avoid phonological clashes in their rhymes so that Veldeke did not use obviously useful rhymes like Low German *tît* 'time' (MHG *zît*) with *wît* 'white' (MHG *wîz*) in his courtly epic, the *Eneit*, which was aimed toward a wide audience at various High German speaking courts, where the corresponding High German forms would not rhyme, while he did rhyme them often in his earlier *Saint Servatius* which was written for local Limburg consumption. This no doubt real desire for a social-literary court norm is inferred mainly from the avoidance not only of dialect rhymes but also of dialect forms, e.g., no Bavarian dual forms of the pronoun come to us from early medieval documents, but we know that they must have existed from their presence in modern Bavarian as plural forms *enk* and *ös*.

Present-day German dialects continue along lines marking the political territories of the late Middle Ages since later religious, cultural, and economic development was controlled by the princes, both ecclesiastical and temporal, who headed these states. The old feudal society had been oriented beyond local dialects; at least its poetry seems to have tended toward linguistic normalization though by no means as far reaching as the normalization which the Germanistic editors of the nineteenth and early twentieth centuries conjured in their normalized editions. But with the fall of the old knightly class, the old tendencies toward normalization ran dry.

At the same time the cities were growing in strength, and their interterritorial and international interests provided a strong impetus and basis for standardization. Together, the imperial and royal government offices or chanceries, the religious, especially the reformational centers, the printers and the universities with the various city interests shared a need for communication beyond and above dialects. No one of these would by itself have had the singleness of purpose nor the cohesive force to bring about standardization. Thus, for example, business interests alone would not have been enough. The great business community of the north, the Hansa, had a Low German trade language while those of the Swabian and Franconian South had another, Upper German trade language.

There is no reason to assume that the so-called *Sondersprachen* or jargons of sailors, soldiers, thieves, hunters, miners, and so on contributed toward the standardization of German. On the other hand scientific and technical writings in German were published in large editions, read by a geographically widespread public and so, it has been claimed, had more influence than literary or even most religious works. Evidence of their popularity is not only the large number of manuscripts and versions of books like those on veterinary medicine but also the fact that they were translated into the other languages of western and even eastern Europe as well as, of course, into Latin. It may well be, as Gerhard Eis says, that their contribution to the standardization of German has been inadequately presented.[8]

At the same time that knighthood, the leading social institution in western Germany, was losing power and influence, the colonization of eastern territories was being intensified. Starting in the twelfth century settlers from western Germany came to the area around Leipzig and Dresden in large numbers and formed along with those from Upper German areas a new colonial language with a mixture of features. This new land with its rich natural resources was to blossom into a political, economic and cultural configuration that gained ascendancy over all of Germany in the next centuries. It was only here that the phonological, morphological, and lexical features that mark Standard German apart from any of the dialects are actually found in the local dialects: the *-r* and *-ch* forms of the personal pronouns (*mir, mich, dir, dich, er, wir, ihr, euch*) of the South for the Northern forms reminiscent of English *me, thee, he, we, ye,* and *you*; diminutives in *-chen* of Middle German for southern *-li, -le* (*Stückchen* versus *Stuckli, Stuckele*); the forms with *e* rather than *a* in the stem, *gên* and *stên* of the Southeast for *gân* and *stân* of the Southwest and West; the long simple vowels of Middle Germany in words like *lieb* and *gut* for the diphthongal *liab, guat* of the South; the full schwa of Middle German in prefixes and endings for the syncopated and apocopated forms of the Southeast: im *Grunde, bestellt, gestohlen* as well as, of course, the diphthongized southeastern forms like *Haus* and *Zeit* for *hûs* and *zît* of the Southwest or *hûs* and *tîd* of the North. Only in East Middle German do all of these standard language phonological and morphological features appear together even in the local dialects alongside such standard lexical items as *Bettstelle* for South German *Bettstatt* 'bedstead' and Western *Bettlade* to name only one, and the Middle German feminine gender of *die Luft, die Butter* versus *der Luft, der Butter* of the South.[9]

In addition to the selection of dialect features found in the Middle German and East Upper German dialects, New High German is marked by these basic changes in the morphology. In the verb, the distinctly marked third person plural indicative (*-ent*) is given up so that the form without *-t* of the subjunctive, the past tense, and the modal auxiliaries becomes completely general. Also during the early New High German period the distinction of singular and plural in the past tense of strong verbs (*bleib – bliben; sang – sungen*, etc.) was abandoned. And thirdly, the new "mixed" declension of feminine nouns (MHG *vrouwe* in the nominative singular versus *vrouwen* in all other cases, NHG *Frau* in the singular versus *Frauen* in the plural) gradually became a regular feature of Standard German.

The selection of certain dialect features and changes in the phonology but especially in the morphological system in colonial East Germany is a good example of the way in which colonial languages change when in dynamic contact with other dialects or other languages.[10] What has been a rigid or invariable rule in the traditional dialect becomes variable or uncertain as speakers in Middle Germany have contact with other forms of the underlying language while the relatively static West Upper German tends to conserve old forms. This observation does not of course rule out innovation and change in the local dialects. We know, for example, that the use of umlaut and of the ending *-er* as a plural marker in nouns came first and most extensively in Upper German dialects,[11] perhaps because the loss of final *-e* left the plural unmarked in many nouns otherwise. However, Standard German also extended the use of those two plural markers while retaining the final -e as well (NHG *Hände* UG *hänt*).

In some of these features, a long period of uncertainty and variation preceded the regularization in the seventeenth and eighteenth centuries. Even the classical authors of the eighteenth century had to go to their Adelung dictionary[12] for a ruling.

A clarification of the share of the various dialects in the emerging standard language has come recently from the work of Werner Besch.[13] His maps of variants from manuscripts of the fifteenth and sixteenth century show the extraordinarily great strength of Southeast German (Bavarian-Austrian) and the relative weakness of the old Southwest (Alemannic) and even of the West (Franconian) which lost the battle over *gân/gên, brengen/bringen, born/brunn,* and *otmuot/demuot.* A coalition of East Middle German and East Upper German was almost always decisive. Besch's conclusion against Theodor Frings's position was that literary written language considerations are overriding in determining the features that survive in Standard German while true dialect factors and the language of the rural population play a subordinate role. The chancery language of the fifteenth and sixteenth centuries was eclectic and operated on a different social-cultural level from that of the dialect speakers of the area. In this respect, Arno Schirokauer's view receives needed support: "The peasant element had a minimal influence on the determination of written language features." The chancery language of East Middle Germany had some basis in the spoken language of the settlers, but Early New High German or what we know of it was a literary language and rested on the chancery and school languages of East Middle German and East Upper German.

While older views saw in Martin Luther not only the dominant religious and cultural figure of the sixteenth century but also the originator and founder of Modern Standard German, recent scholarship has shown him to be a link—to be sure a most powerful and important link—in a chain of linguistic development beginning almost a century before his time and continuing long after his immediate influence and even after his gigantic contribution, the Luther Bible, was no longer the major literary-linguistic influence on Standard Written German.

Luther's contribution lay not so much in his furtherance of the East Middle German–East Upper German amalgam in sounds and linguistic forms, for to tell the truth, Luther himself paid very little attention to these details of his published works, but in the fact that he more than any other freed written German from its slavish dependence on and imitation of Latin grammar and style. He sought his model for vocabulary and syntax not in the twisted and broken close renderings of Latin originals as did Niklas of Wyle (1410–1478), for example, but in the informal and simple language of sermons and religious tracts. The close translations which we find in the pre-Luther Bible or in scholastic texts or even in literary works like Wyle's *Translatzen* (1461–1478), renderings from Latin originals or Latin translations of mid-fifteenth century humanistic works, are all but incomprehensible at times without the Latin text as a guide to their intention. And it was in this stylistic, syntactic, literary sense that Luther was the founder of Standard Literary German. He wanted a Bible that could stand by itself syntactically and lexically and be understood correctly by monolingual Germans without keeping an anxious eye on the Latin text as was surely necessary with the pre-Luther Bible. This has been pointed out often.[14]

We have learned most forcefully from Werner Besch that Luther's own language does not win out in New High German against a unified Upper German position, where Bavarian is supported by Alemannic and East Franconian, as for example Middle German *brengen, die hulfe*, initial *sl-* versus *schl-* in words like *schlange*, etc., *quam, werlt, twingen, born* cannot hold up against Upper German *bringen, hilfe, Schlange*, etc., *kam, welt, zwingen, brunn*. Either Luther's genius or that of his printers recognized early that they could not win and switched to the Upper German forms. In a few cases Middle German ultimately did dominate eventually against a solid Upper German, e.g., *ich gebe* versus *ich gibe* or *ich gib*, but the battle continued into the eighteenth century.

The often cited examples of shift in grammatical gender between MHG and NHG in favor of MG and Luther usage are actually examples of the rejection of the isolated Alemannic and hence literary MHG form, e.g., *der andacht, daz zît*, in favor of forms in use in Low German, Middle German, and East Upper German, *die andacht, die zît/zeit*. Such cases were decided early. In cases where Upper German was split, the choice between the variants was left open for a long time, so, e.g., in favor of *sonne, fremd, die toufe, ich danke dir* versus *sunne, frömd, der touf, ich danken dir*. Nor were all victories East Middle German. The feminine *die gewalt* is a WMG form while EMG and UG had the masculine. Luther used his native masculine in early writings but he or his printers prefer the feminine overall. Yet the masculine holds large sway throughout the sixteenth century. Only the seventeenth century probably with the help of the grammarians and by analogy with *die Macht, die Kraft* brings the full breakthrough of the feminine and later Luther form.

An interesting phenomenon in the history of German is the struggle over the so-called Protestant final *-e* which among other features exercised spirits like Gottsched and Wieland not to mention lesser lights especially in Bavaria. August Langen writes: "The Upper Saxon literary language met most resistance in southern Germany. The denominational contrast may not have started the language controversy but it certainly sharpened it. Catholics, especially the religious orders often rejected not only Luther's teachings but often their medium as well; the content and the Middle German linguistic garb were inseparable."[15] He provides a detailed discussion of the situation in the eighteenth century.

It is an amusing sidelight that the apocope of final *-e* of Bavarian, which could thus become a shibboleth in the struggle between the confessions, was itself a relative innovation having begun in the thirteenth century. It was probably the conflict between apocopating and non-apocopating dialects in East Middle German that led to the hypercorrect preterite forms of strong verbs which mark Luther's writings: *sahe, flohe, lase, schluge*, forms in which the so-called Luther grammarian Johannes Clajus refused to follow his model.[16]

It was thus in the sense in which we have presented it that Luther's often cited and much disputed table talk pronouncement should be understood. It was not the 'gemeine teutsch' of the Southeast of Emperor Frederick III (r. 1440–1493) or, as Luther says, of Emperor Maximilian (r. 1493–1519) alone, nor the East Middle German Wettin dynasty chancery language of Prince Elector Frederick the Wise (r. 1486–1525) alone, but both together, which conditioned Luther's choices and that of New High German.

In sum, the details of standardization in sounds, linguistic forms, and vocabulary resulted from countless human decisions and were decided in the three hundred years following the Reformation. The grammarians of the sixteenth and especially the seventeenth century (Johannes Clajus, Fabian Franck, Schottelius, and others) helped to codify them. In the eighteenth century, authors turned to Gottsched's *Deutsche Sprachkunst* (1746) and Adelung's *Lehrgebäude* (1782) as well as to his dictionary for verdicts. As the title of that dictionary stresses, it was grammatical and critical. Although the seventeenth-century poet and poeticist Martin Opitz sternly forbade that southern apocopy of final -*e*, Wieland (1733–1813) broke a lance as late as 1782 (*Was ist Hochdeutsch?*)[17] for freedom of choice for poets between Adelung's prescribed Middle German '*Hochdeutsch*' and forms with a syllable more, or one less, from Upper German:

> But we can never allow the critic to arrogate to himself the right to lay down arbitrary rules, and to put genius, wit and whimsy in chains so long as they do not palpably abuse that freedom which is the only element in which they can survive. . . . An archaic word, a dialect word for which *Hochdeutsch* has no full equivalent is sometimes in the place where it is used the only one that has the shade of color which is right for his purpose and on which the whole effect depends. Sometimes the Upper German word is a syllable shorter or longer, or has different vowels or consonants etc. than the *Hochdeutsch* and the poet achieves by that very thing the greater euphony of a verse, the better rounding of a period etc. And if it is moreover a word which Luther or Opitz already used, who is to insist that he should reject it merely because it was not current in Southern Electoral Saxony between 1740 and 1760?[18]

It was not until the late nineteenth century that the concept of Standard German was extended from a literary or written to a spoken norm with the preparatory discussions and plans and finally the publication in 1898 of Theodor Siebs' *Deutsche Bühnenaussprache*. As the title shows, this book was designed to provide a standard for stage pronunciation, thus a logical extension of a literary norm so that actors from various parts of German speaking areas could perform together with a natural effect. It was not until 1922 that the subtitle of the work reflected in the use of the word *Hochsprache* or 'elevated language' the step from regularizing stage pronunciation to providing a standard for speakers at large. Only in 1957 did the word *Hochsprache* move into the main title and *Bühnenaussprache* become relegated to the subtitle. With the 1969 edition the title becomes simply and without apology or pretension:

Deutsche Aussprache (German pronunciation). This bibliographical history is symptomatic of the standardization process in German, which had no Paris as its cultural center and no French Academy as its century-long arbiter of linguistic normalcy, not even its "Oxbridge" to set the tone and accent. It is worth noting that German dictionaries traditionally did not even undertake to provide a guide to pronunciation unlike our *Webster* (else Siebs would not have needed to try). Neither Adelung nor Campe nor Grimm nor Paul nor even the most recent German-German dictionary modeled on American dictionaries of the Webster type, Wahrig, gives pronunciation of native German words. Only the Siebs and since 1962 the *Duden Aussprachewörterbuch* undertake this task which, as the dustjacket says, is "unerläßlich für die hochdeutsche Aussprache" (indispensable for standard German pronunciation).

We have come a long way from the Germanic tribes and their variety of dialects with Latin as the *lingua franca* for cultural purposes. Even Zwingli was so afraid that his Swiss German would be incomprehensible that he proposed conducting the Marburg Religious Conferences of 1529 in Latin, and Luther complained that it cost him some sweat to understand Zwingli's German. There is still not complete standardization of spoken German and even in writing a South German author may write *ist gestanden* instead of *hat gestanden*. The everyday home and street language of Bavaria is incomprehensible to a North German. The amusing passage in Thomas Mann's *Buddenbrooks* in which a Lübeck lady tells of her experience in Bavaria is just as true in 1970 as it was in 1901:

> And when I say '*Frikadellen*,' she doesn't understand me, because it is called '*Pflanzerln*' here; and when she says '*Karfiol*' then a Christian person is not very likely to guess that she means '*Blumenkohl*'; and when I says '*Bratkartoffeln*,' she keeps screaming "What?" until I say '*Geröhste Kartoffeln*.'[19]

Even the literary written norm without which German cultural, economic, and political unification would have been impossible was achieved far more slowly in reality than in idea and hope and much later than when Luther made his famous statement:

> I have no certain, specific language of my own in German; rather I use the common German language so that both Highlanders and Lowlanders can understand me. I speak after the Saxon Chancery, which all princes and kings in Germany follow;

all Imperial Cities and Princely Courts write in accordance with the Saxon Chancery of our Prince, and that is why it is the most common German language. Emperor Maximilian and Prince Elector Frederick, Duke of Saxony, etc., have thus brought the German languages in the Roman Empire into one certain language.[20]

4. The Eighteenth Century: Foundation and Development of Literary Criticism 🖎

E. Allen McCormick

I

The general state of German literature and criticism in the second half of the eighteenth century is admirably if somewhat charitably summed up in Goethe's famous assertion that when he was eighteen Germany too was just eighteen. From the perspective of more than two centuries it is tempting to object that so far as literature is concerned Goethe may be confusing adolescence with backwardness, for the seventeen-forties and -fifties are clearly a time of painful struggle against an entrenched tradition of Renaissance and Baroque poetics, the bawdy improvisations of the theater with its *Hanswurst* (harlequin), a generally poor state of poetry, and a quarrelsome uncertainty as to whom to imitate, since imitation seemed to many the only solution.

If mid-century literature seemed impossibly mired in sentimentality, vulgarity, and rule-mongering, any imaginative attempt to strike out along new paths, to innovate as well as liberate, must have had the effect of violent revolution. And it is surely in this spirit that we should understand Goethe's feeling that in his own youth literature was experiencing its birth as something both liberating and truly national. Goethe's assessment of the literary state of affairs is summed up in the seventh book of his autobiography, *Poetry and Truth*:

> The literary epoch into which I was born developed from the preceding one by way of contradiction. Germany, flooded for so long with foreign peoples, subject to the mastery of other nations, forced to use foreign tongues in scholarly and diplomatic affairs, could not possibly develop its own language. . . . If one looks closely for what German literature lacked one finds that it was content, a national content.

The challenge of improving the "chaotic condition" and "pitiable state" of which Goethe speaks was not to be the work of a single writer, although it is to but one, Gotthold Ephraim Lessing

(1729–1781), that the major credit is usually given. Three works in particular, the drama *Miss Sara Sampson* (1755), the comedy *Minna von Barnhelm* (1767), and the aesthetic treatise *Laocoön* (1766), were of vital importance in bringing about the new climate of liberation and the resurgence of German literary spirit. We may turn again to Goethe for succinct assessment of the impact that two of these works had in eighteenth-century Germany:

> One must be young to picture the effect Lessing's *Laocoön* had on us in snatching us out of the region of mere observation into the free realm of thought. The long misunderstood "ut pictura poesis" was removed at one stroke, the difference between plastic and literary arts was made clear, and the peaks of both now appeared separately, no matter how close their bases might be. . . . All the consequences of this splendid thought were illuminated as though by a flash of lightning, all previous legislative and judicial criticism was cast off like a worn-out coat.

And about *Minna von Barnhelm* he says:

> You may imagine how the play affected us young people when it appeared during that dark time! It was truly a flashing meteor, making us realize that there still existed something higher than anything dreamed of by that weak literary epoch.[1]

The third work, *Miss Sara Sampson*, is Germany's first domestic or middle-class tragedy ("bürgerliches Trauerspiel"). It has aptly been called an important essay in practical criticism in that it was written to serve as a model for the new kind of drama Germany needed.[2] More important, it dealt a fatal blow to prevailing dramatic theories, most of which had derived from Gottsched and his group.[3]

Since both criticism and modern German literature in its broader sense may be said to begin during and immediately preceding Lessing's time, his critical and historical achievement is best appreciated when seen against the bright and dark spots on the literary landscape of eighteenth-century Germany. To be a poet or critic in the early years of the century meant to accept the authority of Martin Opitz's *Buch von der deutschen Poeterei* (*On German Poetics*, 1624) and its Baroque predecessors, that is to say to accept in the main the (borrowed) principles laid down and constantly reiterated by these aestheticians. This overbearing tradition of legislative criticism, based on the optimistic conviction that the writing of poetry was teachable, must be borne in mind when assessing the achievements of Lessing's predecessors. Admittedly, the original contributions made by such men as Gottsched, Bodmer, and Breitinger were exceedingly modest; however, they began the slow task of reinvigorating German intellectual and cultural life by combatting the excesses of some Baroque poets and effecting reforms in the German language, in drama, and in standards of taste generally.[4]

A first, somewhat awkward step towards fruitful critical and literary discussion was taken by two Swiss writers: Johann Jakob Bodmer (1698–1783) and Johann Jakob Breitinger (1701–1776), whose weekly *Discourse der Mahlern* (*Discourses of Painters*) appeared from 1721 to 1723. Modelled on the English moral weeklies, especially the *Spectator,* the *Discourses* aimed at sweeping cultural reforms; the level of taste among the middle classes was to be raised, life was to be imbued with spiritual values, and in the process the bourgeois was to be properly entertained. Relatively few of the ninety-four essays comprising the *Discourses* deal directly with literature, at least in any real critical sense. However, some important matters are at least touched upon—the different ways in which the poet and painter imitate nature, and the clumsily expressed insight that the poet also portrays "the mechanism of the mind and its own thoughts," i.e., the poetic imagination, are the two principal ones—and the ground is thus laid for later and larger aesthetic studies.

The third important forerunner to Lessing, especially in the field of criticism, was Johann Christoph Gottsched (1700–1766). For a time one of the most respected and feared men of German letters, this literary dictator is a further example of the fact that the first half of the eighteenth century was overwhelmingly an age of theory and rule-making rather than poetry. During a crowded literary career of over forty years Gottsched managed to produce no less than five periodicals, two large drama anthologies, a number of poetic works, and four hefty textbooks. His chief concern as self-appointed reformer of the German language, literature, and the theater—Bodmer and Breitinger were after all Swiss, and their language, according to Gottsched, was horribly "disfigured" by dialect—was to write prescriptive criticism, to lay down hard and fast rules for writing comedies and tragedies. His first periodical, *Die vernünftigen Tadlerinnen* (1725–1726), enjoyed greater popularity than its Swiss predecessor, and linguistic and literary problems are given more attention than in the *Discourses* or the other weeklies that sprang up in Germany in imitation of the English. Intended to raise the moral level of its feminine readers and to introduce them to poetry, Gottsched's journal offers some vague, derivative theorizing about the nature of the poet (in order to write poetry "one must know almost everything"), poetry's need to adhere rigidly to nature as its model, and the way to write comedies. Occasionally Gottsched gets down to actual literary criticism and examines specific poems.[5]

The object of such criticism is often better than the criticism itself, but we must remember the novelty of the enterprise as well as the laudable aims of the moral weeklies. In a time of general literary stagnation the *Tadlerinnen* served the dual purpose of offering the culturally deprived German public reading material of the highest quality (virtually for the first time since the Thirty Years' War) and of laying the foundation for Gottsched's major critical achievement.

The *Versuch einer Critischen Dichtkunst* (*Critical Poetics*), first published in 1730, is not only Gottsched's major statement on criticism, it is the most important single work of its kind since Opitz's *On German Poetics*. Later revisions brought this compendious handbook of poetics to its final size, slightly more than 800 pages in the 1751 version. It attempts to answer two essential questions: what is the nature of poetry, and how does one "make" a good poem? Gottsched frequently relies on the writings of other critics, which is to say that his work is a compilation of leading statements on poetry from Aristotle to Neo-classicism, with an occasional valiant attempt to synthesize and arrive at a consistent aesthetic.[6] The stated goal of the *Critical Poetics* is to "show that the inner nature of poetry consists in the imitation of nature." Proceeding from this conviction, virtually as old as criticism itself and still the heart of all theory in eighteenth-century Europe, Gottsched begins his work with a translation of Horace's *Art of Poetry*, for which he supplies a commentary, and then turns to theoretical problems, which comprise the first part of his work. A second part deals with the various kinds of poetry.

According to Gottsched, the poet is a "skillful imitator of all natural things." Among his special qualifications a strong imagination and great sagacity are listed foremost; but the first requirement, that of imagination, must always be held in check by reason or common sense. As for the marvelous, it must always remain "within the limits of nature and not climb too high," by which he means that it must unfailingly remain credible. Clever poets, he insists, remain with what is probable, that is, with "human things and with those the probability of which we are able to judge."

Gottsched leaves no room for the possibility that poetry may go beyond imitation or art beyond nature. Nor does he see that calling imitation a "faithful reproduction of reality" on one occasion and a "representation of the possible" on another is a contradiction. These are failures which his Swiss opponents were quick to seize upon in their attempt to restore respectability in Germany both to the marvelous in poetry and to English literature generally. Before turning to the "quarrel" and its outcome we may inquire briefly into Gottsched's activities as a practical critic and his contribution to German criticism as a whole.

As early as 1725 Gottsched had resolved to bring about sweeping changes in the German theater. His attack on German drama was three-pronged: against the *Haupt-und Staatsaktionen,* a term coined by Gottsched to denote those plays presented by the itinerant troupes in the years after 1700 which customarily dealt with historical or political subjects and offered sensationalism, improvised comedy, numberless intrigues, and a moral ending; against the harlequin or *Hanswurst* tradition that provided for a comical character even in the serious plays, to interrupt the action, address the audience and engage in banter with it, and generally to entertain by bawdy improvisation; and against the opera, which in Gottsched's day was a formless and for the most part tasteless court entertainment.

Realizing that theatrical reform could not succeed by means of criticism alone, Gottsched undertook to supply the theater with a new, improved repertory. In addition to numerous translations (mostly from the French), some original German plays were written, the first, *Der Sterbende Cato* (performed in 1731) by Gottsched himself. The play is a strange mixture of Gottsched's ideas, an awkward translation of Deschamps' *Caton D'Utique* (1715), and an adaptation of the ending of Addison's *Cato* (1713). In the preface Gottsched seeks to justify his audacious attempt at verse tragedy. It is not faith in his unique qualifications which impels Gottsched to revive verse tragedy in Germany but rather a sense of frustrated waiting. The Germans do not lack great and sublime spirits, he asserts, and yet no one has appeared to remedy the situation. Examining his sources he praises Deschamps' *Caton* at the expense of Addison because the French dramatist followed Aristotle much more closely. In Addison's play, on the other hand, the scenes are too loosely connected, the characters enter or exit without reason, and the stage is often left empty even when no action has been concluded. Gottsched also objects to Addison's plot and, above all, to the marriage Cato must witness before dying. In favor of Deschamps he cites the logic or probability of the whole. Caesar's presence in Utica, for example, is made probable by having him rush to the Parthian queen, whom he loves, rather than from any desire for peace. From Addison's play Gottsched borrows the concluding action. Deschamps lets the great Cato die in desperation rather than in wisdom; in Addison, on the other hand, Cato sees Caesar's army approaching and, realizing that resistance is impossible, kills himself. Two subplots weaken both the unity and plausibility of the English play, and so Gottsched simply drops them. The result of all this mechanical manipulation is, in Gottsched's view, a theatrical success. "Believing myself to have observed most accurately the classical rules for tragedy," he writes in the preface to the first edition, "I have had the pleasure of seeing a performance of this play well received by both the lettered and unlettered, from both of whom tears were wrung."

It is difficult to assess Gottsched's place in literary criticism, especially since his faults and limitations are so glaring as to obscure much that is significant. For the most part his overall achievement is an historical one. Both respectable theater and criticism of the theater were virtually non-existent in the years preceding Gottsched's first decade of activity as professor of poetry in Leipzig. His ideas concerning restoration of rules to tragedy and comedy are neither original nor especially acute, and his ideal of a German theater modelled upon Corneille and Racine was in no way realized. But at least he made the attempt. He led the way in moving from a rulebook of poetics to a critical poetics, without, however, being able to renounce rules and the mechanical method of producing poetry. More important, he also tried to move from theory to practice, to apply some of those long-standing (though never fully understood) rules to living theater. For all his vagueness and exaggerated sense of what is proper, he is rather close to his texts, as close, that is, as his limited critical talent and his larger sense of a personal cultural mission would permit.

Gottsched's quarrel with the Swiss has been compared to a storm, whose first mutterings were heard about 1738 and whose full fury was unleashed in 1740, with the publication of Bodmer's

Critische Abhandlung von dem Wunderbaren in der Poesie (*Critical Treatise on the Marvelous in Poetry*) and Breitinger's *Critische Dichtkunst* (*Critical Poetics*).[7] Though the analogy is apt, one emendation is necessary: disagreements go back virtually to the beginnings of Gottsched's literary activity. As early as 1723 Breitinger published a pamphlet mocking a Leipzig imitation of the *Discourses*. His ire had been aroused by the fact that Gottsched had borrowed liberally from the Swiss periodical while at the same time attacking its language and the presence of those very excesses now being roundly condemned in Baroque poetry. Bodmer replied with a stinging criticism of Gottsched's *Tadlerinnen*, to which he added a defense of his own style in the *Discourses*. In 1727 the Swiss collaborated on an essay called *Von dem Einfluß und Gebrauche der Einbildungskraft, zur Ausbesserung des Geschmacks* (*On the Influence and Use of the Imagination, for the Improvement of Taste*), which was dedicated to Christian Wolff, upon whose philosophical method the essay was based. Within weeks after reading this essay Gottsched offered his reply (in his periodical *Der Biedermann*). Not finding much to disagree with, he had to content himself with pointing out that his own concepts followed Wolff's philosophy more closely than those of the Swiss. Silenced for a time, Bodmer and Breitinger devoted themselves to a systematic inquiry into the nature of poetry. Bodmer published his *Briefwechsel von der Natur des poetischen Geschmacks* (*Correspondence on the Nature of Poetic Taste*) in 1736—the earlier essay on imagination had been largely Breitinger's work—and continued his work on English literature, principally a translation of Milton's *Paradise Lost*. From about 1732 until 1739 relations between the two camps were actually friendly.

A second series of attacks and counterattacks began in 1740. No less than four significant works were published by the Swiss in this and the following year, among them Bodmer's study of the element of the marvelous in poetry and Breitinger's *Critical Poetics*. Gottsched reviewed Bodmer's work in his *Critische Beiträge* (*Critical Contributions*) and attacked its "vain author" for calling the Germans unappreciative and uncomprehending. He accused Bodmer of incompetence in translating and clumsiness in his use of German. Sides were quickly taken, with most writers espousing Gottsched's "cause"; but by 1742 the balance had already begun to shift in favor of the Swiss, and by about 1745 Gottsched's reign was definitely at an end.

It is all too tempting to stress the inconsequential and often purely personal nature of the great quarrel. Certainly, on a number of issues Gottsched and the Swiss were essentially in agreement. Both sides stressed reason and praised rules, both believed in the moral and didactic function of literature, both subscribed to the theory of imitation (borrowing equally freely from classical antiquity on), and both railed against the excesses of some Baroque poets. Their disagreements, however, are of importance to eighteenth-century German literature. Gottsched defended the cause of drama and French classicism; Bodmer and Breitinger were more interested in epic poetry and the fable, in older works from their nation's past, and in English literature, notably Milton. More important, Gottsched is less interested in literature as such than the Swiss, and he is decidedly uncomfortable with a literary text except as it serves to illustrate some theory or other. As for his theoretical criticism—and most of his non-philosophical work may be called that—it is based largely on the ideas of others. Bodmer and Breitinger (especially Bodmer) are well read; their writings betray genuine enthusiasm at times, and their "system" suggests considerably more direct contact with literary works.

The major difference between Gottsched and the Swiss is in the place they assign to the supernatural in poetry. Bodmer and Breitinger claim for the marvelous the highest role in literature. It is, as Breitinger argues in his *Critical Poetics*, the fountainhead of all poetry and represents the highest stage of the new, a clear echo of the Italian critic Gravina's *la novitá é la madre della meraviglia*.[8] These two concepts, novelty and the marvelous or supernatural, are examined in their relation to truth and possibility, and their essential difference is found in how they suggest probability to the audience. Whereas novelty, which may be at variance with our ordinary experience, does not exceed the limits of the true and the possible, the marvelous casts off all pretense of truth and possibility and appears as frankly false and at odds with our experience. But this deception, which pleases us, is a matter of appearance rather than reality; for the marvelous must always be based on real or possible truth if it is to be distinguished from pure lying. Otherwise the biggest liar would be the best poet. Breitinger concludes that the marvelous is in fact merely a disguised "probable." The poet's task is to present us with a semblance to truth, since our minds are open only to what we can believe.

No one in German criticism had so convincingly pleaded the

case for the element of the marvelous in poetry until this time; and because Bodmer and Breitinger were in the main aware that many of their ideas had been current in European criticism for some time it is likely that they did not grasp the full impact of their liberating aesthetic view for the future of German criticism. As dutiful rationalists they were of course concerned to reconcile their theory with respect for the laws of nature: "The marvelous can neither please a clear head nor afford delight unless it is artistically combined with and based upon the probable." In the eighteenth century, poetry is still an imitation of nature, but the truth of which Bodmer and Breitinger speak is that inner truth which represents the realm of genuine poetry. Consequently poetry becomes a matter of fantasy and imagination rather than reason. With the Swiss we thus take a step away from Gottsched's pragmatic realism in the direction of idealizing. Poetry need not correspond to the external appearance of things; if it is *internally* true, if it expresses the inner logic or regularity of the world, then its fidelity to nature is of a higher kind: it will express the typical and essential rather than the individual or particular. It is an idea that was later to become dear to the hearts of the German classicists; Bodmer and Breitinger, however, do not yet draw the final conclusion from their insight. Realism in the form of the mimetic theory is still granted supremacy even while the products of the imagination are praised as true poetry.

The Swiss aesthetic appealed to a generation of rationalists who had had enough of Gottsched's rigid law-making. It did not itself exert the same influence that either Opitz's or Gottsched's position did, but the unreconciled clash between reason and imagination which marks their essential contribution had its effect. After Gottsched and the Swiss both literature and criticism turn into more fruitful channels.

II

At mid-century, in 1748, the same year that young Lessing went to Berlin to begin his career as a critic, Friedrich Gottlieb Klopstock (1724–1803) published the first three cantos of his *Messiah*. Bodmer had encouraged the young poet to compose an epic poem on a national theme or one dealing with Columbus' exploits; instead, Klopstock turned to the timeless subject of the redemption, using Milton as his model. Goethe's remark to Eckermann that in his youth he had venerated Klopstock ("I revered whatever he had done, and never thought of reflecting upon it, or finding fault with it") is typical of the time,[9] at least so far as admiration is concerned: not even Goethe's own *Werther* was to arouse a greater degree of enthusiasm than that which greeted these three cantos. Subjectivity, sentimentality, and piety, vivid flights of imagination—in sum, the wild effusions of poetic genius—appear to have been the missing ingredient in German literature until then.[10]

Lessing himself was not unaffected by this new and in many ways revolutionary work. His lengthy review of 1751 is generally sympathetic and, more important, favorably disposed towards the violations of rules that are everywhere evident in the *Messiah*. Just one month earlier, in the April issue of the same periodical *Das Neueste aus dem Reiche des Witzes* (*The Latest from the Realm of Wit*), Lessing had attacked Gottsched for his slavish obedience to rules and his failure to appreciate genius. There are too many writers, exclaims Lessing in undisguised disgust at Gottsched's followers, who believe that "a limping heroic meter, some Latin structures, and the avoidance of rhyme are enough to raise them above the poet rabble." They are simply unaware of that spirit which lifts the ardent imagination above these trivialities and leads it to the great beauties of fantasy and feeling.

Lessing's commitment to genius and the right to strike out in new directions is not to be his last word as critic; he is in fact more conservative (and often closer to Gottsched) than this, but the timing is at once crucial and symptomatic. At mid-century we are about to witness the culmination and crystallization of those forces and ideas we have been describing. Literary criticism in its higher and more precise sense is ready to emerge and assume its role in the shaping of modern German literature.

Lessing's criticism defies meaningful generalization. He never developed an aesthetic system: of his three major critical undertakings two are collections, a series of unordered notes for a book ("Collectanea") and scattered "Fermenta cognitionis," to use his own words. Furthermore, one is a periodical, to which some of Lessing's friends contributed, another remained a torso, and the third represents accounts of day-to-day theatrical performances intermingled with, and gradually changing to, serious dramatic criticism that is often abstract and primarily concerned with theoretical principles.

To name them in the order indicated, *Briefe, die neueste Literatur betreffend* (*Letters Concerning Contemporary Literature,* generally referred to as *Literary Letters*) appeared in the years 1759–1765, *Laocoön* in 1766, and the *Hamburg Dramaturgy* in a two-volume edition in 1769. These works established Lessing as the first great critic Germany had produced, but they nevertheless do not indicate either the scope or richness of his critical and theoretical writings. As theologian, philosopher, classical philologist, aesthetician, literary critic, and book and play reviewer he covered so vast a field—and in most cases covered with impressive competence—that George Saintsbury, himself a critic of great breadth of interest, writes of him:

> There is nearly always something that Lessing prefers to literature, constantly as he was occupied with books. Now it is the theatre, now it is art—especially art viewed from the side of archeology; now it is classical scholarship of the minuter kind; now philosophy or theology; now it is morals; not infrequently it is more, or fewer, or all of these things together, which engage his attention while literature is left out in the cold.[11]

This overstates the case. Even in the *Laocoön*, that landmark of aesthetic inquiry in the eighteenth century, Lessing never forgets his most genuine concern, literature, be it Homer or Virgil, Shakespeare or Thomson, Gessner or Ewald von Kleist. And his numerous reviews of specific works by German authors range from the Baroque poets to the newest writers of his own day. Nowhere else in the century do we get such extensive criticism in the literal sense of the term.

Several major concerns emerge from Lessing's critical writings as a whole. First, his concern with the German theater, both in terms of acting and stagecraft and the plays themselves; then, his abiding interest in the theory of literature; and lastly, his insistence on direct, concrete criticism of literary works. Permeating all these is his conviction that the larger, moral view of literature is paramount. Not in the rather limited sense of Gottsched's moralizing but in the deeply ethical one of seeing in literature a humanizing force, which springs from an informed tolerance. In this conviction Lessing is less direct than two of his greatest successors: Herder with his goal of humanism or Schiller with his stress on the harmonious development of man's potential, but the faith in *humanitas* is nonetheless everywhere present in his work.

The modernity of his stand as a critic is expressed most clearly in the 105th letter of his *Letters Concerning Contemporary Literature*:

I have always believed it to be the duty of the critic, whenever he undertakes to judge a work, to limit himself solely to this work; to give no thought to the author in doing so; to disregard the question of whether the author has not written other books, worse or better ones; and to tell us forthrightly what opinion we can reasonably form of him solely from this work.

Lessing is not rejecting biography; his *Life of Sophocles* (1760) would alone disprove that. He is simply expressing—at a surprisingly early period in the history of German criticism—what has today become an overworked truism: the private life of a writer is often ill-used when made to supply explanations of a particular work. As Lessing puts it in the 17th literary letter:

Of what concern to us is the private life of an author? I have no use for deriving elucidations of a work from the author's life.

The *Hamburg Dramaturgy*, somewhat less known and certainly less read than the *Laocoön*, shows Lessing in his best light as a critic. Though there is a good deal of ephemeral writing in the 104 pieces comprising the *Dramaturgy*, both his theory and practice of criticism emerge in it in exemplary form. Since Lessing wrote this work in his capacity as critic-consultant to the newly created "national" theater in Hamburg and much of his duty lay in reviewing the performances of plays, he focuses almost exclusively on questions of drama: what is its nature, what rules govern it, how is it to be performed, what is tragedy? Proceeding from concrete examples, usually the performance of a mediocre play the evening before, he turns straightway to these questions, confronts Aristotle, draws comparisons, offers occasional line-by-line analysis, and ultimately produces a simple but effective view of the literary form he had long considered the high-point of literature.

The picture that emerges from these dramaturgical pieces, i.e., the view we get of Lessing the critic, is that of a faithful but by no means blind Aristotelian. He sets himself the task of examining the contemporary stage, primarily in France since that is where most neoclassicists looked in Lessing's and of course Gottsched's time, and of measuring its achievement against Aristotle's rules which he finds infallible.[12] Lessing saw it as his duty to arrest what he calls this fermentation of taste, caused, so he felt, by the delusion of regularity of the French stage. According to him no nation had so misunderstood the rules as the French. Corneille himself, after fifty years of dramatic production, "ought" to have sat down and studied Aristotle more diligently *before* undertaking his commentary to the *Poetics:*

> He appears to have done this only in so far as the mechanical rules of dramatic art were concerned. He left essential points disregarded and when he found at the end that he had sinned against Aristotle, which nevertheless he had not wished to do, he endeavored to absolve himself by means of explanations and caused his pretended master to say things which he never thought. (No. 75)

The intent of statements like the foregoing seems to imply a return to Aristotle; and Lessing points out at least once that this philosopher must be studied thoroughly. Yet he is also fully aware of the achievement of the English, and in admonishing the Germans not to throw away all rules in favor of genius he clearly has Shakespeare in mind. Lessing has relatively little to say about Shakespeare directly, but he has him serve on occasion as the model one should study in pursuit of moderation, of the middle way between tradition and genius. Study Shakespeare, he urges, do not plunder him.

In the *Hamburg Dramaturgy* Lessing investigates tragedy and comedy, analyzes the Aristotelian concepts of pity and fear and their supposed misinterpretation by the French, and inquires into the dramatic art and aesthetic phenomenon of illusion. Furthermore, the book offers several insights which pertain to literature specifically. In a discussion of Lope de Vega and mixed forms (tragi-comedy and comi-tragic drama) he digresses long enough to make an acute statement on the principle of selectivity in art:

> The purpose of art is to save us . . . abstraction in the realm of the beautiful, and to render the fixing of our attention easy to us. All in nature that we might wish to abstract in our thoughts from an object or a combination of various objects, be it in time or in place, art really abstracts for us, and accords us this object or this combination of various objects as purely and tersely as the sensations they are to provoke allow. (No. 70)

On the subject of artist and poet as opposed to critic and observer, Lessing offers a view which occasionally appears in criticism from antiquity to the present. He has studied the art of dramatic writing, he declares:

> and studied it more than twenty who practice it. I have also practiced it *so far as it is needful in order to be able to speak my say*; for I know well that as the painter does not like to be blamed by one who does not know how to hold a brush, so it is with the poet. (Nos. 101–104; italics mine)

His speculations and observations—made, it is worth repeating, in no systematic way—cannot be reduced to a simple formula. Still, it is relatively easy to discern one of Lessing's key convictions about literature: the essence of poetry is action; it presents us with inner perfection which arises from great passions in their freedom of movement. It is an insight won from Aristotle but modified and blended with Lessing's concept of truth as embodied in the natural order and recreated in the work of art as structure or form. It pervades his criticism and recurs in such unexpected places as the detailed review of a minor play or its performance. One such play, *Richard III*, by a now forgotten dramatist named Weiss, occasioned lengthy discussions of Aristotle, Corneille, Dacier's commentary on Aristotle, and literally dozens of other matters. And just when it appears that Lessing has forgotten his example and task, he returns to it by criticism of the most practical sort:

> Now if not one of the personages in Richard possesses the necessary qualities which they ought to have were this work a real tragedy, how has it nevertheless come to be considered an interesting play by our public? . . . If it occupies the spectators, if it amuses them what more do we want? Must they needs be amused and occupied according to the rules of Aristotle? (No. 79)

Lessing is here a devil's advocate, a role he often plays in his attempt to anticipate and dispose of all opposition. He now proceeds to supply his own answers:

> Even if Richard is no tragedy, it remains a dramatic poem, even if it lacks the beauties of tragedy it may yet have other beauties: poetical expressions, metaphors, tirades, bold sentiments, the spirited dialogue, fortunate situations for the actor to display the

113

whole compass of his voice, the whole strength of his pantomimic art, etc. (No. 79)

No better example could be given of Lessing's peculiar gift: to remain at, or return to, the most practical level of criticism, even to reviewing, while insisting constantly on calling our attention to the larger theoretical issues. We close this brief discussion of the *Hamburg Dramaturgy* by permitting Lessing to raise one more point. Richard is an abominable villain, says Lessing:

> but even the exercise of our disgust, especially upon imitation, is not wholly without its pleasures. . . . everything that Richard does is horrible, but all these horrors are committed for a purpose; Richard has a plan, and wherever we perceive a plan our curiosity is excited. (No. 79)

This is not appreciably different from what we read in Aristotle, and a full quarter-century earlier than the *Hamburg Dramaturgy* Johann Elias Schlegel expresses very much the same thought when he speaks of the pleasure aroused by perceived order.[13] Lessing's use of the word 'plan' has to do with plot, to be sure, but it is just as apparent that he is here betraying strong interest in motives and theories underlying form in the literary work. To these things he addresses himself more systematically in the *Laocoön*.

As subtitle *Laocoön* bears the promising line "On the Limits of Painting and Poetry." Since the time of Martin Opitz, critics had generally equated the two arts, so far at least as their aims and achievements were concerned. Such writers as Simonides (poetry is a speaking picture and painting a mute poem) and Horace (*ut pictura poesis*) had established a tradition in which clear lines of demarcation were almost totally erased.[14] Lessing now attempts to restore poetry to its proper place among the arts. His *Laocoön*, he explains, is written to counteract poor criticism and false taste, both of which have led to a mania for description in poetry and for allegory in painting (Preface).

Taking as his starting point a reference made by the classical archeologist and art critic Johann Joachim Winckelmann in his *Thoughts on the Imitation of Greek Works in Painting and Sculpture* (1755) to the figure of Laocoön as he appears in Greek sculpture and in Virgil's *Aeneid*, Lessing proceeds to demonstrate that the differences in artistic presentation of the suffering Trojan priest are due to inherent differences in the two arts, viz., in their means of representation. The poet has Laocoön cry out since a scream is consonant with a noble spirit and since poetry, moreover, may depict the ugly as well as the beautiful. The plastic arts, on the other hand, see beauty as their highest law. And so the Greek artist was forced to soften the priest's scream to a sigh—as all violent emotions must be so reduced in the visual arts—in order to obey this supreme law. The plastic arts, says Lessing, must by virtue of their material limitations confine themselves to one single moment, not necessarily one of greatest emotional intensity but one that enables the observer to grasp the true significance (theme or symbolic intent) of a work of art. There is nothing to compel the poet to compress his picture into a single moment:

> He may, if he so chooses, take up each action at its origin and pursue it through all possible variations to its end.[15]

The prolonged cries of a statue would be revolting, while in narration a scream (which we do not *see* in all its ugliness) is transitory and hence quite endurable:

> Virgil's Laocoön cries out, but this screaming Laocoön is the same man whom we already know and love as a prudent patriot and loving father. We do not relate his cries to his character, but solely to his unbearable suffering. (Chap. 4)

The second half of the essay attempts to draw general conclusions from these differences. Painting is a spatial art; hence, objects existing in space (figures and colors that coexist) are the subject of painting. Objects that follow one another (articulated sounds in time) are called actions, and these accordingly are the subjects of poetry. Concerning time in relation to the two arts, Lessing says that

> painting can use only a single moment of an action in its coexisting compositions and must therefore choose the one which is most suggestive and from which the preceding and succeeding actions are most easily comprehensible.
>
> Similarly, poetry in its progressive imitations can use only one single property of a body. It must therefore choose that one which awakens the most vivid image of the body, looked at from the point of view under which poetry can best use it. (Chap. 16)

Homer demonstrates the truth of these propositions. He represents nothing but progressive actions, depicting objects with a single trait only when they contribute toward these actions. Juno's chariot or Achilles' shield are not described ready-made but as they are formed before our eyes. Enumerative description is wrong, Lessing declares, for this is to attempt to transfer the coexisting objects of nature to the consecutive quality of words.

Much of what Lessing says in the *Laocoön* has been reduced to aesthetic commonplaces by later generations. In the eighteenth century, however, it was, as Goethe put it, a ray of light breaking through dark clouds.

The *Laocoön* and the *Hamburg Dramaturgy* are chiefly responsible for Lessing's enduring place in criticism. His other major critical effort, the *Literary Letters*, were a joint venture of Lessing, Mendelssohn, and Friedrich Nicolai. Because they came first in the chronology of Lessing's criticism, they must be considered important for having prepared the way for the more substantial later works. The fifty-four letters (about two-thirds of the entire enterprise) which Lessing contributed to the periodical deal mostly with contemporaries or immediate predecessors. Wieland's works come in for lengthy discussion, translations from various literatures are judged, Klopstock is admired and English literature defended as being more faithfully Aristotelian than were Corneille and Racine.

The seventeenth literary letter contains Lessing's spirited attack on Gottsched's "Frenchifying" theater reform. He argues that Gottsched ought to have seen from Germany's older dramatic works that German taste was closer to English than to French. Lessing is convinced that if only Shakespeare's major plays had been translated it would have been more advantageous for the German stage. For Shakespeare is a much greater tragedian than Corneille despite the fact that the Frenchman knew the ancients and Shakespeare did not. As proof that old German dramas were closer to the English Lessing provides the reader with a scene from his *Doctor Faust*.

Any attempt to assess the place and importance of this *Faust* fragment in Lessing's critical and poetic work must remain at the level of speculation. There is too little to go on; we have only the scene from the *Literary Letters*, a prose sketch, and a few references to two versions Lessing worked on intermittently between 1755 and 1767. Beyond pricking our curiosity, however, the bare bones of a

Faust drama by Lessing have strong implications for his creation
and use of a literary work as an exercise in practical criticism. We
recall the admission Lessing makes in the *Hamburg Dramaturgy*
that he has practiced dramatic writing so as to be able to have his
say as critic.

Shortly after moving from Leipzig to Berlin, Lessing began
his first serious critical work, the *Beiträge zur Historie und Auf-
nahme des Theaters* (*Contributions to the History and Improvement of the Theater*, 1750), in collaboration with his friend
Christlob Mylius. In this quarterly, which lasted for only four issues,
Lessing hoped to open Germany's eyes to a theater on a genuinely
European scale. The attention that had been paid to the French
theater had led to a degree of monotony on the German stage
which could only be relieved by attention to the plays of Italy,
Spain, Holland, and classical Greece and Rome. Special emphasis
was to be placed on English and Spanish drama.

Two other early writings, *The Latest from the Realm of Wit*
and the *Kritische Briefe* (25 "Critical Letters," written in 1753),
may be seen as sequels to the *Contributions* and as illustrations of
Lessing's rapidly maturing critical powers. The first of these contains
the detailed commentary on Klopstock's *Messiah*, the attack on
Gottsched for his failure to appreciate genius (reference to both has
been made), and a number of moralizing stories. The *Critical
Letters* are noteworthy for the early example they offer of Lessing's
rehabilitations or vindications of unjustly treated or neglected predecessors.

One Simon Lemichen, poet and contemporary of Martin
Luther, had once been so imprudent as to praise one of Luther's
enemies. Lessing traces in detail the unfair persecution to which
Lemichen is subjected, Luther's excessive zeal in damning the poor
epigrammatist, the proceedings instigated against him, and Lessing's
reasons for adjudging the whole affair a miscarriage of justice.
Although the occasion, an all but forgotten sixteenth-century poet,
can hardly seem any more urgent today than it must have been in
Lessing's time, the sides of Lessing's character, critical as well as
moral, displayed are vital to our full understanding of the man.

Another vindication *Rettungen des Horaz* (*Rehabilitations
of Horace*, 1754) shows the same sense of fairmindedness, of the
need to uncover the truth and present it conscientiously and
thoroughly, which is indeed the *movens* of most if not all his
polemical writings also. The details of his quarrels with several

contemporaries—notably Pastors Lange and Goeze, and Professor Klotz—need not concern us here; but we should not fail to take note of Lessing's keen awareness of professional standards and the constructive ends towards which satire, irony, invective, aggressiveness verging on bullying—there are few such weapons that he failed to use—are turned. But to say that the ends—exposure of ignorance, superficiality, dishonesty, or simply poor scholarship—justify the means is not to suggest that Lessing ever descended to personal levels of attack. His was exclusively an intellectual anger, and the thought of personal or moral defamation was abhorrent to him.

Directly or indirectly, the preceding pages have stressed intellectual and analytical qualities of the man as well as of his criticism. No small part of Lessing's greatness lies in having recognized in himself certain limitations which, in the context of literary criticism and for German literature as a whole, have had as deep and lasting a significance as the very best of his critical efforts. He was obviously aware that his early plays were primarily extensions of his critical efforts; they were written to inspire other playwrights and show them what a German repertoire could contain. They are not profound. *The Free-Thinker* borrows its idea and much of the plot from a French play; *The Jews* is quite openly propagandistic, and *The Treasure* is a rather bald imitation of Plautus' comedies.

Faust too was apparently chosen for extrinsic reasons; it seemed to be an ideal subject for the national German tragedy Lessing had been calling for. Only someone with a genius equal to Shakespeare's, we are told, could have conceived many of the scenes in *Doctor Faust*; one of them, offered in the seventeenth literary letter, is supposedly taken from an old draft or outline given to Lessing by a friend. The ruse is not important, but we are curious as to why Lessing never finished the play, why this one short scene should strike him as adequate rebuttal of the French in favor of Shakespeare, and what the many great things (*viel Grosses*) are that Lessing finds in it. The scene (the third of Act II) relates Faust's encounter with the seven spirits of hell, from whom he will choose the swiftest to serve him. Each appears in turn, and only the last is found worthy; his swiftness is "no more and no less than the transition from good to evil." But the fifth devil, who is as swift as human thought, almost qualifies. Faust admits, "that is something!—but man's thoughts are not always swift. Not when truth and virtue summon them. How slow they are then!—You can be swift when you want, but who will guarantee that you will always want to? No, I trust you no more than I should trust myself."

Most of the old Faust puppet plays include this scene, but it is the devil as swift as thought whom Faust chooses. In Karl Simrock's well known edition Faust's reply to this devil (Mephistopheles) is a tame: "You are my man. Swift as man's thought? What more can I demand than that my thoughts be realized as soon as I think them."[16] Evidently the eighteenth–century rationalist demanded more; there is, needless to say, nothing whatever about a transition from good to evil in the chapbook versions, and the sophistication of logic apparent in Faust's reflections on human thought is too typically Enlightenment, too characteristically Lessing to belong to the German chapbook tradition.

Although this scene, written in 1755, cannot say all that Lessing obviously intended it to, no further Faust material was forthcoming except for a brief prose sketch comprising some forty-odd lines of text and a short prelude. References to a Faust play in his correspondence and conversations indicate, however, that he intended to have the finished work performed in 1767. He was, as he tells a friend, working at the play with all his powers. Yet eight years later he is quoted as saying that both of his Faust versions need only the final touches![17] We need not dwell further on this unusual and aborted genesis; Lessing later lost or (more likely) burned the manuscript, leaving this important subject to Goethe, who himself needed a half-century to master it.

To return to the question of why Lessing could not finish his *Faust*, it would appear evident that Faust's condemnation ran counter to the rationalistic thinking of Lessing's day.[18] Furthermore, the use of magic, i.e., Bodmer's marvelous, must have left Lessing decidedly uncomfortable, for there is evidence that Faust's temptation and pact with the devil were to have been only a dream intended to warn against immoral action. Yet a domesticated, enlightened, and most undemonic Faust could have little to do with the figure that has traditionally so stirred the German mind. Lessing realized this, for though he accepts the supernatural in theory—and sometimes in the works of others; for example, in Shakespeare's *Hamlet*—it is with the proviso that the poet can thereby "create a poetic illusion" and that it not detract in any way from the larger issues. These latter, we should remind ourselves, were in the 1750's primarily moral ones and still subservient to the need for rules.

119

If in *Faust* we are confronted with a reluctant subject onto which Lessing was unable to graft his ideas, *Miss Sara Sampson*, written a short time before Lessing began his *Faust*, proved to be a more successful experiment. Here too the approach is much the same: Lessing searches for a subject or character to express certain ideas. Then he proceeds to build up the action, flesh out the characters, and let them perform within the rules of drama and the conventions of the age. *Faust* is neither bourgeois nor realistic, and so there could be little genuine congruity between character and overall dramatic conception; *Miss Sara Sampson*, on the other hand, did not suffer from this initial incompatability. Lessing found his plot, setting, and characters in English literature, in works such as George Lillo's *The Merchant of London* (1731) and popular novels like Richardson's *Clarissa Harlowe* (1747–1748). The new kind of tragedy that Lillo's play represented was, Lessing felt, quite suitable for the German stage; and unlike English comedies, which he found too "rich and complex,"[19] their tragedy is relatively uncomplicated and fulfills the main requirement of the genre: "to arouse as much pity as possible in the spectator."[20] Princes and heroes contribute very little in this regard; Lessing looks rather to those whose misfortunes most resemble our own, for "they penetrate most deeply into our hearts, and if we pity kings, we pity them as human beings, not as kings."[21]

With the production in Hamburg of Lillo's *Merchant of London* in 1754, and exactly two years later Lessing's *Miss Sara Sampson*, middle-class tragedy was successfully established on the German stage. In borrowing "foreign treasures" Lessing produced a work not completely satisfactory artistically, to be sure, but the effect of this first domestic tragedy on German literature more than offsets this. By extending his criticism from precept to practice he gave actual demonstration of the correctness of his theories: not French but English drama, not French but English taste, not meter but natural prose dialogue, and not heroic and noble but everyday characters—these are Lessing's innovations.

Even his failures were later turned to successes. The national theme which he found in *Faust* but could not express artistically is brilliantly realized in *Minna von Barnhelm* (1767), and the spirit of tolerance and humanity, coupled with a desire for moral betterment, is evident in *Nathan the Wise* (1779), some of the fables, and *Emilia Galotti* (1772). With the publication and performance of *Minna von Barnhelm*, Lessing's importance shifts from that of a critic to that of the father of the modern German theater. The play, one of the few excellent comedies written in German, captures the atmosphere of Prussia after the Seven Years' War in a sequence of vivid scenes and above all creates several unforgettable characters. The fast-moving action which revolves around a potentially tragic conflict is resolved by Minna whose love conquers all obstacles and cures Tellheim of the hubris of his excessive pride.

In *Emilia Galotti* Lessing created a play of almost perfect symmetrical construction which moves inexorably toward the final disaster. Emilia's tragic death on her wedding day seems the result of several psychologically well motivated circumstances: the weakness and immorality of the Prince who desires her and orders her abduction, the rage of his former mistress, the plotting of his evil adviser, the stern morality of Emilia's father, and finally her own decision. Basically, however, the tragedy reveals that man's relation to man has become impossible because truth has vanished from life. Emilia finds herself in a world without compassion or equity. The prince, the highest judge in this world, is evil. And Odoardo, despairing in his effort to find justice on earth, sacrifices his daughter and can only hope for a judgment after life. Thus Emilia is defeated by forces beyond her control. The play's final scenes breathe the air of death.

Nathan the Wise, structured around the parable of the ring, is a magnificent testimony to Lessing's humanitarian ideals. In the parable three sons appear before a judge, each claiming that their father had secretly bequeathed him a magical ring which made its possessor beloved of God and men. They learn from the wise judge that only their actions can prove the authenticity of their ring's qualities. The highly successful "dramatic poem" actually established blank verse as the meter most commonly used by German playwrights. *Nathan* presents a picture of a world in which man finally conquers his instincts, listens to reason, tolerates other beliefs, and loves his brother. Thus it introduces themes which Lessing emphasized again in his essay *On the Education of the Human Race* (1780), themes which become also a challenge for Goethe and Schiller.

All in all, it would therefore be wrong to isolate Lessing's literary criticism from his varied activities as playwright, fabulist, and moralist-theologian. Goethe surely speaks for his time, or more precisely, for his own as well as succeeding generations, when he says:

We want a man like Lessing. For how was he great, except in character—in firmness? There are many men as clever and as cultivated, but where is such character?[22]

This is Lessing's legacy to German literature, inseparable from criticism and drama alike. As reformer, critic, playwright, and man, he firmly established the tradition Germany needed and made possible the literary climate from which Storm and Stress and Classicism were to grow.

III

The first of these movements, Storm and Stress, is often regarded as one of Germany's great literary revolutions. Despite some innovations and marked shifts of emphasis in literature and criticism, however, the notion of revolution suggests a more decisive rejection of Enlightenment ideals and a sharper turn to new ideas than literary history can fully justify. Human rights, the power of intellect, and a respect for rules had been salient characteristics of the German Enlightenment; and except for the last (a high respect for authority as expressed in rules), these attitudes were taken over by the Storm and Stress writers. Their chief contributions, as far as literature is concerned, lay in raising Klopstock's and (in lesser degree) Lessing's acceptance of the emotions to a level of supremacy hitherto undreamed of. Originality and genius, not unknown to the Enlightenment but by no means key concepts, were now united in the single word *Originalgenie*; the artist was finally rescued from the 'tyranny' of the Opitz-Gottsched tradition; and *Natur* and *Volk* were rediscovered for literature.

Criticism could hardly be called a vital force in the 1770's, when Storm and Stress crystallized into a movement. Of the scant dozen Storm and Stress writers of any stature only three, Lenz, Gerstenberg, and Herder, merit serious consideration as literary critics; and of these three, it is unquestionably Herder who best represents the period both in its new directions and its continuation of Lessing's critical achievements. Johann Gottfried Herder (1744–1803) is Germany's second great critic, and it is scarcely surprising that much of his work is a direct confrontation of his famous predecessor. It has even been said that most of his critical theory is essentially a series of variations on Lessing's norm. Certainly, Lessing's presence can be felt in much of what Herder wrote during the decade from about 1765 to 1775, when the bulk of his criticism was produced.

But the matter of influence is by no means that simple. Rejecting the main premises of neo-classical criticism—propriety, decorum, clarity—he pleads for a literature which would be spontaneous, natural, sensuous. In an essay entitled *Über Ossian und die Lieder alter Völker* (*Ossian and the Songs of Ancient Peoples*), published in 1771, he bestows uncritical praise on the vitality of primitive, savage man, whose poetry is both lyrical and natural. While Herder never actually advocates a Rousseauistic return to nature, he does insist on the creation of a national literature based upon the remnants of German folk poetry, its songs of the past.

The views expressed in the Ossian essay reveal Herder's dual concern in literary matters: the emotional or subjective attitude, and the constant insistence upon viewing literature in an historical context. Both this dual view and his overall concept of poetry as an integral part of the history of mankind, are enunciated as early as 1764 in his *Versuch einer Geschichte der lyrischen Poesie* (*Essay Toward a History of Lyric Poetry*), a work which serves as a kind of introduction to the *Fragments on More Recent German Literature* and the later *Treatise on the Origin of Language*. Of these three works, the *Fragments* makes its point most clearly. Published anonymously in 1765, it purports to be a continuation of and running commentary on Lessing's *Letters on Contemporary Literature*. However, one is struck rather by the differences between the two works. Lessing's primary concern was theory, not criticism directly; Herder is likewise only slightly interested in criticizing, but his concern is less with literary theories than sweeping ideas which place poetry in its proper relationship to language and then bend them both into the central theme: the observation of man as he expresses himself in language and literature. Language, Herder claims, was originally the means for expressing basic human emotions. During its early period poetry arose but later became estranged from its genuine self by striving for artistic beauty and regularity. True poetry, which Herder defines as the mother tongue of the human race, is to be found in the utterances of the people. Poetry that gives expression to the natural feelings of the people, that is to say folk poetry or poetry written with the naturalness of folk poetry—Homer, Ossian, Shakespeare—represents the hope and source of a true national literature.

Another theme explored in the *Fragments* is criticism and the critic. After asserting that the first critic was nothing more than a reader of sensitivity and taste, Herder discusses his relationship to the reader and the author:

> To the reader [he is] first servant, then confidante, then physician. To the writer first servant, then friend, then judge; and to all of literature either uniter or helper or the master-builder himself . . .
>
> What is the critic to the author? His servant, his friend, his impartial judge. Try to get to know him, study him thoroughly as your master, but do not attempt to be your own master . . . It is difficult but essential that the critic should put himself in the mind of the author and read him in the spirit in which he wrote. (*Fragments* I)

Herder's major tool is empathy. Whereas Lessing approached a literary work from the outside and tried to understand the theoretical principles governing it, Herder is concerned to enter into the work, to 'feel' its beauty. Lessing thinks, Herder intuits. As to the act of criticism itself—which involves originality, genius, and above all empathy—Herder demands that it subordinate itself to the work and keep its main purpose always in mind: to advance the cause of national culture by interpretation and explanation.

Another major theme of the *Fragments* is the logical application of Herder's belief that national literature must look back into its own past, collect its 'monuments' and emulate them. Language is an organic growth; both language and literature can be understood by the conditions under which they came into being and developed: environment, geographical, political, and cultural factors hold the key to the (re)creation of a first-rate literature. This theme is not fully developed in the *Fragments*, but it is clear enough that poetry—which, Herder claims, must be looked at from within and for its own sake—is really being pressed into the larger service of cultural history.

The three *Groves* (a fourth was planned but not published) that comprise the next important work, *Kritische Wälder* (*Critical Groves* or *Criticae Sylvae*, 1769), offer further elaboration of Herder's historical approach to literature. Like the *Fragments*, this new collection uses Lessing as a point of departure, this time the *Laocoön*. In moderately polemical tones Herder chastizes Lessing for having drawn hasty and ill-founded generalizations from his reading of Homer. The first chapter of the *Laocoön* points out that "a cry is the natural expression of physical pain. Homer's warriors not infrequently fall to the ground with a cry." But, insists Herder, this is simply untrue. He then cites several instances from the *Iliad* which show Homer's heroes giving utterance to spiritual pain, for "those are sufferings of the soul, and noble tears, with which crying and wailing over a wound simply cannot be compared" (*Grove I*).

For Herder the point is not an insignificant one or a display of mere pedantry. Behind his objections to Lessing's explanation for Homer's weeping heroes is his conviction that the combination of heroism and tears is not at all a meaningful distinction between Greek and barbarian, or for that matter between one national soul (or temperament, climate, etc.) and another. It is rather a question of the Greeks having reached a certain cultural level, a borderline situation which might best be characterized by the word elegaic. When Lessing points out that to master all pain and die laughing is a trait of old Nordic heroism, and then insists "not so the Greek," Herder retorts:

> Not so the Scot, the Celt, the Irishman! He gave utterance to his pain and sorrow; he was not ashamed of any human weakness. And so I have said everything for my barbarians that Lessing said for his Greeks in contrast to the Nordic barbarians.

The supposed typicality of one nation or time is rejected in favor of what might be called a cultural phase lying between nature and artifice or refinement. Both the Greeks and the Celts have, according to Herder, one thing in common, their naturalness. Homer is essentially a nature poet, in contrast to the refined or artistic poet (*Kunstdichter*) which Lessing believes him to be; and his modern counterpart is Ossian.

The implications of such a pairing were profound for German literature. Homer is 'rescued' from classical authority, put into the company of (a non-existent) Ossian, Shakespeare, and all manner of folksongs. They all express nature before it was ruined by art; they all reflect the popular style with its vigor, natural genius, and breadth of imagination. Nature versus art now becomes, by implication at least, emotions versus intellect. Anyone who reads Homer with a healthy mind, Herder asserts, will find far less art in him than his commentators, who put it there. He is "noble flourishing nature—like Ossian." And towards the end of *Grove I* he introduces the notion of poetry as energy, that is to say as a spontaneous outpouring of the poet's soul.

Having pushed literary criticism into unexpected new channels, Herder next turned to his task of rejuvenating German literature—a concern that often appears to border on the obsessive from Gottsched until well into the nineteenth century. He called upon critics ("who can count syllables and scan so well") to go out among the people and collect their songs, which may scan and rhyme badly but which nevertheless are in no way inferior to Percy's *Reliques* in liveliness, rhythm, simplicity, and vigor of language.

Another important impetus to criticism and literature was Herder's adoption of Shakespeare. He was of course not the first German critic, or even the first Storm and Stress writer, to 'discover' the English dramatist for German letters; but his departure from Lessing's view of Shakespeare does represent something new. Whereas Lessing had looked at Shakespeare with the eye of the dramaturgist, Herder is looking for a worthy representative of the new *Zeitgeist*. As he had done with Homer, Herder produces a very personal Shakespeare; through direct (i.e., emotional) experience rather than aesthetic contemplation or intellectual comprehension he arrives at the conclusion that Shakespeare's plays are history, are the great happenings of human fate. His essay entitled *Shakespeare*, published in 1773 as part of the little volume V*on deutscher Art und Kunst* (*Of German Nature and Art*), makes the claim that Shakespeare's art grew out of the popular tradition. His dramas thus have nothing to do with the tradition of classical antiquity, as Lessing had suggested, but were created in the wider world of the north with its far more complex conditions of social, political, and cultural life. However, in one important point the north and south, i.e., Shakespeare and such a writer as Sophocles, coincide: in their effect on the reader's soul. Both are poets of nature, and both grew organically from the multiple conditions of their own soil and culture.

Formal questions of structure, the unities, and classification are in Herder's view irrelevant:

> What would one have with the subdivisions tragedy, comedy, history, pastoral . . . Not a single play would be Greek tragedy and comedy and pastoral. Nor should they be. Every play is history in its broadest sense . . . and at bottom every play remains and must remain what it is: history!

It is thus primarily the dramatization of history and the interpretation of nature and the universe which make Shakespeare so meaningful to Herder and the period in general. When Herder asserts that stage, actor, props and the like disappear when he *reads* Shakespeare, he is expressing a view typical of his time. While the French might lament Shakespeare's lack of form and his failure to live up to the rules, Herder is quick to point out that the rules based on Aristotle have little or nothing to do with English and German theater. Shakespeare and his England were one, just as Homer had represented the organic oneness of another age, and it is this new, incomparable period of world history that opens the way for a resurgence of German literature. As tenuous as this argument may be, the insistence that foreign rules be largely ignored in favor of the innate genius and soul of one's own nation performed its mission; Germany's national literary consciousness was awakened and the groundwork for Romantic poetics is laid.

To have completed the task of liberating German literature from French neo-classicism and an exaggerated adherence to classical models must therefore be called Herder's major achievement. It might be pointed out that such an accomplishment falls rather more in the realm of literary and cultural history than in that of criticism proper. But it is as unfair to demand of Herder what he did not intend to do as it is difficult to find him speaking or writing in other than broadest theoretical terms. When he does address himself to a specific work it is primarily as an empathetic critic in search of genius—the genius of the work, or of its creator, or of the national spirit from which it sprang. Criticism is rarely understood as a reporting of the contents of a work but rather as a repository for ideas. Formal literary analysis could hence have little purpose for Herder. Realizing that the Germans had "absolutely no living poetic literature upon which our modern poetry might grow," he set out to restore the glory of Germany's popular poetic past. His literary history was, as René Wellek aptly says, "one of broad vistas, wide sweeps, bold generalizations."[23]

IV

It was just such sweeps and vistas that profoundly impressed the young Goethe (1749–1832), who met Herder in Strassburg in 1771 and joined him in the rediscovery of Germany's folk tradition in literature. Goethe who did not consider himself a literary critic has been dismissed as offering "rather stale" critical wares (Saintsbury). At the other extreme, however, Matthew Arnold praised him as the "supreme critic." Predictably, he may be said to fall somewhere between the two views. Of too random a nature to represent a coherent body of critical thought, yet too sensible and full of insights to be dismissed as purely peripheral activity, his criticism exerted an influence on German literature as profound as it is difficult to separate from his impact as man and poet. There is a further complication, that of accessibility. Despite a large number of essays and studies on literary works and problems, and almost as large a number on questions of art in general, it cannot be said that such more or less direct discussions offer an adequate picture. His autobiography *Poetry and Truth*, the *West-Eastern Divan*, *Wilhelm Meister*, the correspondence with Schiller, the *Xenien*, and many of the *Maxims and Reflections* are equally important in any fair assessment of Goethe's critical activity. In our sketch we may slight chronology and renounce comprehensiveness in the attempt to suggest answers to three basic questions regarding Goethe's role as critic: what are the obvious ways in which Goethe continued the critical tradition, what are his outstanding innovations in criticism, and what are his chief characteristics as practicing critic?

Goethe's friendship with Herder, begun in the 1770's, was marked by excessive enthusiasm for Shakespeare, popular poetry, praise of nature and genius as opposed to rules and intellect, and a rejection of French classical theater. An early speech, printed as an essay, *Zum Shakespeares Tag* (*On Shakespeare*, 1771), is, strictly speaking, not criticism at all but merely a panegyric. In addition to praising Shakespeare for having opened his eyes to nature, Goethe slips in an attack on the French habit of using Greek subjects: "What do you want with Greek armor, it is too large and heavy for you," and draws a favorable comparison between Shakespeare and classical antiquity. There are also some three dozen reviews, written during the years 1771–1772 for the *Frankfurter Gelehrten Anzeigen*, but they are almost without exception as uncritical as the Shakespeare essay.

Another testimony to Goethe's Shakespeare-worship in his early years is the novel *Wilhelm Meister*, which appeared in 1795 but offers substantially the same view of Shakespeare as an earlier version, begun about 1778. The hero of the novel offers a detailed analysis of Prince Hamlet, a role he intends to act, and no less than sixteen chapters are devoted to a critique of the play. Although it is perhaps an exaggeration to say, as James Boyd does, that the Hamlet discussion in *Wilhelm Meister* is Goethe's most significant contribution to the criticism of English literature,[24] it is nevertheless an excellent example of his critical stance during the pre-Weimar period. Speaking of the poetic merits of the play, Meister (who is neither to be simply identified with Goethe nor removed too far from him as critic) observes that:

> all the anticipations I ever had regarding man and his destiny, which have accompanied me from youth upwards often unobserved by myself, I find developed and fulfilled in Shakespeare's writings. It seems as if he cleared up every one of our enigmas to us.

Inadvertently Meister is pleading the traditional cause of the classics as the proper study of man, a shift of emphasis in early literary criticism (e.g., in Horace) from imitation and emulation of nature to imitation of great classics, which themselves are nature.

As an actor Meister feels that he must penetrate into the spirit of the character, "to take upon myself the load of deep melancholy under which my prototype was laboring." His method is to investigate Hamlet's character *before* his father's death, to show "what most probably the young man would have been had no such thing occurred." Although Meister does not speak purely and simply for Goethe, especially where *Hamlet* is concerned—and indeed some would deny altogether that he does—we should also bear in mind that this particular mixture of psychological criticism and the attempt to get at the intentions of the author is a typical feature of Goethean criticism. It undergoes modification, various refinements, and here and there a toning down, but it remains an essential critical habit—one might call it an instinct—throughout Goethe's life. As late as the 1820's Goethe is still stressing author intent and the need to project oneself into the author's mind and spirit:

> Constructive criticism asks: what did the author set out to do? Was his plan reasonable and sensible, and how far did he succeed in carrying it out?

And about the same time he asserts that "the critic must judge a work of art more for the sake of the author than the public."

Accompanying this is an insistence on the validity of what

129

must be called the subjective view. Recognizing that "sympathy and enjoyment in what we see are in fact the only reality," Goethe turns a personal admission into a critical generality:

> Some of my admiring readers have told me for a long time that instead of expressing a judgment on books, I describe the influence which they had on me. And at bottom this is the way all readers criticize.

When a book is, in Goethe's estimation, good enough or important enough, he goes so far as to recommend that criticism leave it alone for a time and show instead its goodwill, interest, and sympathetic appreciation. The occasion for such a remark was the famous anthology *Des Knaben Wunderhorn* (*The Boy's Magic Horn*) by Arnim and Brentano. Goethe's review of this work, dating from 1806, shows that he has not lost his enthusiasm for folksongs and the popular tradition generally. Poetry of this kind, he exclaims, is as true as poetry can possibly be. In place of criticism of the book as a whole, Goethe offers a series of what he calls impromptu characterizations, some forty in all. There is no trace of theory here, nor even of description in any expected sense; criticism simply cannot judge, it must appreciate. A poem called *Drought* bears this entry: "Thought, feeling, presentation everywhere right." *Nocturnal Musicians* is called "droll, extravagant, inimitable." *Tell and His Child* is "honest and solid." And about a poem entitled *Cradle Song* Goethe says "rhyming nonsense, perfectly suited to put one to sleep."

Beyond all suggestion of variety and disparity, there is a level at which such criticism—reviews, casual pronouncements, Shakespearean analysis, folksong study and the like—is of one piece. Shortly before his death Goethe is quoted as saying, "At bottom we are all collective beings, pretend as we may. For how little we have and are, that can be called our own in the purest sense! We must all receive and learn, both from those who were before us and those who are with us." This statement to Eckermann in February 1832 betrays Goethe's central concern both in literature and criticism. And such a concern is surely the reason why so little of his criticism is literary in the stricter sense. The art work is a work of nature, Goethe believes, and as such it possesses a higher inner form (*Old German Folksongs*, 1806). This may be arrived at through an examination of the outer form, which in an organic entity is the product of forces working within. There is an apparent paradox in the dual assertion that a work must be seen as an independent phenomenon while it is at the same time the expression of the whole and directly related to it. Goethe himself was aware of the "eternal lie about the connection between nature and art," but he nonetheless insists on his own distinctive kind of relativism: the independent writer or work of art *within* the suprapersonal stream of western culture:

> There must be such a happy conjuncture of outer and inner circumstances that he will not have to pay dearly for his mistakes, but that in the prime of his life he may be able to see the possibilities of a great theme and to develop it according to some uniform plan into a well arranged and well constructed literary work.

Goethe, like Herder, is often more interested in culture and in a broader view of cultural interrelations than in the strictly literary view of poetry. In his *Conversations with Eckermann*, recorded from 1822 to 1832, he expresses several times the conviction that the principal criterion for a work of art is its validity as a statement on human nature and the ordering forces behind man's world. His ideal is a universal culture to which poetry as the universal possession of mankind can contribute substantially. Not as a sum of individual works or as national literature—for as Goethe says, "Left to itself every literature will exhaust its vitality if it is not refreshed by the interest and contributions of a foreign one"—but as a genuine world literature. Goethe first uses this term in 1827: "national literature is now rather a meaningless term. The epoch of world literature is at hand, and everyone must strive to hasten its approach." The wording indicates that Goethe does not mean simply the accumulation of great works of literature of the past—his word for this is *Weltpoesie*—but the still-to-be-attained ideal of unhampered spiritual and intellectual intercourse between nations. Such contact will have the effect of stressing the universally human aspects of national culture and eventually of bringing about a synthesis which will be truly cosmopolitan.

Goethe's own interests and reading habits qualify him as a worthy proponent of world literature. As early as 1765 he was studying Greek art and attempting to learn modern Greek; during the seventies and eighties he read and re-read all the major classics, and the early years of the nineteenth century were filled with aesthetic and art studies: Greek sculpture, the Elgin marbles, the Parthenon reliefs, etc. Articles in *Kunst und Alterthum* illustrate his interest in

Spanish, Italian, French, and of course German literature. Finally, his enthusiasm for Shakespeare and a number of eighteen–century writers completes the picture of a man passionately interested in both ancient and modern cultures. His deepest concern was hardly descriptive or practical criticism but rather the larger view we have called cultural. Both his numerous opinions on literature and his somewhat more modest examples of critical practice are subservient to that view.

V

It has often been remarked that Goethe and Schiller (1759–1805) are the great antipodes of German literature, and it is in fact difficult to conceive of sharper contrasts of mind and temperament within a common age and literary movement. But differences of background, constitution, temper, outlook, and general view of art could prevent neither a friendship that brought substance and greatness to German letters in the decade from 1794 to 1805 nor a degree of mutual understanding and cooperation in literary matters unparalleled in eighteenth–century Germany.

Cooperation does not necessarily mean identity of views, however, as the Goethe-Schiller correspondence and other publications demonstrate. Schiller emphasizes *idea* and is altogether more critical and analytical; Goethe is committed to *experience* and is tempted to reject theory as a hindrance to true enjoyment. Yet both men are ultimately brought together by a common desire to establish principles by which art can be evaluated. It is perhaps fair to say that Goethe looked to such principles and the establishing of objective standards as corroboration of his own nature, as a surer base for his poetic instincts, whereas Schiller responded to rules as to an inexorable necessity. For Goethe principles and laws are to be the watchdogs and guidelines for literature; for Schiller they are the very structure that promises objectivity in criticism and improvement of one's own poetic production.

Without doubt Schiller is the more theoretical of the two; he is also more readily convinced that a school of art and poetry can supply "regulative laws" and thus "correct feelings by means of laws." Goethe too can be convinced of this, but intuitive insight remains basic to his conception. Common to both men, and perhaps ultimately more important than such obvious differences, is their lasting interest in the problem of art's relationship to nature. Goethe is convinced that art is art precisely because it is *not* nature. The artist can give us the *illusion* of reality but not the reality of life itself; therefore he concludes that the work of art is above nature, even as it appears natural and supra-natural (*übernatürlich*) simultaneously. Yet the work of art is in the final analysis a work of nature as well, for it arises from the same spirit that acts in nature.[25] The form which art takes possesses a higher truth (the truth of idea), to be sure, but in its artistic form it realizes the intent that seeks to fulfill itself in the processes of nature.

Schiller argues with different terminology but with essentially similar ends in view. He is, for example, convinced that every work of art is answerable only to its own rules for beauty, and is hence subservient to no other demands (letter to Körner, 1788). But beauty is general though concealed truth, and the artist's attempt to attain beauty thus becomes the attempt to express an ethical or moral value as well, which is the kind of truth that Schiller relates to nature. Poets, he tells us elsewhere, are the custodians of nature—and where they are not actually nature themselves, they will seek it. Schiller's critical works are in substantial part concerned with such aesthetic questions as the one just raised. Two major attitudes are apparent, and it is hardly a coincidence that Goethe figures in both. The essay *On Naive and Sentimental Poetry* (1795–1796), Schiller's most important piece of criticism, is in part a defense of his kind of poetry against what Goethe represented. Another cornerstone of Schiller's aesthetic, the *Letters on the Aesthetic Education of Man* (1795), attempts to reconcile the Kantian opposites of reason and the senses, of morality and sensuality, and to give to art the vital role of reconciling man and nature.

Schiller's other aesthetic and theoretical writings offer valuable insights into certain of his critical preoccupations. Two of these essays are devoted to tragedy, *Über den Grund des Vergnügens an tragischen Gegenständen* (*On the Cause of Pleasure in Tragic Subjects*) and *Über die tragische Kunst* (*On Tragic Art*). Both were published in 1792; beginning the following year certain emendations to his theory of tragedy were made, in *On the Pathetic* (1793) and *On the Sublime* (1801). Another work of aesthetic significance, *Über Anmut und Würde* (*On Grace and Dignity*, 1793), is too little concerned with literature to justify inclusion in a discussion of the criticism.

Turning to criticism proper, we find little. Some of Goethe's works are critically examined: *Wilhelm Meister, Egmont, Iphigenie;* there is a review of Gottfried August Bürger's poems (*Über Bürgers Gedichte,* 1789), a discussion of Friedrich Matthisson's poetry, of German theater, of two of his own plays, and a modest number of lesser, more topical items. There is, finally, the correspondence with Goethe, which, while offering no extended criticism, is an imposing array of critical views on a wide variety of writers, works, and literary problems. If, however, we add to this criticism the aesthetic treatises already mentioned, the result is a fair-sized body of work, profoundly influential among nineteenth–century Romantics but rarely in sufficiently close contact with actual literary works to qualify as major criticism. There is surely something stuffy in Saintsbury's verdict: "Schiller does not seem to me a great critic, or even a good one," though in a narrower sense this does have a degree of validity. But what is unfair in such a judgment is the refusal to grant some of Schiller's theories (on tragedy, genres, art, etc.) an intrinsic importance almost as great as the historical. It is worthwhile to examine briefly some of the major points made in the aesthetic as well as the critical studies.

The *Letters on the Aesthetic Education of Man* ask the question, what role does art play in human life? The title itself suggests Schiller's answer, which is to stress the civilizing influence of art and its function as healer and mediator. Modern man, Schiller claims, is moving along two false roads and is in consequence a prey to coarseness, exhaustion, and depravity. The beautiful must bring him back from his double error. Since the state affords us no instrument for overcoming the fragmentation of society, we must find another. Our salvation can be found in cultivating the fine arts, which is what Schiller means by aesthetic education.

A series of antitheses runs through the *Letters,* as through much of Schiller's theoretical thought altogether. Aesthetic education is in effect a synthesizing or fusing of the artistic and the ethical, which is to say of man's two fundamental interests, the aesthetic and the moral. Man's basic drives, from which comes his dual nature, are the sensuous impulse and the formal impulse. Since they are in constant opposition our task is to reconcile them and thereby restore unity to human nature in such a way as to preserve the importance of both. Schiller proposes a synthesis that raises both sensual and formal impulse to a higher plane. This higher spiritual synthesis he calls the *play impulse,* which expresses the pure idea of humanity. Man's play impulse responds to the living form, "a term that serves to describe all aesthetic qualities of phenomena, and what people style in the widest sense, *beauty*."

Feeling that the reader will reproach him for confining beauty to mere play, Schiller offers a series of explanations. In play, by which Schiller means free aesthetic activity, man is free of all connections with practicality and can therefore permit his own nature to expand to its fullest. The split between intellect and the senses is healed in this new realm of play: "By beauty the sensuous man is led back to form and thought; by beauty the spiritual man is brought back to matter and restored to the world of sense" (Letter 18). In the aesthetic condition, the realm of play and appearance, man finds himself in a state of beauty, i.e., life and living form, where spirit is reconciled with nature and matter with form. In this aesthetic state man places himself outside the world and contemplates it; by means of art he frees himself. "While having no claim to promote exclusively any special human faculty, the aesthetic state is favorable to each and all without favoritism." Such neutrality, Schiller concludes, is what gives art its great positive value, opening as it does the way to morality.

The essay *On Naive and Sentimental Poetry*—second in importance only to Lessing's *Laocoön* in German criticism—is a brilliant exposition of Schiller's reformulated version of the Quarrel between the Ancients and the Moderns. The terms have been changed, to be sure, but the equations naive = Greek and sentimental = modern are everywhere apparent. Schiller begins his essay with the observation that we feel a kind of love and touching respect for certain aspects of nature: plants, minerals, animals, landscapes, and human nature in children. The man of refined feeling reacts this way when face to face with simple nature in "civilized" (non-natural) situations. Two conditions must obtain if we are to have this interest: the object that arouses us must really be nature or something we take for nature, and it must be naive, that is, it must present the contrast between nature and art and put the latter to shame. Schiller defines nature as existence in a state of full freedom, as the existence of things in and of themselves, as existence according to its proper and immutable laws.

However, we do not love objects for their own sake, but rather for the idea represented by them: the inner necessity of things, the eternal unity of their own nature. "They *are* what we *were*; they are what we *must be* again some day. We were nature as they are, and culture must bring us back to nature by following the way of reason and freedom." Schiller sees a victory of nature over art, not by blind force but in virtue of its form as moral magnitude and as inner necessity.

Turning to the question of who is naive, Schiller attributes naiveté of feeling to the man who in his judgment of things passes over the artificial aspects and sees only simple nature. Children and childlike men are naive; and "every true genius must be naive, or else he is not a genius." In speaking of the greatest geniuses Schiller mentions Sophocles, Archimedes, Hippocrates, Ariosto, Dante, Tasso, Raphael, Dürer, Cervantes, Shakespeare, Fielding, and Sterne. As for poets in general, they are the guardians of nature. "They will either *be* nature, or they will *seek* it if it is lost." The former write naive, the latter, sentimental poetry. Both Homer and Shakespeare were naive, but in this artificial age such genuinely naive poets are scarcely in their place any longer. Society will always produce such men, who will appear "as strangers, who excite wonder, or as ill-trained children of nature, who give offence. . . . The critics, as regular constables of art, detest these poets as *disturbers of rules or of limits."* Goethe is never expressly mentioned in the essay, but clearly Schiller sees him as naive, as a survivor of a happier age when humanity's ideals were realized.

In his discussion of the sentimental poet, Schiller comes to the defense of the moderns. The goal that man strives to reach through civilization is preferable to that which he actually attains through nature. The sentimental poet *reflects* on the impression produced on him by objects, and his poetic force is based exclusively on this reflection. Having two modes of representing objects, the real and the ideal or the limited and the infinite, he is in a position to choose his treatment. The naive poet, on the contrary, follows simple nature and confines himself to imitation. Which of the two is superior? Schiller does not decide. The naive poet gives us nature at first hand, the sentimental poet raises it to the ideal; the one is great by limitation, the other by infinity; both are seen as stages in a natural evolution, and both complement one another.

Returning to the choices open to the modern, i.e., sentimental or reflective, poet, Schiller asks: "Shall the poet attach himself to the real or the ideal? To the real as an object of aversion and disgust, or to the ideal as an object of inclination?" The answer to these questions is worked out in his discussion of the three modes of feeling which the sentimental poet betrays in his writings. He is elegaic when he measures his reality against the ideal and finds it wanting, i.e., imperfect and contrary to nature. His poetry will express this conflict between the ideal and the real. He is satirical when he regards the imperfection of reality in a spirit of mockery or censure. The sentimental poet may, thirdly, be idyllic, in which case he will show that he has overcome the conflict in his imagination and is consequently able to depict the idea of an innocent and happy humanity. Schiller's perfect idyll is the idea of humanity definitely reconciled with itself.

As critic and theorist Schiller was naturally most concerned with the stage and, more specifically, with tragedy and theories of the tragic. His two earliest plays, *The Robbers* and *Fiesco*, were each followed by a short essay in which he attempts to outline his views on the dramatic art. *Über das gegenwärtige deutsche Theater* (*On the Contemporary German Theater*, 1782) and *Die Schaubühne als eine moralische Anstalt betrachtet* (*The Stage as a Moral Institution*, 1784) see the theater as a sister of morality and religion, and it is to the latter that the stage can most meaningfully be compared: "The uncertain nature of political events, rendering religion a necessity, also demands the stage as a moral force." Its virtues form an impressive list: it curbs vice by terror, acts as a guide to civil life, is a key to the mind, teaches us to be more considerate, etc. Contrary to Goethe's view of the stage as a means above all of personal expression, Schiller wants to turn it into an organ of mankind, an instrument of the state which can have "a great influence on the national temper and mind by helping the nation to agree in opinons and inclinations."

Four essays written in the 1790's—*On the Cause of Pleasure in Tragic Subjects* (1791); *On Tragic Art* (1792); *On the Pathetic* (1793); *On the Sublime* (1795)—are the essential sources for an outline of Schiller's conception of tragedy. Echoing Moses Mendelssohn and Lessing, Schiller sees as the principal object of tragic art the arousal of pity. Tragic art must imitate actions especially adapted to arouse pity. To create tragedy, three conditions must be fulfilled: First, the object of pity should belong to our own species, and the action tragedy seeks to interest us in, must be a moral one (i.e., an action comprehended in the field of free will). Second, suffering, its sources and degrees, should be fully communicated by a series of connected events. Third, the object of the emotion must be rendered present to our senses directly and through action, not indirectly and by description. Schiller then defines tragedy according to these principles—and evidently with an eye to Aristotle. Tragedy, he says, is a poetic imitation of a coherent series of particular events forming a complete action, an imitation which shows us man in a state of suffering, and which has for its end to excite our pity. He follows up this brief definition with his own paraphrase, each part of which is supplied with a running commentary.

The essays on the pathetic and the sublime amend this view. Schiller begins *On the Pathetic* by declaring that simple suffering is not the end of art but rather a *means* for attaining its end. He admonishes the poet not to try to attain the pathetic by depicting suffering in the most vivid manner, and he repeats his qualification: "suffering in itself can never be the final end of imitation, nor the immediate source of the pleasure we experience in tragedy. The pathetic has aesthetic value only in so far as it is sublime."

His essay *On the Sublime* carries the ennoblement of man a step further, and it is in some ways a further removal from the strictly tragic. An earlier and less important essay, *Vom Erhabenen* (*The Sublime*, 1793), defines a sublime subject as one in regard to whose perceptive nature our sensuous nature feels its limitations but our reasonable (i.e., understanding) nature its superiority and freedom from limits, and against which we are inferior—but *morally* (i.e., through our ideas) superior. In *On the Sublime* Schiller argues that man is surrounded by numberless superior forces, but by his very nature he aspires not to have to suffer injury at their hands. To be free, man must oppose force with force, must command nature as nature himself; or he must destroy the very idea of violence by the *idea*, issuing from nature. He must, in other words, annihilate as an idea the violence he is obliged to suffer in fact. Such a man, Schiller says, will be entirely free. Having been fashioned by moral education, he is either superior to nature as a power, or he is in harmony with it. Yet true harmony is not possible; nature is capricious, defiant of logic, and deviant from intellectual laws. And since nature cannot be explained by nature's laws themselves, the mind is driven to the world of ideas. As for the sublime, it is a higher stage than beauty: "Beauty is useful, but does not go beyond man. The sublime applies to the pure spirit."

At this point Schiller has left tragedy behind, or rather he has turned it into an exercise of fate:

Happy he who learns to bear what he cannot change! There are cases where fate overpowers all ramparts, and where the only resistance is, like a pure spirit, to throw off freely all interest of sense and strip yourself of your body.

Such a pronouncement removes us from the consideration of the tragic as it applies to literary works and returns us, "like a pure spirit," to the realm of pure aesthetics or philosophy.

As a practicing critic Schiller has limited himself to about twenty reviews, a scant dozen short pieces on drama and the theater, and a moderate amount of editorial activity: prefaces, introductions, etc. In a review of Matthisson's poems he rather badly overestimates this sentimental versifier, a view he later amended considerably; and his treatment of Bürger, which is haughtily unkind but not really unfair, is rather more a personal statement on the problems and processes of the poet than a discussion of Bürger's poetry. But such 'lapses' into the general and theoretical come as no surprise; Schiller is first to last a man concerned with ideas, with the aesthetic realm in its relation to the ideal and the moral. When he practices criticism it is almost inadvertent, in the sense that criticism serves only as an illustration of, or departure from, his own ideas.

Beyond their usefulness as examples of Schiller's kind of criticism the two reviews just mentioned, together with a scattering of remarks in some of the essays and in the correspondence with Körner, can be compressed into what might pass for a theory of the lyric. Schiller laments the indifference with which his philosophizing age regards literature. Of the three genres—dramatic, epic, lyric—it is the last which has suffered most, and Schiller speaks several times of the decline of lyric poetry. Returning to his favorite theme, the attainment of nobility of character, knowledge, and truth, he demands that the poet possess the "enthusiasm of a cultured spirit." What is wrong with Bürger's poetry is that it lacks a manly spirit, is uneven in taste, and does not spring from a mature, fulfilled mind. Such virtues as poetic force, richness, power of language, and beauty of verse are not lacking in Bürger's poems, and Schiller is more than generous in this respect. But when weighed against the grander concept of nobility of spirit or the ideal, they cannot prevail. Schiller accuses Bürger of not having felt poetically enough: "That which Lessing established as law for the tragedian—to present no oddities, no strictly individual characters and situations—applies far more to the lyric poet." In demanding the non-specific, the objective, and generally human, Schiller is a true classicist. As a critic he is obviously applying the wrong set of criteria to a more personal, and even naturalistic, kind of poetry.

Similarly before accepting Friedrich Matthisson's poetry—and indeed the lyric genre itself—Schiller feels that he must establish a connection with human nature. "There are two ways by which inanimate nature can become a symbol of human nature: either as representation of emotions or as representation of ideas." Emotions, says Schiller, can be expressed in landscape poetry by music, that is, a musical effect, which is a valid representation of man's power and feeling. Since music can accompany and symbolize inner states of feeling by means of external analogies, it is also able to express the same necessity that governs the inner emotions of human nature. The composer and landscape painter need only to study (external) analogues to become true "soul-painters."

Nature in landscape can be brought into the human context by making it express ideas. Not those which are dependent upon the haphazardness of association, but those which result from the laws of a "symbolizing imagination." Man's reason constantly strives to make this free play of imagination conform to its own processes, and when it discovers some manifestation of the imagination that can be grasped and treated according to its own (practical) laws, it transforms it into a symbol. "The dead letter of nature becomes a living language of the spirit, and the outer and inner eye read the same script . . . in a different manner."

Proceeding from the truism that it is never the subject but always the technique which makes the artist, Schiller turns to the poet directly and demands that he give our imagination free play. At the same time, however, the poet must produce a certain feeling in us. Schiller has the poet resolve the dilemma by letting our imagination have full freedom within the framework of its own laws; and such freedom, attainable through nature, can be found, paradoxically, in precision or exactitude. What happens is that the poet controls the reader's associations or chains of ideas. Schiller now reaches two general conclusions: everything in a poem must be *true* nature; and only in the "discarding of the fortuitous and in the pure expression of necessity" can we find the true style. Thus Schiller essentially uses Matthisson's poetry for a careful and very classical appraisal of the poet's function, an approach consistent with his criticism.

Schiller's actual criticism, samples of which we gleaned from a few reviews and the aesthetic treatises, is in no way proportionate to his achievement as measured by his impact on German letters, his talents as a philosopher, and his ability to ask important general and theoretical questions about literature. It is above all the last which must be singled out: to question penetratingly the entire issue of literature and to insist clearly and confidently on the close relation of literature to civilization and morality. This more than anything else makes him one of Germany's best examples of what a first-rate poet-aesthetician can do for literature.

VI

The foregoing account, will have indicated, first, that literary criticism has been from the outset so heavily concerned with theory, speculation, and aesthetic questions as to make the few examples of extended literary analysis, i.e., descriptive criticism, veritable oddities on the German scene. However, even from the perspective of the present age of formalism, textual analysis, and various approaches employing descriptive techniques, one cannot fairly lament this 'lack' in the early history of German criticism. For the need to rehabilitate literature, to free it as a genuinely national expression, and to ponder and engage in dialogue about the nature, forms, and possibilities of literature was so great as to make the particular critical emphasis we have observed both justifiable and necessary. Indeed, one wonders if such figures as Lessing, Herder, Goethe or Schiller could have advanced the cause of German letters in any comparable way had they been less abstract, less concerned with essentially extra-poetic matters, and more 'critical' in the modern sense.

There is, second, the strong emancipatory effort common to the critics of these founding years: Gottsched wanted to free German literature from its own chaotic mediocrity; Bodmer, Breitinger, and Lessing from overzealous imitation of the French in the name of Milton and Shakespeare; Herder and the young Goethe in the name of Shakespeare and Germany's own popular tradition; and Schiller, finally, joins Lessing, Herder, and Goethe in their espousal of literature as the expression of human culture.

While such a formulation ignores the multiplicity and complexity of views and subjects in the critical writings discussed here, we have seen nevertheless how two or three central ideas emerge with sufficient force to give criticism its continuity. It is therefore no accident that despite enormous differences of outlook and historical circumstances each of the critics examined builds successively upon the other. Schiller's ideal synthesis remains of course unattained, but it is far more important to see in the successive echoes, one of the other, a continuity that later periods and critics were not to disrupt substantially. Friedrich Schlegel's "progressive universal poetry," to conclude with an example that leads from Classicism to Romanticism and into the nineteenth century, is still close enough to Schiller to remind us of that essential continuity we call the German critical tradition.

5. Classicism 🖋

Horst S. Daemmrich

I

While the Storm and Stress movement (1765–1780) still dazzled the eyes of contemporaries with startling bursts of productivity, the group had already lost Johann Wolfgang Goethe (1749–1832), their greatest and most original genius who had achieved world renown with the publication of *Werther* (1774). In 1775 he had joined the court of Grand Duke Karl August of Saxony-Weimar (1757–1828). The first months of wild escapades, hunts, drinking bouts, and amours seemed to justify the fears of court and citizens that the young poet had come to establish a fountainhead for the group of irresponsible young poets. But Goethe, as inscrutable as ever, began slowly and carefully to guide the young Duke toward more responsible behavior. When in 1776 Jakob Lenz (1751–1792) and Friedrich Klinger (1752–1831), inspired by the idea to make the city the intellectual center of the Storm and Stress movement, suddenly arrived in Weimar looking for a haven, Goethe remained deaf to their wishes. Could they have imagined that their former companion was to become a strong-willed statesman or a hard-working commissioner of public works who practically singlehandedly revived the mining industry in the state, and that, for all practical purposes, he would suppress his creative urge for a decade while he served the state and its citizens? Could they have guessed that his life during these years would perfectly exemplify the themes of self-realization and renunciation of personal desires which figure dominantly in his later works?

Meanwhile, in and around Weimar another concentration of forces was gradually taking place: on Goethe's advice Johann Gottfried Herder (1744–1803) was called to the small city; Goethe's relationship with Christoph Martin Wieland (1733–1813) who had been Karl August's tutor, became more amicable; from 1787 onward Friedrich Schiller (1759–1805) lived alternately in Weimar and Jena; there he met Wilhelm von Humboldt (1767–1835), who saw in Schiller's and Goethe's works an expression of his own humanistic ideals and later as Prussian minister and founder of the University of Berlin tried to instill them into the Prussian educational system. From this principality which otherwise would have sunk into historical obscurity a literature began to radiate, a literature which holds forth answers to our most searching questions.

German Classicism (*die Klassik*) is generally thought to include Goethe's literary creations since his first Italian journey (1786–1788) and Schiller's works after 1794.[1] Of special interest are the years of the enormously stimulating and remarkably productive friendship between Schiller and Goethe which lasted from 1794 until Schiller's death. The reader will be disappointed if he expects in German classicism the regularity of form (metric cadence, structure of sentences, restricted use of language) or even a strict adherence to Aristotelian unities typical of French classicism. Instead, Goethe and Schiller strove for an organic form, one in which subject matter, action, themes, and stylistic characteristics were fused. Furthermore, they expressed a view of man and his relationship to the world which Friedrich Hölderlin (1770–1843), for instance, did not share. This is one of the reasons why Hölderlin, though he reached perhaps greater formal perfection in his poems than Goethe or Schiller, is not considered to be part of the classical movement. Classicism is one phase of a general intellectual development in Germany which saw an unprecedented ascent in creative forces and is characterized by a distinct acceleration of stylistic and cultural change. During the brief span of 1770 to 1830 three literary movements, Storm and Stress, Classicism, and Romanticism reached their apexes. The music of Gluck, Haydn, Mozart, and Beethoven captured Europe. Taking into account the impact of geographic location, socio-political forces, and political events on the evolution of styles, Herder laid the foundation for a new appraisal of myths, folklore, and literature. Immanuel Kant (1724–1804) formulated a philosophical system which was to dominate completely the thought of the nineteenth century. As an unintentional result of his and Johann Gottlieb Fichte's (1762–1814) investigations, the theocratic view of history, already questioned during the Age of Reason, fell into further disrepute. In addition, anthropological investigations, the growth of the scientific spirit, and the beginning of comparative studies of religion nurtured an increasingly skeptical attitude toward religious dogma, with its proofs of God's existence, as well as toward theism itself. Suddenly man had to adjust to the idea of a transcendental God in a transcendental world.

During this period the political scene was characterized by

unstable and temporary relationships among states and principalities. Prussia and Austria struggled intermittently for the dominant influence over the rest of Germany. The French Revolution (1789) not only generated ferment in ideas but also led to the War of Intervention. Goethe, who accompanied Karl August to the battlefield (1792–1793) personally "experienced the enormous upheaval and frightful disintegration of all order and social conditions." The threat of violent changes, the disruption of the old culture, and a sudden flux in the social order form the background for four of Goethe's works: *Conversations among German Emigrants* (1795), *Hermann and Dorothea* (1797), *Eugenie* (*Die natürliche Tochter*) (1803), and *Campaign in France* (1822). At first the modern reader may find that these works are conservative, even unrealistic attempts to stem the tide of sweeping change. Nothing could be further from the truth. The apparently secure world that forms their background is threatened by potential disaster, and man sails a dangerous sea of seething undercurrents. Man cannot look backward but must reach a new and unexplored shore. These works express Goethe's strong faith that mankind ultimately will be able to control the forces it has unleashed and master its own fate. Though both Goethe and Schiller sympathized with the causes of the French Revolution, they lost their enthusiasm for it as violence spread and as the idea of a universal brotherhood was smothered by nationalism and by purely political maneuvers.

A characteristic aspect of the period is the failure of rulers and statesmen alike to lay the foundation for a unified German nation. Many of the small principalities depended on subsidies from France for their existence, a situation which did not change even after Napoleon's rise to power. Many princes, grand dukes, and dukes paid little or no attention to the welfare of their subjects, were intolerant of their aspirations, and ruled them arbitrarily. Compared with Frederick the Great, who had always supported social reforms and advanced the cause of religious toleration ("in this country every man must go to heaven his own way") by opening Prussia to refugees from all over Europe, they appear unenlightened. Thus Karl Eugen of Württemberg forced Schiller's father to send his son to the academy ("Militärische Pflanzschule" later "Karlsschule") he had founded. Though the judgment of contemporaries and historians is conflicting, some arguing that the academy provided an excellent education for financially disadvantaged students, others pointing out that it was simply a pet project of a ruler who habitually squandered large sums on his mistresses, there can be little doubt that Schiller's thinking was profoundly affected by this arbitrary decision. What was detrimental to German national development, however, often had distinct advantages for cultural life. To be sure, the peak of achievement in architectural design had been reached in the preceding decades with the construction of the palaces and residences Sanssouci, Dresden, Würzburg, and Vienna, but most rulers of the small states still vied with each other in their support of the arts. Their interest in the growing art galleries deserves special mention.

At the same time the rising aspirations of the middle class and the cultural ideals formulated by literary artists and philosophers came into conflict with the existing order. And while the ideas expressed by Herder, Goethe, and Schiller were in a sense too imaginative and personal to constitute a "theory of culture," they acted as the unifying factor first in the cultural and later in the political life of Germany. The history of ideas has rarely seen another concept which so completely dominated the mind of a people as the German concept of culture. In 1773 a collection of essays entitled *Of German Nature and Art* (*Von deutscher Art und Kunst*) appeared on Germany's literary scene. The book comprised Herder's interpretations of Ossian and Shakespeare, Goethe's essay "Concerning German Architecture," a reprint of Justus Möser's introduction to his *History of Osnabrück*, and Paolo Frisi's "On Gothic Architecture." These essays, declarations of independence from prevailing conceptions, stressed three ideas of major consequence: first that nature, culture, and art follow the same evolutionary path (an idea of organic growth); second, that great art is based on common cultural values (appreciation of the Middle Ages); finally, that a variety of forms, called nations, develop in the evolutionary process of man (the measure of cultural progress differs from nation to nation). No doubt, Rousseau's idea of the supreme worth and dignity of man as well as his criticism of cultural achievements linger in these essays. Goethe himself readily admitted in his conversations with Eckermann how difficult it had been for him in his youth "to maintain" his "own ground and true relation to nature" when he was confronted with ideas that stirred everyone's imagination. Yet, there is a striking difference in his and Herder's attitude toward the emergence of culture and its role in the formation of man's consciousness. For, although the times were not considered a period of fulfillment, both felt that man could neither escape historical development nor negate his own achievements.

Herder saw the universe as a vital, living organism governed by the laws of growth and decay. Life merges into life and no fixed categories seem to exist in nature. Still each organism seeks that form which fits it most completely and which enables it to act reciprocally upon the environment. By analogy, cultures evolve into diverse patterns, clearly recognizable in national states. For Herder, each nation has its unique quality and character. In his *Outlines of a Philosophy of the History of Man* (1784–1791) he developed these ideas most consistently and restated his firm belief that the pure national spirit is to be found in a people's myths, sagas, songs, and rituals. All the people of a nation constitute an integral collectivity, united by a common historical past, a common contemporary culture, and common interests in the future. In his criticism of poetical creations, Herder took the view that man forms what is prompted by his age, the climate of his country, his needs, and world destiny. But it is important to remember that Herder's outlook was cosmopolitan. His collection of folk-poetry and songs shows that the study of national cultures was a means of gaining a knowledge of the best which had been thought and said in the world with the ultimate aim of transmitting mankind's heritage and thus furthering human perfection.

Goethe expressed the theme of self-improvement consistently in his autobiographical writings, letters, and conversations. Acutely aware that a momentous cultural change was taking place and, after he had seen how a "Werther fever" had seized Europe's youth after the publication of the book, especially sensitive to the effect of literature on young minds, he felt obliged to evaluate old and new beliefs before becoming their spokesman. Typically, his interests ranged from architecture and other arts, to botany, morphology, mineralogy, and meteorology. Despite the fact that he viewed history essentially as intellectual history, he accepted technical and industrial developments as important steps in man's progressive quest for self-liberation.[2] His view similar to Herder's involves the assumption of the continuity of cultural development from the state of savagery to that of civilization. However, since Goethe was basically interested in man, he saw a recurrence of fundamental problems, even if the change in historical scenery had lent them a distinctive coloration. He had more faith in man's creative ability to meet the ever-new, yet ever-recurring, challenges of life than in any

147

progressive cultural development. His view of the systolic-diastolic movement in nature and of man's growth resembles Toynbee's pattern of challenge and response; the notable difference is that Goethe had more confidence than Toynbee in man's ability to rejuvenate himself. In general, Herder and Goethe show a marked tendency to attribute greater importance to achievements in the realm of the creative spirit than in the sphere of technical advances and material progress, thus commencing a trend in historical speculation which stressed a duality of natural cultural history and unnatural conventions in civilization. The concept of civilization was subsequently used by cultural historians such as Troeltsch, Meinecke, and Spengler to characterize the late or final stage in the cycle of a culture, a stage in which veneration of technological processes has almost become a spiritual necessity and in which materialistic values and philosophies dominate intellectual life.

The cultural heritage presented itself to Goethe not as fact but as a challenge. Its validity and ultimate significance depended entirely on man's ability to awaken the past and infuse it with new life. Goethe's approach was one of active participation; he felt that true insight not only into cultural phenomena but also into history and nature could best be gained by establishing an almost personal relationship to objects. Thus he transformed them into subjects with whom he could enter into a dialogue. A cathedral became an intimate friend, a great artist of the past, his brother, and nature the primeval mother who nourished him. Such continuous communication, for instance, generated the great immediacy with which he experienced antiquity during his Italian journey. Indeed Goethe felt that through a dialogue of this kind which demands constant reflection and reappraisal of one's own position, the individual could expand his cultural consciousness and thereby ultimately gain self-knowledge. That Goethe disdained orthodoxy whose unbending dogma had suffocated the true spirit of love and humanity can hardly be surprising. But much of his dislike for the scientific methods of Linnaeus and Newton can also be traced to his mode of thinking: in contrast to the investigation and classification of isolated phenomena, Goethe perceived associations and interrelations. He invariably looked for the total structure.

He was likewise interested in the entirety of cultural achievements. A hallmark of cultural distinction would be the coexistence of a variety of forms which together seek to express everything that is dignified and worthy of humanity. And just as the artist had an obligation to preserve and enhance cultural values, so the educated citizen should seek to mediate between various cultures.[3] Perhaps the most important aspect of the individual's interaction with his cultural environment is the necessity for an unceasing effort to learn and try to improve himself and for the culture to provide standards and values which enable him to realize his potential fully and harmoniously.[4] Since Goethe felt that a culture grows over the years through the creative contributions of numerous individuals, the notion of a cultural determinism remained meaningless for him.

Schiller's and Kant's thoughts revolved around similar convictions. To both, history demonstrated that man was advancing from an original natural condition to a rational maturity of self-imposed laws. Kant's evaluation of culture was not based, as were Rousseau's and Locke's, on the judgment of pre-historic man as a noble savage, but on the investigation of civilized man. Kant accepted the reality and validity of historical cultural achievements. In sharp contrast to Rousseau's deification of nature and his view that civilization had enslaved and corrupted man, Goethe, Schiller, and Kant appreciated the arts and sciences as vital, creative factors for the progress of humanity, rather than as impediments hindering its development. Man cannot create the order of nature of which he is part, but he can establish his own moral laws and freely set up universal standards for all men.

Schiller saw culture primarily as a regulative process which was at once liberating and restraining. Culture as such is a system of institutions devised by man for the promotion of his existence and welfare. These institutions are historically created designs for living; explicit, implicit, rational, and irrational.[5] The ultimate aim of culture would be to enable man to cultivate all his faculties. Therefore, political and social institutions have to be evaluated by their practical consequences in fulfilling this end: "In judging political institutions we can generally apply the following rule: they are only valuable and praiseworthy insofar as they further the growth of all of man's faculties, insofar as they advance the development of culture or at least do not impair it."[6]

The totality of cultural patterns and their changes are one dynamic, interdependent complex. According to Schiller the historian selects and interprets from it certain events in order to make history intelligible. The only standard of selection is the relative importance of the events judged by the degree of influence they had, directly or indirectly, upon the total life of society and by their

149

impact in shaping "the contemporary age." If the student of history were not able to grasp the underlying factors and tendencies of the past, it would remain an aggregate of isolated historical facts ("ein Aggregat von Bruchstücken"). For only by defining their relationship to the emergence of culture can he hope to understand his own time.[7] It should be clear that Schiller's view of universal history is an idealistic one and that some historians may question his synthesis because it disregards the complexity of each age. Yet Schiller's historical studies, *The Revolt of the Netherlands* (1788) and *The Thirty Years' War* (1791–1793), prove that he tried to ascertain all the available facts before reaching conclusions on historical periods. Whatever shortcomings his method may possess (which for instance did not prevent his outspoken partisanship for the Netherlands), it provided the foundation for his imaginative recreation of periods and events in his dramas which admirably capture the spirit of the past, at the same time infuse it with new life and raise it to universal significance. Perhaps we should remember that Schiller's interest in history was essentially prompted by his profound concern for man's plight in his contemporary culture. Schiller's *Letters on the Aesthetic Education of Man* (1794–1795) indicates clearly that he spoke as a son of European culture which he loved, in which he believed, and for which he had high hopes.

In his investigations Schiller argued that a distinction has to be made between the material progress of mankind and its effect on the individual. Through technology man has mastered nature and transformed his environment. Yet these intellectual victories only aggravate his spiritual disharmony.[8] Looking at society, Schiller finds "on the one hand, a return to the savage state; on the other, to complete lethargy: in other words, to the two extremes of human depravity, and both united in a single epoch!" No wonder man longs for a golden age in the past. But Schiller points out that historical awareness ought to prevent an excessive admiration for the past and to check our desire for returning to a projected "state of innocence and bliss." In contrast to Rousseau, Schiller considers primitive man far from being a blissful, noble creature: all indications point to the fact that he had been ruled by instincts and enchained by customs and traditions. History seems to reveal a development of mankind from a condition in which it was governed by brute necessity to a state of reason. In accordance with the spirit of his age, Schiller believed that in classical Greece, Western man had achieved for the first time an equilibrium between individual desires and the demands of society, between sensuous needs and intellectual capacities. The unsurpassed cultural achievements of Greece can be attributed to this fact. Although Schiller questions some of the conclusions reached by Johann Joachim Winckelmann (1717–1768) in his enormously influential *Thoughts on the Imitation of Greek Works in Painting and Sculpture* (1755) and *The History of Ancient Art* (1764), he agrees with his genetic account of the evolution of styles and ideas, especially with the view that an interrelationship exists between socio-political forces and the arts. Based as it is on the "noble simplicity and calm grandeur" of Greek sculpture, Winckelmann's picture of the harmonious Hellenic personality seems overidealized. Yet, as compared to the fragmentation and specialization of modern life with its internal tensions and external conflicts, Greek culture can teach an important lesson, for it shows how man could reach a harmonious balance of all his faculties and desires.

In essence Schiller's and Goethe's humanistic views have the same intention: to focus on the whole man. Their works show how man could and should live. Again it is important to stress that neither had an inclination for a utopia patterned after the Greek model. They realized that no matter how adversely the cultural development had affected the individual, man could not abrogate it. Perhaps the Faustian drive for knowledge was the only possible road to progress for the species. But materialistic concerns, the search for knowledge or the fetish of scientific and industrial progress should never dominate the lives of men. Goethe and Schiller despised the rhetorical phraseology of progress and felt that the emphasis on the so-called "economic and technical realities of life" would eventually lead to mediocrity. The "great society" they envisioned was one of truly free men; it looked forward but was enriched by the thought of the past; it had been reformed from within and not from without; it had been humanized by art, and in it man could live in harmony with himself and with others. "Lasting reforms must begin with man's character. . . . The state, political freedom, and civil rights depend on the character of the citizen. . . . Political freedom and civil liberties will always remain our most sacred possession, the highest goal to be achieved, and the magnificent center of all culture. But this marvelous structure can only be built upon the solid foundation of man's ennobled character. It will be necessary to educate citizens for a constitution before you can give a constitution to citizens."[9] Thus the question troubling the nineteenth century which is still of the gravest concern today was raised during the period of German Classicism: can a culture survive the rift between man's spiritual aspirations and the technical and economic realities of life? The thought of Goethe and Schiller, Herder and Kant provides an answer. It is for us to reappraise their ideas by asking: Have we really tried? How do we measure up to their views of man and society?

II

A number of dominant themes in classical literature are related to the ideal of self-realization and self-transcendence. From *Prometheus* to *The Elective Affinities*, from *Don Carlos* to *Demetrius*, man's ultimate success or failure is measured in terms of his ability to master life—a major challenge since both Goethe and Schiller see man as an autonomous being no longer safely cradled by the old religious ethos. Although the scenes shift from play to play and the configurations differ in poems and novels, the concern with the human condition, the search for a new basis of existence and conduct, and the quest for identity give an overall continuity to the works. The artistic representation and resolution of problems embrace a wide spectrum ranging from the praise of life, the joy of power, and the exuberant delight in freedom, to tragic error and ultimate failure.

It took years for Goethe and Schiller to perfect the measured cadence of the style we associate with their classical works. But the high pathos and the prophetic voices of their early poems cannot detract from the fact that they already capture the essence of the problem, though in a style which is responsive to the exuberance of youth. In Goethe's poems from 1772 to 1774 the pictures of the wanderer and the beckoning shelter, the contrasting imagery of "heart" and "convention," "mist" and "clarity," the hymnic praise of nature's healing power and the defiance of her destructive force, the song to the loving cosmic father and the challenge to the gods who have deserted man, support the basic theme of man in search of a new order. "Wanderer's Storm Song" (1772), the poet's dialogue with his muse, conveys the defiant determination to withstand the elements and create even under the most adverse conditions. In the midst of storm, rain, and hail the poet espies the warm glow of a hut's hearth and suddenly perceives the seductiveness of the shelter. Has his age not substituted a deceptive, physical security for the reassurance of inner satisfaction? Has it not abandoned all struggle before victory was won? The poet realizes that just as he himself must become worthy of the grace bestowed upon him by the muses through complete dedication to his work and ceaseless striving, so man merits security only when he has complete faith in his own self. Only then will he have the strength and endurance to master life. In "Prometheus" (1773) the feeling of self-reliance is conveyed even more forcefully. Now God is challenged by autonomous man, who asserts his freedom, his will, his power. In contrast to "Ganymede" (1774), which conjures up a beautiful vision of cosmic harmony in which man becomes completely united with nature and God, "Prometheus" bares the enormous rift between God and man. "You must leave/My earth standing,/My cottage, too, which you did not raise,/And leave my hearth/Whose glow/ you envy."[10] The earth-heaven antithesis remains essentially unresolved in these poems. Even the bliss of the union with the universe in "Ganymede" is overshadowed by Werther's harrowing insight that the resulting expansion of consciousness is momentary, that man cannot give his experience eternal duration. Still, the underlying systolic-diastolic rhythm between self-assertion (I, sacred glowing heart) and transcendence (upward thrust of the hymns) suggests a positive view: life's cycle is dynamic, not static; consequently man must always seek new solutions. The question of how a person can realize his full potential can only be answered after he has discovered his true self.

"The Wanderer" (1772), "To Coachman Cronos" (1774), and the tragedy *Egmont* (1787) point toward one possible solution to man's search in the form of a total commitment to life. The quiet, balanced cadence of the "Wanderer" differs sharply from the tone of the other poems and is in accord with its positive resolution. The wanderer, confronted with the overgrown ruins of a temple, initially reproaches nature for her unfeeling destruction of man's work. "Is this how you esteem man's masterpiece/Crumbling, without feeling a sanctuary in your honor/Sowing thistles there?" It seems as if all attempts to give a lasting quality to the brief span of life are doomed. But then, perceiving a flowing spring, a hut atop the ruins, and a slumbering child, the wanderer becomes conscious of the timeless cycle of birth and death. His stance towards nature changes. He feels rejuvenated and hopeful because the spirit of the past will be transmitted to the child and will "bear fruit" again.

Thus, even if man's creations crumble, nature nourishes new life and provides the energy for fresh achievements. In contrast to Werther who despairs, the wanderer accepts life: the earth is his and he will build his home on it. "To Coachman Cronos" breathes the spirit of dynamic life. Though death inexorably awaits the traveler, he accepts the fact courageously. Indeed he is enriched by this knowledge which gives a greater intensity to his living. The most characteristic aspects of the poem are a cheerful tribute to nature, an enthusiastic faith in man's ability to master his destiny, and an enormous energy unleashed in the process of self-realization. Thus when the traveler, the "fiery sea of foaming light in his eye," rushes into Orcus, he not only has conquered death but has also converted it into powerful life.

In *Egmont* Goethe was perhaps most successful in portraying a dynamic personality who at every moment lives his life to the fullest. *Egmont* certainly embodies the aspiration of the Dutch people for political freedom, but at the same time the play's historical dimension is finely interwoven with the exposition and development of Egmont's character. His cheerful exuberance, his confidence in his own strength, and his complete disregard for anxiety and fear are admired by others who are attracted by his frankness. Indeed, his vitality, his love of freedom, captured by Goethe in the image of the horseman galloping on his prancing steed through life, and the unwavering faith in his ability to master life make him the symbol of a new generation. Yet, his strength is also his weakness. Untroubled by solicitude and caution, basically not concerned with the problems of tomorrow, Egmont acts instinctively and is reluctant to reflect on the consequences of his actions. "Does the sun shine for me today, so that I may ponder on what happened yesterday? So that I may fathom and link that which is not to be fathomed or linked—the destiny of a future day? . . . As though whipped by invisible spirits, the horses of the sun, Time's horses, run away with the light chariot of our destiny; and we have no choice but to grip the reins with resolute courage . . . to live for safety's sake is to be dead already. I shall act as I must."[11] We associate Egmont with Antaeus. He seems to be one with the steaming earth and the glistening heaven. Yet, though he has conquered fear and is truly free, he shrinks from the "terrible freedom" that knows no laws, that "rages like a hailstorm through meadow, field and forest, wreaking destruction, and knows no bounds that human hands have set." The freedom he envisions is based upon respect for life. For ultimately Egmont believes in a society in which men can listen to the voices of their hearts and remain true to themselves.

Margaret of Parma, Spanish regent of the Netherlands and a minor character in the play, once observes that the very existence of such a person whose behavior cannot be gauged by conventional motives threatens the established order more than the rational planning of its other adversaries. The accuracy of her judgment becomes most evident in the great encounter between Egmont and Alba, the icy rationalist and statesman, who attempts to save the old order. Alba, the king's most reliable servant, capable of planning, commanding, and executing military and political designs, fears the "arbitrary whims" of a people not held in strict order. "Far better to hedge them in, to treat them like children, so that one can lead them to their own welfare like children." He is convinced of the necessity to subjugate them for their own good. When Egmont points to their just desire for freedom, Alba replies: "What is the freedom of the freest? To do what is right!" Unlike Egmont he does not hear the voice of his heart and cannot distinguish right from wrong; thus Egmont emerges as the wiser statesman because his view is more humane. Alba may temporarily assert his will and fell Egmont, but his world is doomed because it lacks compassion and tolerance.

During their confrontation Alba asks Egmont: "What is permanent in this world?" And the audience, seeing the failure of Alba's design, realizing that he who seemed invincible is compelled by an unfathomable fate to abandon his plans, and finally witnessing the destruction of Egmont's noble mind, may wonder what hope there is for man whose destiny is weighed by inaccessible "silent judges on black scales." The final act of the tragedy provides an unequivocal answer however. Alba's son comes to the prison, confides to Egmont his deep admiration for him, and remonstrates with the fate which destroys his hopes by taking the man whose name "shone like a star of heaven." Egmont's reply clearly justifies the form into which he has shaped his life. Destiny's caprices make life uncertain at every step and there were moments when he pursured his dream like a "sleepwalker, balanced on the knife-edge of a roof top." But holding fast to the careening chariot of time, his energies at their highest pitch, he has always responded to the challenge of life with cheer. Now he calmly accepts death, suddenly aware that not only his life but also his death have a symbolic significance, perhaps even realizing that his almost demonic energy will survive in a future generation. "If my life to you was a mirror in which you liked to contemplate yourself, let my death be the same . . . Every day of my life I was glad to be alive, every day I did my duty with quick efficiency, as my conscience demanded . . . I cease to live; but at least I have lived. Now live as I did, my friend, gladly and with joy and do not shun death!" Thus he remains free and at peace with himself even in death.

The poem "Sea-Voyage" (1776) breathes a similar spirit of commitment to life. At first, the reader will be puzzled by a shift in emphasis which almost seems to negate the Promethean mood of the earlier poems. Whereas Goethe had previously exalted man's autonomy, "Sea-Voyage" as well as "Limits of Mankind" (1781) and "The Divine" (1783) raise the question of whether man's newly won independence can survive in harsh reality. At the same time these poems consider the individual's obligation in his relation to others. The central theme of shipwreck as well as the images of the helmsman and the heart already point ahead to *Iphigenia in Tauris*, a play in which Goethe resolves the competing claims of autonomy and restraint, of individual freedom and social order. The skipper in "Sea-Voyage" who has patiently waited for favorable winds sets out confidently on his journey. But the joyous picture of swelling sails, cheerful activity, and a sun "beckoning with fiery love" changes to gloom as "God-sent changing winds" and a storm threaten the ship. Indeed, soon "Wind and waves/play with the anguish-laden ball." The skipper's attempt, to remain faithful to his goal while trying to balance the scales tipped against him, fails. Yet he does not rebel against fate, curse the Gods or abandon his course but remains at the rudder. "On the fierce depth he looks, a master/ And trusts, sinking or landing safely/In his Gods." The calm assurance with which the poem ends, essentially reflects the skipper's confidence in himself. For as we hear in "The Divine" and *Iphigenia*, the Gods should be considered a symbol for man's aspiration to understand the voice of a mysterious world order, an order that is the voice of life itself in which man must take his place. "According to laws eternal,/Inexorable and mighty/All of us/Must round/Our existence's circles." And the Gods, creations of man's imagination, can reveal themselves only in his conduct and actions: "His example teach us/To believe in them!"

In "The Divine" Goethe proceeds from the Golden Rule as the basis for man's conduct to the reflection that the truly ennobled man's actions are altruistic and inspired by love. Through the spirit of humility and reverence for life we simultaneously become truly human and approach the realm of the Gods. In the poem Goethe actually inverts the Biblical idea that man was created in God's image. Instead, God appears as a vision of man's desire to become a more ennobled, humane being. This ideal in turn affects the further course of human conduct since it encourages us to seek constantly to improve our behavior. Thus the Gods—it is noteworthy that Goethe consistently uses the plural in these poems—reflect man's growing awareness of himself and of his place in the universe. And while our conception of the Gods evolves over the centuries and may differ from people to people, they do have permanence as symbols illuminating the provinces of human life. "Limits of Mankind" gives a hint of this thought: "What distinguishes/Gods from man?/Countless waves roll/Before them/An eternal stream/We are raised by the wave/Engulfed by it/And sink."

One of the central themes in *Iphigenia in Tauris* (1786)[12] rests upon an almost passionate belief in the idea of a new humanism grounded in a revolt against the debasement of human life. This humanism necessitates the clarification of man's image of God and the establishment of new human relationships based on truth and brotherly love. The call for a new order is tested in Iphigenia's confrontation with old beliefs. The traditional German view of the play as a *Seelendrama*, that is, one characterized by internal conflict, is quite applicable since it focuses attention on Iphigenia's inner struggle and on the development of her character. The reader has to realize, however, that once Iphigenia is convinced of the validity of her belief, she gains the strength to act accordingly and through her humanizing influence shapes the life of others, indeed ultimately even the course of society. The play poses a number of important questions: What customs and institutions are worth preserving? Must man bow to fate or can he control his destiny? Is the notion of fate as man's scourge really an excuse behind which he hides his unwillingness to accept the responsibility for his actions?

The opening scene reveals Iphigenia torn by conflicting emotions. She has acquiesced in the will of the Goddess Diana who saved her life. However, she would prefer to dedicate her life freely to Diana's service and deplores a fate which has cast her to the shores of a land inhabited by a wild, uncivilized race. Doubtful that she has been able to soften the Taurians' hearts, she longs to be liberated and return to Hellas. Yet it becomes immediately evident that her civilizing influence has already been felt by the Taurians. She has tempered their wild instincts and persuaded King Thoas to abolish the custom of sacrificing strangers at Diana's altar. Her behavior is all the more remarkable since she springs from a family whose wild passion and barbarous acts, be they adultery, incest, murder, or fratricide, equal the Taurian savagery. But whereas her ancestors believed that they were cursed by the Gods and refused all responsibility for their actions, Iphigenia sees the Gods in a different light. "Whoever assumes that the Gods are bloodthirsty, misconceives their nature; he only attributes his own cruel desires to them." She has faith in man's ability to conquer his primitive instincts.

Iphigenia's faith is rooted on one hand in her innate desire to remain pure, on the other in the revelation she experienced when she herself was to be sacrificed and then saved by Diana. In a sense she was the first individual in her family chain to fathom the significance of a symbolic act: to be sacrificed is to renounce and transcend the old self. Goethe expressed this idea, to which he returned throughout his life, most poetically in the poem "Joyous Yearning" (1814). Employing the ancient symbol of the butterfly, he suggests that the cycle of death and rebirth is applicable to man's growth in maturity. Viewed from this perspective, Iphigenia's initial insight is but one step in her development. She has to transcend her self again when she is confronted with the choice between saving her brother but betraying Thoas or remaining true to her vision but seeing Orestes die. For at this critical moment Thoas threatens to reintroduce the sacrifice of strangers unless she marries him, the first captives being her brother and his friend Pylades. Thus Iphigenia's intuitive vision of ennobled man has to be implemented by her own just action.

The easiest and all-too-human course for her to follow would be to satisfy her personal desire and flee with her brother to Greece. But once Pylades' cunning has further drawn her into the plan to betray Thoas and escape, she is overcome by apprehension and remorse. "Alas! I see I must consent to follow like a child. Detested falsehood/it does not free like words of truth." The feeling of being caught in a web of deceit and flung into the hands of forces over which she has no control overpowers her. Helplessly writhing in her chains, forced by an unrelenting fate to break with her vision, her hope for human relationships built on truth shattered, she begins to doubt herself and her image of the Gods: "Let not finally abhorrence rise/Within my heart! The titans/The old Gods' hate toward you/Olympians seize my breast with vulture talons! Save me/And save your image in my soul!" After this outcry she chants the Parcae's Song, until then a faint memory but suddenly laden with the tragic foreboding that man is flung into the world, chained to the wheels of brutal life, and forgotten by indifferent and amoral Gods.

The song marks the climax of Iphigenia's doubt and inner conflict. It also ushers in her resolute break with tradition. For in the final confrontation with Thoas she dares the impossible. She listens to her heart, transcends her emotions, speaks the truth, and reveals the plan to escape to Thoas at the risk of losing everything. This action not only convinces Thoas but also heralds the beginning of a truly human relationship between individuals. Iphigenia's existential commitment unmasks the curse of the Gods as a fearful projection of man's inner weakness and his unwillingness to assume the responsibility inherent in freedom. Thus the play, one of the world's most civilizing works of great beauty, perfect symmetry, and moral truth, transforms the stark tragedy of antiquity into a victory for man's humane spirit.

In contrast to this assurance, *Tasso* (1790) seems to be a bitter indictment of man's failure to resolve the conflict between art and life, between artist and society, as well as of everyone's inability to rise above the thousand abrasive little incidents of daily living which endanger humanity's very soul. The play is perhaps especially tragic because none of the characters is evil; all attempt to help Tasso but lack the strength to renounce their own desires completely. Above all, their fear to show true emotions coupled with the complete inability to understand another person leads to a groundless suspicion that constantly destroys the trust and love necessary for human relationships. The play opens with a tranquil, sunlit morning scene—during which Tasso is crowned with a laurel wreath for his poetic achievement. But the hour of triumph is followed by one of bitter despair and the joyous picture of bright sunlight fades into a symbolic grey mist enveloping the court when Antonio, the reserved statesman arrives and precipitates in Tasso an emotional outburst which reveals the poet's tragic solitude, his inner tension, and the gulf that separates him from the court. The play ends with the image of shipwreck. The work of art, born of anguish, endures and is immortalized but the artist clings in tormenting grief to his visibly moved adversary: "Broken is the helm, the ship bursts on all sides. And beneath my feet the planks tear asunder!"

In *Tasso* Goethe created almost an archetype of the suffering artist. Certainly the play's dominant themes, the insight into the artistic temperament, and the symbolic significance of the artist's figure for a secularized society helped to establish the tradition of the artist-hero in modern literature. The conflict between Tasso and the court is deeply rooted in his personality and also in the conventions of the society that supports him. Like the poet-prophet in Hölderlin's works, he is inspired by God. He alone can face the beam of truth emanating from above, but he is also in danger of being destroyed by the light. Tasso's life is dedicated to the effort of casting man's highest aspirations into literary form, of surrounding his contemporaries with symbols of excellence, of moving their hearts through the beauty of poetry and thus by ennobling them to transform the world. He has no sympathy for compromises, be they of an aesthetic or ethical nature. He ceaselessly works to perfect his literary creation; still, he is haunted by an almost obsessive fear of his contemporaries' criticism and history's judgment. This anxiety together with his feeling of not being accepted as a free man among equals further heightens his inner tension and accentuates the solitude imposed upon him by the process of artistic creation. Leonore, visiting her friend the Princess at the court, observes once that Tasso seems hardly aware of the actual world but instead lives in a magic circle of his own creation, listening to nature's harmony, appraising history, and focusing his attention on man's unfulfilled potential. The Princess agrees but also points to Tasso's love lyrics as evidence of his strong attachment to the world. Leonore objects because she senses that love is a metaphor for Tasso's ideal. What she does not see is that for Tasso this ideal exists; in the Princess it has assumed the form of an unattainable woman, one he nevertheless intensely loves and yearns to possess. And the Princess, by persuading him that his fears to lose her are unfounded, actually nurtures his passion. Yet she is utterly helpless and unable to break with convention once Tasso expresses his love.

His desire intensifies the existing conflict which finally erupts in the confrontation with Antonio. Tasso and Antonio not only crystallize the two positions of artist versus statesman, contemplation versus action, and uncompromising vision versus political arrangements, but also represent two poles of human experience and self-realization—two poles, we might add, which seek, need, and complement each other, which if harmoniously united would fulfill mankind's dream of humanism. In the play, however, the conflict between the laurel and the oak wreath remains unresolved. Tasso envies the experienced statesman who is wont to control the fate of states with ease. Antonio begrudges Tasso's position as a favorite of the court which in his eyes rewards Tasso excessively for a "gift of blind fortune," for light play that entertains society or at best may praise men of notable achievements. He fails to understand Tasso's faith in the redeeming power of art and does not see the demonic menace inherent in Tasso's calling. When Tasso impulsively offers his friendship to him ("heart and hand"), Antonio hesitates and remains cool. The heart remains in his view a too emotional and unstable basis for friendship. A lasting relationship can rest only on serenity of mind gained by experience and firmness of character tested by time: "Self-knowledge comes from knowing other men;/ Only life reveals to each his worth." The conflict between word and deed, heart and mind culminates in Tasso's emotional outburst in which he challenges Antonio to a duel. Tasso's instinctive, elemental, and perfectly understandable action threatens the code of restraint which holds civilized society together. Tasso has transgressed the dictum, "Permitted is what is proper." All attempts by Duke Alphonso to protect Tasso and also to save society's code are doomed, for he too does not comprehend the enormity of the offense against Tasso's yearning for recognition, love, and truth.

The complete stagnation and the inability of everyone to find the redeeming word is reflected in the barren world of the third act. Confined to his room, Tasso does not appear at all. Trying to communicate in a language that veils their emotions and thoughts the others admit their guilt. The voice of the heart is completely silenced in the following act when Tasso in tragic isolation and utmost despair hides his true self behind deceptive conventional phrases. The artist as well as his work cease to speak. Just as Werther wearies of life, Tasso becomes increasingly alienated from the world. But other parallels frequently noted between *Werther* and *Tasso* also point to a more tragic conception of the basic conflict. Werther yearned for annihilation since he could not eternally cling to fleeting moments of cosmic awareness and because he failed to cast his subjective feelings into artistic form. Brimming with emotions and vague sensations which barely disguised his inner vacuity, he was destroyed by his own subjectivity. The key to

Tasso's tragedy is the inability of both society and artist to understand each other. Essentially in this play the faith in the power of love and the belief in man's dignity founder.

Indications of this tragic possibility, envisioned by Goethe as a threat to humanism, are also present in other of his works. But the pessimistic view is always balanced by a courageous acceptance of life, by faith in man's ability to increase his self-insight and by a trust in love's healing power. "Whatever as either truth or fable/In myriad volumes you have spied,/Is all but as a Tower of Babel/Unless by love it's unified." Certainly it is no coincidence that Goethe's genius was first recognized in his unforgettable love lyrics. Judged by most readers as intensely personal, these poems reveal a universal dimension and symbolic significance which becomes increasingly pronounced with the *Roman Elegies* (1790). The reader will find it rewarding to consider seriously Goethe's statement in "Maxim 1002": "Poetry points to the secrets of nature and tries to solve them through the image." Numerous poems that breathe the spirit of love not only reflect the poet's immediate experience but also paint a picture of pulsating life. Already the "Sesenheim-Songs" (1770–1771) capture this dimension. Nature herself sings in joyous exclamations of "Welcome and Departure," "May Song," and "With an Embroidered Ribbon." These poems, timeless expressions of human emotion, affect us through a magic quality which springs from the artist's gift to perceive and hear the essence of life in nature. It is present in the fleeting tension, expressed in the contrast between morning sun and the pain of departure, in nature's powerful transformation by spring, captured in the image of "blossom's haze," or in a playful atmosphere, the sudden recognition that a ribbon may change into a lasting bond.

In the *Roman Elegies* the impassioned spontaneity is tempered by the distichs' quiet flow. A centrifugal-centripetal movement provides the basic structure for this cycle of poems. The inner sphere, formed by the individual's sensuous love, expands to embrace the myths of antiquity and develops into a dialogue with God. Then the circle contracts to celebrate the rites of love only to move outward again when the initiate is overwhelmed by a feeling of almost cosmic consciousness. Love breathes life into streets, palaces, and ruins. The Isis-Osiris cult, the Eleusinian Mysteries, and the harvest rites blend into an organic unit to reveal the secret of life, death, and transcendence. Thus the discourse with the past enhances the present and intensifies the artist's self-knowledge. Indeed, it leads to the poetic confession that only love can inspire art's most essential quality: a profound reverence for life.

Between 1814 and 1819 Goethe wrote another great homage to love as the force that creates, shapes, and transforms the world. The love lyrics in the *West-Eastern Divan,* comparable in scope to the *Roman Elegies,* also display a complete fusion of experience, image, and idea. The extraordinary vitality of these poems rises from a loving dialogue with the present, the artist's own past, and a different civilization. The poet's youth, fresh in his memory from the work on *Poetry and Truth* (I–III, 1811–1814), seems to recur in his friendship with Marianne von Willemer. Only now his love is enriched and enhanced by the insight that life neither was then nor is now the raw material for his poetic creations, as some critics had charged, but was always filled with poetic form. That he saw this form on the Rhine, in the works of the Orient, and now in his own life gives an almost spiritual clarity to the erotic, sensuous poems without ever diminishing their immediacy. The motto to the "Book Suleika" must have appealed to Goethe since it contrasts the soft glow of the past (images of haze and darkness) with the clarity of the present; "I thought in the night/That I saw the moon in my sleep;/But when I awoke/The sun unexpectedly rose."

The polarity of darkness and light, past and present, separation and union, expansion and contraction sustains the movement in "Reunion." However, the tension is resolved by Goethe's attributing a universal perspective to the personal experience. As the core of the poem he presents a myth of creation in which he envisions a rapidly expanding universe after the spirit has burst into the existing chaos. This cosmos, soundless and devoid of emotions, lacks a life-giving, unifying force. It remains dead until God sends love in the form of a "red dawn." Now the world begins to pulsate, assumes new forms, and sustains itself in the systolic-diastolic rhythm. "Allah now may rest his hands/We create his world." And just as love has united the universe, it will also join the two lovers. The powerful yearning for the moment of complete fulfillment becomes the dominant theme in the "Night of the Full Moon." The dialogue between servant and lady and the simple structure of verse and refrain are especially well suited to convey the woman's emotion; under the spell of her desire, anticipating the instant of the meeting, she can only whisper: "I want to kiss! Kiss!" But though she remains oblivious to the world, the glowing, starlit night seems to be set afire by her love. If we finally ask the sixty-six-year-old poet whether the coming of dawn ("Morgenröte"), this eternal, rejuvenating process, is nature's ultimate gift to troubled mankind, we hear a strong yes. Goethe's response in "Hold me, locks, securely caught" is plain: through Eros man can break his tragic loneliness. Only then can he hope for the self-realization or transcendence, envisioned by Classicism. And only then may he experience *caritas*, the true love, based on renunciation, and succeed in directing his life.

These themes are broadened in *Wilhelm Meister* (1795–1829), Goethe's great novel of human development in which he traces the life of a merchant's son who has aspirations as an artist, joins a theater group, and later becomes a physician. The novel, of considerable influence on Goethe's contemporaries and later authors, helped initiate the genre of the *Bildungsroman*. Clearly expressing the humanistic ideal of the classical period, it did much to establish in the German mind the concept of what constitutes a model education and spiritual growth. If we ask how Goethe conceived of human development, we are confronted by a most timely question. Goethe's answer, however, may prove unacceptable to many, if only because his basic idea has been analyzed to death by present day cultural critics and seems too difficult to be put into practice. In *Wilhelm Meister* Goethe sets forth his view of a free man's education which is inseparably linked to the development of a free society. The institutions of society seek to civilize man by enabling him to realize freely his potential and thus fulfilling his entelechy, but they can only function if the individual foregoes all purely egotistical desires. Perhaps even more significantly, the novel shows how Meister learns to live though his dreams are crushed and his achievements fall short of his ambition.

In contrast to Faust, Wilhelm Meister is a less problematical and more average personality. But by characterizing him as a person who might easily lose direction and be ruled by chance events, Goethe has created a figure with whose failure and success the reader can readily identify. During the phases of his development—youth (apprenticeship), search for meaning in life (travels), and maturity—Wilhelm is exposed to numerous formative influences. They comprise passion and love, the theater and the arts, friendship, the intellectual currents of the past and of his time, and the study of medicine, a scientific discipline intimately familiar with life and death. Wilhelm's growing self-insight is best illustrated by his changing perception of himself and his role in the world. Initially troubled by the question: Who am I? he later wonders: what is man? and is finally guided to ask: how can we live? Though man remains the center of interest, Wilhelm's thinking progresses from a concern for the individual to one for all men. Wilhelm Meister's success can be attributed primarily to the community of sympathetic friends whom he meets during his life's journey. The bonds of these friendships are mutual respect, a common effort, and a deep reverence for life. But above all they help Wilhelm see himself objectively by providing him with wise counsel, constructive criticism, and a mirror in which he can observe the effects of his actions.

Friendship proves to be an objectifying experience. It teaches Wilhelm that the statement, "Know yourself," is not to be interpreted in an ascetic sense, for all introspection or brooding only magnifies the subjective element in one's thinking. True self-insight becomes possible only through knowledge of the world, through the constant exchange of ideas: "Remember to live." This recognition paves the way for Wilhelm to face the world in a new spirit and resign himself to the fact that ultimate truth escapes man and lies shrouded in mystery. Friendship also fosters in him the awareness that "every ability is valuable and ought to be unfolded." Once he has realized the statement's full significance, he can face failure and still remain productive. Finally, the mutual confidence that characterizes the atmosphere of his friendships provides the basis for his investigation of the moral, social, and political aspects of the relationship between individual and society. Rejecting an escape from the world into introspection, but also the rhetoric of political action, he finds his way into a community built upon a common respect for life.

Romantic artists initially hailed the novel since it developed several themes and motifs (search for self-realization, friendship, artist-hero, and travel) with which they were preoccupied. They also saw in the novel's structure, especially in the almost independent narrations scattered throughout, a vindication of their own poetic tendencies. But they came to realize that Wilhelm Meister's ethos of resignation, his acceptance of reality, and his comprehensive view of the world, which not only precluded the alienation of the individual from society but also the separation of humanistic and scientific values, contrasted sharply with the romantic cult of individualism and its underlying conviction that the individual could comprehend the mysteries of the world only in his subjective visions. To be sure, Wilhelm's inner development and growth is almost total but it is coupled with a constantly increasing awareness of reality. The world we experience in *Wilhelm Meister,* though not lacking in dark overtones, precludes the tragic possibility of the ultimate failure of either man or society whenever distrust and doubt slowly undermine all human relationships. That Goethe saw this danger becomes evident in *The Elective Affinities* (1809), a novel planned originally to be a part of *Wilhelm Meister.*

While the world portrayed in *The Elective Affinities* is one of polite society in which behavior is governed by civilized conventions, the atmosphere is laden with feelings of uncertainty, suspicion, and complete helplessness in the face of forces which seem to be uncontrollable. All meaningful activity has ceased. Even the cultivation of nature has been reduced to an attempt to eliminate the last trace of her power and wildness. But the desire for artificial order, just as the proclivity to deny death, betrays a deep fear of latent forces that threaten to destroy the deceptive harmony. Indeed, the artificial landscape reflects the inner barrenness which manifests itself most strongly in the all-pervasive boredom that seems to affect everyone including the unwary reader. When the little world finally crumbles, when passion proves as illusory as morality, and adultery as confining as the bonds of marriage, we are nevertheless moved instead of being relieved. Why? Do we fear that the trap in which these people are caught is waiting for us? Do we feel that Goethe's pessimistic portrait of life in *The Elective Affinities* corresponds more closely to reality than the chiliastic vision expressed in the *Novelle* (1827)?

It is no coincidence that we should think of the *Novelle,* for there too a small, highly civilized community is menaced by dark undercurrents. But the persons in the *Novelle* gain new insight from their experience, grow, mature, and can resolve their tensions through love. They are capable of renouncing desires which conflict not so much with the common good but with their conception of their own entelechy. This alone constitutes the true augmentation and progressive refinement of one's own potential. It is the realization of the self, the will to live, health. In contrast, even Ottilie, the most touching figure in *The Elective Affinities,* falters in her valiant attempts to cultivate and strengthen her inviolable human integrity. With a silent gesture of submission she too resigns herself finally to forces beyond her control. She can only hope for transcendence in death. While living she is compelled to listen to her demon and follow her inner nature. And while a martyr's halo seems to encircle her, the picture of the gods, symbols of man's spiritual growth, fades away. Thus we also hear in this novel, faintly to be sure, a restrained plea for change and liberation. But to return to our questions, the ominous overtones are so strong that the fear man may lack the courage and strength to humanize the world creeps into our minds.

Goethe continued to the end of his life to probe and search for illumination about man's destiny. The tensions between error and clarity, guilt and innocence, dark demonic threats to existence and the promise of harmonious fulfillment, self-realization and transcendence, salvation and damnation, come to a climax in Goethe's most incommensurable poetic creation: *Faust*.[13] Goethe worked intermittently from 1773 to 1832 on the tragedy which, in his own judgment, "should remain a riddle and delight men forever." The enormous literature devoted to the work testifies to its appeal, importance, and mystery. In the non-German speaking world the tragedy has been generally considered to be romantic in structure, themes, and scope. Germans, who usually view the play in the light of its symbolism, have felt that it could not be measured in terms of narrow classifications. If anything, they have esteemed *Faust* as the poetic recreation of man's ceaseless struggle and final redemption (*Erlösungsdrama*). Many saw in it a mirror of all of man's aspirations, life itself as it were; many agreed with Spengler who saw in *Faust* the essence of Western spirit; some critics felt that Mephisto was more moral than Faust, ignoring Goethe's almost painful objectivity, for when the Devil speaks, he *is* right; and a reader today turns in horror from the work, feeling that "the new ethics personified by Faust are evil and destructive, and the human organism rejects them with that hidden sense St. Thomas Aquinas said preserves cows from eating poison herbs."[14] But he forgets that Goethe created a work of art, not a moral tract, and that when the artist held up his mirror, saying "Ecce homo," judgment was passed upon all of us. If today we sense more keenly than ever before the danger inherent in the passionate will to knowledge which "laughs at the limits of time and space" and ultimately transforms the world, we have all the more reason to contemplate the scene in which Faust, apparently master of technological progress, reclaims land from the sea in order to expand man's living space. He joyously listens to the clanking spades. "I work that millions may possess this space,/If not secure, a free and active race./Here man and beast in green and fertile fields,/Will know the joys that new-won region yields." He does not know that the lemures are digging his grave, while Philemon and Baucis, parents of the race that will inherit the promised land, were sacrificed to progress. How could Faust know? *He is blind!*

Yet if progress is blind, can we ignore Faust's dream of a society united by the common will to live in freedom on its land or Goethe's final vision of love which has conquered the beast in man? Faust dies the very instant he realizes that, by dedicating himself completely to the living, his own life has been fulfilled. "This is the highest wisdom that I own,/The best that mankind ever knew,/Freedom and life are earned by those alone/Who conquer them each day anew." Faust's struggle spans the history of Western civilization from the Hellenic period to the scientific age; he wreaks tragedies, experiences the depth of nihilism but also of creative joy, transforms passion into love, evil into good. With Helena he enjoys a brief dream of Elysium. Yet ultimate satisfaction seems impossible, for absolute truth still eludes him. He almost discovers the secret of life's origin, but when Homunculus springs from the test tube, Faust learns that the creation begotten by pure intellect will remain sterile without love. So shedding his old self, rising above his limitations, born and reborn, ever striving and forever becoming, he, the symbol of man's soul, continues to struggle, actively searching for values.

When Faust has died, Mephisto, cynical and nihilistic, concludes that all creation is doomed to be annihilated: "Now it is over. What meaning can one see?/It's as if it had not come to be." But, if anything, Faust's experience proves that man can lend continuity, even permanence, to his visions by generating in others the will to continue where former generations have left off. Thus life, of necessity cyclical in its course, could be spiral in achievement and effect. In the figure of Faust Goethe expanded the picture of the wanderer to titanic proportions. Faust's desire to grasp the spirit of the Western world, his search for the cosmic essence, and his challenge to God and Mephisto surpass all individual limitations. During his life he suffered the fury of hell but also the bliss that results from the expansion of the mind. In the end he is redeemed by an act of love and grace. "Who ever strives with all his power,/We are allowed to save." For Faust the barrier between him and heaven had long since disappeared. Only peace awaited him. With the dawning of a new age, men will certainly contemplate once more his enormous driving force; they might even shape their existence in the spirit of the work: Be not afraid to live!

III

Friedrich Schiller differed greatly in temperament and philosophy from Goethe. Basically an idealist, he brooded over society's social and political ills, but above all over the futility of any life that lacked ethical norms. Ever ready to call for a new order based on his ideals, he delighted in portraying intrigues, outrageously evil characters, and situations of fierce conflict. Though criticized for creating at times literary figures who seemed more allegorical than real, he has also been praised for his almost uncanny psychological insight into human motivation. Convinced of art's healing power, he nevertheless appraised realistically its efficacy. And despite having been exalted by one generation as Germany's eminent poet-philosopher, he is best remembered today as the great dramatist.

Schiller's poetry lacks much of the sensuous immediacy the reader finds in Goethe's lyrics. His poetic diction is essentially dramatic: the poems are structured around conflicts, contrasts, and oppositions. In their upward thrust their movement appears apogean, frequently also triadic when the rise is followed by a sudden downward plunge. Schiller's idealism led him to explore the poetic possibilities of spiritual adventures. In the epigram "Accord" he tersely defined the difference between his and Goethe's stance toward the world as being basically visual or visionary. "We both seek truth, you outside in life, I within/The heart; we both shall find it./If the eye is sound, it will meet the Creator out there,/If the heart is hale, it will mirror the World." When he, bred in a cheerless world, tormented by disease, and burdened by the knowledge of early death, looked within himself or into the hearts of others, he found a passionate yearning to transcend the unnatural barriers separating men and discovered a new ethical basis for existence. He also realized that man's tragic situation was better suited for dramatic action than for the poetic allegorization of the ideal. Thus the suffering heroines Amalia (*The Robbers*), Elizabeth (*Don Carlos*) and Thekla (*Wallenstein*) who embody his vision are almost overshadowed by such ambiguous but powerful figures as Fiesco, Wallenstein, and Maria Stuart.

169

The early poems and plays, uneven and teeming with revolutionary pathos, like Goethe's, reveal several themes and motifs that came to full fruition during the classical period. "The Evening" (1776) casts the poet not only in the role of a mediator between the world and eternity, sunset and everlasting light, but also in that of the prophet who reminds man of God's existence. Even the vivid descriptions of individual scenes strongly suggest that Schiller is more interested in conveying abstractions (man, universe, God) and an impression of the desire for transcendence than a lyrical mood. The poem's somber overtones are unmistakeable despite its powerful, almost "baroque" assertion of God's greatness. For the poet recognizes that even during the loftiest flights of fantasy man fails to unlock life's secrets. The feeling that man's search is halted by the confrontation with infinity also pervades "The Greatness of the World" (1782). The poet's imagination, envisioned as a traveler in space, seems to approach the source of creation on the wings of light. The flight of fantasy is brought to a sudden halt. The poet realizes that the goal is unattainable and plunges back to reality. But as "The Conqueror" (1777) shows, the earth offers little consolation. Here the poet rises in fury against evil, hurls his curses against tyrants, and demands their eternal damnation from a God who is no longer the all-loving father but one of judgment and wrath. The immense energy unleashed to reach God, the inability to find him in nature and merely a faint symbol of his essence in the order of the stars, clearly reveal man's isolation in a despiritualized world.

This theme which found its most poetic expression in "The Gods of Greece" (1788) also figures prominently in the three plays that precede Schiller's classical works: The Robbers (1781), Fiesco (1783), and Intrigue and Love (1784). In "The Gods of Greece" the poet mourns man's loss of the once intimate relationship with his Gods, idealistic creations of his imagination, who had animated the universe and mirrored his high aspirations. The poem's mood, the feeling of sadness and permanent loss, are strongly reminiscent of Hölderlin's poetry. The bright days when Gods roamed the world have passed forever. Now in these "barren times" only the poet dreams of the past. In the plays Schiller paints a stark picture of the unbridgeable gulf that separates man's life from the world of his dreams. Society is in a state of dissolution; even the family, its smallest unit, is torn by conflicts, feuds, intrigues, and hate. The recurring motif of the struggle between brothers (I and you) and

son and father (man and God) reflects a rebellion of man's
instincts against his former symbols of excellence, a rebellion which
threatens the basis of all existence. The scene is bleak indeed. On
one hand we see monstrous characters such as Franz Moor and
Gianettino Doria, who are ready to commit any crime or a weakling
like von Walter, who sacrifices his son's happiness and ultimately
his life for political advantage; on the other hand we behold revolutionaries, as for instance Karl Moor and Fiesco, who fight the
corrupt social order but lose sight of their goals and fall prey to the
lure of power. The others seem but helpless victims in the claws of
an infernal process that seizes and destroys them. To see the
struggle and end of these persons simply in terms of their tragic
guilt or fate does not do full justice to the plays. Schiller apparently intends to castigate a situation in society in which mutual
confidence already requires an act of courage of which few persons,
if any, are capable. Thus society falls apart because individuals
cannot establish the relationship that Martin Buber envisioned as
the encounter of "I" and "you" and Schiller as the "meeting of
hearts."

But as the *Aesthetic Letters* indicate, man can listen to the
voice of his heart only if he is neither chained by his instincts nor
dominated by his will, but remains free from all external constraints. Fiesco's tragedy, which foreshadows those of Wallenstein,
Maria Stuart, and the brothers Don Cesar and Don Manuel in *The
Bride of Messina*, is caused by his inability to achieve the serenity
that seems absolutely necessary for such existential commitment.
Fiesco is characterized as a person who seeks to retain his freedom
of action even while he plans to overthrow the government. He
responds almost playfully to the challenge of the conspiracy, remains unperturbed when disaster threatens, and proves magnani-
mous when his enemy shows greatness. But since his life is not
discernibly oriented toward any ethical norms, his freedom, though
it may be total, amounts to the irresponsibility of a gambler. In the
end when he could free the people with one gesture, an idea
Schiller developed in the variant Mannheim stage version of the
play, he risks everything instead by succumbing to the lure of
power. When he knowingly rejects his friend Verrina's plea to
remain faithful to the republican ideal, he unknowingly gambles his
life and loses it.

The gambling motif recurs in the form of a play with human
hearts in *Don Carlos* (1787).[15] The dishonesty of courtiers and

politicians who are only interested in their own advantage will hardly surprise the audience. What enforces the play's profoundly tragic tone is the fact that, with the exception of Elisabeth, everyone fails at one time or another to speak the truth. Even Posa, "the citizen of a future age," cannot resist the temptation. He keeps his plans secret out of consideration for Don Carlos but also because he is blinded by the "vain desire" to cut the thread of the intrigue completely alone and in so doing save his friend, and the Queen, and through them, his vision of an ennobled world. The resulting misunderstanding leads to the catastrophe. To be sure, Posa transcends himself and becomes truly free when he sacrifices himself for his friend. But his act cannot save Don Carlos; it actually dooms all hope for the state's citizens, since it extinguishes in King Philip's soul the last ray of light and "spark of truth."

Instead of love the silence of the grave reigns over man's dreams at the play's end. Yet everyone longs for honesty, understanding, and compassion. Even Philip, the icy statesman, experiences the emptiness surrounding him and the terrifying barrier separating men, a barrier which language can no longer penetrate. At the height of his despair when he is confronted with apparently irrefutable proof of his wife's and his son's betrayal, he pleads with providence to "send him a human being, a friend" he can trust. He finds Posa. Later Philip admits that he looked into Posa's eyes and became mortal again. Thus confidence is possible. All Posa has to do is to open the King's eyes to the truth. What weighs heavier: the evidence of the letter, as deceptive and treacherous as the oaths and assertions of loyalty which always underscore in Schiller's plays the failure to communicate, or the voice of the heart? King Philip, deeply moved by Posa's honesty, his vision of a truly humane society, and his demand to restore "mankind's lost nobility," is willing to listen. Perhaps the world is ready for Posa's ideal. But at this critical juncture Posa fails. He lacks confidence in the "hardened" old monarch—"What can I be to the King? In such arid soil, no rose of mine could bloom"—and only trusts the seed of hope for millions he has planted in Don Carlos' soul. Posa struggled and succeeded in combining his compassion for mankind with his love for his friend, but in his confrontation with the King he only sees the future of humanity and remains blind to that of the individual. How tragically he erred becomes evident in one of the play's most memorable scenes (V, ix) when Philip mourns his loss: "One spirit, one free man arose in this whole century—one alone—

he despises me and dies . . . I loved him, loved him very much. He was dear to me as a son. In this youth a new, beautiful dawn rose before me."

Now not even the beautiful example of the enduring friendship between Don Carlos and Posa can affect the King. By handing his son to the Grand Inquisitor he finally dissolves all bonds of nature. Don Carlos' fervent wish to be loved by his father, to be accepted by him as a human being, to rule with him a free realm, has been denied. But guided by Posa's example, he transcends himself by purifying his emotions, by overcoming his passion for the Queen which had poisoned the atmosphere, and by facing her in the spirit of true love. Though man's desire for freedom is temporarily crushed and the threat of the Grand Inquisitor's statement, "It is better to labor for the grave than for freedom," lingers, Schiller's chiliastic vision has found a monument in the spirit of friendship and humanity realized at the threshold of death by Posa, Don Carlos, and Elisabeth. The tragic insight is momentarily softened in the hymn "To Joy" (1786) and the ballad "The Hostage" (1799), in which Schiller holds forth the promise of fulfillment in life by joyously proclaiming the brotherhood of all men. In "The Hostage," the love and loyalty of two friends converts a tyrant to their ideal; in "To Joy" all of mankind is reconciled by love. The hymn, Schiller's most moving expression of his hopes for man, glorifies joy as the divine power that descends from heaven to soothe man's sorrow by embracing and uniting all men in love. As joy softly stirs the hearts, God's breath is felt: all conflicts cease, "men are brothers," death loses its terror, and man's soul, free at last, rises triumphantly to the stars.

The stars, bright symbols of love and harmony, grow dim and finally disappear altogether in *Wallenstein* (1800), leaving the world in spiritual darkness. As in other historical dramas by Schiller, a comparison with the actual historical events sheds little light on his artistic achievement. The trilogy, Schiller's greatest work, pictures Wallenstein at the zenith of his power and his subsequent fall, his quest for self-realization and ultimate failure. It also shows the coming-of-age, the love, and heroic death of Max Piccolomini, the tragedy's most admirable character, whose faith in his two spiritual mentors, his father and Wallenstein, is shattered when he realizes that they are neither truthful nor capable of listening to their own hearts. Finally, the tragedy captures in a series of tableaus the essence of war itself, a war begotten by men but now assuming a life of its own, bewitching weak and strong alike with its frightful nihilistic freedom:

> Looking death in the face, as only he can,
> There's none but the soldier who is a free man.
>
> . . .
>
> Up then, comrades, saddle your steeds,
>   With hearts in battle delighted!
> Youth seethes, life foams! So onward to deeds
>   Before the spirit is blighted.
> Till life has been staked for the rise or the fall
> Your life will never be won at all.[16]

Wallenstein stakes his life on a daring venture that is to secure his place in history. The admired and lauded, but also feared and envied leader of an army which rallied to his name and whose full allegiance he seems to command, now plans to use his men to bring peace to the ravished land and at the same time fulfill his personal ambition. The picture of the powerful general, strangely compounded of admiration and antipathy that emerges from reports and conversations of soldiers, officers, confidants, and antagonists, assumes new dimensions with Wallenstein's appearance. Is he really the sober rationalist and capable politician who can execute the plan? Inscrutable and indecisive, he plays with the idea of breaking his allegiance to the emperor, uniting his troops with the Swedish army, and after victory, turning on the Swedes to force them off the continent. At the same time he tries to remain uncommitted and thinks of forcing the emperor's hand while he retains his favor. He hopes to impose a new order upon the world in which there is no room for the real evil in life that springs from man's lethargy and unwillingness to accept change: "the eternal yesterday,/What always was and always comes anew,/What holds good for tomorrow just because/It held good for today." He looks to the stars for guidance since they reflect the order for which he yearns. But as he searches for the right path, he loses sight of the stars' symbolic significance, waits for favorable signs, and becomes dependent upon planetary constellations. Forgetting his own belief that man's deeds are not dictated by chance, he sees in the stars omens for random success or failure. He remains undecided, perhaps even unaware of his own motives until events over which he has lost all control force his hand. Even after he has lost Max, his only truthful and faithful friend who could have shown him the path to *true order,* he remains puzzled about his course of action. "If I had known before what was to happen,/That it would cost the dearest of my friends,/And if my heart had spoken as it speaks now,/Maybe I would have been more cautious—maybe/I wouldn't." Thus Wallenstein, surrounded by adventurers who sack the land and gamble their fortune on his name, plays a dangerous game himself and shares their fate. Deceived to the end by those he trusts blindly, he is murdered at night. No star is to be seen.

Octavio Piccolomini stakes his fortune on the survival of the old imperial Austrian order which in his opinion can secure a lasting peace. But his motives too appear in a questionable light. As his son Max suspects and as the last scene proves, he can expect a personal reward from the emperor. He betrays Wallenstein's complete confidence to achieve his goal and realizes too late that his action forever alienates his son, who believes in truthfulness and despises his father's cunning and deceit. Max passionately longs for peace and a better world, but one built upon the solid foundation of man's honesty and integrity: "My path must be straight." He feels that reforms of lasting value can only begin after the individual has learned to listen to the voice of his heart. Too late he realizes that neither his father nor Wallenstein live up to his ideal. The brief moments of happiness in his life, when Thekla, Wallenstein's daughter, responds to his love and stands firm with him in the midst of deception, are overshadowed by the knowledge of the impending disaster.

In the final confrontation between Max and Wallenstein man's purest impulses, symbolized by the voice of the heart, come into conflict for the last time with the will to power, broiled in the fires of hell and stranded in political quicksand. Wallenstein pleads with Max not to leave him while he still plays with the idea of seeing a crown on Thekla's head. Thus he demands that Max sacrifice his ideal while he himself is incapable of rising above his desires. Max, torn in agony, offers to stay if only Wallenstein would renounce his ambition. When it becomes clear that Wallenstein must follow his path to the end, Max, encouraged by Thekla, remains true to himself and to his ideal. He leaves in a scene in which Schiller captures the full horror of war, a scene in which all bright dreams turn to ashes and the force unleashed by man returns to scourge him: while Max struggles with himself and pleads with Wallenstein to look him into the eyes for a last farewell, his cavalry men take over the stage. The horns begin to call. More and more soldiers crowd into the action. As the music grows more challenging Max turns, is surrounded by his men and swept away. The theme of "Naenia" (1800), that beauty also must die, characterizes his death: the same evening he is killed in battle with all his men. As the horses trample him to the ground, the promise of a bright future for mankind fades away. What remains is Octavio, a dishonest, tired old politician facing a world without hope or beauty.

In *Mary Stuart* (1801)[17] Schiller underscores the idea that force and fraud poison the atmosphere not only in times of war, but whenever man lacks compassion. Implicitly he rejects the notion that man is the prisoner either of blind forces or of his own institutions, even if they seem to gain their own momentum and evolve a will or reality of their own. They reflect man's weakness or strength. At the same time the tragedy exposes the almost insurmountable difficulty of reconciling individual freedom with the interests of the community. The threats to individuality and liberty arise as much from persons who abuse their power (Leicester) or firmly believe that it is better to sacrifice an innocent person than endanger the state (Burleigh), as from the ever-changing public opinion. Shrewsbury, Queen Elizabeth's forthright and honest counselor, sees most clearly that it is especially the so-called general interest of the public and government which serves as an excuse for refraining from unpopular decisions or arriving at independent judgments. As opinions clash around Elizabeth, it becomes obvious that she alone must decide whether Mary Stuart, sentenced in the interest of the state, shall be executed or pardoned. Her decision demands complete integrity, freedom from hate and fear, and, above all, compassion. By focusing on Elizabeth's and Mary's personalities Schiller translates the political struggle into a human confrontation which enables him to develop his major theme of guilt and atonement.

The tragedy's opening scenes unmask Mary's real guilt. Dominated by wild passions, she had encouraged the murder of her second husband Darnley, had married his assassin Bothwell, and had forced Parliament to acquit him of the crime. After a nineteen years' imprisonment she is still haunted by guilt feelings and views her unjust detention and trial as a punishment meted out by fate for her offense. Indeed she seems composed and willing to accept the verdict, though she knows herself innocent of the accusation to have ignited the torch of civil war in the land. The sudden promise of liberation renews her inner turmoil. Indeed, the alternately rising and diminishing hope not only creates the mounting suspense in the play but enables Schiller to communicate Mary's inner experience and the ultimate triumph of her mind over hate, fear, and despair. Three possible roads for saving her open up: Mortimer offers to free her forcibly; Leicester, Elizabeth's suitor and confidant, can use his influence; finally Elizabeth may be moved by a personal plea. Mary discourages Mortimer, afraid that he will only lose his life like others before him; she believes that a meeting with Elizabeth who has never seen her, will soften the Queen's heart; but she expects the most from her appeal to Leicester's heart.

Elizabeth is deeply but only briefly touched by Mary's letter. Mary's disaster arouses her pity and fear. But she sympathizes more with herself than her suffering sister when she realizes that the same misfortune could have befallen herself. Urged by Leicester "to follow the soft dictates of her heart," she vacillates only to implore Mortimer in the next scene to murder Mary so that she may be relieved of the hated "duty" to sign the verdict. Though she views herself as a person who has sacrificed her whole life to the interest of the state, her attitude toward Mary is determined by strong emotional undercurrents of hate and envy. At the fateful meeting between the two queens, Elizabeth cannot rise above her emotions. She denigrates Mary, delights in her power, and is in turn humiliated by Mary, who is flushed by passion and pride. The violent clash of the two seems to infect the others with primitive emotions. Mortimer lusts after Mary and appears willing to kill his uncle in order to free her. But his plan as well as the attempted murder of Elizabeth is foiled. When Leicester, fearful for his own life, finally betrays Mary, her fate is sealed. Yet, Elizabeth's struggle between signing and not signing the death sentence continues. Overwhelmed by hate, she finally signs the document but refuses to the end to accept the full responsibility for her action. Mary on the other hand transcends herself before dying; ascending the last steps on the ladder of suffering, she gains true self-knowledge. She realizes that in the past the turmoil of the world had deafened the voice of the heart and that she failed again in the confrontation with Elizabeth because she could not renounce her pride. In the spirit of love she can even forgive Leicester and Elizabeth and becomes truly free in the hour of her death.

In Mary's apotheosis, the new ethos is clothed in Christian symbolism. But as she renounces the pleasures of the world as illusory, her victory becomes elusive to the living who are left with the picture of Elizabeth standing in tragic loneliness at the center of the stage—ruler of a world harder than granite. One wonders whether the spark of hope, albeit false, is not essential for man's self-realization. Perhaps the conscious acceptance of man's ultimate annihilation demands a heroism of such tragic dimensions as to make humane relationships impossible. Indeed, in the light of "Cassandra" (1802) and *The Maid of Orleans* (1801) such lives seem more cursed than heroic. Both blessed and cursed by a God to foresee the future, Cassandra clearly sees the inexorable end awaiting everyone. Whereas the others remain blind to the truth but enjoy the pleasures of the day, her knowledge dooms her to a somber, isolated existence: "Who can ever in life take pleasure,/ Once he has seen its dark abyss?" In her life, no room remains for the present. Though Joan of Arc seems tied to a world of battle and strife and almost exhilarated by the glory of her deeds, she is totally committed to the idea that she was chosen to execute God's will. Her mission, but also the knowledge that she will die once she has fulfilled it, sets her apart from the world. Possessed or inspired by her idea she destroys life like a demonic, fateful angel of revenge. She knows no pardon: "Why fear death? Fight and die!" She is touched only once by love. And as the fear that she has betrayed her cause seizes her, she loses her power. But when she conquers her emotion, she breaks all shackles, defeats the enemy, dies in a last great battle, and ascends to heaven. The audience can only wonder what thundering God has sent her. For her joyous acceptance of His will and her fate only nurtured a stern and ruthless post-Christian ethos that left no room for peace, love, or even compassion.

In *The Bride of Messina* (1803), a fierce tragedy of passion and murder, Schiller returns to man's struggle for light in the darkness of his own creation. More so than any other work this play leaves the impression that man's existential tragedy is determined by a malevolent fate and enigmatic Gods. Each character feels that he innocently suffers a curse: the many attempts to surmise the right course of action by seeking oracles or interpreting omens and dreams only lead to the conclusion that man cannot escape his destiny. "It is impossible/To reach to gods who dwell on high, just as/One cannot shoot an arrow to the moon./The future is from mortals walled apart/And no prayer penetrates the iron sky."[18] However, with the exception of Don Cesar in the hour of his death, everyone is unwilling or incapable of drawing the right conclusion from this insight: If the Gods are so distant that their commandments can no longer be heard, man has to shape his own destiny

178

and accept the full responsibility for his actions. Instead, the leading characters blindly follow their instincts, seize upon fortune's pawn as guarantee for ultimate success, and denounce the "demon envy" and fate when disaster finally strikes. Thus it can be argued that all attempts of the dramatis personae to break the tragic curse are doomed because they pursue a path strewn with suspicion, deception, error, and guilt.

The plot is stark and simple. Conflicting interpretations of dreams prophesying the salvation but also the destruction of the family by a new-born daughter commence the chain of events. To stave off the impending disaster the father orders the child's death. The mother Isabella saves her daughter and hides her in a convent. Isabella's sons Don Manuel and Don Cesar, who have been feuding since childhood, meet Beatrice. Unaware that she is their sister, they both propose to marry her. On the joyous day of their reconciliation Don Cesar finds his brother with his sister and murders him in a jealous rage. Even after he knows the truth he persists in his passion and takes his own life. The closing scene shows a bereaved mother and sister in silent embrace.

The human situation in *The Bride of Messina*, reminiscent of other plays by Schiller, is one of conflict and tragic solitude. The brothers' feud is magnified in the war between their men. Though its origin dates back to childhood when they vied for their mother's affection and though Don Cesar's life is poisoned by the fear that his mother has always preferred his brother, the fight seems to express a primitive instinct and need. The warriors themselves are undecided: peace beckons but war offers the extraordinary, a gamble with life, release of passion, unlimited freedom, and honor. What they fail to see is that they are slaves to their emotions and, unable to reflect upon their motives, are forever fearful of fortune's changing tide. Thus Manuel who is loved by Beatrice remains apprehensive and finally abducts her to insure his success. Don Cesar, overpowered by compulsive passion for Beatrice when he briefly sees her at his father's funeral, haughtily declares her his wife when he finds her again in order "to seize the chance and ward off demon envy." This deep-seated fear, contrasting strangely with the iron will of the brothers, bears the evil fruit of secrecy and dishonesty which blights the whole family. Isabella, also afraid of demon envy, never told her sons that their sister was alive. Beatrice grows up unaware of her true identity. When Isabella informs her sons on the day of their reconciliation, they are preoccupied with their own secrets. After all, each hopes to bring his bride, whose name he does not know. Furthermore, Don Manuel had concealed his name from Beatrice, an action which has clouded their pure relationship. And Beatrice shares his guilt by fearfully remaining silent that she attended their father's funeral where a stranger had fallen in love with her. Her secrecy delays Don Manuel's discovery that she is his sister at the most critical point when the truth might have prevented his murder.

Any true human relationship based on honesty and love would be impossible in this atmosphere, in which everyone is fearful, preoccupied with his own desires, and essentially alone. Beatrice expresses the feeling of the tragic solitude that envelops all when she sees herself as "a leaf torn from the tree and flung into the world" which she cannot comprehend. This world is not ready for Isabella's plea: "Dare to look into your eyes." For to see man as brother requires honesty, self-knowledge, and love. Don Cesar's fratricide only gives finality to the existing situation. However, he accepts the full responsibility for his deed and atones for it with his death. As in Schiller's other tragedies, man's failure to realize the ideal of a humane existence has led to destruction.

The skeptical audience may wonder how a universal brotherhood of men can be effected in a basically evil world or how an honest relationship between two persons could exist if one persists in his egotistical ways. Of perhaps more immediate concern is the question of what happens when a peaceful people who are willing to listen to the voice of their hearts are threatened and coerced by unethical and powerful individuals. Schiller probes these and related issues in *William Tell* (1804), his last completed play. His answer is clearly not that of a pacifist who would forgive his enemy and gladly suffer at the stake. Instead Tell's action shows that if man desires to shape his destiny in accordance with his ideal he must eliminate the evil menacing him by force, if all peaceful recourse has been exhausted.

In a series of scenes Schiller portrays how the "hand of tyranny" oppresses the land. Imperial bailiffs and burgraves try to impose the Austrian rule, upon the Swiss people. In the hope of breaking the people's will to remain free they finally resort to terror. No one seems to be safe from their brutality and arbitrary interpretation of the laws: homes are invaded; women are no longer safe; a father is blinded for his son's minor transgression of the law; a hat, symbol of the Austrian rule is erected in the town square and is to be revered by all men; finally, the bailiff Gessler gambles with a child's life to bring Tell and with him the land to their knees. Gessler severs all "bonds of nature" when he asserts his monstrous will, leaving Tell no choice but to aim at the apple on his son's head. Tell pleads with Gessler and offers to pay with his life for his disobedience of the new rule to salute the hat. But Gessler enjoys his gamble and persists: "You will die *with* the boy unless you shoot. . . . I do not want your life, I want this shot." Schiller shows ever so carefully that Tell's further action is not based on revenge but the conscious recognition that Gessler must be eliminated because he is an enemy not just of freedom, but of life itself. Tell acts in the same spirit which had characterized the meeting of the Swiss people under the bright stars when they looked up to the symbols of a universal order and swore to restrain themselves with sword in hand, prevent bloodshed, and simply drive the tyrants away.

But Gessler's demand far surpasses all other tyrannical acts. When he taunts Tell with the words "A man cannot complain of a harsh sentence,/When he is made the master of his fate," he strikes at the very root of man's ability to choose the right path; for Tell has lost all freedom to act in accordance with his beliefs. Tell, consistently portrayed as a person who extends his helping hand to others, cannot sacrifice his son and must risk his life to save him. Thus Gessler not only transgresses all laws of morality but also tries to destroy man's inner freedom and identity. The "new law" of which Gessler speaks when Tell's arrow strikes him, the law he *wills* is one under which man has become an object without human emotions. Tell's monologue before the deed clearly shows that he must kill Gessler to protect himself, his children, his wife, but above all, the soul of humanity. The Parricida scenes comparing Tell's action with a murder that originated from passionate, egotistical desires simply mirror Tell's innocence once more. He can raise his "hands freely up to heaven" knowing that he restored man's hope for a humane existence.

Goethe, fascinated by the Tell legend, had originally planned to write an epic poem on the subject. In the year after Schiller's death he thought about the project again but finally abandoned it, just as he had to resign himself to his inability to complete Schiller's *Demetrius* fragment. The differences between the two authors in conception and execution of a work were too great.

Still their works show a common perspective of the challenge confronting man as well as similarities in themes and even imagery that give Classicism its unifying features. The questions raised are still with us today. They indicate that this literature was born of a crisis in man's self-knowledge. Once the assurance which theoretical knowledge had provided in the preceding century had been dissipated, man had to search for a new basis of his existence. The answers given by Goethe and Schiller were not restricted to a simple faith in the good, true, and beautiful, but opened up new vistas that were, for instance, further explored in our century by Thomas Mann, C. G. Jung, and Martin Buber. Of special concern for us should be the idea which Goethe and Schiller set forth in so many of their works: Man cannot realize his self, liberate himself from the forces threatening his inner freedom, or become really civilized until he has become conscious of his motives and has the courage to accept life and live with his brother.

6. Romanticism 🖋

Raymond Immerwahr

In the history of European literature German Romanticism plays a paradoxical role. It is the original Romantic movement, the creator of the Romantic[1] literary and critical program, and the most thoroughly Romantic movement of the Western world. Nevertheless, it represents a less radical break with its immediate precursors than is the case with other European Romantic movements. The key to this paradox lies in the fact that the great revival or regeneration associated with Romanticism elsewhere had been initiated in Germany by earlier writers and movements: Hamann, Herder, Goethe, Schiller; Storm and Stress and Classicism. Indeed, from a wider European perspective German Classicism and Storm and Stress belong to the international Romantic movement as much as German Romanticism. Until fairly recently, a Frenchman or Englishman asked to name a German Romanticist would have been more likely to mention Schiller or Goethe than Novalis. Moreover, there are three writers in the chronological period of German Romanticism—the most widely read and influential novelist, the greatest philosophical lyric poet, and the one great dramatist (Jean Paul Richter, Hölderlin, and Kleist)—who cannot unequivocally be classed as Romanticists but who are far too important for us to ignore.

German Romanticism shares some important tendencies with both Storm and Stress and German Classicism:

1) a recognition of the non-rational elements in the human personality as elements and sources of poetic creation;

2) the conviction that individual artistic creations as well as entire national cultures grow from within according to organic principles analogous to those governing plants and animals but, like the latter, are conditioned by their environment;

3) an emphasis on sensuous imagery and a tendency to use images as symbols with indefinite ranges of connotation;

4) a conviction that the artist or poet has or ought to have a constructive influence on culture and society.

Romanticism resembles Classicism more than Storm and

Stress in its conviction that artistic creation requires an interaction of intuitive inspiration and the conscious, formative intellect. But in the following tendencies Romanticism is closer to Storm and Stress: first, an interest in the historic past of Germany; second, a predilection for folk literature; third, a tendency to see human life, cultural history, and artistic creation as striving toward an infinite, never fully attainable goal.

Another tendency, incipient in both Storm and Stress and Classicism but much more pronounced in Romanticism, is the affirmation of antithesis, paradox, and incongruity as principles of life, culture, and artistic creation. This tendency, known as "Romantic Irony," is observable in all the Romantic movements but most strikingly in German Romanticism. An important aspect of it is the special Romantic relationship of intuition and consciousness: In addition to forming and curbing the inspiration out of which the work of art grows, the Romantic intellect consciously reflects upon the whole creative process, and the author expects this of the reader. The emotional experience of the work is at one moment intensified, at the next interrupted, by conscious reflection. This is the special sense in which Romantic literature is "subjective." But there is also a special quality to Romantic irrationality: The Romanticist tends to be a dreamer, giving himself over to his free associations and allowing his visions to merge with sensory perception and even religious experience. He is inclined to fuse rather than differentiate consciousness, the sub-conscious, the external world, and what he may feel to be ultimate reality.

The German Romanticists transformed the popular notion of the Romantic into a highly sophisticated, albeit complex and amorphous, critical concept. In the Middle Ages words like *roman, romaunt, romance,* were used to describe narratives designed for popular entertainment and, for that reason, written in the vernacular *Romance* languages instead of Latin.[2] Such literature imitated in the Germanic languages was still denoted by these terms. The famous German courtly verse epics and their French prototypes were part of this tradition, as were the English romances of King Arthur and his Round Table. Such books were rambling in structure and full of incredible deeds and adventures. But from the thirteenth through the sixteenth centuries courtly verse romance degenerated into even more extravagant and artistically cruder prose romances and chapbooks suiting the tastes of the new and much larger middle-class reading public. Meanwhile, in Italy and Spain romance was again taken up in both verse and prose by more sophisticated authors, who consciously indulged and more or less subtly satirized its extravagance and incongruity. The most famous examples are the *Mad Roland* (*Orlando Furioso*) of Ariosto (1474–1533) and the *Don Quixote* of Cervantes (1547–1616).

The word "romantic" was coined in England in the year 1650 to mean fictional or fictitious, but it was almost immediately extended to any person, situation, or event in any way reminiscent of romances. Although the word was first applied in a derogatory sense, it quickly took on favorable connotations as well. If the reading of romances was a dangerous habit, it was nonetheless a delightful one, and so was the indulgence of romantic tendencies in life. Soon also a great variety of attractive or interesting scenes in the landscape came to be felt as romantic, partly because they reminded the viewer of scenes in romances, partly because of his feeling that they had an analogous effect upon his imagination and emotions. Reading extravagant romances and viewing lush, wild, and contrasting landscapes liberated the imagination and met deep emotional needs that were not satisfied by the formalized and rigidly ordered society of the eighteenth century. This also accounts for the special popularity of the literature of travel and exploration, which took its readers to strange, distant, and exotic lands and introduced them to emotionally spontaneous, primitive peoples, often applying the word "romantic" to such contexts.

The enjoyment of wild, irregular, varied, and contrasting scenes in the natural landscape soon came to be reflected in gardening and landscape architecture. A new informal style of gardening stressing these qualities and their subjective enjoyment by the viewer developed in England before the middle of the eighteenth century and shortly afterwards spread to the continent.[3] In gardens and in scenes of the natural landscape the most striking contrasts of quiet pastoral and wildly sublime beauty were felt to be especially romantic. Since literary and historical associations could enhance the romantic appeal of any scene, it became fashionable to install imitation Gothic ruins, artificial grottoes, "hermitages," Greek temples, and Chinese pagodas; garden emblems like these became favorite symbols in the literature of Romanticism.

All of these developments tended to enrich the aesthetic values associated with the word "romantic" and to enhance its prestige. More importantly the term was extended to cultural history about the middle of the century, first in England but within a few years in Germany as well. The Middle Ages, long deemed an era of "Gothic" savagery, now came to be recognized as an age of chivalry, lofty idealism, adventurous action, beautiful folk poetry, and heroic "bardic" epics. The English cultural historian Thomas Warton conceived the idea that the most romantic aspects of medieval culture and literature had been imported from the Orient, an idea quickly taken over by Herder. In this way the romantic associations of the Middle Ages were enhanced by those of the mysterious and exotic Orient. Attention also began to be directed to medieval institutions and ideals surviving in primitive societies of modern Europe, such as the clans of the Scottish Highlands and Hebrides. The vogue for primitive and medieval folk poetry made possible the most sensational and influential literary forgery of all time: the publication in 1760 by James Macpherson of melancholy and sentimental prose poems allegedly translated from the songs of a medieval Scottish bard named Ossian.

All these developments are reflected in a characteristic psychological and aesthetic pattern observable in the context of the word "romantic" in England and Germany in the latter part of the eighteenth century. What is romantic is not merely a quality of the object contemplated but a special relationship involving the contemplating viewer, the intervening visual medium and spatial or temporal perspective, and the contemplated object. The object—a character, landscape, cultural epoch, or region—may seem endowed with grandeur, power, intense energy, luxuriant vitality, variety, irregularity, change, and paradoxical incongruity. Obscurity or dazzling radiance in the intervening visual medium enhances these qualities in the imagination of the viewer, as do suggestions of remoteness in space or time. His imagination is set off, so to speak, on a boundless flight and he is cast into a state of tremulous emotion—yearning, melancholy, or a pleasurable horror.

When the German loan-word *romantisch* first emerged around 1700, its connotations were derogatory. But in the 1760's translations of English travel literature and the emulation of the English style of informal gardening familiarized German readers with the favorable connotations of the word as applied to landscape. At this period the concept of the romantic Middle Ages was being taken over from English cultural historians by Gerstenberg, Wieland, and Herder. Writers of this period tend to use the word with an ironic ambivalence. They considered their own enlightened culture superior to the Middle Ages but had a feeling that medieval culture was somehow aesthetically more satisfying than theirs. In Wieland especially, one also notes the interplay of derogatory and favorable connotations that the word had carried in England almost from the beginning. He considered the indulgence of romantic imagination, idealism, and mysticism a peril to reason and to a well-ordered, happy life, but he himself could not help being fascinated by them.

Before turning to the first generation of German Romanticists, we must devote some attention to two of their contemporaries, Friedrich Hölderlin (1770–1843) and Jean Paul (1763–1825). Hölderlin is the greatest philosophical poet of German literature. His odes and hymns in ancient Greek lyric forms bring to culmination a tradition developed especially by Klopstock and Schiller, revived more recently in varied forms by poets like Rilke. The last half of Hölderlin's life was passed in hopeless mental illness; but the transitional period in which his psychosis was first becoming manifest, the first few years of the nineteenth century, was the time of his supreme poetic achievement. Hölderlin's profound admiration for ancient Greek culture, his striving for formal perfection, and above all the humility and resignation with which he came to accept human limitations generally and his own tragic destiny are classical. With the Romanticists he shares a belief in the supreme mission of the poet in relation to the culture of his age and a feeling that the state of this culture—the rationalism, utilitarianism, pettiness, and insensitivity of both middle-class and court society—made the poet's mission desperately urgent.

But Hölderlin differs from the Romanticists in the tragic tone of his creation and of his attitude toward life. At least in the early German Romanticists, one notes a soaring faith in the ability of poetry and even criticism to regenerate culture. Hölderlin believed that such regeneration would be accomplished, but he was not sure when and had increasing doubts in his own ability to contribute to it. Nor did he share the view of the brothers August Wilhelm and Friedrich Schlegel and Novalis that poets and critics could accomplish this task through their own energies. He believed rather in a historic destiny which brings cultural regeneration at the appointed time but then also brings cultural decay. In other words, the early Romanticists' view of cultural history is chiliastic[4], that of Hölderlin is cyclical.[5] He calls the civilization of ancient Greece from Homer to the age of Pericles a "Day." Later antiquity and the Christian era up through the eighteenth century he regards as a "Night." However, he sees signs of an approaching dawn in the social, political, and military upheavals resulting from the French Revolution as well as in the philosophical and literary revolutions currently taking place in Germany. In some of his great odes he expresses the hope that Germany may play a decisive role in ushering in the new Day.

Hölderlin's cyclical view of history is one aspect of his mythic view of nature and life, which though it may appear at first sight to be a revival of ancient Greek mythology, is in fact new and profoundly personal. Hölderlin experienced nature as alive, and he symbolized this experience in divine forces. In eras of cultural Day man is in active, harmonious communion with the gods; in eras of Night they are withdrawn from his view and he is out of touch with them. The foremost of these divine forces, the Father god, is Aether, the spirit manifest in the life-giving air but also in the lightning bolt that may bring death as well as inspiration. The Earth is a Mother goddess, herself in loving union and interaction with the Father. The Sun brings light and inspiration to cultures and poets; the Moon brings rest, dreams, consolation, and the stirrings of new cultural growth during the Night. Sometimes, to be sure, the names of ancient Greek gods are transferred to Hölderlin's deities, especially Zeus (for Aether) and Apollo or Helios. Love is not a special god or goddess but a universal force manifest in all the gods and in man. If cultures are closest to these gods in eras of Day, the individual is closest to them in childhood and in love:

> Once when I was a boy
> A saviour spared me
> From the clamor and violence of men:
> And safe and serene I
> Played in the flowering grove,
> The airs of the heavens
> Played over me.[6]

Hölderlin's first work, the poignantly beautiful novel *Hyperion* (1797–1799),[7] has a heroine named Diotima, a woman of modern Greece who is loved by the titular hero, a young revolutionary. Diotima is a personality of complete beauty, in harmony with herself, her fellowmen, and the divine forces in nature. In loving her, Hyperion, who is otherwise restless and turbulent, partakes of this harmony and feels its healing influence. Like most of Hölderlin's important creations, *Hyperion* underwent several drastic revisions, but the heroine acquired these qualities and was given the name just *before* Hölderlin met the woman who was to be his great personal love and who was to be called Diotima in his lyric poetry. What is more, we can verify from her own letters to him that the personal Diotima, Susette Gontard, was in reality precisely the kind of complete, harmonious, and cultivated personality that Hölderlin had conceived in his fictional heroine. Unfortunately, she was the wife of a banker in Frankfurt and the mother of several children; as their tutor Hölderlin lived in the Gontard household for about a year and a half in 1797 and 1798. His position became untenable because Gontard was totally unable to appreciate the sensitivity of Hölderlin's personality and the cultural contribution he was giving the children. He treated Hölderlin simply as a household servant. This and the hopelessness of his love led to Hölderlin's departure and, not long afterwards, to the breaking off of all contact with Susette. Here again, biographical events were anticipated by the novel: Just as Hyperion and the Greek Diotima are separated and she shortly afterwards dies; so Susette Gontard died a few years after Hölderlin's departure, just at the time when Hölderlin was suffering his first severe onset of mental illness.

The novel *Hyperion* and the tragedy *Empedokles* (of which Hölderlin wrote three quite different fragmentary versions during the last three years of the eighteenth century) approach the problem of the prophetic leader's relation to society from almost opposite directions. Hyperion fails in the attempt to lead the modern Greeks through regeneration to a successful revolution, but in spite of this failure and Diotima's death he wins through to a higher level of insight. Empedokles was an ancient Sicilian philosopher-poet who, according to legend, cast himself into the crater of Aetna. Hölderlin interprets the legend to mean that Empedokles attempted to lead the Sicilians according to his own prophetic vision but identified himself too closely with the gods and had to expiate this hubris with a sacrificial death. Although each of Hölderlin's three dramatic frag-ments conceives this problem quite differently, we can say that, whereas the emphasis of the novel is on the shortcomings of the people, that of the tragedy is on the high responsibility of the leader. A similar shift of perspective may be seen in the development of Hölderlin's lyric poetry from about 1795 to 1803. The poem "Applause" ("Menschenbeifall"), for instance, still written when he was living with the Gontards, reflects both the ennobling influence of his love for Diotima and his despair of any understanding from the public. But in the great odes and hymnic poems written in the

189

first few years of the nineteenth century the poet wrestles with the question of his own fitness for the prophetic mission of proclaiming the advent of a new cultural Day, with the fear that he may be stricken by the gods for false or premature prophecy.

During these years Hölderlin drew closer to Christianity and attempted to reconcile his personal religion with it. Doing justice to the earthly mission of Christ is the central concern of "Patmos" and several other poems, such as "Bread and Wine," "The Only One" ("Der Einzige"), and the long and enigmatic "Peace Festival" ("Friedensfeier"), the complete text of which was finally discovered in 1954. In these poems Christ is recognized as a god or demi-god of the same order as Hercules and Dionysos. Like Dionysos, he was sent by the higher deities to prepare man for the long Night that was beginning to fall and to strengthen him with the sacramental bread and wine. Christ cannot supplant Father Aether, but Hölderlin feels that the devout study of the Christian Scriptures may be the highest duty of man during the long Night of the Christian era. And so, at the end of "Patmos," Hölderlin considers how he, as a German poet, may prepare for the return of the supreme gods in the new Day by fostering Christian tradition.

During the first half of 1802 Hölderlin had a tutorial post with a German family in Bordeaux. He returned home that summer suffering from acute schizophrenic symptoms, which were, to be sure, intermittently relieved during the next few years. The impressions of the southern French landscape are preserved in "Remembrance" and in the first strophe of another poem which sums up succinctly the tragic significance of this mid-point of Hölderlin's life:

"The Half of Life"

Laden with yellowing pears
And with wild roses filled
Lies the land in the sea:
Beautiful swans,
Drunk with your kisses you
Dip your heads in the
Saintly sobering water.

Alas, where can I find, when
Winter arrives, the flowers? Where
The light of the sun

And the shadows of the earth?
The walls arise
Speechless and cold: in the wind
Clatter the banners.[8]

Hölderlin's position in German literature is so unique that his relation to any one literary movement seems irrelevant. The case is quite different with the novelist, Johann Paul Friedrich Richter, who called himself Jean Paul. Although several years older than most of the early German Romanticists, he is close to them in spirit and style, a fact clearly recognized by their greatest critical spokesman, Friedrich Schlegel. Personal circumstances and Jean Paul's tremendous popularity as a novelist, which made the Romanticists proper, both envious and distrustful, have prevented his full recognition as part of the Romantic Movement. The success of his novels—of which *Hesperus* (1795), *Siebenkäs* (1796 f.), *Titan* (1800 ff.), and *Adolescence* (*Flegeljahre,* 1804) are the most important—is all the more remarkable in view of their length, their extremely involved style, and the bizarre humor depending in large part on displays of strangely inconsequential erudition. In twentieth-century Germany, Jean Paul is quoted a great deal more than he is read, but his contemporaries revelled in the involved wit, lofty idealism, and tearful sentiment of his books. Jean Paul combined two traditions, both of which were introduced into European literature by Laurence Sterne (1713–1768): the cultivation of sentiment (*A Sentimental Journey through France and Italy,* 1768) and the deliberately bewildering involvement, confusion, and interruption of the narrative line (*The Life and Opinions of Tristram Shandy,* 1760–1767). Jean Paul's use of the latter technique is illustrated by the complete titles of some of his novels and by the different terms used to designate chapters in each. *Hesperus oder 45 Hundsposttage* (*Hesperus or 45 Canine Mail Deliveries*) takes its title from the conceit that the author is writing the book on an island from manuscript materials carried to him by a spitz who swims over each day from the mainland.

Jean Paul's characters tend to fall into certain types: starry-eyed young idealists, profoundly wise sages, decadent voluptuaries, cynical sycophants, and whimsical eccentrics. A common feature is the pairing of either similar or contrasting characters: the idealistic Albano (the "Titan") and the depraved Roquairol; the two eccentric friends, Siebenkäs and Leibgeber, who exchange identities when

Siebenkäs fakes death to escape from a tedious wife; the respectively experienced and naive brothers Walt and Vult (short for Gottwalt and Quod Deus Vult) in *Adolescence*. Such pairs tend to suggest the duality of the human personality, foreshadowing the alter egos (*Doppeltgänger*) appearing in some of E. T. A. Hoffmann's work. Jean Paul is preoccupied with the contrast of earthly existence and the Hereafter, which he depicts ecstatically but in fairly traditional Christian terms. His idealists feel themselves to be outcasts on this earth; in dreams and visions they enjoy rapturous moments of reunion with departed friends and lovers. The author also likes to symbolize his aspirations in daring literal metaphors: characters soar from the earth in balloons to anticipate their experience of immortality or float from one point to the next to look down upon a variety of petty earthly concerns in proper perspective. A boy is made to spend his childhood in darkness so that when he first sees the light of day he will have a foretaste of his ultimate awakening from earthly life to immortality. Behind the intense fervor of the episodes concerned with immortality we sense an anxious insecurity in the author's faith. Its most remarkable expression is "The Dead Christ's Speech Down from the Firmament That There Is No God," in which Jean Paul depicts the desolation and meaninglessness of a life without faith.

Whereas Jean Paul derives ideologically and emotionally from German Pietism, stylistically from the eighteenth-century novel, the German Romanticists of the early Berlin-Jena group derive intellectually from the critical idealism of Kant; their literary and artistic ideals are derived from the Middle Ages and the Renaissance, and to a considerable extent also from German Classicism. The principal members of this circle were Wilhelm Heinrich Wackenroder (1773–1798) and Ludwig Tieck (1773–1853), both of Berlin; the brothers August Wilhelm and Friedrich Schlegel (1767–1845, 1772–1829), born in Hannover and active at this period (1797–1802) in Berlin, Jena, and Dresden; F. E. D. Schleiermacher (1768–1834), a pastor and theologian active at this time in Berlin; the Kantian philosopher F. W. J. Schelling (1775–1854), at this period a professor in Jena; Friedrich von Hardenberg (1772–1801), known as Novalis, member of an old aristocratic family in central Germany, employed as a mining official in an area near Jena. The two most important women of the circle were Karoline (1763–1809), wife of August Wilhelm Schlegel and later of Schelling, and Dorothea Veit, daughter of the Jewish philosopher

Moses Mendelssohn, mistress and later wife of Friedrich Schlegel. Everybody in this group had close personal ties with the others except for Wackenroder, Tieck's boyhood friend, who died too young to meet any of the others. Most of them were together in Jena a good part of the time around the turn of the century.

Wackenroder was the principal author of the first critical manifesto of Romanticism, *Herzensergießungen eines kunstlieben-den Klosterbruders* (*Outpourings from the Heart of an Art-Loving Friar*, 1796–1797), a work that applies Romantic principles, not to literature, but to painting and music. Tieck who also contributed a few chapters published a sequel, *Fantasies on Art* (1799), after Wackenroder's death.

Wackenroder introduces his work by assuming a role singularly appropriate to his own sensitive, shy, and retiring personality. The ostensible author is a humble Catholic friar who has become interested in art, read some sixteenth- and seventeenth-century writings on the Renaissance painters and has withdrawn from the bustle of the world to write these sketches. He approaches art and the artists in a spirit of reverent awe, rejecting the coldly critical analysis of eighteenth-century art criticism. The first essay, "Raphael's Vision," demonstrates (by Wackenroder's own apocryphal invention) that great art is directly—in this case miraculously—inspired by God, an idea ultimately derived from Plato. As in a musical composition, this initial theme of the book soon becomes interwoven with other, equally important themes. Two of the essays are devoted directly to such themes rather than to individual artists: "A Few Words on Universality, Tolerance, and Humanitarianism in Art" and "On Two Marvellous Languages and Their Mysterious Power."[9] In the first of these the Friar contemplates the infinite variety and heterogeneity of art in a spirit of rapt admiration. Ultimately all artistic feeling emanates from God as "one and the same heavenly ray," he proclaims; but like light striking the variously polished surfaces of a multi-dimensional prism, this ray is refracted in the various zones of space and time into "thousands of different colors":

> Just as every mortal eye has a different image of the rainbow, so a different image of beauty is reflected from the surrounding world upon every eye. But the universal, original beauty, which we can name only in moments of transfigured perception and cannot dissolve into words, is shown only to Him who has made both the rainbow and the eye that sees it.[10]

It is precisely this affirmation of endless variety in mankind and in the world that characterizes the Romantic—as distinct from the Classicist—view of humanity.

The essay "On Two Marvellous Languages" is devoted to symbolism. The two "languages" are nature and art. God manifests Himself directly through His own creation in nature, and He has endowed the human artist with a sympathy enabling him to understand the various natural manifestations through which He speaks. But man cannot reduce the Divine language to rational terms; he can only "fold his hands in adoration." In art, however, God has given man a "hieroglyphic script" which can express the spiritual and super-sensory in inspiring visual images. This language of art "discloses to us the treasures in the human heart, directs our glance into our souls, and shows us the Invisible, everything novel, great, and Divine, in human form." The essay closes with a proclamation of a fundamentally aesthetic view of life and reality typical of Romanticism:

> Nature, or what a mortal eye can glimpse of nature, is like fragmentary oracles from the lips of Divinity. But if it is permissible to speak of such things in these terms, one might perhaps say that God may well view the whole of nature or the whole world in the same way that we view a work of art.[11]

Wackenroder's interest in Renaissance art and culture had been kindled on walking trips with Tieck in east central and southeastern Germany during university vacations. One such tour introduced them to the German art of the Middle Ages and the Renaissance preserved in the sculptural and architectural monuments of Bamberg and Nürnberg. In Bamberg these two north German Protestants also had their first sight of a Catholic religious procession with its synthesis of medieval and Baroque traditions. In 1796 they saw the great art treasures from the Italian Renaissance in the Dresden collection. Wackenroder's impressions of sixteenth-century Nürnberg are immortalized in the Friar's "Memorial to Our Venerable Ancestor Albrecht Dürer." The biographical approach of this sketch, with its stress on the simple virtues, reverence, and diligence of Dürer and the cultural integrity of sixteenth-century Nürnberg, is in some respects naive and uncritical. Nevertheless, this chapter, together with one on Leonardo, balances the mystic-intuitive bias of "Raphael's Vision" with a recognition of the part played in artistic creation by study, observation, even analysis. Aside from its contribution to interest in the German cultural heritage, the most significant element of this essay is its praise of the varied individuality of the human countenance and the concrete reality of man's environment that are manifest in Dürer's art. It thus anticipates a realistic current in European Romanticism generally, one which Friedrich Schlegel was soon to recognize in principle for literature but which was to enter into the literary creation of only the younger Romanticists.

The childlike simplicity of the Art-Loving Friar must not blind us to another side of his creator's personality, one that was sophisticated and complex, as we can see in the long semi-autobiographical sketch at the end of the collection: "The Remarkable Musical Life of the Composer Joseph Berglinger." Here, the dilemma of the Romantic artist clearly manifests itself. In order to enter upon his career as a musician, Berglinger must break all family ties and accommodate himself to the unhappy lot of the eighteenth-century musical director, dependent on the whims of princely patrons and a fickle public and subject to the debasing conditions of professional rivalry: "This bitter discrepancy between his innate ethereal enthusiasm and the earthly lot in the life of each human that forcibly drags him down from his dreams each day tormented him throughout life." But additional obstacles to fulfillment are imposed by the art itself. The composer must mold his inspiration into the rigid forms of an artistic "grammar": the laws of harmony. At the moment of his greatest professional triumph, Berglinger again comes in contact with his family, to find his sister in rags and his father dying: "Why did Heaven ordain that his whole life long he was to suffer from the conflict between his ethereal enthusiasm and the base misery of this earth, a conflict which was finally to tear apart his dual being of body and spirit?" For Wackenroder himself, there was no solution to this basic predicament of Romantic artistry, and like Berglinger he was destroyed by it, for he lacked the ability of the great Renaissance artists to "weave his lofty visions boldly and firmly into the fabric of this earthly life."

Ideas of Berglinger on music as the symbolic language of human emotion are further developed in Wackenroder's contributions to the *Fantasies*. But the most interesting piece in this latter collection is the "Marvellous Oriental Tale of a Naked Saint." Although this tale may just possibly have been written by Tieck, it beautifully symbolizes Berglinger-Wackenroder's view of the artist's predicament. The Saint suffers from the delusion that he hears the incessant roaring of the Wheel of Time and is condemned to keep turning it. Anyone who comes near and distracts him with other activity drives him into murderous rage. One beautiful moonlit evening two lovers come down the river, and an ethereal music resounds from their boat. At the sound of this music, the figure of the Saint is seen dancing up into Heaven. Music, love, and the magic of the moonlight have liberated him from his maddening enslavement to the conditions of temporal existence.

Ludwig Tieck, in some ways a more troubled and problematical temperament than Wackenroder, had a resiliency which his friend lacked. Throughout his career, he worked to stimulate German familiarity with the Elizabethan dramatists. He became editor of the Shakespeare translation begun by August Wilhelm Schlegel, translated *Don Quixote,* and wrote numerous excellent novellas.

Tieck's most original contributions to Romanticism were in the genre of the psychological art tale and in the fantastic comedy. But even where he is least original, he is one of the best examples of the links between Romanticism and the imaginative popular fiction from which the word "romantic" had been derived. He first revived the German versions of the old prose romances of chivalry, some as free adaptations in modern German, some in new treatments of the same material in both prose and dramatic form.

Tieck's remarkable ability to adapt his talents to the spirit and style of other writers is evident in his contributions to the works conceived by Wackenroder. Before Wackenroder's death, he and Tieck jointly projected a novel on the German sixteenth century, the fictitious biography of a student of Albrecht Dürer. Wackenroder did not live to collaborate in this work, *Franz Sternbalds Wanderungen (The Wanderings of Franz Sternbald,* 1798), and Tieck never quite finished it. It is interesting to observe the gradual shift in its spirit from the idealistic reverence of Wackenroder toward erotic hedonism. It is the first novel to give vent to the ideal of free wandering as an expression of the untrammeled spontaneity of the Romantic imagination. Tieck's friend Friedrich Schlegel, generally one of his more severe critics, acclaimed *Sternbald* as the first truly romantic creation since Cervantes. What appealed to Schlegel was an indefinable aura which he could only compare to the hazy atmosphere over a landscape painting and the vibrancy aroused in the soul by music.

But Tieck had already written one important novel before

this, *Geschichte des Herrn William Lovell* (*The History of Mr. William Lovell*, 1793–1796). Inspired by an eighteenth-century French popular novel, it belongs to the tradition of horror literature but is essentially an original work and one more deeply personal than *Sternbald*. Published virtually at the same time as Goethe's *Wilhelm Meister*, it is a novel of development in reverse, an account of the progressive moral disintegration of a human personality that has fallen prey to persons diabolically conspiring to that end. But the corruption of Lovell is made possible by the moral vacuum existing in his soul: he doubts whether anything in life has meaning or value, and wonders whether reality exists either in the objective world or in the subjective soul. The novel, written at the dawn of German Romanticism, exposes the reverse side of what might otherwise appear to be the most idealistically affirmative of literary movements.

A similar fascinated horror at the mysterious depths of the human psyche runs through the art tale *Blond Eckbert*,[12] written a few months after *Lovell* was finished. When a publisher whom Tieck was supplying with pot-boilers and Gothic thrillers asked if he would soon have something new ready, Tieck pulled this title out of the air and then sat down to write the story in a few hours. The result was the most irrational and yet the most concentrated, authentic, and meaningful piece of writing ever to come from his pen.[13] *Blond Eckbert* and other tales by Tieck contributed to the tradition of the forest as the ideal setting for the German Romantic imagination. Growing up in a flat and sparsely wooded region, Tieck had been fascinated since childhood by images of forests and mountains; the landscapes of the Harz and of eastern Bavaria which he came to know as a university student gave substance to the paradisiac as well as to the terrifying aspects of the forest. In this story the forest and mountains appear as a domain of isolation from ordinary human society and as a refuge of the escapist poetic imagination, nourished by "spinning" and reading, inspired by images of beauty and richness.

Whereas *Eckbert* was written at a time when Tieck had no contact with other Romanticists except for Wackenroder, his later tales reflect the influence of Novalis, Friedrich Schlegel, Schelling, and other writers of the Romantic movement. *The Runenberg* (1802)[14] has similar but more readily interpretable symbolism. Its hero, Christian, is torn between a domestic, agrarian domain and a demonic realm of mountains, crags, and minerals, symbolized in a supernatural being who appears first as a man, then as a woman of stately beauty leading Christian to her subterranean castle in the Runenberg, later as an old hag. In the end Christian is won back to her domain by the seductive influence of gold, returning only briefly and in an insane state to see his now destitute family in the village. Although the nature of the conflicting drives in Christian's soul is much more, obvious, we are left wondering which of his loyalties are the right ones.

Tieck also wrote several comic and serio-comic adaptations of well known folk tales in dramatic form. His comedy *Puss-in-Boots* (*Der gestiefelte Kater*, 1797) made a drastic break with conventional eighteenth–century theatrical style and dramatic technique. Tieck and other Romanticists abhorred the sentimentality, shallow utilitarian ethics, bourgeois milieu and values, and trivial realism then popular on the German stage. The publication of a ponderous treatise praising among other things the histrionic style of a prominent actor inspired Tieck to make fun of all such contemporary theatrical foibles in this fairy-tale comedy. Tieck, extremely fond of the traditional German clown (*Hanswurst*) who had taken refuge in the puppet theater since his banishment from the legitimate stage by Gottsched, restored him in his comedy to his proper place. At the same time, Tieck's great familiarity with European theatrical literature convinced him that there should be something better than the tearful middle-class comedy with its slavish adherence to the "illusion" of a miniature reality on the stage. His *Puss-in-Boots* was intended to defy realism, plausibility, and "illusion," make fun of pathos and sentimental idealism, let the spectators' or readers' imagination play as freely as in a fairy tale, and above all arouse laughter rather than tears or sighs. The ostensible dramatic action is the familiar fairy tale from Perrault's French version, but this is only a play within a play. The frame or outer play is the theatrical world on both sides of the footlights: spectators and dramatic critics with the typical prejudices of the contemporary German theater, objecting even when characters from different countries understand each other's language, actors who repeatedly fall out of their roles, the terrified Poet, and the Property Man who tries to placate the audience with elaborate fire-and-water spectacles. In a mad climax the characters engage in a debate on the merits of this very play with the clown as the comic adversary. Tieck tried to outdo the nonsensical jest of this comedy in two sequels, which are even more irrational but less spontaneous; numerous other German writers emulated him in subsequent generations.

The brothers August Wilhelm and Friedrich Schlegel were primarily scholars and critics. The older brother made a monumental contribution to the German literary heritage in his superb translations—in prose and verse like the originals—of sixteen plays of Shakespeare between 1796 and 1801 and one more in 1809. Friedrich Schlegel, however, was more original as a critical thinker; he and his close friend Novalis must be considered the architects of the Romantic program.

Friedrich Schlegel substantially modified his critical ideas in the course of his career, but we shall limit ourselves to a few of his central concepts and tendencies in the period when he and August Wilhelm were preparing and editing their epoch-making literary and critical journal, *Das Athenäum* (1798–1800). The most important of these concepts was that of the "romantic" itself. Precisely because Friedrich Schlegel made the word *romantisch* the keystone of a critical and cultural movement, it must be made clear once and for all that *he did not apply this term primarily to himself, his friends or their program but to a past age and culture*. To quote from his *Dialogue on Poetry* (1799):

> This is where I look for and find the Romantic—in the older moderns, in Shakespeare, Cervantes, in Italian poetry, in that age of knights, love and fairytales in which the thing itself and the word for it originated.[15]

Friedrich Schlegel uses this adjective in a broad sense to distinguish the entire Christian era since the fall of the ancient Roman Empire from Greek and Roman antiquity. Nevertheless, at the time of this *Dialogue*, he sees the core of romantic culture and literature in the period extending from Dante to Shakespeare and Cervantes, about 1285 to 1620 A.D. A little later his historical concept of the romantic is expanded backward to include the lyric poetry and narrative romance of the eleventh and twelfth centuries and forward to encompass Pedro Calderón de la Barca (1600–1681). Subsequent modern literature ought to have remained romantic but in fact had not. This historical demarcation of the romantic from the ancient or classical age cannot be regarded as a rejection of classical culture. Friedrich Schlegel started his career as a scholar in ancient Greek and Roman literature and had very recently written important treatises in this field. He retained his love of ancient Greek literature but recognized comparable, though very different, merits in the literature of the romantic era. Ancient Greek culture and literature aimed at and briefly realized an ideal of complete beauty and harmony within circumscribed limits, then began to disintegrate. In contrast romantic culture and literature aspires to ideals which can never be realized precisely because they are boundless, "infinite." They could never become perfect but would always remain changing and "progressive," even though there are temporary aberrations and retrogressions. Such an aberration was the imitation of external features of ancient Greek literature practised by some writers of the Italian Renaissance, in seventeenth-century France, and throughout Europe in the eighteenth century. Friedrich Schlegel did not, however, reject classical values as such for modern times; his ultimate ideal was a synthesis of the classical and the romantic, a synthesis toward which he thought some works of Goethe, such as *Wilhelm Meister* and *Hermann and Dorothea*, were pointing. We could therefore say that Friedrich Schlegel's literary program for his own age was a synthesis of the poetic values of the romantic age with those of Goethe's.[16]

Friedrich Schlegel's historical concept of the romantic also has aesthetic and typological implications. Apart from the deliberately paradoxical aphorisms the most important references are to be found in the *Dialogue on Poetry*, particularly in the sections *Brief über den Roman* (*Letter on Romance*) and in a *Talk on Mythology*.[17]

In the *Letter*, Schlegel emphatically distinguishes between the *Romane* of the Middle Ages and the Renaissance (romances) and the *Romane* of the eighteenth century (novels). The former are treated almost ecstatically, the latter ironically. Schlegel's conception of the ideal romance was approximated from varying directions in the poetic creations of Dante, Petrarch, Ariosto, Boccaccio, Tasso, and Cervantes; its spirit, though not its form, was very closely approximated in the dramas of Shakespeare. It is a poetic work that encompasses all categories and rises above the prosaic concerns of everyday life through a suggestion of the ultimate, divine spirit which pervades, animates, and encompasses reality, a reality poetically so transfigured that it appears to us like the haze over a landscape painting and evokes a subtle musical vibrancy in the soul.

When the central section of the *Letter on Romance* proclaims: "That is romantic which presents a sentimental theme in a fantastic form," the sentimental element is precisely this reference to the Divine, the poetic spirit which the romantic poet senses within and above the phenomenal world. Schlegel most emphatically differentiates this sentimental quality from everything "maudlin and lachrymose." It is "not a sensual but a spiritual feeling. The source and soul of all these emotions is love, and the spirit of love must hover everywhere invisibly visible in romantic poetry."

The "fantastic form," on the other hand, is closely tied to Schlegel's principle of irony. The romantic poet knows that the spirit of divine love can only be dimly felt and imperfectly expressed by any human being. He is therefore aware of the limits of his creation as he creates and communicates his awareness to the reader, a feat accomplished by subtle exaggeration of these very limitations, by a paradoxically witty synthesis of antitheses manifest in the whole structure of his work, and by a playful treatment of his own artistic form. Typical examples are the deliberate exaggeration of the incongruities of romantic plot in Ariosto's *Orlando Furioso*, the whole structure, style, and spirit of *Don Quixote*, with its "charming symmetry of contradictions," its contrast between the impractical idealism of the hero and the earthy cunning of his squire Sancho Panza, and the reflection of this contrast in its episodically inserted novellas. In the art of painting, examples are afforded by the "grotesques" or "arabesques" that frame some murals by Raphael and other Italian Renaissance painters. The sportive play with human and animal forms in these borders makes the viewer more conscious of the materials with which the artist is working in the central painting and affords an ironic contrast to its serious content. Schlegel implies that there is something analogous to this arabesque technique in the great romances of the Renaissance, and his *Letter on Romance* itself has a playfully ironic double frame around its serious core.

Friedrich Schlegel believed that Shakespeare, whom his brother was translating at this time, was the most romantic of all poets. He and August Wilhelm both found in Shakespeare the all-important element of idealization, an awareness of the limitations and paradoxical incongruities of life and art, and a pronounced tendency to make the theater a subject of the play itself. Nevertheless, Friedrich Schlegel preferred narrative romance to drama. Even though no other romantic poet could equal Shakespeare, the book written to be read, he felt, has a greater romantic potential than the play intended to be performed; the author of a book can establish a more subtle and varied relationship with his readers than the playwright with an audience. *Don Quixote* comes closer than any one Shakespearean play to Schlegel's ideal of an all-encompassing poetic category with constant reference to the contrast between human limitations and the Divine ideal.

In most novels of the eighteenth century Schlegel finds little merit other than the unintentional comedy in the author's involuntary portrayal of his own foibles and those of his social milieu. The only way eighteenth-century novels could become romantic in such an "unromantic age" is by being "arabesques" or "grotesques." In adapting this concept to literature, Schlegel is thinking of a playfully rambling and inconsequential narrative line, analogous to the playful succession of figures in the borders of Renaissance murals; but he is also thinking of the particular kind of playing with the medium that occurs when the conditions of telling a story or writing and publishing a book get mixed up with whatever other content the work may have. His chief examples are the novels of Laurence Sterne, Jean Paul, and Denis Diderot's *Jacques le fataliste.* The tone of these sections of the *Letter,* both before and after the central portion on the literature of the romantic age, is ironic. The approach to Jean Paul might almost be called praise by loud damnation; certainly part of the damnation is ironic because Friedrich Schlegel was attracted by Jean Paul's arabesque technique more strongly than he was repelled by his lachrymose sentimentality.

Elsewhere Friedrich Schlegel also applies the term "arabesque" to the comedies of Aristophanes (to which he had devoted a laudatory essay a few years before),[18] also to *Puss-in-Boots* and other fantastic farces by Tieck. It is correct to associate these techniques with Friedrich Schlegel's famous principle of irony but misleading to equate the two concepts. He regarded irony as a universal principle. The irony of the great romantic poets and of great writers and thinkers in many different fields in all ages of man is a recognition of the paradox inherent in the infinite being manifest in finite forms. It is ironic for an infinite God to create a finite universe and for any one human being to communicate anything of universal significance from his particular niche in the phenomenal world to another individual occupying a different niche. Friedrich Schlegel did not invent or even discover irony; it was invented by God and discovered by Socrates. The principle is most clearly enunciated in two *Fragmente* a year earlier than those of the *Athenäum* and published in 1797 in another periodical:

Socratic irony is the only entirely involuntary and nevertheless completely conscious dissimulation. . . . It contains and incites a feeling of the insoluble conflict of the absolute and the relative, of the impossibility and necessity of total communication. It is the freest of all liberties, for it enables us to rise above our own self; and still the most legitimate, for it is absolutely necessary.

Philosophy is the true home of irony. . . . In this respect, poetry alone can rise to the height of philosophy. . . . There are ancient and modern poems which breathe, in their entirety and in every detail, the divine breath of irony. In such poems there lives a real transcendental buffoonery. Their interior is permeated by the mood which surveys everything and rises infinitely above everything limited, even above the poet's own art, virtue, and genius; and their exterior form by the histrionic style of an ordinary good Italian buffo.[19]

Irony is first of all a fact, or rather *the fact*, the predicament, of finite existence. It is secondly a feeling, a mood, a spirit. Externally it is manifest in myriad forms, styles, and techniques, all of which bear some analogy to the clown of Italian popular comedy making fun of theatrical portrayal. However, Schlegel's specific examples in literature (Goethe's *Wilhelm Meister*, the works of Boccaccio, Cervantes, and Shakespeare) make it evident that even outwardly irony can be expressed by more subtle techniques than the outright violation of so-called "illusion."

An equally important and even more famous part of the *Dialogue on Poetry* is the *Talk on Mythology*. For most eighteenth-century writers, mythology had been a dead relic of past cultures to be used as ornamentation. Friedrich Schlegel proclaimed mythology as the living sub-stratum of poetic literature. It expresses the fundamental beliefs, insights, and values of a culture in an organically unified symbolic complex. It is therefore the living ground from which each individual poetic creation draws its symbols. Every living culture must have its own mythology, not simply try to borrow bits of dead myth from the past. Schlegel saw signs that a new mythology was about to be born in his time. It would be, he thought, a mythic expression of the great new philosophical discovery of the age, Kantian philosophy, particularly in the Idealistic form given it by Schlegel's friend Johann Gottlieb Fichte (1762–1814), at the time a professor in Jena. Fichte's Idealism dispenses with Kant's *things-in-themselves*, the external source of our experience whose existence Kant was willing to adjust even though all we can know is the content, forms, and laws of our own minds. According to Fichte, the individual mind or ego creates or "posits" its own objective world, or non-ego, without any such outside help, thereby repeating within itself the process by which the Absolute Ego creates the whole physical universe. But Schlegel could see that Fichtean Idealism was too abstract to inspire mythic images, and he therefore forecast a new synthesis of this Idealism with the older Realism—as Schlegel calls it—of the seventeenth-century philosopher Spinoza (1632–1677), one in which the spiritual and physical worlds, what he called "Nature creating" and "Nature created" (*natura naturans* and *natura naturata*), were two sides of the same thing. Actually, such a synthesis was being provided at the time by F. W. J. Schelling (1775–1854), another philosopher who was even more intimately associated with the Schlegels and Romanticism than Fichte. Perhaps because he hoped to accomplish this philosophical mission more satisfactorily himself, Friedrich Schlegel consistently slighted Schelling's philosophical achievement. Schlegel was also unaware of the new mythology of Hölderlin, a fellow-student of both Schelling and Hegel.

Schlegel saw another potential source of mythological symbolism in the recent discovery by the Italian physicist Galvani (1737–1798) of electricity in the animal nervous system. The Romanticists thought that both the physical and psychological discoveries (hypnosis) of their age pointed to a common mystic life force or "magnetism" animating the physical, biological, and psychological realms. Although Schlegel's expectation of a new unified mythology common to all the poetry of the age was not to be realized, the *Talk on Mythology* justified and helped stimulate the development of new mythologies by individual poets.

Friedrich Schlegel's most important creative effort was a fragmentary novel, *Lucinde* (1799). This book evoked quite a scandal because it advanced theories of free love. What is more, it presented intimate details of the personal relationship of Friedrich with his mistress Dorothea Veit, also of the past loves and personal friendships of each. Whatever we may think of the literary achievement, the intent of this book is serious. It expresses a mystic vision of erotic love also found in Novalis, Blake, and Shelley. Two lovers becoming one in body and soul heighten to that extent their partaking of the ultimate unity of all being. But friendship of each with other men and women can bring them still closer to mystic union. In

form the novel is an arabesque. There is no consecutive narrative to
the book as a whole. Its various chapters taken together exemplify
the union of the greatest variety of literary forms: ecstatic monologue, dialogue, dream, revery, prose poem, retrospective narrative,
and so on. The shortcomings of this novel result from a lack of
judgment both in the treatment of personal relationships and in the
application of literary principles. The one Romanticist who grasped
the serious intent behind the book and publicly came to its defense
was the theologian F. E. D. Schleiermacher, a close personal friend
of Friedrich Schlegel. Schleiermacher was the founder of modern
liberal Protestant theology, a champion of complete freedom of
conscience, who centered religious experience in a feeling of personal dependence on God rather than in a creed, written Bible, or
Church. He published a book designed, as its long title indicates, to
make religion meaningful again to the intellectuals who had become
estranged from it: *Reden über die Religion an die Gebildeten unter
ihren Verächtern* (*Lectures on Religion to the Educated Atheists,*
1799).

Mystic union achieved through erotic love, the poetic transfiguration of personal experience, and the self-reflective treatment
within the poetic work of its underlying principles are prominent
features of the most remarkable and most profoundly mystical of all
the German Romanticists, Friedrich von Hardenberg, known as
Novalis.[20] He prepared himself by the study of law, accounting,
and mineralogy for service as an assessor of salt-mines in Thuringia,
an occupation which enabled him to be a frequent visitor in the
common household of August Wilhelm, Karoline, and Friedrich
Schlegel and Dorothea Veit in Jena around 1799. Having been
brought up in a somberly devout Pietistic home, he was delighted
when his work took him late in 1794 into another aristocratic
household animated by hearty warmth and social conviviality. Here
he fell in love with the stepdaughter of his host, Sophie von Kühn,
who at this time was not quite thirteen. Very soon they were engaged, but then Sophie became ill and in March, 1797, she died.
Before her illness Sophie had been a lively, spirited, and thoroughly
practical girl, not the least bit interested in mysticism or—for that
matter—literature. In the advanced stages of her illness she took on
a quality of ethereal beauty. However, her transformation in
Novalis's poetic work into a mystic being, the very spirit of cosmic
wisdom (the meaning of Greek *Sophie*) must be attributed entirely
to the poetic imagination of her bereaved fiancé. This process of

transformation may be observed in his letters even some weeks
before her death; but the central, crystallizing experience took place
on May 13, 1797, when he visited her grave and felt for a moment
that she was about to appear to him. This experience together with
impressions gleaned from *Romeo and Juliet,* Edward Young's
(1683–1765) *Night Thoughts,* also from Herder and Jean Paul,
inspired a *Hymn to the Night* in lyric prose:

> Once, as I . . . stood lonely by the barren mound which in
> narrow and dark room hid away the form of my life . . . , and
> clung to fleeting extinguished life with infinite yearning—then,
> out of blue distances, from the pinnacles of my old blessedness,
> there came a twilight shudder, and all at once the bond of birth
> broke the Light's fetters. . . . Thou Night-inspiration, slumber
> of heaven, didst come over me: the region gently rose aloft and
> over the region hovered my released and newborn spirit. The
> mound became a cloud of dust and through the cloud I beheld
> the transfigured features of my Beloved. In her eyes reposed
> eternity. . . . Millennia passed off into the distance, like storms.
> . . . It was my first and only dream, and since then only have I
> felt everlasting, immutable faith in the heaven of the Night and in
> its Light, the Beloved.[21]

The grave of Sophie has become a portal leading out of the
temporal world of Day into the eternal world of Night, illumined by
the light of her spirit. In the next two years, this poetic germ grew
into a cycle of six *Hymns to the Night* alternating between rhythmic
prose and verse. In them personal experience merges with mystic
philosophy and Christian imagery into a rich mythology. The most
important single philosophical source was the German mystic Jakob
Böhme, in whose writings Sophia figures as the Bride of the Soul,
bringing Divine Light to the reborn human spirit.

The theme of these *Hymns* is the antithesis between finite,
temporal Day and mystic, eternal Night; they are introduced by a
rhapsodic praise of Day, of the radiant beauty and endless variety of
the whole finite universe over which man reigns as glorious king.
Then the poet turns "to the holy, ineffable, mysterious Night." Now
the world seems far off, "sunken in a profound tomb." Although he
regrets the departure of Day and of the joys of earthly life, the poet
becomes aware of the deeper joys of the infinite Mother, Night. She
is at once the primal source of all being and the Virgin Mother of
Christ. She sends him his personal beloved as Sun of the Night. The

first hymn ends in a paean to Night as an eternal, mystic-erotic love death. In this lyrical prose, one image constantly flows into the next, each taking on ever new and wider symbolic connotations. Everything is at once aerial and ardently erotic. The unconsummated love for the earthly Sophie von Kühn has become an eternal Night of ecstasy. But the poet still lives on earth and returns each morning to the business of the Day.

The second hymn praises every experience of earthly existence that anticipates the mystic wonders of Night: the intoxication of wine, the influence of opiates, the maiden's readiness for motherhood. The third (chronologically original) hymn and the fourth are the core of the whole cycle. In the fourth, the gravemound of the poet's personal bereavement is transformed into the Holy Sepulchre; to it he has borne the Cross on a long and arduous pilgrimage. But the same gravemound also becomes a mountain range dividing temporal, finite existence from eternity: "Whoever has stood up there on the watershed of the world and gazed across into the new land, into the dwelling place of the Night—truly, he does not return to the doings of the world. . . ." Although the poet still observes the beauty of the earth, symbolized in the radiant clock of the sun, he looks forward to the time when that clock will point to the end of time, when the Cross will triumph.

In relating personal experience to Christian symbolism, Novalis gives a new interpretation of Christ's death: it demonstrated that the grave is the gateway to an eternally consummate love and mystic union. In the fifth and longest hymn, this new interpretation of Christian tradition is projected mythologically upon the history of human civilization: In ancient Greece the world was the home of the gods. The "all-kindling living Light" of the sun dwelt beyond the morning hills in the "womb of the sea." The life of man was a radiantly happy spring festival. Yet he was ruled by an ironic destiny; his soul was bound in a dark blindfold: the dread of death. As "the old world waned," its "pleasure garden" withered, the gods and their retinue departed. Man ceased to be childlike and attempted to solve the mysteries of space. Nature was left desolate, bound by the iron chains of rigid measure, the dry numbers of scientific intellect. The soul of the world withdrew to await the dawn of a new era in the depths of the human spirit.

The radiant beauty of ancient Greece giving way to a cold, desolate age of darkness reminds us of Hölderlin, but Novalis attaches a higher significance to Christ. With the advent of this "son of the first virgin and mother, infinite fruit of mystic embrace," the barren darkness of rationalistic late antiquity gives way to a new Christian Night which is "the mighty womb of revelations." The fifth hymn ends in rhymed verses celebrating the resurrection not from but *to death*, the Marriage of Cana which is a wedding of man with death. The sixth hymn, entirely in verse, expresses a plaintive longing both for the eternal Night to come and for the past age when Christ gave his sweet life for man. Its concluding images of mystic love—death fuse Sophie, Jesus, and the Virgin Mother into one.

Closest in spirit to the *Hymns* is a collection of *Spiritual Songs* (*Geistliche Lieder*) which became a living part of the German Protestant liturgy despite their undercurrents of eroticism, theosophical mysticism, and Catholic adoration of the Virgin. Novalis' most ambitious effort was the fragmentary novel *Heinrich von Ofterdingen*. Even if his work on it had not been cut off by his fatal illness, it is scarcely conceivable that his plan for its completion could ever have been realized, so cosmic is its scope, so mystically supernatural the projected action. The novel almost exemplifies Friedrich Schlegel's ideal of a universal romance combining lyric, dramatic, novellistic, and fairy-tale elements and opening up boundless vistas to the imagination. The completed first part however has a cohesive and concentrated structure with a well defined historical and geographical setting.

Heinrich von Ofterdingen (1802), the first Romantic work inspired by the High Middle Ages, has as a major theme the awakening and developing of the poetic imagination. Heinrich, age twenty, has glimpsed in a dream a blue flower with a face of a beautiful maiden in its chalice. The Blue Flower has become the central symbol of ineffable Romantic longing in German thought. In the novel it is a symbol of love and of ultimate mystic union with God but more importantly, it symbolizes the unifying and transfiguring function of poetry. Heinrich grasps the significance of the blue flower and sets out to fulfill his mission by finding it. Much like a musical composition, the first part of the novel progressively varies, develops, and expands its unifying theme: the mission of poetry in the world. This theme is central to two legends Heinrich hears as he journeys to Augsburg. The first tells of an ancient Greek bard, Arion, who, plundered and cast into the sea by sailors, so charms a sea monster that it carries him safely to shore where all his treasures are miraculously restored. The second tale also depicts the triumph of poetry and love. To the despair of his realm, the proud King of Atlantis, a patron of poetry, can find no suitor worthy of his daughter's hand. As the Princess rides in the forest one day, practising her songs, she meets a quiet, earnest youth who, with his father, devotes himself to the study of nature. Their love is consummated later in a grotto where they take refuge from a storm. The court, troubled before is now plunged into grief by her disappearance. One day a bard sings of the Golden Age when all beings were united by love, of the subsequent period of strife and hatred, and of a Golden Age to come. The court acclaims the singer who then sings a song of his own love. As he concludes, he lifts the veil from the woman beside him: the singer is the youth, the woman is the Princess who carries a beautiful child; the land becomes a festival of happiness. The youth's first song crystallizes the whole tale, which in turn summarizes the novel and, indeed, Novalis' total creation: love unites poetry and the study of nature; their union overcomes all strife and ushers in a new Golden Age.

As they travel, the group meets returning crusaders, whose song of the liberation of Christ's Tomb stirs Heinrich deeply. Yet he finds a captive Saracen woman even more fascinating; her accounts of her ancient, mysterious culture reveal that the Saracens are also poetic and romantic. When Heinrich arrives in Augsburg, he is betrothed to the daughter of another minnesinger, Klingsohr. The figure of Klingsohr and his wise counsel to Heinrich are reminiscent of Goethe at this period: the poet should base his work on careful observation of life, temper the expression of emotions, and in general "practise poetry as a strict art." Klingsohr warns against writing fairy tales in youth, but then narrates a tale he had written as a young poet. There is some irony in his inconsistency and in the contrast between his advice and Heinrich's mystic conception of the poet's mission. Still, irony is less conspicuous in Novalis' works than in those of most Romanticists. Unlike Friedrich Schlegel, he believes that the poet—or the philosopher, historian, scientist—can fully realize his mission. What strikes us as ironic is the conviction that the goal can be reached from different, even seemingly opposite directions. Both Saracens and Crusaders are unwittingly fighting for the same clause: historic destiny. Klingsohr and Heinrich are both right: the Classicist and the Romanticist can each in his own way achieve the poetic transfiguration of human experience. But it should be noted that in part one of *Ofterdingen*, Novalis has himself applied some of Klingsohr's and Goethe's principles and achieved a control, discipline, and formal unity reminding us more of *Wilhelm Meister* than of *Lucinde* or *Sternbald.*

Novalis's novel *The Novices of Sais* was left in an even more fragmentary state than *Ofterdingen.*[22] In it the mysteries of nature are personified in the image of the Veiled Goddess (Isis). Sais is the seat of a kind of scientific academy; novices gather specimens of plants and mineral crystals, arranging and organizing them in different patterns as though they constituted problems in cryptography, which is precisely Novalis's view of natural phenomena. The teacher acknowledges a variety of approaches to the mysterious language of nature and realizes that some of his novices—those with childlike, contemplative, or poetic temperaments—can penetrate these mysteries more deeply than he with his empirical methods. And it is a poetic novice who narrates the beautiful little tale of *Hyacinth and Rosebud* which restates one of Novalis's basic themes: In the age when all of nature, including man, was in happy communion, the intercession of the intellect (in the form of a book left by a stranger) temporarily destroys this harmony for the youth Hyacinth. He deserts his love Rosebud and sets out on a long journey to the Temple at Sais. On his arrival he lifts the veil from the image and finds himself in Rosebud's arms, and he as well as the reader realize that the hidden mystery of the natural universe is love.

A short essay entitled *Christendom or Europe* became one of the most controversial works of Novalis.[23] Like the fifth *Hymn to Night,* it presents a dialectical view of cultural history, but in this case the Golden Age is the Christian Middle Ages. Intended as a poetic discourse on the ideals, not the realities, of medieval Christendom, the essay idealizes the medieval Church, the Holy Roman Empire, and the feudal system as an ideal state of spontaneous, creative harmony and unity. The voracious intellectual curiosity of Novalis is reflected in the thousands of pages of aphorisms and notes on his scientific and philosophical studies which cover every imaginable subject. Particularly interesting today are his insights into the symbolic character of language. The illness and death of Sophie von Kühn inspired ideas about the possible control of the body and its physical environment by the mind, ideas anticipating modern psychosomatic medicine but going far beyond it into a realm which Novalis properly termed "magical idealism." Quite a few aphorisms are concerned with *Romantik,* a discipline analogous to *Mathematik, Physik,* or *Ethik.* Hence its English equivalent would not be "romanticism" but "romantics," analogous to "mathematics," "physics," or "ethics." *Romantik* is the discipline of writing and evaluating *Romane* (novels or romances) and of viewing and portraying human life, indeed the whole universe, romantically, as a romance. This involves a twofold process: One step is to see every individual personality, object, or phenomenon in its universal aspect as a symbol of ultimate, universal reality, to "raise it to a higher power" (*potenzieren*). The other is to conceive every abstract or universal idea in concrete terms, symbolically, to "find its logarithm" (*logarithmisieren*). Both sides of this process are encompassed in what the English poet Blake called "to see the world in a grain of sand." Novalis wanted to point out the deeper import behind precisely the connotations of *Roman* and *romantisch* in popular usage. In the marvellous and surprising coincidences, the revelations of concealed identities, the magic talismans and other devices contributing to the suspense of eighteenth-century popular fiction, Novalis saw clues to the kind of mystic interpretation of phenomenal experience which he practised himself. He also saw a deeper meaning in the application of *romantisch* to the landscape:

> The unknown, the mysterious, is the *result* and the *beginning* of everything. . . . Nature is incomprehensible in itself. . . . Distant philosophy sounds like poetry—because every call into the distance becomes vocalic. . . . Distant mountains, distant people, distant events, everything becomes romantic. . . .[24]

In other words, Novalis wanted everything, great and small, profound or trivial, to be experienced with a sense of wonder, with an intuitive awareness of a deeper, mystic meaning beneath the surface of phenomena. He and the other writers we have come to call Romanticists became convinced that the whole of life and culture ought to be experienced romantically—imaginatively and with a sense of wonder—and that serious poetry should be written in a romantic spirit. Life, culture, philosophy, poetry, and art were to be experienced and practised the way previous generations had read or written popular romances, viewed, painted, or imitated romantic landscapes.

However, the Berlin-Jena Romanticists did not call themselves *Romantiker* nor did they consider *Romantik* a literary movement. Jean Paul Richter noticed the word *Romantik* in the posthumous 1802 edition of Novalis's writings published by Friedrich Schlegel and Tieck, and gave to the word a new meaning in his *Primer of Aesthetics* (1804): "the romantic," not a discipline but an abstract quality. The word *Romantiker*, which for Novalis meant a practitioner of the discipline of "romantics," Jean Paul applied in a derogatory sense to Tieck, a poet who "writes in a romantic vein without bothering to convey any meaning." Hostile critics of the younger Romanticists seized upon these words for polemic purposes, making *Romantik* a collective noun for a new Romantic school of poets, the *Romantiker*.

The German Romanticist who did the most to spread the principles and tendencies of this movement beyond the borders of Germany was beyond question August Wilhelm Schlegel. His great translation of Shakespeare was interrupted by another, very different task which absorbed nearly all his energies from 1804 to 1817 but which was itself to have epochal significance for Western culture. In the year 1804, after he was divorced from his wife Karoline and had delivered a very successful series of public lectures on the history of world literature in Berlin, he was introduced there to the most brilliant and forceful woman of the age, Mme. Germaine de Staël-Holstein. Keenly interested in the revolutionary developments of German culture in the past generation (Storm and Stress, philosophical Idealism, and Classicism), she was preparing to write a book about German culture and society. She also needed someone to supervise the education of her children. Recognizing that August Wilhelm Schlegel was ideally suited to serve as both a cultural informant for her and a mentor for the children, she offered him a generous salary and packed him off to her castle at Coppet on Lake Geneva. There he conveyed to her the philosophical, literary, and cultural knowledge she needed for her influential book *On Germany* (*De L'Allemagne,* 1810), which introduced the whole rich German cultural heritage to France and the Western world.

A few years after her return to Coppet with August Wilhelm Schlegel, Mme. de Staël and her court had to flee before Napoleon's advancing armies. They first stopped in Vienna, where August Wilhelm held in 1808 his second series of public lectures *On Dramatic Art and Literature* before a brilliant audience of famous authors, artists, scholars, scientists, statesmen, generals, and royalty. These lectures were soon afterwards published in many languages and spread a German Romantic view of literary history around the world. Of particular importance are his evaluations of Shakespearean and seventeenth-century Spanish drama, the propagation of the Romantic concept of the symbol which we have observed in Friedrich Schlegel and Novalis, and the attack on the view that the theater, poetry, or any art is an imitation of nature. According to August Wilhelm, the one thing any true artistic creation has in common with nature is that it grows organically. Poetic or artistic "illusion" has valid meaning only as the heightened state of consciousness which we experience when we contemplate a work of art.

Soon after 1800 the circle of the "older Romanticists" dissolved. Wackenroder and Novalis died, Tieck moved to other parts of Germany, and the Schlegels left the country for several years. The "younger Romanticists" were no longer as close a group as the older Berlin-Jena circle. They were active in many different groups and in virtually every region of Germany. In contrast to the Berlin-Jena circle the "younger Romanticists" were less innovative though by no means less creative. Though they were not a homogeneous group they share certain common tendencies. They are more concerned with their German national heritage, particularly that of the Middle Ages: they are intensely interested in folk literature and folklore but not in literary criticism as such; their criticism is intended to promote their cultural, social, and political ideals. Whereas the Berlin-Jena Romanticists started out as admirers of the French Revolution but gradually moved toward political and social conservatism, most younger Romanticists are conservative throughout their periods of influence. All of the Berlin-Jena Romanticists were Protestants, although Friedrich and Dorothea Schlegel later became converted to Catholicism. A considerable proportion of the younger Romanticists were Catholics to start with or became converted.

The differences in literary style are even more striking. The imagery and language of the early Romanticists tend to be either generalized and idealized (under the influence of Goethe) or fluid and ethereal. The imagery of the later Romanticists becomes immeasurably more concrete and particularized; their writing has a much greater number and variety of symbols. Although realism in and for itself never becomes a goal of the younger Romanticists, their imagery moves closer to actual sense experience. They express the ideal, the mystical, and the supernatural right along with and often as a concrete part of the actual world, and in consequence their symbolism borders quite frequently on the grotesque. They also have a more diffident view of their own poetic mission than did

213

Friedrich Schlegel or Novalis. Sometimes they express an ambivalent view of poetic genius or of poetry as a formal vocation.

The first of the younger Romanticists was Clemens Brentano (1778–1842). Son of a wealthy Frankfurt family of Italian origin, he was raised a Catholic, drifted away from his religion, and then underwent a profound reconversion in his late thirties. As a student at the University of Jena, he became a disciple of the Schlegels and Tieck, who never reciprocated his esteem. By temperament he was passionate and unstable. Behind the guilt-ridden voluptuary of his young manhood and the penitent and devout believer of his later years, one always senses a wistful, fanciful child longing for its mother's arms. This longing for a lost mother, the theme of much of Brentano's writing, can be explained by his absence from his own very beautiful mother during a large part of his childhood. We see it in the title of Brentano's early novel: *Godwi or the Mother's Stone Statue* (1800–1801), which bears the equally revealing subtitle: *A Novel Run Wild* (*Ein verwilderter Roman*). It combines an eroticism much more passionate than that of Friedrich Schlegel's *Lucinde* with an arabesque narrative technique closer to that of Jean Paul. The pseudonymous author Maria (Brentano's middle name) becomes a character in the second part, and his fatal illness and death are related by his own literary characters.

Brentano's great poetic gifts, an amazingly rich sensuous imagination and an uncanny ability to evoke poetic impressions through the mere sound of words, are only partially apparent in *Godwi* but are fully manifest even at this early period in his lyric poetry and later in his novellas and fairy tales. The latter are in large part adapted from the Italian author Giambattista Basile (1575–1632), but in their richly imaginative detail they are really original creations. Brentano's greatest contribution to German literature was the folk songs which he and his friend, later brother-in-law, Ludwig Achim von Arnim (1781–1831), collected: *The Boy's Magic Horn* (1806–1808). Arnim and Brentano freely adapted many of the songs and also interspersed original poems of their own. Nevertheless, the collection included enough authentic folk material to serve as the foundation for the more scholarly collections of our own time. It profoundly influenced subsequent German lyric creation, including Brentano's own. In this connection two other monuments to the German Romantic interest in folk literature should be mentioned: the famous collection of fairy tales (*Kinder- und Hausmärchen*) published by the brothers Jakob and Wilhelm

Grimm, which was carefully compiled from peasant informants. And in 1807 Joseph Görres (1776–1848), a friend and associate of Brentano and Arnim, published a collection of popular German chapbooks of the fifteenth and sixteenth centuries, *Die teutschen Volksbücher,* including both prose romances and late medieval prose versions of the German heroic epics.

Scholars in our century, notably Emil Staiger, have carefully analyzed Brentano's poems and found that in images, themes, and musical quality they are to a considerable degree representative of Romantic poetry. One especially revealing image is the boatman borne along on a drifting current, the wraith of his dead sweetheart in the vessel over which he has lost control ("Auf dem Rhein"). Other early poems show the poet in passive communion with the living forces of nature ("Sprich aus der Ferne"). Sometimes Brentano's childlike temperament, fascination with little animals and birds, and the rich fantasy of his fairy tales are also reflected in his lyrics. But one of the more common themes of his poems is the obsessive spell of erotic passion, a theme for which his habit of repeating and rearranging lines and images is singularly appropriate ("Der Spinnerin Nachtlied"). Eroticism as a demonic force destroying both the sorceress who lives under its curse and the men whom she unwillingly victimizes is the subject of the ballad "Zu Bacharach am Rheine." The theme of the ballad was taken up by other Romanticists, notably Eichendorff, and achieved its final form in Heine's famous "Lorelei." Brentano's most intense and deeply felt lyric creation, "A Servant's Cry in Spring Up from the Depths" ("Frühlingsschrei eines Knechtes aus der Tiefe"), dates from 1816, when the great emotional and religious crisis culminating in his return to the Catholic faith the following year was well under way. The poem portrays the poet as helpless servant in desperate need of his Master's help, for he is sinking down in a well or shaft (his own sinfulness) and its muddy walls are caving in upon him. The season which each year brings new life and hope to other humans and to the whole earth is threatening him with spiritual annihilation. But the tidings of the redeeming Blood of Christ bring the hope at the end that the poet may be rescued.

Brentano's finest novella, *The Story of Honest Kaspar and Fair Annerl,* likewise written a year or two before his reconversion, is also concerned with guilt, perdition, and redeeming grace. The novella's main locus of interest, however, centers on the clash between human pride and a transcendent code of honor. As the story unfolds the reader comes to recognize that man's worth is determined neither by the judgment of others nor by his conduct in life but will be judged by God alone according to His inscrutable principles. The difference between the spirit of this work and the views expressed in Classicism is all the more striking because Kaspar and especially Annerl also fall prey to an inexplicable fate, a fate which cannot defeat Divine Grace, but seeks its victims on earth.

Brentano's friend and collaborator Achim von Arnim wrote only narrative prose, which tends toward a bewildering complexity of structure and grotesquely bizarre symbolism. It contrasts strangely with his balanced, healthy, and seemingly uncomplicated personality. Although his work achieved much less popularity than E. T. A. Hoffmann's, with whom he has some stylistic affinity, Arnim was one of the German Romanticists most admired by other creative writers. The complex plots of his two novels, *Guardians of the Crown* (*Die Kronenwächter*, 1817) and *Isabella von Ägypten* (1812) are of less interest than the weird figures, strange episodes, and the sombre, often bizarre, atmosphere that pervades both narratives.

A shorter novella with an eighteenth-century setting, *The Mad Veteran at Fort Ratonneau* (*Der tolle Invalide auf dem Fort Ratonneau*, 1818), introduces a technique that became increasingly common in late Romantic literature: a remarkable sequence of events for which alternative supernatural and rational explanations are provided.

A much more influential writer, especially outside of Germany, was Ernst Theodor Wilhelm Hoffmann (1776–1822), who replaced the third name with Amadeus in tribute to Mozart. Hoffmann was himself a composer and music critic as well as an author and also practised a third art, painting. He served briefly as musical director and later stage designer for the theater in Bamberg, but most of the time he supported himself as a legal official in the Prussian civil service.

Hoffmann's parents were divorced early in his childhood, and owing to the mental illness of his mother, he was raised by his maternal grandmother, aunts, and uncles in the culturally isolated, provincial city of Königsberg. The family environment provided little stimulation for an imaginative child. Hoffmann found release from the detested milieu in the instruction in painting and music he received at school and later in the independent musical studies he pursued as a law student. His works reflect the resulting tendency toward a sharp dichotomy in his mind between an ideal world of poetry, art, and music—a world of heavenly beauty and harmony—and the actual world of the urban middle class. Another experience which apparently influenced Hoffmann's artistic production almost disrupted his life when he was in his early thirties. Married for some years to a faithful but uninspiring wife of Polish lower middle-class background, he fell deeply in love with Julia Marc, a girl to whom he was giving vocal lessons. His love and disillusionment when she married can be traced in the image of a beautiful but inaccessible woman which recurs in several stories.

Hoffmann sought release from the frustrations and tensions of his life in drinking, a habit which he enjoyed but one that occasionally gave rise to hallucinations. But instead of succumbing to delusions, Hoffmann very successfully exploited the pathological side of his personality in his writing. Not only are a number of his characters insane; the theme of diabolical obsession runs through a large part of his work, most conspicuously the novel *The Devil's Elixirs* (1815); in this novel the peculiar motif of the diabolical alter-ego, symbolizing the duality of the human personality, also figures prominently. There is no other author in whom the romantic yearning for a heavenly ideal is so frequently juxtaposed with the romantic fear of infernal forces. If we are to say that in many of his stories Hoffmann tends to contrast the sterile, prosaic world of the bureaucratic middle class with an ideal realm of poetry and music, we must add that there is frequently also a third realm of infernal, diabolical powers. Sometimes, as in *The Golden Pot* (1814), this diabolical realm is allied with the bourgeois middle class and simply means doubt in the validity of the higher realm and the temptation to accept bourgeois values. But there are other tales in which the creative genius of the poet or artist is allied with or animated by diabolical forces. In the last analysis, Hoffmann's view of creative genius is ambivalent. His own allegiance is to the artistic temperament, but there is an underlying uncertainty as to whether genius is controlled by heavenly or infernal powers.

A few characteristic stories will illustrate Hoffmann's varying treatment of this problem. In *Ritter Gluck* (1809), the narrator who is listening to a third-rate band concert at a Berlin sidewalk café, gets into conversation with a stranger. The man shows a profound musical insight particularly into the music of Gluck (1714–1787). We soon notice that he conceives Gluck's music in daring new variations going beyond Gluck's actual achievement. He also speaks of a journey through an agonizing realm of dreams to a mystic domain of ideal harmony, where he experienced ecstatic moments in the chalice of a sunflower. Since then his life in Berlin has been like that of a departed spirit condemned to wander through a void. On a later meeting, the stranger takes the narrator to his apartment, where he announces, "I am Ritter Gluck." Hoffmann conceived this as a story of insanity, but we see that the madman who takes himself for Gluck has musical insights superior to those of sane musicians.

The student Anselmus, hero of *The Golden Pot*,[25] is torn between Veronica, the beautiful daughter of a school official, and a serpent-girl he hears whispering in an elder-tree by the Elbe River in Dresden. Serpentina is one of the daughters of Archivist Lindhorst, who soon employs Anselmus to copy rare manuscripts for him. Lindhorst generally appears as a bitingly ironic bureaucratic official, but for occasional brief moments he reveals his true identity as a Salamander, a prince of the realm of spirits who traces his ancestry back to mythic beings who participated in creation itself. His relation to Anselmus is that of a severely critical taskmaster, insisting on absolute perfection in the copying of the strange characters on his Oriental manuscripts. Anselmus' service under Lindhorst is, in short, an apprenticeship in poetry and Serpentina a symbol of poetic inspiration. But for all his love of the ecstatically beautiful singing of Serpentina, Anselmus cannot easily resist the temptations presented by Veronica: an attractive wife, a comfortable existence, and a secure position in the bureaucracy, perhaps even with the enviable title of Court Councilor. In her effort to win Anselmus away from Serpentina, Veronica enlists the aid of the Apple Woman, a former servant of Veronica's family but in reality a spirit of the lower realm (man's base instincts) hostile to Lindhorst. When Anselmus wavers once during his work in his loyalty to Serpentina and contemplates the advantages of life with Veronica, his inspiration leaves him and he ruins one of Lindhorst's manuscripts. Trapped in the oppressive atmosphere of bourgeois life, symbolized by the glass bottle into which he is banished, Anselmus yearns for release. His love for Serpentina finally conquers all other emotions; the walls of his prison shatter; Lindhorst wins a great battle over the Antaean forces, Anselmus weds Serpentina and moves with her to an estate in Atlantis, the land of poetry. Hoffmann has thus revived a fundamentally mythical theme of Novalis: the role of poetic imagination in restoring unity and harmony to the world and triumphing over the forces of doubt, separation, hatred, and conflict. Unlike Novalis, however, Hoffmann introduces his mythical characters and their supernatural deeds right into the everyday world of nineteenth-century Dresden with its salons, river boats, amusement parks, and coffee houses. The Apple Woman becomes a grinning face on a door-knob; the Archivist-Salamander lights a pipe by snapping his fingers; and finally even Veronica's father, the Vice-Rector, champion of prosaic rationality, proclaims the reality of the Salamander. The cosmic battle is waged with pages of parchment, and the Archivist smothers his foe in his damask sleeping gown and turns her into a parsnip. Hoffmann is also unlike Novalis in conceiving the ideal harmony as something to be achieved in and through the poetic imagination alone; it can never change the face of the everyday world. On finishing his fairy tale, the author intrudes into his own work and laments that he must work on in his attic room, engulfed in the trivialities of his penurious existence. But he is consoled by the recognition that reader and poet alike experience moments of cosmic harmony in the contemplation of art.

Hoffmann's most masterfully constructed novella is *Mlle. de Scudéry* (1818). The scene is Paris during the reign of Louis XIV, when Paris was in the throes of a terrible wave of poisonings and other heinous murders. The elderly poetess Mlle. de Scudéry stands out against this background of hatred and violence with her universally esteemed virtue, serenity, and kindness. She becomes involved in the crimes when she coins an epigram at court that seems to ridicule lovers who are afraid of falling victim to a mysterious new wave of murders: Purchasers of the most magnificent creations of the jeweler's art, the work of the highly respected master goldsmith René de Cardillac, are silently murdered as they bring the jewels to their brides. It turns out that the murderer is Cardillac himself, who so admires his own creations that he cannot endure the thought that they are in the hands of others. At a time when his own guilt is still unsuspected, he sends Mlle. de Scudéry one of his masterpieces in gratitude for her epigram. Everything comes to light after Cardillac himself is murdered and Mlle. de Scudéry comes to the aid of a young man unjustly accused of the crime. Here the great creative artist is a ruthless criminal. And attractively as Hoffmann paints Mlle. de Scudéry and the other innocent and virtuous characters of the story, it is dominated by the demonic figure of the artist-criminal Cardillac.

Hoffmann has always been widely acclaimed as the German

author who wrote the best tales of crime and suspense. But many of them also show a deep awareness of man's ontological insecurity and reflect a profoundly pessimistic spirit.[26] Often enough, to be sure, this may seem relieved by a happy ending, by the playful use of "arabesque" narrative techniques (in the sense of Friedrich Schlegel), or by the ironic extravagance of Hoffmann's mythic fantasy. In three novellas, *The Story of Krespel* (1816), *Mlle. de Scudéry*, and *The Sandman* (1815 f.), doubt is cast upon the artistic imagination as a redemptive force in human life. An underlying pessimism is particularly evident in Hoffmann's two novels, *The Devil's Elixirs* and *Tomcat Murr's Views on Life* (1820–1821), as well as in his last narrative creation, the long "fairy tale" *Magister Flea* (1822). All three are essentially tragic tales of man's lonely quest for self-realization. We have seen that *The Devil's Elixirs* focuses upon the pathological depths of the human soul. This theme is combined with that of the tragic predicament of the creative artist in the semi-autobiographical novel of the composer and *Kapellmeister* Johannes Kreisler, which—after the fashion of Jean Paul—has become haphazardly mixed in the print-shop with the satiric journal of a smugly philistine tomcat. In *Magister Flea* the characters lead a dual existence in nineteenth-century Frankfurt am Main and in an exotic mythic realm. Unlike *The Golden Pot*, which it thus outwardly resembles, this fairy tale achieves a happy resolution only by the last-minute introduction of an implausibly perfect heroine. Its negative import encompasses not merely modern urban culture but the state, justice, the scientific exploration of natural phenomena, communication between human beings, even love. In outlook, description of abnormal psychological patterns, and the artistic experiment of reproducing disconnected dream sequences, Hoffmann was far ahead of his time and is perhaps the Romantic writer who has the greatest appeal today.

Whereas Hoffmann's popularity in the nineteenth century was primarily outside of Germany, the Romanticist most loved by German readers was the Silesian nobleman Joseph von Eichendorff (1788–1857), one of the greatest German lyric poets. Many of his *Lieder* have been set to music by composers like Mendelssohn, Schubert, Schumann, and Hugo Wolf, themselves rooted in Romanticism. The folklike quality of much of his poetry—of which "The Broken Ring" ("Das zerbrochene Ringlein") is the most famous example—and the spirit of joyous *Wanderlust* animating his *Memoirs of a Good-for-Nothing* (*Aus dem Leben eines Taugenichts*) long prevented a critical appreciation of Eichendorff's subtle artistry. But in his seemingly naive use of romantic clichés—marble statues and fountains in the moonlight, grotesque neglected gardens, larks soaring in song at daybreak, wanderers gazing out from lofty heights, carefree young people embarking on river boats—scholars have come to recognize an artfully organized symbolic expression of the poet's philosophy of life, which manifests itself simultaneously in the characters and action of his narratives.

Throughout his life Eichendorff was a profoundly devout Catholic Christian, unquestionably the most deeply and genuinely religious of all the German Romanticists. His religion is essentially a piety toward life, toward human beings and their relationships, and toward all of nature as creations of God. Some of this feeling is captured in the poem "Morning Prayer" ("Morgengebet"):

> O silence, wondrous and profound!
>   O'er earth doth solitude still reign;
> The woods alone incline their heads,
>   As if the Lord walked o'er the plain.

> I feel new life within me glow;
>   Where now is my distress and care?
> Here in the blush of waking morn,
>   I blush at yesterday's despair.

> To me, a pilgrim, shall the world,
>   With all its joys and sorrows, be
> But as a bridge that leads, O Lord,
>   Across the stream of time to Thee.

> And should my song woo worldly gifts,
>   The base rewards of vanity—
> Dash down my lyre! I'll hold my peace
>   Before Thee to eternity.

Despite the orthodoxy of Eichendorff's Catholicism, his religious feeling, as it is expressed in his poetry, is akin to Schleiermacher's sense of dependence on God and to that of such twentieth-century religious thinkers as Martin Buber.

Although Eichendorff lets many of his characters enjoy quite an adventurous love life in their youth, he draws a sharp line between Christian love, the love of one human person for another as such, and obsessive eroticism, which he sees as a love of one's own passions and sensations, using the other person merely as an instrument. He does not condemn erotic love as such but demands that it be combined with true love of the other person and oriented in a religious attitude toward the whole of life. This antithesis between Christian and erotic or pagan love is the theme of all of Eichendorff's work and the organizing principle of his symbolism.[27]

Consequently Eichendorff sees himself as a champion of the true, Christian Romanticism against a false, pagan Romanticism or the decadent salon Romanticism that was fashionable during the first two decades of his adult life. But he also is a champion of the spontaneous poetic imagination nourished by the love of God, of one's fellow-man, and of nature, against a prosaic, utilitarian attitude toward life. He considers energies expended wholly on family concerns, economic security, and vocational responsibilities just as wasted as those devoted to the gratification of egocentric sensations. In actual fact, the kind of poetic life which Eichendorff envisioned as an ideal was no longer feasible in his time—if indeed it ever had been—and he was himself a conscientious civil servant and a dutiful husband and father. Thus the *Wanderlust*, the free, poetic life embodied in his *Good-for-Nothing*, is portrayed with considerable irony. But he implicitly believed that one could remain free and Romantic in spirit even while accepting the responsibilities and limitations of life in practice.

Nearly all of Eichendorff's narrative prose is either mythical or frankly allegorical. Indeed the *Good-for-Nothing* and a shorter novella likewise published in 1826, *The Marble Statue* (*Das Marmorbild*), are pre-eminently mythical expressions of his view of life. *The Marble Statue* presents the conflict between the two opposing Romantic attitudes toward life as a struggle within the soul of a youthful poet named Florio who must choose between the pagan goddess Venus and a chaste, modest young girl named Bianka. Florio first sees them as two identically costumed figures at a garden masquerade party. The more stately, indeed more beautiful one is Venus; the smaller, more retiring, more winsome girl is the pure and innocent Bianka. Later he is introduced to Venus' mansion by a pale, gloomy, and dissolute-looking man who has long since fallen victim to her spell. For according to an old legend, at certain times Venus comes alive in the Christian world and lures unsuspecting men into her domain. Near the end of the story Florio is about to become hopelessly enslaved by Venus when he hears his friend, the happy, outgoing Fortunato, sing a song of devout faith from outside Venus' garden. Venus pales at the sound; the beautiful decorations of her mansion turn to hideous insects, and then everything disappears. Florio rejoins his friend Fortunato and shortly finds himself wandering with him and Bianka down the road toward "Mailand" (the old German word for Milan, equivalent to "Mayland").

The titular hero of *Memoirs of a Good-for-Nothing* is a miller's son who, tired of the tedious life at home and his father's beratings, sets out on a life of sheer *Wanderlust*. The plot of this story is a fairy tale of the impossible come true, the tale of the simpleton (*Dümmling*) who wins a princess. He is given a ride to the outskirts of Vienna by two ladies in a carriage, then employed at their castle as gardener's helper and tollkeeper. He falls in love with the younger of the two "countesses" but in consequence of a disappointment leaves and wanders to Italy. A great variety of adventures ensues from his initial misconception, for the "countess" he loves is actually a girl of simple origin. Subsequently both are exploited by a pair of eloping lovers. There is rich irony, not merely in the deliberate implausibility of the episodes, but even more in the way the Good-for-Nothing relates the whole sequence of events which he does not understand, in the first person. Rome appears as a city of contrasts: It is the Heavenly City of a childlike Christian faith as it shows itself to the Good-for-Nothing on his first approach to it. But it is also potentially a source of erotic temptation and spiritual peril, against which, however, the innocent Good-for-Nothing is happily secure. Eventually he wanders back northward to the Alps and returns with a gay party of students on a river boat to his castle, where he finds his wedding to the "countess" already prepared.

Eichendorff began and closed his literary career with two novels. The first of these, *Presentiment and Actuality* (*Ahnung und Gegenwart*, 1815) is primarily cultural and social criticism, portraying the decadence of pseudo-Romanticism at a German princely court and in the literary salons, but also expressing the author's hopes for the regeneration of Germany under the leadership of a responsible aristocracy. It is also concerned with the country's liberation from the Napoleonic yoke, which was not yet broken at the time Eichendorff wrote it. The other novel, *Poets and Their Companions* (*Dichter und ihre Gesellen*, 1837), interweaves four

223

very different love stories to contrast the author's conception of the true Christian poetic spirit with three variants of decadent Romanticism.

Two other younger German Romanticists contributed each a single narrative that won lasting fame. Baron Friedrich de la Motte Fouqué (1777–1843) was the descendant of French emigrés of an earlier generation. His *Undine* (1811) expresses the antithesis between human society and man's deeper roots in nature in the story of a medieval knight's love for a water-nymph. She demands more than usual faithfulness from her mortal lover, and he is finally destroyed when he betrays her for a noblewoman. *Undine* was twice made into an opera in the nineteenth century, the first time by E. T. A. Hoffman. In our own time the dramatic adaptation by the French author Jean Giraudoux has achieved world-wide success. Adalbert von Chamisso (1781–1838) was born in France but emigrated to Germany with his parents, who tried to escape the French Revolution. His novella *The Wonderful History of Peter Schlemihl* (1814) is the story of a man who wins worldly wealth by selling his shadow to the Devil, then vainly tries to win it back. The story gains in force from the realistic portrayal of the contemporary world and from the very ambiguity of its theme, which somehow seems to express, not simply the loss of something everyone takes for granted, but the destiny of the person set off from his fellow-men by greater depth, sensitivity, and imagination.

With the exception of Tieck's fantastic comedies, which have enjoyed limited success on the stage, the Romantic writers were not successful as dramatists. Tieck and numerous others, including Brentano, Arnim, and Eichendorff, tried their hand at a variety of dramatic forms, particularly those mingling comic and tragic elements in emulation of Shakespeare; but all of this was frankly intended to be read rather than acted. Zacharias Werner (1768–1823) achieved significant theatrical success in the historical drama in his time, but he is all but forgotten today.

The one great German dramatist of the Romantic period is Heinrich von Kleist (1777–1811). And it is precisely the dramatic power of his work, its movement, intensity, and concentration, that makes us hesitate to call Kleist a Romanticist. Kleist was actually a member of a Romantic circle, collaborating with the Romantic philosopher, aesthetician, and political theoretician Adam Müller (1779–1829) in the publication of a periodical. His little essay *On the Marionette Theater* (1810) presents in its most striking and concentrated form the dialectic view of human culture characteristic of Romanticism: the marionette, which moves from its center of gravity with a grace impossible for the self-conscious human dancer, symbolizes an intuitive harmony with its own being which man has lost as a result of his civilized intellect but will ultimately regain through a higher self-consciousness. Nor is there anything in Kleist's human personality setting him off from the Romantic temperament. He was keenly sensitive, moved restlessly from one place, vocation, personal relationship, and plan of life to another, finding personal fulfillment in none. He fluctuated violently between extravagant hope and bottomless despair, finally to end his own life in a grotesque suicide pact with a casual acquaintance.

The underlying theme of Kleist's work is the need for the human soul to realize itself in constructive and reliable interrelationships with other human beings and the tragic—or comic—situations arising from the frustration of this need. Such frustration sometimes springs from the failure of others to understand or sympathize with these basic needs, sometimes from deliberate hatred, cruelty, or injustice of individuals or of society. But frustration also arises from the blinding intensity of man's own drives and passions, from the inability to understand one's own situation. Thus we can say that the fundamental theme of Kleist's work is man's weakness. In the violence of the tensions that often accompany the imbalances in human relations which he portrays, Kleist resembles the dramatists of Storm and Stress, without sharing their revolutionary tendencies. In his ideals of fairness, harmony, and confidence in human relationships as well as in his achievement of concentrated, unified form, he is close to Classicism. His sympathy for the yearnings and drives of his characters and his recognition of the irrational in the human make-up sometimes bring him close to Romanticism, even closer, in fact, than the historical settings, adventurous activity, and supernatural episodes that not infrequently occur in his work. His keen observation of the actual world sometimes brings him close to realism, but this is no more an end in itself for Kleist than for any other poet of the Romantic era. In addition to his dramas, Kleist contributed one of the greatest German historical novellas, *Michael Kohlhaas* (1810), and is the founder of the German short story.

Kleist's greatest dramatic effort was a historical tragedy dealing with the Norman Sicilian ruler Robert Guiscard. He wrote a large part of the work, then destroyed it, and sometime later again wrote a short fragment, which shows the hero struggling to conceal from his followers the fact that he is dying of the plague. Kleist never quite recovered from his failure to realize his conception of this tragedy. *Amphitryon*, written 1805–1806, is an adaptation of a comedy by Molière going back through the Latin comedy of Plautus to ancient Greek myth. The god Jupiter falls in love with Alkmene, wife of the Theban ruler Amphitryon, comes to her bed in the shape of her husband returning from the wars, and begets the demigod Hercules. Kleist richly develops both comic and tragic potentialities of the situation. Not satisfied to be loved simply as Alkmene's husband, Jupiter wants her to distinguish between the husband she was used to and the Amphitryon now returning from his absence as an ardent lover. Alkmene does in fact love the new heightened image of the husband-lover differently from the husband of the past and becomes increasingly troubled by this difference, especially after the real Amphitryon returns and his visits and dialogues with her alternate with those of the god. Potentially tragic—but also comical—is the desperate bewilderment of the real Amphitryon. The secondary action involving Jupiter's assistant Mercury in the form of Amphitryon's servant Sosias is a source of broad comedy.

Penthesilea (written 1806–1807) is a tragedy of consuming erotic passion. The heroine is an Amazon queen who violates the code of her nation by falling desperately in love with a man before she has defeated him in battle and taken him captive. The object of her uncontrollable passion is Achilles, and her desire to possess him becomes so fierce that it is at once a drive to destroy him. Achilles too falls in love with Penthesilea, but he loves her with a happy self-confidence that blinds him to the peril he faces from her demonically obsessive passion. He deludes himself with plans to win Penthesilea by feigning defeat at her hands. He does in fact defeat her in preliminary encounters, only to fan her into an even more raging frenzy of passion. Finally he challenges her to personal combat and approaches her unarmed with the intention of surrendering himself to her. She, however, literally joins with the pack of dogs she has brought along in tearing him apart. After this she is in a trance for a time, but when she realizes what she has done she kills herself with the very intensity of her grief.

Kate of Heilbronn or the Trial by Fire (written 1807–1808, produced and published 1810), has the subtitle *A Great Historic Drama of Knighthood.* It is, in fact, an attempt to create a romantic drama with a medieval setting in the sense understood by the Schlegels and unsuccessfully attempted by Tieck, Brentano, Arnim, and other Romanticists. The titular heroine is a young blacksmith's daughter who for unknown reasons follows a knight, the Count vom Strahl, in self-abnegating, unswerving devotion, despite all efforts to separate her from him. It is eventually disclosed that she had seen him in a dream as her destined husband. He too had had an identical dream but failed to understand it because of her seemingly humble origin (she turns out to be the Emperor's daughter of his dream). Once again, Kleist portrays a character who is guided by feeling and intuition in defiance of all reason. But Kleist's very merits as a writer for the theater, his instinct for vivid situations and action, the clarity and concreteness of his symbolism, and his dramatic concentration, are inappropriate to the romantic conception of this play, which is so much like a fairy tale or a saint's legend. The superhuman devotion of the heroine and the supernatural evidences of her innocence and destiny require the kind of romantic aura or patina of which a Tieck, say, was capable, but which is scarcely compatible with vivid theatrical action.

Like many others of his generation, Kleist reacted to the Napoleonic conquest of Germany with patriotic fervor. He expressed his pride in the German national heritage and his hatred for the foreign oppressor in the *Battle of Arminius* (*Die Hermannsschlacht*, written 1808), a historic drama on the victory of the Germanic tribes under Hermann (Latin Arminius) over the Roman legions in the Battle of the Teutoburg Forest in the year 9 A.D. A more mature, but specifically Prussian patriotism animates *Prince Frederick of Homburg* (written 1809–1810).[28] Here the problem is how to achieve a balance between the drives and emotional needs of the individual and the law and order required by a state and its armies. The titular hero is a general under the Great Elector Frederick William of Brandenburg, to whom he also has close personal ties. In the night before the Battle of Fehrbellin (1675), in which the forces of the Elector broke the power of the Swedes in Pomerania, the Prince is discovered by the Elector and his niece, Nathalie, in a somnambulant state, dreaming of military glory and of winning Nathalie's hand. A few hours later, when the generals receive their battle orders, he is still absorbed in reveries of this kind, a fact for which the Elector and Nathalie are partially responsible, and pays no attention to the order not to join in the battle until expressly commanded to do so. He attacks the Swedish forces prematurely and helps win a great victory. But the Elector orders his execution for violating his orders, earnestly believing that in so doing the Prince had undermined principles essential to the survival of any state. The Prince is at first so shaken by the prospect of death that he is willing to sacrifice everything, including his love for Nathalie, just to live. When Nathalie reports this to the Elector, the latter sends Homburg a pardon that is conditional upon the Prince's inability to recognize the justice of his death sentence. The Elector's letter awakens the Prince to his responsibilities; he regains his moral courage, sees the justice of the Elector's sentence, and is prepared to die. After the Elector has decided to pardon Homburg anyway, an older officer helps him see that states and armies cannot survive by rules alone but must also take cognizance of the feelings of subjects and soldiers. The play has a romantic, happy end in which the dream becomes reality.

Kleist's other dramatic masterpiece is *The Broken Jug* (1811),[29] one of the very few great German comedies. An indolent and incompetent but crafty village judge in the Netherlands, whose name Adam epitomizes his human weaknesses, is put in the position of having to try a crime of which he is the real culprit. He broke a village woman's treasured jug while fleeing from an unsuccessful attempt to seduce her daughter. For a time the judge cleverly manages to make others appear guilty, even though his alert clerk has very quickly apprised himself of the real facts. The judge has contrived to keep the girl from disclosing his guilt by threatening to have her fiancé sent to military service in the Indies. Her temporary concealment of the truth, in turn, shakes the youth's confidence in her faithfulness—something which she feels she has a right to demand of him despite all appearances to the contrary. This one intrusion of a tragic element in the play illustrates the importance Kleist attaches to mutual trust and harmony between human beings based on intuition rather than empirical evidence and intellect. Eventually the judge is caught in his own wiles and flees ignominiously from the scene. In the portrayal of the milieu, the characters, and the requisites which remind us of the sixteenth-century paintings of Pieter Bruegel the Elder, Kleist comes closest to realism. But the whole dialogue is in blank verse, and Kleist makes copious use of thematic images and words with symbolic connotations going beyond their immediate meaning.

The problem of justice treated comically in this play and the problem of the balance between the individual and society are the themes of Kleist's novella *Michael Kohlhaas*.[30] The titular hero was an historical personality of the sixteenth century whose remarkable history was recorded in a contemporary chronicle. In Kleist's words at the beginning of the story, he was "one of the most upright and, at the same time, one of the most terrible men of his day." A prosperous and respected horse trader, he suffers grave injustice when a nobleman lawlessly seizes some of his best horses. Attempting to secure justice, Kohlhaas turns from one state authority to another; when all efforts fail his desire for justice turns into a passionate thirst for revenge, and he becomes a ruthless outlaw and rebel. The precarious balance between individual and state is restored after the horses are returned to him while he, facing the executioner, repents. In several fine shorter narratives Kleist deals with similar imbalance and discord in human relationships and human passions. There are brief moments when love, trust, and harmony prevail in individuals or even whole communities, but more often blind, destructive passion seems to prevail.

The Romantic Movement in literature was the result of a reaction on two distinct cultural levels against the rationalistic, utilitarian, and formalized culture of the Enlightenment. On the lower cultural level this reaction originated in the stimulation and release afforded the imagination by fictional narratives of chivalry and by such other popular arts as the literature of travel and exploration, the painting and sketching of landscape, and the reproduction of picturesque scenes in parks and gardens. It was in such contexts as these that the word "romantic" first took on favorable connotations and developed aesthetic values. In the course of the late seventeenth and eighteenth centuries, this new taste for the romantic gradually spread upward on the cultural scale but remained a genteel pastime rather than a serious mission.

On the higher cultural level, the reaction was manifest in the intellectual and literary movements which we know by the names of Irrationalism and Storm and Stress, both nourished by the religious phenomenon of pietism. Authors like Hamann, Herder, Wilhelm Heinse (1746–1803), Heinrich Friedrich Jacobi (1743–1819), and the young Goethe and Schiller emphasized the importance of feeling and intuition, stressed spontaneous "organic" development, and prized the literary and cultural manifestations of primitive peoples.

The rediscovery in the 1760's of the cultural values of the

romantic Middle Ages fused these two currents of revolt against the Enlightenment and prepared the way for a programmatic Romantic Movement in the next generation. This new movement, beginning in Germany in 1796, acclaimed the romantic imagination, the romantic sense of wonder, romantic intuition, aspiration, and yearning as valid principles, not merely for the creation and enjoyment of art, but to provide the foundation of an entire new culture. To be sure, most German Romanticists were aware that this cultural ideal could never be completely realized; after all, a smiling awareness of the gulf separating the ideal from reality had been associated with the word "romantic" from its inception. The very recognition that limitations and contradictions were part and parcel of all human aspiration and communication might, so they hoped, make these limitations bearable, transcending them in principle, if not in fact. But there were only a few Romanticists for whom this sense of irony could really afford a satisfactory solution for the ironic predicament in which they found themselves.

There was a fundamental difference, however, in the way the early and the later German Romanticists faced this dilemma. The early Romanticists started, at least, from the premise that their aspirations ought to be realizable; the younger Romanticists were prepared to compromise from the outset. They knew that this earthly life and their temporal culture could never be completely transfigured by romantic ideals, but only hoped that the latter could be a source of rejuvenation and renewal. Some younger Romanticists, in fact, sought nothing more than a haven of beauty and harmony—an "Atlantis"—that might provide the soul with the sustenance it needed to endure its existence in the dreary world of actuality.

But even all these compromises could not keep the culture rooted in wonder and yearning alive beyond the third decade of the nineteenth century. Moreover, the two greatest literary artists of the Romantic generations, Hölderlin and Kleist, could find no fulfillment in Romantic aspiration. The one recognized that any new Golden Age must await its destined moment in history, that the poet and cultural leader could only prepare his countrymen for its coming. The other achieved poetic greatness only in a domain where human fragility struggles to achieve a perilous equilibrium through renunciation and restraint.

We may say, then, that the attempt to found a culture upon romantic aspiration, yearning, and wonder was a failure. But in falling short of its set goal, Romanticism nevertheless succeeded in making literary art an expression of the total human personality, of feeling, dream, and reverie as well as intellect. And for a time it also succeeded in making modern poetic literature what romance had been two centuries before: a popular art.

7. Realism and Naturalism 🖉

Sigfrid Hoefert

The general social and cultural tendencies underlying the development of literature in Germany and Austria, after
the Romantics had made their mark, are manifold. The regime of
Prince Metternich ruthlessly fought the forces of liberalism, being
bent on suppressing political discontent, national aspirations, and
the widespread desire for more liberty. But these actions brought
about only a temporary stagnation; they could neither dispel the
unrest of the age nor halt the tide of progress. During this period of
German history significant changes occurred in many spheres, especially in that of socio-economic and technological endeavors. The
forces of nature were being harnessed to an ever greater degree; new
machinery and sources of power were introduced, steel was being
cast, railroads were built and communications improved. New in-
ventions helped to increase production in industry and agriculture.
Industry, in particular, expanded rapidly; new branches of manufac-
turing were founded and developed quickly. With this economic
expansion socialism became a fact. The rise of a new class, the
proletariat, upset the balance of the social order. In the sphere of
man's spiritual inquiry, natural science and historiography took the
lead over philosophical speculation. A strong anti-clerical trend
became evident (David Friedrich Strauss, 1808–1874; Ludwig
Feuerbach, 1804–1872), pessimistic thought came to reign after the
middle of the century (Arthur Schopenhauer, 1788–1860), and the
last great philosophical system, that of Georg Wilhelm Friedrich
Hegel (1770–1831), was given a definite turn to the left. Karl Marx
(1818–1883) and Friedrich Engels (1820–1895) utilized what they
could of it in their study of economic and social changes and came
forth with a doctrine that grew more and more influential in the
course of century. In the early sixties Darwinism made its appearance and somewhat later Friedrich Nietzsche's (1844–1900) criticism of society and man could be heard.

If we survey the course of German history during the nineteenth century, two events stand out: the failure of the Revolution
in 1848 and the achievement of political unification in 1871. These

232

events also left their imprint on German literature and may serve as convenient landmarks when charting the course of literary endeavor during the Realist-Naturalist phase. They do not signify a break in the development of literary form and perspective, but are signposts. Literature in Germany and Austria during the period under consideration was one continuous movement. It reaches from the days of Metternich to the late nineties and can be seen as the gradual approximation to an ever more conscious striving for realistic portrayal.[1]

Literary activity prior to the Revolution of 1848 cannot easily be placed under one convenient, independent heading nor can it be reduced to a questionable term such as *Biedermeier*,[2] but it is marked by several trends which prepare for or lead over to the actual Realist phase. A number of writers are still in the wake of Classicism and Romanticism, bewailing, at times, their epigonic fate or giving expression to the attitude of *Biedermeier*, i.e., advocating a retreat into idyllic surroundings and the pursuit of a homespun simple life, such as is reflected, for example, in the pictures of Carl Spitzweg (1808–1885) and Ludwig Richter (1803–1844). Other writers became enthralled by the idea of artistic form or turned toward nature in an attempt to ward off objectionable impressions rooted in the rapidly changing society about them. Yet others grew increasingly militant in their outlook and displayed great zeal in their endeavor to reform the political and social conditions prevailing in Germany and Austria. Among the writers still in the wake of Classicism and Romanticism four deserve special attention: Grillparzer, Lenau, Immermann, and Mörike.

The beginnings of Franz Grillparzer's (1791–1872) literary activity are connected with the Romantic tragedy of fate (*The Ancestress*, 1817) and the Classicism of Weimar. With *Sappho* (1818) the Austrian playwright created an artist drama that reminds us of Goethe's *Torquato Tasso*. In this play the heroine becomes aware of the chasm that separates art from life and seeks death. Behind it stands the author's own awareness of that difference; it marked his life and gave a characteristic note to his work. The treatment of subject matter from antiquity was further expanded in the trilogy *The Golden Fleece* (1821), which portrays the story of Medea and the Argonauts on stage, and in the play *Waves of the Sea and Love* (1831, begun in 1819) which draws on the legend of Hero and Leander. These dramas, just like *Sappho*, show Grillparzer as a masterful creator of character and are indica-

233

tive of the poetic element of his dramatic art; he succeeds in imposing the simplicity and repose of the past literary epoch upon the legendary material and infuses it with gentle melancholy. A trend towards greater realism is noticeable in his historical plays, i.e., in *King Ottocar: His Rise and Fall* (1825) and *A Faithful Servant of His Master* (1828). The play about Ottocar presents the latter's conflict with Rudolf of Hapsburg. Many details were taken from old chronicles, and the figure of Napoleon inspired the author. Although the drama was a tribute to the Austrian monarchy, it was suppressed, for a time, by the censors. When it was finally performed, it was not well received. The case of *A Faithful Servant of His Master* was similar: it appealed little to the public, and the Emperor disliked and tried to suppress it. At about the same time, Grillparzer brought out *Das Kloster von Sendomir* (*The Monastery of Sendomir*, 1828), a tale fraught with Romantic elements, and somewhat later his *Melusina* (1833), a libretto for a Romantic opera.

More and more the influence of the Viennese *Volksstück* and the *Zauberposse*—which had been led to respectable heights by Ferdinand Raimund (1790–1836)[3]—as well as the drama of Lope de Vega (1562–1635) and Pedro Calderón de la Barca (1600–1681) made their influence felt on the work of Grillparzer. His most popular play, the dramatic fairy tale, *A Dream Is Life* (1834), also shows these influences; its hero is purged of his evil ambitions through a dream and accepts the prospect of an idyllic life, an ending quite in keeping with the doctrine of resignation which Grillparzer advocated. A few years later his comedy *Woe to Him Who Lies!* (1838) was performed. It proved a failure, and the author resolved to withdraw from the stage henceforth. His later plays rest on historical and legendary matters (*Libussa, Family Strife in Hapsburg, The Jewess of Toledo*, all in 1872–1873) and their dramatis personae often show traits which can be traced back to the author's own passive and yet assertive nature. This also applies to the story of a Viennese musician, *The Poor Minstrel* (1848), which, more than any other work of Grillparzer, points to the Realism yet to come and throws light on the personality of the author.

The Hungarian-born poet Nikolaus Lenau (actually Nikolaus Niembsch Edler von Strehlenau, 1802–1850) owes much to the Romantics. Byronism and the *Weltschmerz* of the Romantic generation were intensely felt experiences for him, and his lyrics collected in *Poems* (1832–1834) and *New Poems* (1838) reveal his indebtedness to Romanticism. They reflect a pessimistic and melancholy attitude towards life, and often reveal his mastery of mood-imagery, i.e., they illustrate his intent to achieve identity of his mood with nature by endowing it with his emotions. Lenau, a frequent guest of the Swabian circle of poets (Ludwig Uhland, Gustav Schwab, and others), was influenced, for a while, by the mysticism of Justinus Kerner (1786–1862). He failed to find the freedom and peace he was seeking among the Swabians and elsewhere. Dissatisfied with himself and the political conditions in Germany and Austria, he went to America (1832–1833). He did not succeed in the New World, but some of his best poems were written there (e.g., "the Ruins at Heidelberg," "the Postilion"). Several of his poems which have as background the American scene possess local color (e.g., "The Log-Cabin"); in fact, beside the musicality of his verse, the presence of local color distinguishes his poetry, particularly in his *Puszta* poems. After his return to Europe, Lenau led, as he did before his departure, a restless life, beset by doubt and hopelessness, until finally his mind became clouded.

Nowhere else in the literary period is its transitional character so clearly reflected as in the work of Karl Leberecht Immermann (1796–1840). In his early days Immermann, a native of Magdeburg, became known as a dramatist. But although his *Tragedy in the Tyrol* (1828; reworked under the title *Andreas Hofer*, 1834) was lauded by Goethe, he had to realize that he was more gifted as a novelist. Even his most substantial play, the drama *Merlin* (1832), proved weak on stage and showed that he was not very strong in portraying character and feeling. Immermann was an intellectual writer, and the works on which his reputation rests are two novels: *The Epigoni* (1836) and *Münchhausen* (1838–1839). Both present a picture of contemporary life and are rooted in the problems of the day, and the title of the first one, *The Epigoni*, is indicative of the place which the author and some of his contemporaries thought to occupy. That is, they regarded themselves as unfortunate latecomers and deplored that their own literary production seemed not as significant as that of the immediate past. Immermann's *The Epigoni*, which draws on Goethe's *Wilhelm Meister's Apprenticeship*, shows, above all, the struggle between the rapidly degenerating aristocracy and the forces of industrialism which threatened to do away with the hitherto privileged class. The hero survives, knowing that it is only a matter of time before industrialism will prove victorious. The rather pessimistic evaluation of

235

society which Immermann arrives at in *The Epigoni* is also evident in *Münchhausen,* although there, toward the end, an optimistic note is discernible. This humoristic-satiric novel, which owes much to the art of Laurence Sterne and the Romantics, is first of all an attack upon the nobility and the shallowness of their cultural endeavors. The representatives of this class are caricatured and contrasted with the sturdy peasantry of Westphalia in the famous "Oberhof"-episode. The latter—really an independent story but skilfully woven into the body of the novel—brings into play a frequently used motif in literature: that of the regenerative force of nature. Particularly noteworthy are the realistic descriptions of the rural atmosphere and the use of folkloristic elements (a tendency also found in other European literatures of the time, e.g., the *costumbrista* school in Spain).[4] This rustic tale of Immermann's did much to popularize the genre of the *Dorfgeschichte* in Germany, and it greatly aided in establishing Realism there.

The Swabian clergyman Eduard Mörike (1804–1875) is the most unpretentious poet in nineteenth-century German literature. His verse—vivid, melodious, and often close to folksong—shows him as a keen observer of nature and is at the same time proof of his consummate ability to create from his own rich imagination. He seems to have written his poems without any marked effort, and many of them are unexcelled in the history of German poetry (e.g., "On a Lamp," "September Morning," "Prayer," "The Jilted Servant Girl," "Fair Rohtraut," "At Midnight," "On a Walking Tour") and can be ranked with the best of Goethe, by whom Mörike was greatly inspired. Romantic elements can also be found in his work, but on the whole he moved in the direction of Realism. A good example of this is his *Maler Nolten (Nolten the Painter,* 1832), an artist novel in which emotional experiences dominate. This work shows the continuing influence of the Romantics (especially of Ludwig Tieck), but also reaches beyond them because of its realistic descriptions and psychological analyses. Psychology and a supernatural fate compete in *Maler Nolten* as powers that seek to thwart man's quest for happiness. The result is a rather dubious motivation and stylistic ambiguity. This is quite different in his later endeavors, especially in *Mozart on the Way to Prague* (1855), Mörike's greatest prose work. The fantastic elements are gone, and the author comes forth with his best talent: psychological empathy. This masterfully written tale offers a convincing picture of a brief period of Mozart's life. It centers on a creative moment and later dwells on a mood of melancholy, foreshadowing the composer's death.

Close to Mörike but inferior to him are two Franconian poets whose struggles are marked by the desire to achieve primness of form: Rückert and Platen. The first of these, Friedrich Rückert (1788–1866), became known chiefly for his patriotic verse (e.g., German Poems, 1814) and his recreations and translations from Oriental literatures (e.g., The Transformations of Abu Seid, 1826 and 1837; Nal and Damajanti, 1828 and 1838). Worth mentioning also is his Liebesfrühling (Love's Springtime, 1844), a collection of simple verse which enjoyed a certain popularity among his contemporaries. Rückert excelled in imitating the various Oriental modes of lyrical expression (e.g., the Persian ghasel) and gave new impetus to the interest in Oriental culture as displayed previously by Goethe and the Romantics.

August von Platen (1796–1835) also mastered Oriental verse forms (Ghasels, 1821; New Ghasels, 1823), but he achieved excellence mainly through the patterns established in the Classical and Romance literatures. The tendency toward attainment of formal perfection, as was indicated, unites Rückert and Platen, but whereas the latter was also a master of rhythm, Rückert often failed in this regard. There is also more poetic substance in Platen's poems (notably in the cycle Sonnets from Venice, 1825), although they are surrounded by an air of intellectuality. Noteworthy is also his enmity to the Romantics, whose tragedies of fate he parodied successfully in Die verhängnisvolle Gabel (The Fatal Fork, 1826).

The outstanding lyrist among the German Realists is Annette von Droste-Hülshoff (1797–1848); she has often been called Germany's greatest poetess. Several factors influenced her artistic development: the traditions and customs of the class to which she belonged; the relative seclusion of her upbringing (mirrored in "Late Awakening"); the unrequited love for Levin Schücking (1814–1883), an experience from which sprang many verses (e.g., "By the Tower," "To Levin Schücking," "Farewell"); the austere landscape of her native Westphalia; and Catholicism which, however, did not prevent her from being assailed by doubt (e.g., "Monday in Whitsun Week"). Annette von Droste-Hülshoff had written verse as a child. Upon the request of her grandmother she began to compile a cycle of religious poems, the completion of which was delayed and became one of the last tasks in her life. The collection was published after her death by Levin Schücking under the title *Das geistliche Jahr* (*The Spiritual Year*, 1851). Schücking was also responsible for the publication of her last poems: *Letzte Gaben* (*Last Offerings*, 1860).

In 1838 a small volume of Droste-Hülshoff's poetry appeared, entitled *Poems*. It was hardly noticed by the reading public. A second volume *Poems*, published in 1844, contained some of her best lyrics and was reasonably well received. Droste-Hülshoff had, in the meantime, moved to the Meersburg on Lake Constance. The years spent in this castle were creatively the most fruitful. Many of the poems written then reflect the scenery of the Westphalian heathland (e.g., "The Pool," "The Dolmen," "The Founder," "The Boy's Walk through the Bog") or mirror the environment of the Meersburg (e.g., "The Inn by the Lake," "The Old Castle"). Droste-Hülshoff is seen at her best in her nature poetry. Her intimate knowledge of nature, the attention which she bestows on the details of an object, her recognition of the inadequacies of man's perceptual ability, the awareness of her thoughts and pulse beat during the process of observation, and above all the skill with which she renders all this by means of vivid images made her one of the greatest nature poets. Characteristic of her poetry is the passage from inner to outer vision, the compelling harshness of her rhythms, as well as the pronounced visual quality of her verse. The conflicts of the greater world about her were not mirrored in her lyrics; she turned away from the social upheavals that marked her time and exhorted her contemporaries to tread carefully and to adhere to the old ways (e.g., "Hold Fast," "To the Reformers"). Her high poetic stature had, in her own day, been recognized by only a few critics and admirers; nowadays, she rates as having been too advanced for her time.

Of her prose work, *The Jew's Beech-Tree* (1842) merits attention. Set in the hilly regions of Westphalia, it is a well constructed novella of crime and guilt in which heredity and, especially, the prevailing social circumstances play an important role. To be noted also is the author's psychological insight. She succeeds in creating an atmosphere of religious earnestness and portrays the events in a manner that is realistic and also points to man's limitations in his attempts to fathom reality.

The writers who are identified with the Young German Movement[5] sought, above all, more freedom. They were against the old generation, the morals, convictions, and beliefs of its members, and against the indifferentism, displayed by Classicists and Romantics alike, toward questions of the day. A starting point of their polemical activity was the criticism of Goethe's writings by Wolfgang Menzel (1798–1873), an influential literary critic of the time. Ludwig Börne (actually Löb Baruch, 1786–1837), one of the main driving forces of this loosely united group and a master of the *feuilleton*, continued this trend and challenged Goethe because of his apolitical attitude. Forced to go into exile, Börne wrote the *Briefe aus Paris* (*Letters from Paris*, 1832–1834). They portray the political, social, and cultural situation in post-revolutionary France and thereby expose the reactionary nature and untenability of conditions prevailing in Germany. Other spokesmen of Young Germany were Wienbarg, Gutzkow, Laube, Prutz, and Mundt.

Ludolf Wienbarg (1802–1872), the aesthetic theorist of the movement, called in his writings (e.g., *Aesthetic Campaigns*, 1834; *On Recent Literature*, 1835) for an action-directed enthusiasm, demanding that the subject matter of literature be close to life and emphasis be put on what is significant for the present. Almost all the Young German writers were engaged in polemics and produced journalistic contributions; their actual literary achievement suffered from this, and often it was not superior. Karl Gutzkow (1811–1878) caused an uproar with the novel *Wally, die Zweiflerin* (*Wally the Sceptic*, 1835), chiefly because of its attack on conventional morality and its anti-religious tendencies. The emancipation of the flesh which it preached, caught on among his contemporaries and has become a point of departure for a type of literary activity attacking the established ethical norms of society. Gutzkow's rather lengthy novel *Die Ritter vom Geiste* (*Knights of the Spirit*, 1849–1851) is noteworthy owing to the attention bestowed on detail and because of a new technique which the author sought to achieve. Essentially, this technique aimed at presenting a broad panorama of life with emphasis on simultaneity rather than chronological development.[6] Among his dramas the tragedy *Uriel Acosta* (1847) stands out; it centers on the clash of liberal ideas with orthodox tenets. Heinrich Laube's (1806–1884) fame rests on *Die Karlsschüler* (*Pupils of the Karlsschule*, 1846), a play about young Schiller, and on his having been the director of the Burgtheater in Vienna. His main interest was the theater, and his knowledge of stage matters is reflected in several of his works (e.g., *The Burgtheater*, 1868; *The North German Theater*, 1872). Robert Prutz (1816–1872) is still remembered for his comedy *Die politische Wochenstube* (*The Political Childbed*, 1845), a satire on the official Germany of the time, and

239

for his novel *Das Engelchen* (*The Little Angel,* 1851) which deals with the introduction of mechanical looms in the weaving industry and the resulting social and moral decline. Theodor Mundt (1808–1861) is chiefly known for his historical writings and for *Madonna oder Unterhaltungen mit einer Heiligen* (*Madonna, or: Conversations with a Saint,* 1835), a novel centered about the conversion of a young woman to the new ideal of "Free Womanhood."

The authorities in Germany and Austria had eyed the endeavors of these literates with suspicion and on December 10, 1835, they took action against them. The writings of the Young Germans were banned and they themselves were threatened with severe punishment. The same applied to publishers who ventured to further their cause.

Heinrich Heine (1797–1856), like Börne of Jewish ancestry, had been connected with the Young German movement and was mentioned in the official document. He went to Paris and succeeded in establishing himself there. At that time Heine had already gained recognition as a poet and writer; his *Pictures of Travel* (1826–1831) and especially the *Book of Songs* (1827) were considered worthy of note and enjoyed some popularity. Many of the poems in the latter volume were inspired by his unrequited love for his cousin and derive from the folksong and lyrics of the Romantic epoch. They have, however, a distinct ring of their own, be it that the poet's sceptical bent and irony are applied too forcefully to allow him to be regarded as genuinely Romantic, or that one finds in them a combination of lightness and plasticity seldom encountered in German poetry. Some of the verses in this collection have assured Heine's world-wide reputation and brought him lasting fame (e.g., "The Grenadiers," "Belshazzar," "All in the Magic Month of May," "The Loreley," "The Pilgrimage to Kevlaar").

In Paris Heine acted as correspondent for several German and French journals and came under the spell of Saint-Simonism. He wrote about German politics, philosophy and literature, the history of religion in Germany, conditions in France, and also published *The Romantic School* (1836), a work in which he attacked the Romantics because of their flight from reality and developed a program for a literature not divorced from the problems of the day. In the book *On Ludwig Börne* (1840), the polemic poem *Atta Troll: A Midsummer Night's Dream* (1843–1847) as well as in several shorter poems written during that time Heine criticized, at times unjustly, the artistic and political shortcomings of his contemporaries. In 1844 a new collection of verse appeared, entitled *New Poems*. The most famous poem in this work is the strongly political "The Silesian Weavers," which mirrors the threat posed by the proletariat for the existing social order in Germany.[7] Also included in this volume is the long polemic poem *Germany: A Winter's Tale*. In it Heine ridicules the prevailing conditions, particularly the philistine attitude of German citizens. *Romancero* (1850) and *Last Poems* (1853 and 1856) evince an awareness of the demands of the future, but this last phase of his creative activity is overshadowed by the sufferings of the paralyzed poet. There are colorful narrative poems, satirical verse of political and social import, and poems which, despite a note of anguished hopelessness, are testimony to the activist spirit and artistic genuineness of this writer.

Other emanations from the Young German spirit were the endeavors of the political poets: Freiligrath, Weerth, Herwegh, Hoffmann von Fallersleben, and others. They fought for the political and social advancement of Germany and received an additional impulse from the writings of Anastasius Grün (pseud. for Anton Alexander von Auersperg, 1806–1876), who had criticized the Metternich regime in his *Spaziergänge eines Wiener Poeten* (*Saunterings of a Viennese Poet*, 1831). These poets were most active from 1840 to 1848; after the Revolution they produced literature that is only occasionally of interest. Ferdinand Freiligrath (1810–1876) was probably the most genuine lyrical poet among them. He published a volume of rather exotic verse (*Poems*, 1838) and then turned to politics. His poetic activity thus received direction, and he was fired by enthusiasm for the new ideals. The collection *Ein Glaubensbekenntnis* (*A Confession of Faith*, 1844) forced him to go abroad, but other lyrics appeared at intervals, e.g., *Ca ira!* (1846), *Die Toten an die Lebenden* (*The Dead to the Living*, 1848), and *Neuere politische und soziale Gedichte* (*New Political and Social Poems*, 1849–1851). His most famous poem is probably "Up From Below!" which focuses on the role of the proletariat and points to the Revolution that was yet to come. Georg Weerth's (1822–1856) importance had first been proclaimed by Friedrich Engels, who regarded him as the most significant poet of the German proletariat. In his literary work Weerth was influenced, above all, by Heine. His lyrics are typified by their folksong-like quality and social content. Particularly noteworthy are the *Lieder von Lancashire* (*Songs from Lancashire*, 1845 f.). He also distinguished himself as an author of prose, notably with the *Humoristische Skizzen aus dem deutschen Handelsleben* (*Humorous Sketches of German Merchants*, 1845–1848). Georg Herwegh (1817–1875) was admired in liberal circles because of his revolutionary *Gedichte eines Lebendigen* (*Poems of a Living Man*, 1841–1843), an anthology of his best poems. He was driven into exile, failed as a revolutionary leader, but adhered to his radical political convictions. Of his later work the poem "Bundeslied für den Allgemeinen Deutschen Arbeiterverein" ("Workers' Marseillaise," 1863) is noteworthy for its call to strike action.

Apart from these three poets, August Heinrich Hoffmann von Fallersleben (1798–1874) deserves some attention. He was dismissed from his post as professor at the University of Breslau because of his rather political *Unpolitische Lieder* (*Non-Political Songs*, 1840–1841), but later in the century made his peace with the authorities. He is mainly remembered for his patriotic hymn "Deutschland, Deutschland über alles" ("Germany First") which later became the national anthem.

Closely related to Young Germany are two dramatists who were in agreement with or fought for the ideals of the revolutionaries: Grabbe and Büchner. The first notable achievement of Christian Dietrich Grabbe (1801–1836) was *Comedy, Satire, Irony and Deeper Meaning* (1827). In this play, which continues certain trends of Romantic comedy (especially of Ludwig Tieck), the rather unrestrained Westphalian author derides various aspects of society and literary phenomena of his day. There are humor and wit, drastic and grotesque elements, as well as sarcasm and pessimism in this work. It was not performed until 1895; the temper of the Naturalistic period was needed to put it on the stage. Also important is Grabbe's concern with historical tragedy. He wrote a number of dramas which deal with historical figures and events and often use realistic means (regarding psychology, language, milieu, and detail), contributing thus to the development of Realism in German drama. His most successful work was *Napoleon oder Die hundert Tage* (*Napoleon, or The Hundred Days*, 1831). In this spectacle about the return and final defeat of Napoleon Bonaparte the author portrays the hero as the product of time and circumstance. In a sequence of quickly changing scenes with much detail and masses of people he portrays the events vividly, anticipating the efforts of the Naturalists.

Superior to Grabbe's endeavors was the work of Georg Büchner (1813–1837). This Hessian writer, whose eminent stature was not recognized during his lifetime, was to become more and more popular with the passing of time. The Naturalists hailed him as a forerunner of their aims, the Expressionists admired him greatly, and nowadays he has won international recognition and is regarded as one of the most significant dramatists of the nineteenth century. As early as in his student years in Giessen he fought for social justice. He was active in founding a society for supporting the rights of man, the *Gesellschaft für Menschenrechte,* and wrote a revolutionary pamphlet: *The Hessian Peasants' Messenger* (1834). In this pamphlet Büchner attacked the rich, the privileged classes, and their institutions, and turned toward the exploited peasantry of his native Hesse, exhorting them to remedy the situation forcefully. The result was disappointing, and out of his disappointment grew his first drama: *Danton's Death* (1835). In this hastily written and pessimistic work, which makes use of excerpts from the speeches of the French revolutionaries, Büchner seeks to present the French leaders realistically against the background of the people and without regard to idealistic demands or rules of the theater. Danton, an eloquent agitator, libertine, and cynic, is driven into isolation, and his stature is enhanced by Büchner's insight into the mechanism of the Revolution. The author soberly analyzes the fate of his hero and his followers and looks critically at the revolutionaries, creating a historical canvas which is full of life and also reflects his concern with the question of revolution in his own time.

In 1835 Büchner had to flee to Strassburg. He continued his studies of medicine and natural science, took his doctorate, and obtained a lectureship at the University of Zurich. He died prematurely, just twenty-three years old. During the years of exile Büchner wrote some important works: the comedy *Leonce and Lena* (1836) and the prose fragment *Lenz* (1839). In the rather melancholy comedy, which at first sight derides the existence of the many principalities in Germany, the characters become marionettes who move about by the will of their creator, and the play itself becomes the enactment of tendencies reaching back to the days of Romantic drollery. The prose fragment convincingly presents the early stages of J. M. R. Lenz's insanity.

Büchner's best known and perhaps most stirring work is *Woyzeck* (1836), also a fragment. It was not published until 1879 and was first performed in 1913, when it roused the admiration of the Expressionists, just as it had won the esteem of Gerhart Hauptmann and other authors of the *Moderne* before the turn of the century. Based on an actual murder case, the action of this dramatic fragment is dissolved into a series of gloomy pictures. Realistic diction abounds in it. The hero is a common soldier whose actions are determined by his passions and the unjust social order in which he lives. The author's compassion is felt throughout and emphasis is put on the sufferings of the mistreated creature who perishes at the end without a ray of hope.

A quite different type of realistic drama is found in Vienna, in the writings of Johann Nepomuk Nestroy (1801–1862). At first this author was under the influence of Ferdinand Raimund's idealistic fairy plays, but soon he parodied them and in his farces and comedies developed a down-to-earth realism with a distinct social note. Full of intrigue and action, of local satire and drastic humor, and always observant of the requirements of the stage, Nestroy's plays kept the audiences spellbound and secured his fame. Of his many works *Der böse Geist Lumpazivagabundus* (*The Evil Spirit Lumpacivagabundus*, 1835) and *Einen Jux will er sich machen* (*Out on a Spree He Goes*, 1844) are perhaps the best known. Indeed the latter became the model for Thornton Wilder's play *The Matchmaker* (1956).

In the field of narrative prose, interest in the historical novel and the birth of the peasant and regional novel should be mentioned. In Germany the historical novel had had a good start with Achim von Arnim's *Die Kronenwächter* (*Guardians of the Crown*, 1817) and received strong impulses from the work of the historiographers (e.g., Leopold von Ranke, 1795–1886)[8] and from Walter Scott (1771–1832), whose popular novels assured him of some German disciples (e.g., W. Alexis's *Walladmor*, 1824; W. Hauff's *Lichtenstein*, 1826). The most gifted German writer of this genre before the Revolution of 1848 was Willibald Alexis (pseud. for Wilhelm Häring, 1798–1871). The subject matter of his novels was usually taken from the history of Brandenburg-Prussia, and he was able to create realistic situations and figures. His best known work is *Die Hosen des Herrn von Bredow* (*The Breeches of Sir Bredow*, 1846–1848), a humorous tale presenting the conflict of the backward aristocracy of Brandenburg with the Elector Joachim in the early decades of the sixteenth century.

The peasant novel attained a high rank at once through the endeavors of the Swiss pastor Jeremias Gotthelf (pseud. for Albert Bitzius, 1797–1854). Gotthelf, a writer of elemental force, was influenced, above all, by the teachings of his countryman Johann

Heinrich Pestalozzi (1746–1827)[9] and wrote as an educator of the Swiss and of people in general; he did not write so much as a poet with literary interests only. As a result of this leaning he is quite original, but often also inattentive to the conventions of fiction. Thus it is with his first novel: *Der Bauernspiegel oder Lebensgeschichte des Jeremias Gotthelf* (*The Peasants' Mirror, or The Life of Jeremias Gotthelf*, 1837). Conceived in the form of a make-believe autobiography, it shows the development of a young orphan from farmer's helper to free-lance writer and adviser of children. The first part is vivid and forceful; the second part loses some of its élan and becomes too theoretical. Other novels followed, for example, the popular *Sorrows and Joys of a Schoolmaster* (1838–1839), the famous *Ulric the Farm Servant* (1841) with the continuation *Ulric the Tenant Farmer* (1847), and the rather complex *Anne Bäbi Jowäger* (1843–1844) with its attack on quackery. Gotthelf also wrote some novellas of which *The Black Spider* (1842) and *Elsi the Strange Maidservant* (1843) are perhaps his most renowned. Both are rooted in history and present the Swiss environment realistically. His work as a whole is proof of his love for the worker of the soil and of his understanding of Swiss national particularities. Although he was inclined, at times, to sentimentalize rural life, the immediacy with which he describes it stands out in an age of emerging Realism.

Allied with the rise of the peasant novel is the development of the German *Dorfgeschichte*. The origins of this genre lie further back, but various endeavors in the late eighteenth and early nineteenth centuries (e.g., Johann Peter Hebel, 1760–1826)[10] stimulated interest in and led to the creation of the village tale as we know it. This was, in effect, achieved by Karl Leberecht Immermann with his *Oberhof* and by Berthold Auerbach (1812–1882) with his *Village Tales from the Black Forest* (1843–1853). The latter was a popular author whose village tales were widely read. However, with the passing of time only a few of Auerbach's stories have proved to be of lasting value (e.g. *The Story of Diethelm von Buchenberg*).

Mention should also be made of Charles Sealsfield's (pseud. for Karl Anton Postl, 1793–1864) New World tales of which *The Cabin Book, or National Characteristics* (1841) is a good example. It is a series of loosely connected stories describing, in an unorthodox manner, the landscape, conditions, and people of the North American continent. The author uses factual evidence, and through-

245

out remains oriented toward reality. Somewhat less prestigious than Sealsfield's prose was the novelistic work of Friedrich Gerstäcker (1816–1872). Travel and adventure novels such as his *The Regulators of Arkansas* (1846) and *The Pirates of the Mississippi* (1848) enjoyed great popularity, but toward the end of the century they were eclipsed by similar efforts of Karl May (1842–1912) whose adventure novels became popular among German teenagers.

In March 1848 the Revolution broke out in Germany and Austria. In Vienna the Metternich era came to an end, the Emperor had to abdicate, and his chancellor was driven into exile; in Berlin the King of Prussia was humiliated and had to promise a new constitution to the people. There was some fighting in the different states of the Confederation, especially in Austro-Hungary, but the attempt to overthrow the established order was, on the whole, unsuccessful. Some privileges were won by the rebellious masses, but the subsequent lack of unity and efficient leadership soon enabled the old powers fully to regain their position. The years which followed the Revolution brought, nevertheless, some great changes in Germany and Austria, also in the sphere of literary activity. The Young Germans had fallen silent, but a new awareness of reality, political and otherwise, was arising; writers became conscious of the role which the middle class had to fulfill and looked for a closer connection of their work with the world about them.

Looking over the second half of the nineteenth century, we find that Charles Dickens (1812–1870), Ivan Turgenev (1818–1883), and later Emile Zola (1840–1902) were the most important foreign literary influences. The novels of Dickens, in particular, laid claim to the admiration of the men of letters in Germany and Austria; the modernity, humor, and firm stroke of the English author were praised and the German versions of his works greeted with enthusiasm. During this period German literature brought forth two renowned dramatists, Friedrich Hebbel and Gerhart Hauptmann, and several important novelists: Gustav Freytag, Adalbert Stifter, Gottfried Keller, Wilhelm Raabe, and Theodor Fontane. The novels of these writers have by and large failed to acquire wide international significance, such as was attained by the works of, for example, Dickens, Turgenev, Honoré de Balzac (1799–1850), Gustave Flaubert (1821–1880), Fyodor Dostoyevsky (1821–1881), and Leo Tolstoy (1828–1910). They were different from and did not reach the cosmopolitan stature of the Realistic novel

246

elsewhere in Europe, save perhaps the best efforts of Fontane. The range of the German novelists was narrower than that of their English, French, and Russian peers; they withdrew to the area of middle-class endeavor and emphasized inwardness. These novelists and such other writers as Theodor Storm, and Conrad Ferdinand Meyer also excelled as authors of novellas; in fact, this form of narrative prose was most successful and was raised to great artistic heights during this literary period. The aim of these writers in post-revolutionary Germany and Austria was a more conscious Realism; or rather, they wished to labor under the sign of Poetic Realism, as Otto Ludwig (1813–1865)[11] called it, i.e., they sought to present reality as they understood it and strove to embellish it for the sake of art. Lyric poetry did not flourish greatly in the bourgeois age, although some of C. F. Meyer's verse is of high quality. The members of the Munich School were quite active in this genre but achieved little that could be called excellent. Toward the seventies and after the Franco-Prussian War, German literature deteriorated somewhat. Economic wealth and commercial expansion had fostered materialism, and materialistic thought spread and affected the various spheres of intellectual activity. Writers often yielded to the ostentatious spirit of the *Gründerzeit* and produced works of little worth and only ephemeral appeal. The reaction soon set in: Naturalism came to the fore and found in Gerhart Hauptmann its most distinguished champion.

One of the most conspicuous figures of nineteenth-century German literature is Friedrich Hebbel (1813–1863). This energetic writer from the region of Dithmarschen began his literary career as a poet, but his significance in the history of German literature rests on his work as a dramatist and, to some extent, on his theoretical observations. He published a volume of poetry (*Poems*, 1842), several short stories, and also some dramas before 1848. Of these latter, *Judith* (1841), his first success on the stage, may be noted, but the middle-class tragedy *Maria Magdalena* (1844) really stands out; it is Hebbel's only drama dealing with contemporary life and has become one of his best known plays. It continues a line of development marked by Lessing's *Emilia Galotti* and Schiller's *Intrigue and Love* and leads over to Henrik Ibsen (1828–1906) and Naturalist drama. In this work Hebbel uses the analytic technique, i.e., he has the major events antecede the stage action and then reveals them gradually to the audience. The tragic conflict is presented without explanation, reflections, or moralizing. This conflict

247

is rooted in the traditional ideas about honor and arises out of the situation and the characters' inability to adapt to it.

The preface to *Maria Magdalena* is significant since it reflects, apart from polemics and subsidiary considerations, Hebbel's views on dramatic art, its task, development, and relation to his time. Leaning on the doctrines of Hegel and Schopenhauer,[12] Hebbel saw the individual will in conflict with a universal will and sought to portray situations in which the inherent contradictions would be resolved, thus demonstrating the working of the universal in the incidental phenomenon. The thoughts which he presented in this preface were elaborated in his diaries and became part of his "pantragic" view of life.

Hebbel's aesthetic pronouncements to a large measure determined his stature in the history of German literature. His actual dramatic work was frequently considered on a level subordinate to his theory, and often critics dealt with it in an unsatisfactory manner. This applies particularly to some of his later works which were felt to be dramatized ideas and problem-plays. Almost all his dramas are clothed in a historical garb, and usually they are located in a period of history when important changes were about to occur.

In the love tragedy *Herod and Mariamne* (1849) the action is set on the threshold of the Christian era. The necessity for the tragic conflict is bound up with the psychological make-up of the characters. Herod is shown as an egocentric and immoderate despot for whom a wife is mere property; Mariamne displays an equal lack of moderation, but thinks in more modern terms. When her personal dignity is violated, tragedy ensues. In *Agnes Bernauer* (1852), Hebbel's most controversial play, the constellation of characters is arranged differently. The work is set in Bavaria in the early fifteenth century. The love of the young duke for a commoner clashes with the interests of the state; she becomes a victim of a political assassination and the duke has to acknowledge the necessity for the deed. His assent rests on the author's belief that the individual has to yield to the exigencies of a super-individual reality. The tragedy *Gyges and His Ring* (1856) is closer to the spirit of *Herod and Mariamne*. Based mainly on a tale of Herodotus (ca. 490–425 B.C.), it is considered Hebbel's best work as regards dramatic form, but it is not free from improbabilities. In this play the King of Lydia brushes Oriental custom aside and seeks to assert his individuality, allowing Gyges to behold his wife's beauty. The latter, bound by the laws of her forefathers, obtains revenge and commits suicide.

The last major work which Hebbel completed was *The Nibelungs* (1861). It links up the doom of the Nibelungs with the advent of Christianity; the pagan world has to give way so that the new belief can rise. Toward the end of his life Hebbel was working on a play about *Demetrius*; it remained unfinished.

In retrospect it can be stated that for all his talent, psychological insight, and ability to create real people Hebbel's fame has gradually diminished. With great determination he tried to illustrate man's tragic situation as he saw it; but, were it not for the play *Maria Magdalena,* one would be bound to say that Hebbel's work has little appeal nowadays and that it signifies the break between modern drama and that of the past.

Compared to Hebbel the other dramatists of the period seem pale. A great number of plays were written and performed, but only few warrant mention here, e.g., Gustav Freytag's *The Journalists* (1854), Emanuel Geibel's *Master Andrea* (1855), and Paul Heyse's *Hadrian* (1865). The Shakespeare enthusiast Otto Ludwig also wrote some noteworthy dramas, particularly *The Hereditary Forester* (1853) and *The Maccabees* (1854), but they have lost their appeal; his fame rests on his prose work, especially on *Between Heaven and Earth* (1856), a craftsman novel about the fate of two brothers that is impressive for its psychology and vividness. Richard Wagner (1813–1883) is a rather special case. His music-drama was a distinctive contribution to German culture and his high stature as a composer is undeniable. It is also generally accepted that the stage-craft in Germany greatly profited from the production of his operas, but his artistic achievement ought to be considered in a history of music.

The German novel in the second half of the nineteenth century found one of its most successful representatives in the Silesian writer Gustav Freytag (1816–1895). Having been under the influence of Hoffmann von Fallersleben, Freytag sympathized with the aspirations of the Young Germans and carried on the tradition of liberalism after 1848. He became a journalist and also published several dramas, but his fame is mainly based on a book on dramatic technique (*The Technique of the Drama,* 1863), and on the merchant novel *Debit and Credit* (1855). Freytag learned much from the art of Charles Dickens and wanted to become the German counterpart of the English novelist. In our day the limits and shortcomings of his poetic creativity have been recognized and the one-sidedness of his merchant novel has been stigmatized. The basis of

Debit and Credit was provided by Freytag's experiences and his awareness of the growing power of the German middle class. He glorifies the industrious merchant and citizen, showing the ascent of a class that has discovered its superiority over the aristocrats. The aims and operations of a trading establishment in Breslau are presented in detail and the rise of an altogether faultless apprentice to a position of manager and partner is contrasted with the negative development of a young Jew who becomes the villain of the story. The work breathes the self-confidence of the prosperous middle class and emanates the sober-mindedness of the age. The fact that the characterization is often unsatisfactory and the style too artificially elevated did not diminish the appeal of this novel.

In his other works Freytag became engrossed in the cultural history of Germany. He produced a cycle of novels, *Our Fore-fathers* (1873–1881), which enjoyed much popularity among the German reading public. These novels mirror the fate of individuals related by blood from the period of the great migrations to the first half of the nineteenth century. The author seeks to demonstrate the connection of contemporary man with his ancestors and stresses the character traits which unite them. Freytag did not always capture to a sufficient degree the wealth of incident of a given epoch; his development of parallel actions engendered a certain monotony; and the later novels of the cycle lack poetic vigor. Nevertheless, the awareness of historical detail which Freytag displayed in these and other works secured him a prominent place among the writers of his time.

Whereas Freytag had been the representative of the economically progressive and nationally minded bourgeoisie, Adalbert Stifter (1805–1868) presented in his writings middle-class interests of a different nature. This Austrian novelist had frequented the circles of liberals in Vienna, but as they became more radical he distanced himself from the issues of the time. He was concerned about the lack of morality among his contemporaries and about their materialistic outlook on life, and hoped to contribute, as a pedagogue and writer, to the moral betterment of his fellow citizens. In matters of literary technique he was first under the influence of Jean Paul and later under that of Goethe whom he admired greatly and whose classical style he tried to approximate. Only a few discerning critics appreciated his work during his time; Friedrich Nietzsche's high praise of Stifter, and the efforts of some literary historians in the first two decades of this century, finally won him wider recognition. Since then his fame has increased steadily and he is now regarded as one of the great figures of German prose fiction.

Stifter began his career with journalistic contributions. During the years 1844–1850 he published his *Studies,* a collection of tales and novellas previously published in periodicals and annuals. This collection includes such well known stories as *Brigitta, Alpine Forest (Hochwald), Heather Village, My Great-Grandfather's Note-Book,* and others. In another volume, entitled *Bright Stones* (1853), several other stories were published, of which the short Christmas tale *Mountain Crystal* is perhaps Stifter's most popular work. Set in the hilly regions and forests of his native countryside, the Bohemian Forest, it describes the various moods of nature and reveals the author's deep sympathy for children. Noteworthy also is the preface to *Bright Stones;* it contains a summary of Stifter's aesthetic views and stresses the importance of the simple and seemingly insignificant.

Stifter's masterpiece was the educational novel *Der Nachsommer (Indian Summer,* 1857). This lengthy work, set in the preindustrial period in Austria, shows the harmonious development of a young man from an affluent middle-class family. The successive stages of his education are portrayed with meticulous care, and the element of time carries great importance in the unfolding of his personality. Emphasis is put on the role of art and science; they are, in fact, the two most important formative influences in the life of the hero. Art especially is given a prominent place and is intimately connected with love and religion. The hero is exposed to love and art at about the same time of his life. Art is regarded as a parallel to religion: Artists are seen as priests of beauty and beauty in turn as the manifestation of divine laws. Passion is absent from the novel. Its dangers are indicated by pointing to the background of the hero's guide, a former official who was ennobled for the services he had rendered to the Austrian state. This person is shown to have attained, through great personal sacrifice, that sensibility and harmony with his environment sought by the hero; but he is experiencing a serene Indian summer without having truly lived the summer of his life. The value of the family is greatly emphasized; the hero is given to understand that his destiny is to found a family and to lead a well-ordered life.

The novel is permeated with a great sense of order, and the language is stylized and dwells on detail. Stifter is bent on presenting everything in the right proportion; he reduces the action to a minimum and proceeds in a disciplined and leisurely manner which underlines the tranquil serenity that is the mark of the book. Essentially, however, the perfection striven for, the pursuit of this idyllic form of life, is utopian. The social concerns and political problems of the time remain untouched in *Der Nachsommer*, and the people form an élite who have lost touch with the rest of the world. While their particular abode may not be a refuge from reality, it is so much their own that, when measured by the harsh reality outside, it becomes a beautiful illusion, a valiant attempt to brush aside the hostility of real life.

A counterpart to *Der Nachsommer* is Stifter's second great novel: *Witiko* (1865–1867). Here the progress of a whole nation occupies the foreground; the development of the individual is subordinate to it. The novel is carefully constructed and evokes a specific period of medieval history in Bohemia. The emphasis on idea-content, unusual for Stifter, is remarkable. The author is concerned with the historical process and, above all, with the maintenance of order. The main character is not placed in the center of the action, but observes the process and participates in it. The detachment of the narrator lends a certain objectivity to the events portrayed, but historical and other elements rooted in reality are subjected to what may be called an earnest edifying impulse and the desire to maintain ethical appeal. As in most of his works the stream of life is gradually revealed and the narration becomes proof of his conviction that all art is bound up with the religious.

Much closer to the reality of his time than Stifter was the Swiss writer Gottfried Keller (1819–1890). His youth was marked by privations, irregular schooling, and an ill-fated inclination to become a landscape painter. Although he was not without talent in this sphere of artistic activity, Keller gave up painting for the pursuit of creative literature. In 1846 he published a volume of political verse: *Poems*. It won him a stipend and enabled him to undertake university studies. In Heidelberg, Keller was influenced by Ludwig Feuerbach, who had proclaimed the supernatural and God to be projections of man's fancy and to have their origin in man's fears. This materialistic doctrine nourished Keller's anti-religious feelings and shaped his agnostic outlook on life. Moving to Berlin, the author finished the first version of his partly autobiographical novel *Green Henry* (1854–1855). The book was not well received; critics regarded it as an imitation of Rousseau's *Confessions* (1781–1788) and discovered many flaws in it. Keller himself was not satisfied with the work and later revised it. His *New Poems* (1851 and 1854) also appeared during this time. In the latter edition Keller reached his peak as a lyric poet. His first concern in poetry was the substance of the poem, not the melodiousness and even flow of the verse. While he received distinction primarily in the field of prose, he also wrote some excellent lyrics. The "Song of the Evening" is his most famous poem; it typifies Keller's assent to life and awareness of reality, and it led Theodor Storm to call it the "purest gold" of lyric poetry.[13]

In Berlin, Keller also worked on *People of Seldwyla* (1856), a collection of short stories and novellas which belong to the best of German narrative prose. This collection includes the satiric tale *The Three Righteous Combmakers*, a grotesque portrayal of petty bourgeois greed and excessive self-interest; the tragic tale *A Village Romeo and Juliet*, which may be regarded as the apex of the German village story; and several other works of which *Spiegel the Kitten* is to be especially noted for giving free rein to the author's fantasy. The volume was meant to raise the moral and social consciousness of Keller's fellow-countrymen and contemporaries; it satirized their shortcomings and foolishness and greatly enhanced his reputation.

Following his appointment to the position of chief clerk of his native canton at Zurich, Keller's productivity ceased for many years. But in 1872 he published secularized versions of the legends of several saints under the title *Seven Legends* and somewhat later the second volume of *People of Seldwyla* (1874). Of the stories contained in this volume, *Clothes Make the Man* is probably the best known. It depicts the fortunes of a poor tailor and uses the motif of mistaken identity. The hero—unlike the protagonist of other works employing this motif—does not disappear after his true identity has been established but gains a foothold in society. Another collection of narrative prose, consisting mainly of histori-cally rooted tales entitled *Zurich Novellen*, appeared in 1878.

In the late seventies Keller also began to rewrite his *Green Henry* (1879–1880). The revised edition of this novel is justly famous and has become known as the outstanding example of the German novel of development in the nineteenth century. Unlike the first version, which ended tragically, the revised work terminates on a positive note. The isolation of the hero is overcome; he is ready to serve the community and finds a purpose in life. Service to society is the most important thematic element in this work. The artist-figures forsake art and devote themselves to politics or business, and the artist-hero renounces his artistic calling and becomes an administrator in his native canton. That the artist in this novel was to abandon his career and become a respectable middle-class citizen is proof of the progressive spirit of the author. The book reflects the rise of the bourgeoisie to prestige and focuses on one of the main problems of the middle class: that of having to choose "a vocation in accordance with [one's] most promising talents."[14] This in turn is intimately connected with the problem of education and the development of the individual. There is development in various spheres (e.g., love, politics, ethics, religion) and the individualistic plane is gradually superseded by that of social responsibility. Whatever endangers it—e.g., the possibility of marriage in the Dortchen-episode—is circumvented and relegated to secondary place.

Despite the proximity of the narrated events to the author's own life, Keller succeeded in remaining objective and told his story in a leisurely manner, paying attention to humorous effect. As the narrative develops, a loss of precision becomes noticeable and there are incidents which could have been depicted with more skill. Keller is, however, never far from reality; occasionally he changes it slightly or adds a symbolical value or other embellishing feature to it. He writes in a somewhat dense realistic style and strives to maintain a level that is in keeping with the epic temper of the novel.

Of Keller's remaining work *Das Sinngedicht* (*The Epigram*, 1882) is noteworthy. It is a collection of stories which are united by a common theme, the choice of a congenial marriage partner; the tale called *Regine* is the best known of these. His last work, the novel *Martin Salander* (1886), is inferior to *Green Henry*. It is didactic and reflects primarily Keller's concern about the imagined deterioration of the democratic system in Switzerland. The shortcomings of this particular work do not, however, diminish Keller's artistic achievement and his eminent stature in nineteenth-century German literature. His writings are the expression of a humanistic liberalism and reflect the cultural life of the age.

Quainter and less readily accessible than Keller's work are the writings of Wilhelm Raabe (1831–1910), a native of a small town in Lower Saxony. This North German novelist stands in the tradition of Jean Paul and was influenced by Laurence Sterne and other English writers. He became the literary representative of both the provincial and the petty bourgeoisie. His first novel, *Die Chronik der Sperlingsgasse* (*The Chronicle of Sparrow Lane*, 1857), was written while he was still a student in Berlin and brought the author a measure of fame. The book contains a series of arabesque-like episodes held together by the memory of the storyteller, and it is written in a digressive and reflective style. Some of the main characteristics of Raabe's prose are discernible: the preference for characters who have felt the pressure of modern times, the contemplative bent of his narration, the tendency to give way to melancholy musings, and the mingling of realistic description with poeticizing and lyrical impulses.

One of the main issues with which Raabe tried to come to terms was the gulf which he perceived between the strictures of the existing social order and man's awareness of his spiritual freedom. Education, ethics, and humor were to help to overcome this deficiency. This becomes evident, for example, in the tale *Unsers Herrgotts Kanzlei* (*The Chancellory of Our Lord*, 1862), which focuses on the efforts of the bourgeois to assert themselves in sixteenth-century Magdeburg, and in the novel *Die Leute aus dem Walde* (*People from the Forest*, 1863) which throws light on the various layers of city society and stresses the value of education in letting the hero attain mastery of life. Raabe was a defender of bourgeois virtue and looked fondly at the contemplativeness of the past, although later he became aware of its shortcomings. He proved to be a master of the novella and wrote many shorter tales, some of which are rooted in history and at times reveal the presence of the adventurous and romantic (e.g., *The Squire of Denow*, 1859; *The Black Galley*, 1865; *Sankt Thomas*, 1865; *Else of the Fir-Tree*, 1869). As his insight into the social processes which he witnessed increased, his interest in history subsided, and a pessimistic outlook on life, which drew on the writings of Arthur Schopenhauer, came to the fore. This can be seen in his so-called trilogy of novels (*The Hunger Pastor*, 1864; *Abu Telfan, or The Return from the Mountains of the Moon*, 1867; *The Schüdderump*, 1870) and in some of his later stories as, for example, *Zum wilden Mann* (*The "Wild Man" Pharmacy*) and *Die Innerste* (*The Innermost*, 1876). Raabe's trilogy has a central position in his work. The first of these novels, *The Hunger Pastor*, is artistically not too satisfying, yet it proved to be one of the author's most popular works. In it Raabe defends gentleness, innocence, and a thirst for spiritual knowledge. He contrasts the hero's course of life with that of the anti-hero and lets the events culminate in the former's attainment of limited happiness.

The novel suffers from too much inventiveness on the author's part; it contains melodramatic elements and other features incompatible with Realism. While, in this novel, Raabe was still somewhat optimistic regarding man's endeavors, he is beset by doubts and grows more and more sceptical about man's efforts in the other works of the trilogy. In *Abu Telfan* the philistinism of German society is examined and the central character becomes an outsider in the community to which he belongs; in *The Schüdderump* disillusionment prevails and the protagonist has to perish.

At times Raabe succeeds in dispelling the pessimism that colors his work (e.g., in *The Dräumling*, 1872) and gradually reaches a new dimension in his attempt to come to grips with the effects of contemporary industrialization. This dimension is characterized by a reluctantly accepted understanding of the new social order that was emerging. In the novels *Horacker* (1876) and *Alte Nester* (*Old Nests*, 1880) he is still greatly perturbed by the changes arising from the forces of modern life, but in *Pfisters Mühle* (*Pfister's Mill*, 1884) Raabe seems to have overcome his misgivings, insofar as he envisages a compromise between the old and new order. The narrator remains attached to the old ways but allays his dislike of modern industry with the knowledge that there need not be a deterioration of human qualities on account of it. Raabe did not develop beyond this point. His later works portray a world in which a reconciliatory attitude and a place of refuge are the best that can be reached. This is reflected in novels such as *Unruhige Gäste* (*Restless Guests*, 1886), *Im alten Eisen* (*Old Iron*, 1887), *Stopfkuchen* (*Cake Eater*, 1891), and *Die Akten des Vogelsangs* (*The Vogelsang Documents*, 1895). Throughout his literary career Raabe stressed the value of genuine emotions and humaneness. He gave his characters a measure of inner freedom, but distanced them from the turmoil of the world at large.

The work of Theodor Fontane (1819–1898) is firmly wedded to the city of Berlin and the March of Brandenburg which the author called his home. Late in his life he began to write the novels for which he is famous and became the most renowned of the nineteenth-century German novelists. For many years he was active as a journalist and foreign correspondent; he spent considerable time in England; for about a decade he was on the editorial staff of the conservative *Kreuzzeitung,* and later he became the drama critic of the liberal *Vossische Zeitung,* in which capacity he hailed the dramas of Ibsen and Hauptmann.

At the beginning of his literary career Fontane published some ballads and poems. He became better known with the appearance of his *Ballads* (1861) and achieved some distinction in this sphere of literary activity. At times he took the subject matter of his ballads from British and Scottish history, and in some of them he is close to his English models. His language is often intense, straightforward, and somewhat impressionistic. "Archibald Douglas" and "John Maynard" belong to the best ballads in German literature. Commencing in 1862, his *Wanderings through the March of Brandenburg* (1862–1882) began to appear; they describe the countryside of his native region, present some local stories, and demonstrate the author's narrative ability.

Fontane's real significance for German literature rests on his novelistic work. He was almost sixty when his first novel appeared. It is an historical tale of the Napoleonic wars, entitled *Vor dem Sturm* (*Before the Storm*, 1878), and may be considered to be a continuation of the literary efforts of Willibald Alexis; however, its artistic quality outranks the work of the latter. Far superior to *Vor dem Sturm* was Fontane's *Schach von Wuthenow* (1882), a tale also set in the period before the collapse of Prussia in the early years of the century. Its social perspective is significant; the rigidity and conventionalism of the class-code of the Prussian aristocracy are mirrored and shown as destructive of individuality. Fontane had not yet reached the height of his career as a novelist, but some of the characteristics of his prose writings were clearly recognizable: the discreet tone, the skillful building of character and situation, and the accuracy in depicting nuances and milieu, the gift of combining detachment with a sympathetic attitude. Fontane also refrains from emotional appeals to the reader, who consequently retains his intellectual freedom and can think about a problem after he has put the book away.

The influence of Gustave Flaubert and other Realist writers proved beneficial to Fontane's art. His mastery of the novelistic genre became evident in his novels of contemporary life (e.g., *Trials and Tribulations*, 1888; *Mrs. Jenny Treibel*, 1892; *Effi Briest*, 1895). The particular merit of these and other works rests on Fontane's competence in portraying people and their fates realistically and on his ability to render the reality of their time convincingly, i.e., to depict the Prussian society of his day with adequate veracity. Fontane's portrait of society is based on his intimate knowledge of the various social strata. He presents the declining aristocracy (*Effi*

257

Briest; Poggenpuhls, 1896; *Stechlin,* 1899), the well established and newly rich bourgeoisie (*L'Adultera,* 1882; *Mrs. Jenny Treibel*), and the petty bourgeoisie (*Mathilde Möhring,* published posthumously in 1908). He is not given to the presentation of the proletariat, though his interest in the "fourth estate" is clearly evinced and persons from the lower classes appear in his work (e.g., *Trials and Tribulations; Stine,* 1890).

Fontane possessed great talent for characterizing unobtrusively. His figures acquire reality through their actions, reflections, and conversations or through those of others. These conversations do not seem constructed and always fit the situation. He has also been lauded for his subtle psychological empathy; often he succeeds in developing great depth without dwelling on analysis. This is also the case in his most famous work: *Effi Briest,* the portrait of a young woman who marries without love a Prussian official much older than she. More out of boredom than anything else, she has an affair with another man which is discovered years later by her husband. He shoots the offender in a duel; the marriage is ruined, the life of the heroine is ruined, and the husband realizes that he has submitted to the idolatrous conventions of his class. The author tells this story in a detached and slightly ironic manner. He shows sympathy with the culprits and does not judge them, presenting the changing situation of life in the society of his day.

With this novel German literature regained close contact with the great authors of European prose fiction. Indeed, it has won Fontane the reputation of having created the German counterpart of Tolstoy's *Anna Karenina* (1874–1876) and Flaubert's *Madame Bovary* (1857). But while *Effi Briest* has much in common with these novels, it lacks similar scope and excellence. Fontane never had the world-wide appeal of Tolstoy and Flaubert, but he prepared the ground for other German novelists, notably Thomas Mann, to occupy a position of undisputed fame in European letters.

Besides the novelists so far discussed, there are some minor authors of novels in the second half of the century as well as several outstanding writers of novellas and shorter tales. Of Joseph Victor von Scheffel's (1826–1886) literary production the verse epic *The Trumpeter of Säckingen* (1854) and the historical novel *Ekkehard* (1855) should be mentioned. The latter was one of the most successful works of the age; it presents a warped picture of life in Germany in the tenth century and includes a translation of the famous *Waltharius manu fortis* from the Middle Ages. The success of this novel was later eclipsed by that of Felix Dahn's (1834–1912) A *Struggle for Rome* (1876), which depicts the struggle of the Goths in Italy in the sixth century. The national tendency comes strongly to the fore in this work; it is effectively constructed and tries to appeal to the reader by rousing feelings of national superiority.[15]

The most important of these novelists is Fritz Reuter (1810–1874) who, together with the lyric poet Klaus Groth (1819–1899),[16] revived Low German literature and gave it new respectability. After completing the verse narrative *Kein Hüsung* (*Without Shelter*, 1858) and some other literary endeavors, he brought before the public the prose collection *Olle Kamellen* (*Old Stories*, 1860–1868). It contains, among other works, the novels and tales *Ut de Franzo-sentid* (*In the Year '13*, 1860), *Ut mine Festungstid* (*My Prison Days*, 1863), and *Ut mine Stromtid* (*Seed-Time and Harvest*, 1864). In the first of these Reuter tells of the age of Napoleon, in the second about his years of imprisonment, meted out to him for his opposition to the Metternich regime, and in the last he bases the narration on his experiences as agricultural apprentice in his native Mecklenburg. These narratives show Reuter as a master of realistic description; they have secured his reputation as a man of letters and gave rise to the designation "the German Boz" for this writer.

Of the writers of shorter tales and novellas Storm and Meyer are the most outstanding. Theodor Storm (1817–1888) hailed from the North Frisian coast, and one of his most renowned poems, "The City," is a tribute to the place of his birth: Husum. He was influenced in his early poetry (*Poems*, 1852) by Eichendorff, whom he admired and who remained one of his favorite poets. Above all, however, Storm was driven in his lyrics by his love for the beauty of his native region. His range as a lyric poet is limited; he seeks to concentrate on the creation of a mood and tries to capture the shades and hues of the landscape in simple and somewhat restrained verses.

Storm's early novellas, notably *Immensee* (1851), manifest the lyric quality which established his reputation as a prose writer. The composition of this tale suffers from a lack of firmness; it consists of several loosely connected pictures with hazy outlines. The mood is that of wistful resignation, the tone is mournful. Other narratives followed and show Storm advancing along the road of Realism. He treats problems of love and marriage in works such as

259

Angelika (1855), *Späte Rosen* (*Late Roses*, 1859), *Veronika* (1861), *Abseits* (*Aside*, 1863), and he couples these motifs with socially based factors (e.g., the difference of classes) in *At the Castle* (1863), *At the University* (1863), and other novellas.

As time went on, the compositional qualities of Storm's stories improved. They were carefully structured; the characterization grew more accurate, the content more substantial, the expression less vague, and the artistic value greater. Some of the more important later works were *Pole Poppenspäler* (1875), *Carsten Curator* (1877), *Aquis submersus* (1877), *Renate* (1878), *The Sons of the Senator* (1881), *A Chapter in the History of Grieshuus* (1883), and *The Rider of the White Horse* (1888). The most widely read of these are *Pole Poppenspäler* and *The Rider of the White Horse*. The first demonstrates the author's love for puppeteers and dwells on the relationship between art and love, art and entertainment, and art and the bourgeoisie; the second is a vigorous tragic tale that reflects the constant struggle of the Frisians against the North Sea; it received wide recognition and should be regarded as an outstanding achievement of the Realistic novella in nineteenth-century Germany.

Conrad Ferdinand Meyer (1825–1898) made his literary debut with a volume of balladic verse, *Twenty Ballads by a Swiss*, which was published anonymously in 1864. Meyer's poetry, however, was not collected until the eighties; it appeared as *Poems* in 1882 (enlarged version 1892). In our day the excellence of his lyrics has been brought out more distinctly, and he is now considered a forerunner of Symbolist poetry in German literature.[17] Meyer is a master of the condensed form, his verse flows quietly, his language is precise and refined, and there is an abundance of images that acquire symbolic significance. The best of Meyer as a lyric poet can be found in poems such as "The Fountain in Rome," "Two Sails," "Shipped Oars," and "Requiem," as well as in ballads such as "The Feet in the Fire" and "Milton's Revenge." The emphasis in the latter verse form is put on the psychological and the substance is often drawn from history.

History, for that matter, fascinated Meyer, especially the period of the Renaissance, the knowledge of which he derived in part from the writings of Jacob Burckhardt (1818–1897), author of *The Civilization of the Renaissance in Italy*, 1860. Meyer gave preference to the treatment of historical persons, themes, and incidents; his ideal was the fully developed personality of Renaissance times. He strove to avoid subject matter rooted in direct experience and contemporaneity and rather reconstructed the past in his narratives.

His first significant epic work was the verse tale *Huttens letzte Tage* (*Hutten's Last Days*, 1871). It was followed by the novel *Jürg Jenatsch* (1876) and several novellas—such as *The Saint* (1880), *Plautus in the Convent* (1882), *The Monk's Wedding* (1884), *The Tempting of Pescara* (1887)—all of which are noted for their lucid style and plasticity of portrayal. Of these works *The Saint* is one of his best; it centers on the conflict between church and state and presents the life and martyrdom of Thomas à Becket; the emphasis is on the motivation for the sudden change in the archbishop's character. The novella *The Sufferings of a Boy* (1883) also stands out in his prose. Although based on a tale by Saint Simon, it reveals the author's personal involvement and depicts the sufferings of a boy who revolts against the enslavement of his mind by his Jesuit educators. It is one of the few instances in Meyer's work where his understanding of a lone individual is coupled with a reprehensive attitude toward society.

Among the other minor writers of the Realistic period, only Wilhelm Busch (1832–1908) is still read today; his picture stories (e.g., *Max and Moritz*, 1865; *Pious Helene*, 1872) reflect a pessimistic and cruel humor and attest to his gift as an illustrator. Also of interest is a group of writers and poets who became known as the Munich School (*Münchner Dichterkreis*) during the second half of the century. They reacted against political poetry and the advance of Realism; they felt it would encroach upon the purity of art and sought to revive classical traditions. These poets regarded themselves as idealistic defenders of form and beauty, but few if any of them were able to create something worthy of being called great art. The King of Bavaria, Maximilian II, gathered these writers around himself and held symposia with them.

The outstanding representatives of this group were Emanuel Geibel (1815–1884) and Paul Heyse (1830–1914). Geibel is still remembered in histories of literature for his *Heroldsrufe* (*A Herald's Summons*, 1871), a collection of patriotic verse, and some popular poems (e.g., "May Has Come"). Heyse figured prominently as an author of novellas (e.g., *La Rabbiata*, 1855; *The Maiden of Treppi*, 1858; *Andreas Delfin*, 1862; *The Last Centaur*, 1870; *The Embroideress of Treviso*, 1871), but it was as a theorist of this literary form that he gained a position of distinction in German literature. He originated the *Falkentheorie* (referring to the falcon

261

in Boccaccio's *Decamerone* V, 9) which requires that there be in a novella a sharply delineated *Grundmotiv* and specific feature that distinguishes the tale from others.[18]

The members of the Munich School had many enemies. Writers of repute (e.g., Friedrich Hebbel) ridiculed them and the young generation reacted to their endeavors with vigor, labelling the mediocrity of this group as an inadequate artistic expression of the age. The state of literature in Germany, on the whole, depreciated after the Franco-Prussian War. Politically, the establishment of the Bismarckian Empire had consolidated conflicting elements and had satisfied national sentiments; economically, the advance of capitalism had received a strong boost on account of the war indemnity which France had to pay. A period of prosperity was the immediate result, with repercussions on social life. People were primarily concerned with material gains and given to a more unbending pursuit of their personal aims. The literary taste of the public centered on the amusing and pompous and was satisfied with works of doubtful value.

One of the factors no longer to be overlooked in the social life of the nation was the expansion of the working class in the cities. The proletariat had become effectively organized, its power had increased, and socialism was thriving. So far Marxism had made little impact on literature, but in the seventies and eighties its influence could be felt. Together with the doctrines of Charles Darwin (1809–1882) and his German disciples (e.g., Ernst Haeckel, 1834–1919; Wilhelm Bölsche, 1861–1939)[19] Marxist ideas became an important element in the shaping of the materialistic *Weltanschauung* of the new generation. The philosophy of Friedrich Nietzsche also proved influential; his rejection of conventional morality and call for a new man with a new set of moral values appealed to the young intellectuals, though it must be admitted that his teaching found more resonance as the century drew to its close.

Decisive influences came from abroad. In France, Auguste Comte (1798–1857) had paved the way for the theories of Hippolyte Taine (1828–1893) according to which environmental factors were the determining forces of man and historical events. Emile Zola (1840–1902), in his cycle of novels *Les Rougon-Macquart* (1871–1893), saw man, i.e., his nature and fate, as determined by the factors of heredity and environment. Some of the volumes of this cycle as well as his theoretical writings (e.g., *Le roman expéri-*

mental, 1880; *Le Naturalisme au théâtre,* 1881) exercised a profound influence on the young German writers. There were other French authors besides Zola, notably Gustave Flaubert, Guy de Maupassant (1850–1893), and the brothers Goncourt (Edouard, 1822–1896; Jules, 1830–1870), whose works impressed the new generation, but their influence is really not to be compared with that of Zola. In Scandinavia, the writer who exerted the greatest influence on German literature was Henrik Ibsen. Björnstjerne Björnson (1832–1910) and August Strindberg (1849–1912) need also to be taken into account, but it was Ibsen whose dramas revolutionized the German stage and the dramatic technique of the young authors. In addition to these influences the writings of Leo Tolstoy and, to a lesser extent, of Fyodor Dostoyevsky provided noticeable impetus for the endeavors of the German literary avant garde.

The writers and poets who found themselves under the banner of Naturalism in Germany and Austria turned against the existing literature and denounced it as pseudo-art. They wanted to rescue German literature and declared that henceforth the aim of literary activity was to be the exact presentation of contemporary life; it was to include the darker side of man's existence and was not to be colored by the author's intent to poeticize it. Above all, social problems had to be dealt with and art had to be true to life.

The movement started with the establishment of two groups: the Munich Circle and the Berlin Circle. In Munich, Michael Georg Conrad (1846–1927) founded the periodical *Die Gesellschaft* (1885 ff.) and gathered several writers about him. Of these, Karl Bleibtreu (1859–1928) was most active in propagating the new ideas. He is to be remembered for his pamphlet *Revolution of Literature* (1886) which turned out to be one of the most successful programmatic writings of the age. In Berlin, the brothers Heinrich Hart (1855–1906) and Julius Hart (1859–1930) issued the periodical *Kritische Waffengänge* (1882 ff.) and spread the new doctrines. The Hart brothers also originated the idea of publishing an anthology of contemporary verse. The plan was put into effect by Hermann Conradi (1862–1890), Karl Henckell (1864–1929), and Wilhelm Arent (1864– ?). The prefaces contained in this volume, *Moderne Dichter-Charaktere* (*Modern Poets,* 1884), were important; they were not as popular as Bleibtreu's pamphlet, but made substantial impact on the young writers and poets. The group in Berlin grew larger and later became known as the *Friedrichshagener Kreis* (*Friedrichshagen Circle*). Closely connected with it is the literary club *Durch*. It became an important gathering place of the avant garde; problems were aired, concepts discussed, and the term *Moderne* was coined there.

The various theoretical endeavors culminated in the "Consistent Naturalism" of Arno Holz (1863–1929). This writer had found some recognition with his early poetry. Together with his friend Johannes Schlaf (1862–1941), he sought to create the new literary form in which it should be possible to portray in minute detail an event or a conversation. This was the *Sekundenstil* which was put to use in the prose collection *Papa Hamlet* (1889). Their method inspired the other Naturalists, and many found in this collection the necessary equipment for the pursuit of their artistic aims. Later, Holz formulated his theoretical deliberations and published them in the work *Die Kunst—Ihr Wesen und ihre Gesetze* (*Art—Its Nature and Laws*, 1891). In place of Zola's dictum "une oeuvre d'art est un coin de la nature, vu à travers un tempérament" he puts the brief formula: Art = Nature – x; the x standing for the conditions of reproduction and their application.

Surveying the artistic achievements of the Naturalistic movement, we notice that its work is most substantial and important in the field of drama, while the efforts in the field of lyrics and prose do not carry great weight.

As far as drama is concerned, the work of the playwright Ludwig Anzengruber (1839–1889) and the performances of the Meininger, a troupe of actors of the Duke of Meiningen, were an important preparatory stage for Naturalist drama. The Meininger put emphasis on detail and proper requisites; they insisted on natural speech and also introduced the work of relatively unknown dramatists (e.g., Arthur Fitger, 1840–1909, and Ernst von Wildenbruch, 1845–1909). Anzengruber wrote a number of plays which rest on the tradition of popular Austrian dramatic art; they portray real people from the lower strata of society and often are set in the Austrian countryside. Some of his works are marred by a too apparent tendentiousness (e.g., *The Vicar of Kirchfeld*, 1870), but almost all of them effectively capture on the stage the reality of rural life, especially *The Farmer Forsworn* (1871), *The Cross-Makers* (1872), and *The Worm of Conscience* (1874). The drama *The Fourth Commandment* (1877) is noteworthy because of the heredity motif which plays an important part in it; its realism endeared the author to the young generation.

Among the Naturalists Karl Bleibtreu turned to the stage. He was interested in historical drama and sought to erect in his works monuments to outstanding historical personalities. Fascinated by Lord Byron (1788–1824), he wrote a play dealing with the English poet, *Seine Tochter* (*His Daughter*, 1886), in which he underlined the importance of heredity and consequently enjoyed the reputation of having applied the doctrines of Darwin to his work. In his further activity as a dramatist Bleibtreu dealt with problems of contemporary life, but what he produced was of no consequence for the development of Naturalist drama.

Hermann Bahr (1863–1934), John Henry Mackay (1864–1933), Julius Hart, and others tried their hand at the new drama, but the breakthrough came on October 20, 1889, in Berlin when Gerhart Hauptmann's (1862–1946) play *Before Dawn* was first staged. The performance took place at the *Freie Bühne*, an association which had been founded by Otto Brahm (1853–1912), Paul Schlenther (1854–1916), Ludwig Fulda (1863–1939), and others for the furtherance of modern drama and to circumvent the restrictions of the censorship authorities. The young author, who came from the province of Silesia, had become known among the members of the avant-garde with the publication of his tale *Flagman Thiel* (1887) which had appeared in *Die Gesellschaft*. But the performance of his play brought him wide recognition. *Before Dawn* is a study of moral degeneracy and the effects of alcoholism; it seeks to show what the spread of capitalism can lead to in rural areas. The factors of heredity and environment figure in it, the characters are drawn realistically, their dialogue is close to life, the milieu is reproduced in detail, and daring incidents are contained in it. Although the work was severely attacked by the adherents of more conventional theater-fare, it turned out to be a success and marked the beginning of Naturalist drama in Germany.

The next two plays of Hauptmann presented family conflicts. In *The Coming of Peace* (1890) the author demonstrated the workings of environmental factors and heredity; he showed the disagreeable conditions of life in a family whose members distrust each other and whose existence is marred by the constant friction which ensues among them. With *Lonely Lives* (1891) Hauptmann reached a high point in his career as a dramatist. Here he concentrates on the portrayal of a type of man who frequently could be found among his contemporaries: that of a future-oriented intellectual who is unable to rid himself of the shackles of the past and of conventions. Standing between two women, he commits suicide with the realization that the new form of relation between male and female which he dreamt of is an illusion.

The year 1892 saw the appearance of Hauptmann's comedy *Colleague Crampton*, a well drawn portrait of an unambitious artist, and of *The Weavers*. The latter, originally written in Silesian dialect, is Hauptmann's most important dramatic work and the most outstanding play of the Naturalistic movement. The historical background of the events shown was provided by the uprising of the Silesian weavers in 1844, but the portrayal was also inspired by the social problems of Hauptmann's day. Detailed studies preceded the writing of the drama. In February 1893 it was performed at the *Freie Bühne* and much later, after considerable difficulties with the censors, also publicly. The critics debated much the innovations contained in the work, above all the absence of an individual hero. The hero in Hauptmann's drama is the impoverished masses, only in the last act is an individual put into the forefront. The play consists of a series of loosely connected scenes which present the unrelieved misery of the weavers and finally the futile conflict between them and their exploiters. Hauptmann's mastery, his convincing depiction of individual character, is evident throughout. The speech of his dramatis personae is rendered—also in the modified version—with great truth to life, and their milieu is accurately described. The psychological insight of the author, the skill with which he moves the masses about, and the Naturalistic style were lauded greatly and secured the dramatist's fame.

Another important work by Hauptmann is *The Beaver Coat* (1893), a thoroughly Naturalistic thieves' comedy and a satire on the narrow-mindedness of Prussian officialdom, which is represented by a conceited government official who is consistently fooled by an energetic washerwoman. Shortly after the first performance of *The Beaver Coat*, another one of Hauptmann's works was staged: *The Assumption of Hannele* (1893). In this dream-play the author transcends the confines of Naturalism. Fanciful visions of a dying girl are shown against a sordid background, and symbolistic, romantic, and fairy-tale elements are interwoven with reality. The play ushered in a series of works (e.g., *The Sunken Bell*, 1896; *And Pippa Dances*, 1906) which have become identified with other literary techniques of the time, notably that of the Symbolist and Neo-Romantic school. From the rest of Hauptmann's dramatic production several works are still important for Naturalism: the historical tragedy *Florian Geyer* (1896), an attempt to apply the technique used in

The Weavers to the uprising of the German peasants in the early sixteenth century, further the play *Drayman Henschel* (1898), a portrayal of the plight of a Silesian drayman who has broken a promise given to his dying wife, and finally the drama *Rose Bernd* (1903), a stirring representation of the sufferings of a young peasant woman who is pursued by men and driven to commit a criminal act. A latecomer among the Naturalistic works of Hauptmann was *The Rats* (1911), a play in which the society of Wilhelmian Germany is shown in a state of decay. Hauptmann's effort in this and other dramas testified above all that the main driving force of the author was his sympathy with the hardships and sufferings of the poor.

An important contribution to Naturalist drama was made by Arno Holz and Johannes Schlaf with the drama *The Selicke Family* (1890). The veristic dialogue and the minute portrayal of everyday life of an impoverished family in Berlin received much attention and led Fontane to praise it as *terra nova*[20] in recent literary developments. Atmosphere and mood are an effective means of expression in this drama, the action is reduced to a minimum, and the events culminate in the return of the drunken father and death of a sick child. After that the play dwells on the attitude of resignation of the elder daughter. Holz and Schlaf soon separated and went their individual ways. Holz published, among other writings, parts of a cycle of dramas about Berlin and his time, and Schlaf wrote his *Master Oelze* (1892), an intense dramatic work which shows the struggle of a dying criminal with his stepsister, who seeks to extract a confession from him.

Other representatives of Naturalist drama were Halbe, Sudermann, and a host of minor playwrights. The West Prussian Max Halbe (1865–1944) is remembered chiefly for his drama *Youth* (1893). He had brought out some Naturalist plays before that (e.g., *Free Love*, 1890; *Eisgang* [*The Ice Floes*], 1892), but it was *Youth* which made him famous. In this play he portrays the fateful meeting of two young people who come to feel the power of first love and early spring. They accept the consequences of their doings, but the stepbrother of the girl seeks to shoot the intruder. His bullet hits the heroine. The development of these events is conditioned by heredity and environment, the factor of chance plays an important part in bringing about the catastrophe, and the lyrical element gives the play its characteristic stamp. Of the later work of Halbe the drama *Mother Earth* (1897) is noteworthy for its rejection of emancipatory ideas, and the play *Das tausendjährige Reich*

267

(*The Millennium*, 1899) is of interest because of the echo of Haupt-mann's *The Weavers* which can be noticed therein.

The East Prussian Hermann Sudermann (1857–1928) began as a novelist of repute (e.g., *Dame Care*, 1887; *Regina, or The Sins of the Fathers*, 1889) and became renowned as a dramatist with the play *Honor* (1889). It deals with the relativity of the concept of honor and possesses some Naturalistic components. With the drama *Sodoms Ende* (*The Man and His Picture*, 1891) he moved closer to the new literary doctrine, but the venture turned out to be a failure and was, as far as dramatic technique is concerned, one of his weakest efforts. The play *Magda* (1893) was Sudermann's greatest stage success, but it also demonstrated that the author paid homage to Naturalism only outwardly and that he put theatrical effectiveness above everything else. One is merely being reminded of Naturalistic tenets in this and other dramas of Sudermann.

Naturalist doctrine was not favorable to lyrics, and little of more than passing value was achieved in this sphere of creative activity. When the anthology *Moderne Dichter-Charaktere* (*Modern Poets*, 1884) appeared, it was hailed as the beginning of a new lyric poetry, but it soon became evident that only the subject matter had been enriched by some new motifs (e.g., the plight of the worker, social misery in the cities, pity for the downtrodden people, etc.); the verse forms and diction were still traditional. Few of the poets who contributed to this collection are known today, and those who are still remembered (for example Arno Holz) have become famous owing to other achievements, not for their Naturalist verse.

The most important contributions to Naturalist poetry came from the pen of Arno Holz and Hermann Conradi, but the best poet of the time was Detlev von Liliencron (1844–1909). His *Ad-jutantenritte* (*An Adjutant's Rides*, 1883) were lauded by the young generation, but his poetry rather pointed forward to the endeavors of the Impressionists. Arno Holz's *Buch der Zeit* (*Book of the Times*, 1886) was proof of the author's modern and rebel-lious spirit, but it also showed that he was still in the grip of con-vention as far as formal matters were concerned. Holz kept on searching for new forms of lyric expression and thought he had discovered them when he published his *Revolution of Lyric Poetry* (1899), a treatise in which he speaks of a central axis (*Mittelachse*) around which verses are grouped in such a way that the immanent rhythm of the words would be elicited. The resulting poetry (*Phantasus*, 1898–1899) has, however, nothing to do with Naturalism; it points beyond this movement to other literary tendencies. Conradi acquired fame among his contemporaries with his *Lieder eines Sünders* (*Songs of a Sinner*, 1887), a collection of lyric poetry which is marked by the poet's provocative attitude and truth to himself and life.

The prose work of the Naturalists was a little more prominent than their poetry, but in this sphere also little of permanent value was achieved. The outstanding novelists of Naturalism were Max Kretzer (1854–1941) and Wilhelm von Polenz (1861–1903). Kretzer attracted attention as a follower of Zola and shared the latter's interest in social problems. In his tales and novels he mirrors the darker side of city life and the plight of the working classes. Some of the titles of these works are indicative of where Kretzer stands: *Die Verkommenen* (*The Degenerated*, 1883), *Im Sturmwind des Sozialismus* (*In the Onrush of Socialism*, 1884), and *Im Sündenbabel* (*In the City of Sin*, 1886). His masterpiece was *Master Timpe* (1888), a craftsman novel which has as its basic theme the disappearance of the artisan class under the pressure of modern industry.

Polenz succeeded in creating some novels which reflect the changing times and the destructive force of capitalist expansion. In *The Pastor of Breitendorf* (1893) he shows how a cleric gradually distances himself from the church, and in *Der Grabenhäger* (*The Squire of Grabenhagen*, 1897) he focuses on the life of landowners and their attempts to come to terms with the changed situation. The author's best known work is *Farmer Büttner* (1895), a novel which describes the breaking up of smaller estates and the economic decline of a peasant family. The plight of the main figure and the realistic presentation of the events that condition it, prompted Tolstoy to praise the novel highly and to hold Polenz in high esteem.

Of the less important Naturalistic prose writers, Clara Viebig (1860–1952) with her *Kinder der Eifel* (*Children of the Eifel*, 1897), *Das Weiberdorf* (*The Women's Village*, 1900), and other works deserves to be mentioned. She won some acclaim as a writer of narrative fiction in the modern vein of that time, and her concern for the poor and degraded was felt to be genuine.

In looking back upon the Realist-Naturalist phase, we see that it was a period in which established social structures and accepted ideals were gradually transformed, and at times replaced, by phenomena which bore the mark of the ephemeral. This phase of human endeavor lacked a firm set of standards, literary and otherwise, and the development which took place was not one of steady growth; it was marked by upheavals and constant fluctuation. People were torn between adherence to the values of the past and the demands of the future, and the uncertainty thus engendered manifested itself in the works and theoretical deliberations of the writers of the time. They were largely oriented towards the material world but, nevertheless, often still clung to the ideals of the past. Pessimistic and positivistic currents were strong, and Schopenhauer's philosophy proved particularly influential.

In seeking to assess the contribution made by the Realist-Naturalist writers to German literature, we find that their achievements nearly equalled the accomplishments reached during the periods which directly preceded their own. The outstanding literary personalities of this phase strove to re-interpret man's experience of life and to combine various opposites under a unifying point of view. A great number of works of distinct and lasting value were written, but rather than being sustained by a correlative substratum of society as in former times, they were usually the product of the isolated artist.

In summing up within the framework of European letters, it is evident that the results achieved by the Realist-Naturalist writers are not too spectacular, but it is also true that some of them displayed qualities endearing to the modern reader: their fusion of imaginative power and keenness of observation, their valiant attempts to come to terms with the instability of the age, and their desire to bring literature into contact with the social issues of the day remind us of similar struggles of contemporary writers in Germany and abroad.

8. Impressionism and Expressionism 🖋

Penrith Goff

I

While Naturalism was celebrating its greatest triumphs in Germany, the reaction against it had already begun in France. The French novelist Joris Karl Huysmans, whose early work was naturalistic, opened his novel *Down There* (1891), with a debate between Des Hermies and Durtal, the former attacking Naturalism, the latter defending its accomplishments. But Durtal, Huysmans's spokesman, does admit to Naturalism's one-sidedness: "The unsatisfied need for the supernatural was driving people, in default of something loftier, to spiritism and the occult." He concludes that the next direction for literature must be a "spiritualistic naturalism": " 'We must,' he thought, 'retain the documentary veracity, the precision of detail, the compact and sinewy language of realism, but we must also dig down into the soul and cease trying to explain mystery in terms of our sick senses.' " Huysmans's *Down There* is Naturalism applied to the occult. It is a documentary on Satanism. Huysmans's earlier novel *Against the Grain* (1888) had even greater impact and typifies another direction which the reaction took: aestheticism. Its hero, Des Esseintes, is the prototype of the aesthete hero, the man who lives for beauty and gratification of the senses and who, goaded by the banality of life, seeks ever more titillating sensations until his search leads him to perversion. Other French writers—Baudelaire, Rimbaud, Verlaine—both in private life and in their writings made sallies into the realm of mystery, perversion, and evil for which Naturalism had had little interest. The best known novel of English aestheticism, Oscar Wilde's *The Picture of Dorian Gray* (1891), is moralistic—Dorian Gray pays for his orgies with his life—but Wilde himself flippantly insisted on the primacy of art over nature, and in the foreword to the novel declared that "an ethical sympathy in an artist is an unpardonable mannerism of style." The scandal which wrecked his life helped bring the school of English aestheticism into ill repute. The debauchery associated with the French decadents and symbolists cast upon the innocent phrase *l'art pour l'art* a pall from which it has never recovered.

271

These extremes were symptomatic of the general situation in European literary circles in the nineties. The mood had changed— the naturalists' social commitment had yielded to the feeling that art is a realm unto itself, that scientific pretension, political and social programs have no place in literature. The cult of science, the spirit of analysis, positivism were seen as life-robbing attitudes. The naturalists' ideal of truth, which was predominantly ugly, was replaced by the aesthetes' ideal of beauty.

Criticism underwent a correspondingly radical metamorphosis. The new critical approach dispensed with positivism's scrupulous attention to facts. The facts of impressionistic criticism were the nuances of the critic's own aesthetic experience. The English critic Walter Pater, the father of aesthetic (i.e., impressionistic) criticism, emphasized the subjective nature of the critic's task: criticism of a work of art begins with the question, "What effect does it really produce on me?" For Oscar Wilde "the highest form of criticism is in truth nothing more than the record of one's own soul" (*The Critic as Artist*). Wilde's dictum that a work of art should inspire the critic in his criticism to a masterpiece of his own is scarcely an exaggerated description of the impressionist critics' practice. Alfred Kerr, the leading German theater critic from 1900–1920, consciously strove to perfect his critical essays as an art form and claimed to have actually achieved what Wilde only conceived of doing. Behind the virtuoso display of wit, sophistication, and writing skill, there is little to be seen of a critical system: his criticism reflects his personal taste and intuition rather than clearly definable objective criteria.

The willful denial of any ethical prerogative for art encouraged the notion that art was for a chosen few and these few—here Nietzsche gave license—considered themselves beyond the moral precepts which governed the "herd." Their devotion to beauty carried over into everyday life, whose humdrum colorlessness they sought to disguise through intense cultivation of the senses and by attempting to give their lives style. Here, too, they found confirmation in Nietzsche, who had pointed to the Germans' abysmal lack of culture (*Thoughts Out of Season*, I. 1873) and defined culture as "unity of artistic style in all the manifestations of life of a nation." Julius Langbehn in *Rembrandt as Educator* (1890) even expressed the optimistic view that though the present age was scientific, an age of art was imminent. The disdain for the bourgeoisie shown by the naturalists was shared by the aesthetes; but the aesthetes were not concerned with bourgeois hypocrisy and complacency, they were disdainful of the lack of aesthetic sensitivity among the middle class. With their dandyism, dilettantism, their cult of taste and style, the aesthetes deliberately widened the cleft between themselves and the masses. The image of the aesthete in the unsympathetic public eye is reflected in the pathetically comic figure of Bunthorne in Gilbert and Sullivan's opera *Patience.*

The cult of decadence was initiated by Baudelaire and by 1885 had become the leading literary fashion in France, from where it quickly spread through England and Europe. Characteristic of decadence were aestheticism, the inclination for intoxication and perversion, Satanism, narcissism, morbidly over-sensitive nerves, life-weariness, and the feeling of living during the final phase of a culture. It is, in brief, a way of life, a system of values, a pessimistic outlook which can lead only to biological extinction.

In varying degrees the literary characters of German impressionism show these features.[1] They are very conscious of living in a world of appearance. They enjoy life more as spectators than as participants; not merely the tragedy and comedy of other people's lives, even the change of their own moods and feelings is a major source of pleasure. They seek to heighten this enjoyment by careful attention to creating the proper atmosphere in which to stimulate their senses to the utmost. Some derive pleasure from contemplating decay, from aged and decrepit objects.

The melancholy and delicious feeling that one was living in an age of decline, the interest in such late cultural phases as Hellenism or the disintegrating Roman Empire gave currency to the term *fin de siècle* (from the title of a comedy by de Jouvenot and Micard, 1888). The *fin de siècle* mood pervades the world of the Baltic aristocracy presented in the novels and novellas of Eduard von Keyserling (1855–1918). It is a dying world whose people lead elegant but empty lives, resigned to a weary loneliness which is only intensified by their unhappy love affairs. It is a gloomy, Schopenhauerian world of suffering; its people seek release in dreaming, gambling, and adventure but always with a sad awareness that they will not find the life they yearn for.

The decline of an upper-middle-class family is traced by Thomas Mann (1875–1955) in his first novel *Buddenbrooks* (1901). Once a vigorous, enterprising merchant family, the Buddenbrooks with each succeeding generation possess less practical skill and energy; at the same time their aesthetic sensitivity increases. Young Hanno, the fourth generation, is frail, completely uninterested in and unfit for continuing the family business. He loves music and longs for death, and his early death from typhus results directly from his flagging will to live. Similar themes appear in Mann's novella *Tristan* (1902), a parody of Wagner's *Tristan and Isolde*. Like Hanno, Gabriele Klöterjahn comes of an old merchant family; in her, too, sensitivity is combined with frailty and she suffers from tuberculosis. At a sanatorium she meets an aesthete novelist, Detlev Spinell, who fascinates her with conversation about a world she has never known. When he persuades her to play the piano—the love scene in the second act of *Tristan*—he wins her over to his world of beauty, but she has overtaxed her strength and dies.

One of the most powerful sketches of decadence is Mann's *Blood of the Walsungs* (1906). The twins Siegmund and Sieglinde attend "their" opera, Wagner's *Die Walküre*, one last time together before Sieglinde marries von Beckerath, a socially good match but in the twins' estimation a "trivial" man. For the over-refined brother and sister, who are acutely aware of the short-comings of the performance, art can hardly succeed in creating its illusion. Yet it does reach Siegmund, perhaps just because he is not completely under its spell. As he watches the people whose combined labors produce the performance, he is struck by the question "How is a work created?" He reaches the conclusion that "creation originates in passion and assumes the form of passion again." Pondering his own life "so full of words, so void of acts, so full of cleverness, so empty of emotion," he feels a yearning for experience and creation. The final scene of the story portrays Siegmund's breakthrough to inner life: he yields to the only genuine passion he knows, his love for his sister. Incest here is not, as it might have been, a new sensation for a jaded decadent, but is, paradoxically, a positive achievement.

The aesthetes had a horror of the banal and required the illusion of a different reality to shut out everyday life. Music, which the naturalists had rejected as unrealistic, was valued highly. Twilight and evening were favorite settings. The autumnal world mirrored their feelings of decline. In their rejection of the immediate world, they turned to exotic settings. There was a predilection for things Slavic—the word conjured up feelings of desolateness, of being lost. The motif appears in Mann's *Magic Mountain* as a symbol of the forbidden chaos which constantly attracts Hans

Castorp, and in Mann's *Death in Venice* the boy Tadzio, who lures Aschenbach out of a disciplined world into death, is Polish. There was also a fascination with Oriental cultures. Particularly Japanese and Chinese art appealed with their subtlety and artistic economy.

By far the most popular setting at this time was Renaissance Italy.[2] Jacob Burckhardt's great work, *The Civilization of the Renaissance in Italy* (1860), contributed most to providing a total picture of Renaissance culture; Friedrich Nietzsche became its most important interpreter for modernity. Nietzsche saw in the Italian Renaissance a splendid model of aristocratic style with which Germany's decadence and lack of culture might be overcome. Unfortunately the early Nietzsche who admonished the Germans to further their culture (*Thoughts Out of Season*, 1873–1876) was less influential than the later Nietzsche whose superman-ethos seemed to be exemplified in such figures as the Borgias. This misunderstanding of Nietzsche's intention was a fertile one: numerous Cesare Borgia dramas appeared, the Renaissance was widely romanticized as an era of ruthless intrigue, the demonic man, the man of brute strength was idolized. The fashion became so widespread that almost no author failed to treat Renaissance material.

Already in *Gladius Dei* (1902), Thomas Mann satirized the Renaissance cult. A student, Hieronymus, a latter-day Savonarola, demands the removal of an immoral print of the Madonna from a book-shop window. As he gets up after being thrown out, he sees Savonarola's vision of the burning of the vanities and repeats the words from Savonarola's sermon: "Gladius dei super terram . . . cito et velociter." The same theme is treated more fully in the dramatic dialogue *Fiorenza* (1906). Here Savonarola, the life-negating ascetic, triumphs over Lorenzo de Medici, the symbol of Renaissance glory. Triumph is possible because Savonarola is vigorous, whereas the artists at Lorenzo's court are weak; their art, which serves beauty and pleasure but excludes suffering and ugliness, is superficial and leaves the people unsatisfied. Mann expressed his disapproval of the turn-of-the-century infatuation with the Renaissance in his *Betrachtungen eines Unpolitischen* (*Reflections of a Nonpolitical Man*, 1918) and in *Doctor Faustus* (1947) revealed the inherent danger in this "hysterical Renaissance." The discussions of the Kridwiss circle (a group of intellectuals who symbolize the Stefan George circle) cruelly subordinate the fates of individuals to the "beauties" of myth, just as the Nazis were to do later on a catastrophic scale.

275

The reaction to Naturalism in its emphasis on subjectivity was accompanied by distinct changes in style and form. Instead of long novels and carefully structured dramas of four and five acts, the preference was for small literary forms: lyric poetry, verse dramolets, one-act plays, prose sketches, and novellas. The impressionist sought to reproduce his momentary impresssions rather than to give a total account of reality. In contrast to the objective completeness of Naturalism, Impressionism preferred suggestive fragmentariness. The precision of naturalistic observation was applied to subjective impressions; the writer tried to capture and reproduce moods, sensations, impressions in their finest nuance. Thus, one extreme of impressionist style was attained in a style akin to naturalistic *Sekundenstil:* the inner monologue, which attempted to record "all" the sensations and perceptions of an individual. On the other hand, Impressionism, especially of the lyric, is an art of omission. The impressionist tried to say as much as possible in the fewest possible words. Impression follows impression paratactically, producing the effect of fleeting, unconnected perceptions. The impressionist appealed to all the five senses and was aware that stimulation of one sense may evoke response in another. Synaesthesia, musicality in poetry and lyric prose, the play of light and shadow, the abundant use of color are important characteristics of impressionistic style.

Impressionism as a style is not peculiar to this period or to the so-called impressionist writers. The lyric poet Detlev von Liliencron (1844–1909), who remained independent of aestheticist and *fin-de-siècle* trends, was an accomplished master at conveying a picture with a few strokes and a lively rhythm. The style of Johannes Schlaf in *Dingsda* (1892) and of Arno Holz in much of his *Phantasus* poetry is impressionistic. The early expressionists, too, recorded their visions impressionistically. Impressionism is the stylistic expression of intense subjectivism, and thus the natural mode for a generation of writers who saw spiritual values threatened by the relentless spread of materialist views to all aspects of life.

In the fine arts another style developed, an ornate, decorative style which reached its high point about 1900. This was a European development which had its beginning with the English art critic John Ruskin. The most famous, or infamous, representative of the "Modern Style" in England was the brilliant illustrator of Wilde's books, Aubrey Beardsley. His counterpart in Vienna was the painter Gustav Klimt, whose figures are presented in erotic postures against rich backgrounds which vie with them for attention. His pictures have no depth; they are flattened into design. In Germany the style received the name *Jugendstil* from the periodical *Die Jugend* (*Youth*, 1896–1940) which published the work of contemporary artists and writers. *Die Jugend* was expressly against the decadent *fin de siècle* spirit: "We are not living among the last gasps of a dying epoch, we are in the morning of a perfectly healthy age. It is a pleasure to live!" Many important writers contributed to the periodical, though only modestly. Nevertheless its pages of lithographs, drawings, poems, and prose provide an incomparable gauge to the rising tensions and fear in the years 1896–1914.

Though elements of *Jugendstil* are characteristic in such artists as Edvard Munch (emphasis on outline) and Toulouse-Lautrec (flatness, perspective distortion), *Jugendstil* was primarily important in industrial art design, posters, book ornamentation, etc. *Jugendstil* differs from Impressionism by emphasizing lines rather than color, definitive outline rather than blurred contours. But *Judgendstil* line does not promote clarity; it is an end in itself, tending to obscure and devalue content.

The determination to achieve style, the urge to celebrate youth and beauty, the need to find in art a refuge from the problems of everyday life—the forces which led to *Jugendstil*—also gave impetus to much of the literature of the period. Thus, especially in lyric poetry, there is the same over-fondness for ornamentation: complex patterns of assonance, alliteration, internal rhymes which do not serve the content. Many of the motifs of *Jugendstil* art reappear in literature. The earliest *Jugendstil* verse was dance lyric; later poetry depicted Arcadian meadows and woods in which naked men and women romp and make love, worship the sun or weave garlands of flowers on the banks of serene ponds. The landscapes in the idylls of *Jugendstil* literature often featured the same objects which were so popular with the artists because of their voluptuous lines: reeds, poppies, lianas, and other vines, swans, flamingoes, and serpents.

The strain of eroticism running through the *Jugendstil* period is typified by the vitalism of Richard Dehmel (1863–1920). Although Dehmel possessed the naturalists' sympathy for the working class, his concept of art was impressionistic: art is never imitation of nature, it is creation. The purpose of art is to put order into "chaotic impressions of life," to create models for mankind. For Dehmel, art is not elitist; its task is to cause the individual to forget himself and thus to resolve the antitheses between himself and

277

other men, between himself and the universe. Dehmel's central theme is Eros, frankly accepted as natural and not permitted to dominate the individual. His most important work, *Zwei Menschen* (*Two People*, 1903), is a novel in verse divided into three sections, each consisting of thirty-six ballads of thirty-six lines each. This is only an indication of the structural niceties of the work; it is an extreme example of the *Jugendstil* feeling for form. But Dehmel had little concern for technique; his poetry tended to become rhetorical.

In later *Jugendstil* literature the ornamental elements took on symbolic dimension. The fascination with form and design leads quite naturally in the direction of abstraction and expressionism. Max Dauthendey (1867–1918), an impressionist of great descriptive ability, a narrator of exotic erotica, could use color not only impressionistically but also symbolically, much as the early expressionist, Georg Trakl. The worship of the body was continued with great ecstasy by the vitalist expressionists. Like the cult of the Renaissance and the other impressionist poses, *Jugendstil* was an attempt to escape the ugly present. In its idyllic vision of a monistic paradise, *Jugendstil* looked wistfully back to creation, when the world was still innocent. A few years later and somewhat more realistically, the expressionists were to look hopefully ahead to a paradise which would come about through man's regeneration.

II

Stefan George (1868–1933) became a symbol of aestheticism: its exclusiveness, its love of cult, and even its perverseness. He was repelled by Naturalism with its emphasis on ugliness; determined to bring literature back into the realm of spirit and beauty, he sought to bring about a regeneration of German culture. In Paris, he made acquaintance with Mallarmé and French Symbolism. Mallarmé's esoteric art, his elite circle of disciples, his protest against the democratization of the arts, confirmed George's own inclinations. Back in Germany, George likewise gathered an exclusive circle of disciples about himself. Members of the circle published their work in George's periodical *Blätter für die Kunst* (*Pages for Art*, 1892–1919). Statements of their views stressed aesthetic and formal criteria: "The value of literature (*Dichtung*) is not determined by its rational meaning (otherwise it would be learning, wisdom) but by its form. That by no means denotes something external but rather that profoundly stirring element of rhythm and sound by which in every age the men of originality, the masters, have distinguished themselves from artists of second rank." The naturalistic notion that no area of life is unsuitable for literature was rejected vehemently. Social and moralistic intentions have no place in literature; art exists for its own sake. Its purpose is "reproduction not of a thought but of a mood." It does not describe things or events, it "evokes and suggests with the aid of essential words." Literature is "selectivity, measured proportion, and sonority" (*Auswahl, Maß und Klang*). The writer, who must always select from the confusion of nature, seeks to create a "unified impression." His own tact, rather than any rules, governs his composition. Style—an important word for the non-naturalists—is the means by which the artist gives his impress to his material even to the smallest detail. Mature art is symbolic, because seeing in symbols is the natural result of spiritual maturity and depth. The writer must always select the thing which "contains the largest and most beautiful part of the vibrating soul, the part which reflects the others in its deeper being, and which, through its more perfect form, most closely approaches perfect unity, the highest ideal." The poet should avoid a tone of urgency, lest purpose reveal itself. He must remain serene "even on the brink of the abyss." His goal is a "pure, sonorous, austere, and beautiful language."

Under the influence of Baudelaire's parnassian formal perfection, George turned out carefully wrought verse in conventional form. His language, however, with its select vocabulary and stylized syntax has an exalted tone even for the most ordinary subjects. The stylization was carried further: punctuation was sharply reduced, nouns were not capitalized except at the beginnings of lines, and a Carolingian type face was designed for publication of the poetry. Melchior Lechter, a *Jugendstil* artist, drew elaborate designs for the title pages of George's books. George's early poetry shows *Jugendstil* characteristics: a frozen and artificial quality of the landscape, simple and deliberately inexpressive adjectives, verbal music which is decorative rather than expressive, idyllic scenes typical of *Jugendstil* art.

The poetry in George's first collection, *Odes* (1890), expresses with its themes of departure and separation the poet's own

279

leave-taking from the workaday world. As a poet he must renounce life, for the perfection of art is attained only at the price of solitude. Correspondingly, the pictures presented are not an impressionistic enhancement of the natural world, but a deliberate stylization toward artificiality, a conscious fashioning of nature into art.

Pilgrimages (1891) presents in allegorical form George's search for others of similar mind, perhaps even a search for the poetry which will fulfill his ideal. The preciosity of the *Odes* continues; at the same time George turns to traditional forms, the song and ballad ("Stop, o mill, your even sweep"). The search of the *Pilgrimages* continues in *Algabal* (1892), a cycle devoted to the youthful Roman emperor Heliogabalus. The enticements of life are no longer a danger to the poet; he is completely secure in the world of art. The denial of the natural world is complete. Algabal's realm is subterranean, its color is the flash of precious stones but it is a motionless realm in which the birds do not fly and tree trunks are of coal. The Blue Flower of Romanticism finds its extreme contrast in the "somber bloom" which the poet dreams of producing. George, who knew the historical figure Heliogabalus, gives his Algabal decadent features not possessed by the original. Algabal, once a hero, has seen the vanity of human striving and withdraws from political intrigue in order to devote himself entirely to beauty. He becomes so complete an aesthete that he has no feelings left for his fellow human beings. The final poem of the cycle, "Augury," indicates that George has overcome this frightful extreme and that his next poetry will return to the detached restraint of his earlier work. *The Books of Eclogues and Eulogies, The Book of Legends and Lays,* and *The Book of the Hanging Gardens* (1894) present poetry in the costume of three earlier cultures: Greek, Medieval, and Oriental. The poet experiments with the attitudes of the three worlds, sometimes treating the same theme in all three manners with the lyric forms cultivated in each era.

Perhaps most accessible of George's cycles is *The Year of the Soul* (1897), poems organized around the "seasons" of his own soul, from which, significantly, spring is missing. The poems are the poet's dialogue with himself, expressing loneliness, weariness, and resignation, for George's hopes of regenerating German culture had been severely frustrated. But his discouragement is always sung in dignified cadences and tempered by the admonition to himself that he must learn to do without, must not clutch at deceptive hopes:

You reached the hearth, but dwindled
To cinders was the glow.
The moon was all that kindled
The earth with deathly hue.

Your listless fingers crumble
The ashes. If you strain,
And grope in them, and fumble,
Will light return again?

See, how the moon consoles you
With soothing gait,
Leave the hearth—she tells you—
It has gotten late.[3]

With *The Tapestry of Life* (1900) a new phase in George's development began. In the prelude an angel appears sent by "radiant life" (*Das schöne Leben*) to announce the poet's mission. The angel seems almost to be an alter ego and the prelude, then, a sublimation of the dialogue in *The Year of the Soul*. The angel prescribes the future mode of existence for the poet: solitude shared by select companions and spent in Germany. George thus renounces exoticism; he will work henceforth within the German tradition. The poems which follow are vignettes from the "tapestry of life" which "leaps to life" only for the rare elect, the poets. The tone is optimistic; the world of the poetry is not artificial but real, productive nature.

The ideas adumbrated in the prelude to *The Tapestry of Life* are worked out in *The Seventh Ring* (1907). The ideal of the "radiant life" George found incarnated in the boy Maximilian Kronberger whom he literally deified. The figure of Maximin, as the boy was known to the George circle, dominates the book; the center section is devoted to him. George's next volume of poetry, *The Star of the Covenant* (1913) was also meant for the circle. The first book contains the prophecy of approaching catastrophe for German civilization, the second depicts the initiation of the novices into the mysteries and the union of the disciples with God, the third states the rules for George's new order. *The Star of the Covenant* is less lyrical and much more obscure than the earlier poetry, yet by a historical accident—the first public edition appeared in 1914, just before the outbreak of war—it became so popular that George had

281

to explain in the preface to the second edition that he had not meant it "as a breviary for the people and particularly not for the younger generation fighting at the front." In George's last volume, *The Kingdom Come* (1928), for the most part written before 1922, ballads and songs, dialogues, prayers and other traditional forms make up the collection. Once more the lyrical tone of the early poetry is heard; the last song, "You like a flame, unflawed and slender," probably to Maximin, is one of George's finest.

One of the early disappointments of George's career was his meeting in 1891 with Hugo von Hofmannsthal (1874–1929), with whom he had hoped to establish a joint "dictatorship" of letters. Hofmannsthal was too different in temperament for such a partnership. He did agree to contribute to the *Blätter für die Kunst* but while George became increasingly the priest and prophet to an elite few, Hofmannsthal sought an ever broader public. Like the George circle, Hofmannsthal believed that art achieves its effects through symbols but he would not have agreed that symbols are selected by the poet; rather the symbols in a work of art result from the artist's mystic experience of unity with the world and they impart this experience again to the beholder of art.

Hofmannsthal published his first poetry and criticism while he was still attending the *Gymnasium*. Though his lyric production was small—less than 150 poems—much of it is of such quality that he was immediately ranked with George and Rilke. The language of his dramolets is intoxicatingly beautiful; their settings are not contemporary Austria but Renaissance Italy or unnamed places in the early eighteenth century. Nevertheless, they are not escape literature. From the very beginning there is a strong moralistic tone in Hofmannsthal's work.

Especially in his early work Hofmannsthal was influenced by the Viennese physicist Ernst Mach, who taught that reality is not absolute but relative; the world we perceive is a construct of our sense data, and changes, as we ourselves do, from moment to moment. The aesthetes' emphasis on the immediate moment as the only reality poses a dilemma, however, which is the subject of the verse play *Gestern* (*Yesterday*, 1891). This *comédie proverbe* sets out to disprove the contention of the protagonist, Andrea: "Yesterday is a lie and only today is true!" Andrea is an aesthete who indulges every mood, trusts only his sensations, believes only in the present moment, values friends merely as functions of his various moods. But his devotion to enjoyment is ever troubled by doubt: is he perhaps missing something better? And his will is paralyzed at the prospect of making choices because choosing involves relinquishing all possibilities but one. Andrea does not believe in loyalty and he is convinced that if Arlette were to betray him, it would not change their relationship. But when Arlette reveals that she has, unwittingly, betrayed him and asks forgiveness for this "yesterday," he sees the past in a new light: the past "*is* as long as we know that it *was*."

In *The Death of Titian* (1892) a group of students laments their dying master. Titian does not appear—he is within, painting in a feverish final burst of energy—but through the conversation of the students he emerges in sharp contrast to them. The students are aesthetes, not artists; they live for beauty but need the master artist to teach them to see beauty. The play is a fragment; Hofmannsthal had planned to conclude it with a cataclysm sent as punishment for their alienation from life.

Hofmannsthal's moralizing against aestheticism and noncommitment continued in his subsequent verse dramas and in a novella, *The Tale of the 672nd Night* (1905). The story, in an Arabian Nights setting, portrays the wretched end of a man who had refused to engage himself in adult life. Like the verse plays the story is a monodrama: the figures surrounding the merchant's son symbolize life in its variety, and life, Hofmannsthal had written in an essay chastizing the Italian aesthete d'Annunzio, has a "fearful dazing fullness and fearful, demoralizing desolateness. With these two cudgels it beats alternately upon the heads of those who do not serve it."

Hofmannsthal's early works perhaps reflect feelings of guilt for aestheticist leanings of his own, yet he can scarcely be identified with his Andrea or Claudio (*Death and the Fool*, 1893). Nor is the psychological crisis which his fictive Lord Philip Chandos describes in a letter to Francis Bacon ("A Letter," 1901) identical with a crisis Hofmannsthal experienced. In the letter, Chandos explains that he has lost the ability to communicate in abstract language and will probably never write another book. Hofmannsthal himself suffered from infertile periods of depression even during the years when he wrote his best poetry, but, if the fictitious letter is in part confession, it is also, and more significantly, the treatment of a theme which had occupied him even in his earliest poems: the inadequacy of language as a means of human communication. Chandos suffers from too much insight into the depths of existence.

His sudden inability to use abstract language is accompanied by a desire not to use a language which cannot express the complexities of reality. He would prefer instead to "think with the heart." This problem, a constant theme throughout Hofmannsthal's work, was also a problem of his generation, especially of the poets and dramatists who participated in the expressionist movement. The Chandos letter can be seen as an early document of the expressionists' anguish.

After 1900 Hofmannsthal wrote almost no lyric poetry. Attempting to reach a wider audience, he turned to what he called, in contradistinction to his early lyric dramas, "dramatic" drama. His efforts to learn the dramatist's craft by revising older dramas were reinforced by a desire to renew old traditions. His deep awareness of living at the end of an era is not reflected in his work by world-weariness or epigonal frustration, but by a desire to build upon Austrian and European cultural tradition. *Electra* (1903) is an adaptation of Sophocles' play: a monomaniacal Electra has become so wedded to the thought of avenging her father's murder that the only child she can bear is the deed of revenge. But it is her tragedy that she cannot bring herself to lift the ax at the decisive moment, and Orestes must perform the deed. Richard Strauss adapted the play, virtually without textual change, for his opera (1908) and thus began the remarkable collaboration which produced some of the most delightful operas in the modern repertoire: *The Cavalier of the Rose* (1910), *Ariadne in Naxos* (1912, 1916), *The Lady Without a Shadow* (1915), *Egyptian Helena* (1924), and *Arabella* (1929). The texts are sometimes highly symbolic, treating themes of loyalty, commitment to life, transformation through love. Certainly the opera-goer who skims the story from the program just before the curtain rises misses the meaning of these operas.

Hofmannsthal's finest comedy, indeed one of the best in German literature, is *The Difficult Man* (1921), the culmination of his labors with Molière's comedies, yet containing nothing of Molière but the spirit and the form. As the title suggests, it is a character comedy. However, it is not the task of this comedy to chastise a social type, but rather to reconcile the "difficult" man, Count Hans Karl Bühl, with society. The fabric of the play is tremendously complex: the older generation contrasts sharply with the younger, grotesquerie mingles with sympathetic depiction, caricature with profound character portrayal, comic situations alternate with scenes of deep seriousness. Hans Karl, like Philip Chandos, cannot overcome his distrust of language. But that is only symptomatic; he is unwilling or unable to commit himself, to act decisively, to bind himself in love. Helene Altenwyl, much younger but of rare maturity, shares Hans Karl's horror of language, his freedom from petty ambition and desire for esteem. But she can function socially because she is able to transcend her insights. Knowing that Hans Karl cannot admit to himself his love for her, she proposes to him. We cannot say that he is cured and able to assume his proper position of leadership—he had been dodging the duty of addressing the House of Lords—but with Helene's aid, he does find the way to self-fulfillment.

Hofmannsthal's last play, *The Tower* (1925, 1927) is bleakly pessimistic. It began as a revision of Calderon's *La vida es sueño* in 1904; in the final version little of Calderon's play remains. The problem with which Hofmannsthal had begun his writing career, the discovery of the self, is expanded: it is the world which Sigismund discovers, a corrupt place in which everyone seeks power and in which it is almost impossible to escape the taint of violence. The version of 1925 promises regeneration through the coming of a Child King; the final version holds out no such hope. Not only the theme and the messianic element in the earlier version, but also the solemn Biblical tone of the language resemble the expressionist plays of the period.

Arthur Schnitzler (1862–1931), Viennese physician and psychologist, was less concerned than his friend Hofmannsthal with metaphysics; he probed the psychological depths of contemporary society. A series of scenes, *Anatol* (1893), depicts a decadent Viennese playboy who lives only in the present, knows only physical love, and who must set the stage carefully for every mood, in order to live each moment to the fullest. It is daring humor to have Anatol wake up and rush last night's girl into her clothes because this is the morning he is to get married, but the irony of another scene reveals even more tellingly the mentality of decadence. Anatol had bargained with Bianca to break off their relationship if one of them wished to take up with another. But he has, characteristically, not kept his word. He has betrayed her, and after savoring that sensation to the fullest, decides to break the news to her over a suitably lavish dinner. But she has also betrayed him and spoils his evening by telling her news first. The irony with which Schnitzler reveals how even these "emancipated" moderns experience the same emotions men have always felt and how little control they actually have over their feelings and destinies, is typical of many of the novellas and plays he wrote. The decadence of Anatol's world is caught particularly well in Round Dance (1897), a play consisting of ten dialogues. Each is linked to the next when the partner in one reappears in the next with a new partner, the new partner then appears in the next with a new partner, etc. All social levels are represented and their morality is denuded. They swear everlasting love but faith endures only a half-hour. It is a pathetic world which Schnitzler exposes: these people hunger for a meaning in life and hope to find it in love, but they are too self-preoccupied to love. They are afraid of transitoriness and death, but unable to combat them with lasting values. And so they dance from partner to partner in a vicious circle of yearning which always ends in frustration.

In much the same way Schnitzler demasked a socially more acceptable figure in the novella Lieutenant Gustl (1900). Gus is an ordinary officer who has little taste for the concert he is attending when the story begins. It is his exaggerated sense of self-importance, however, which causes him to jostle a baker, who then threatens to break his sword. Convinced he must commit suicide to preserve his honor, Gus spends the night reviewing his situation. The entire story is related in inner monologue, a technique akin to James Joyce's stream-of-consciousness. Gus's thoughts reveal a shabby mental and moral constitution. His soldier's uniform is a façade for cowardice; he places mother and sister on a pedestal of purity but is having an affair with a married woman; the army has presented him with a set of values which he gratefully accepts but which he does not understand. His highest value is honor and he dutifully tries to persuade himself (he forgets repeatedly) that even if the baker were to die, he would have to kill himself to restore his honor. By that customary touch of Schnitzlerian irony, the baker does die; Gus jubilantly forgets his honor. His discourse with his soul has left him totally unchanged. The Austrian Army relieved Schnitzler of his reserve commission.

Sterben (Dying, 1894), one of Schnitzler's earliest novellas, demonstrates man's spiritual dependence upon his body. Paul, given by his doctor only a year to live, offers to break off his relationship with Marie but she insists that she will stay with him to the end and die with him. The description of Paul's decline is detached, precise, clinical; at the same time Marie's feelings undergo a corresponding change. In the end ignoble human nature triumphs; Paul even tries to kill Marie when she refuses to keep her bargain.

Schnitzler shares with the naturalists, scientific detachment and the penchant for unmasking man's true self. Though he does not write of the proletariat—most of his characters are little concerned with earning a living—he does write of moral slums where spiritual poverty triumphs. His world is really more dismal than that of the naturalists because no improvement is possible. The doctrinaire naturalists were basically optimistic, for their study of man's social relationships had a goal: social change. What Schnitzler's analyses usually reveal, on the other hand, is an unattractive and immutable, ego-centered human psychology. The truly selfless devotion shown by Christine in the drama *Light-O'-Love* (1896) or by the blind man's brother in *Blind Geronimo* (1900) is an all too infrequent phenomenon in Schnitzler's world.

In his portrayal of the inner world Schnitzler is, of course, impressionistic. His interior monologue, inspired by Edouard Dujardin's *Les Lauriers sont coupés* (1887), is *Sekundenstil* applied to psychological events. In two of his best novellas he uses the technique masterfully to illuminate psychotic or near psychotic personalities: *Fräulein Else* (1924), whose narcissism clashes tragically with her unyielding middle-class conscience; *Flight into Darkness* (1931), in which the course of paranoia in Robert is pursued from apparent normality to insanity and homicide.

Rainer Maria Rilke's (1875–1926) earliest poetry and his attempt at naturalist drama scarcely hinted at the genius of his later work; he quickly became a poet of undisputed world stature. Rilke's career was a highly conscious personal and artistic development; the perfection of technique when hand in hand with spiritual growth. His first major success was *The Manner of the Love and Death of Cornet Christopher Rilke*, written in a single night in 1899 (published 1906) in lyrical prose. It is an appealing story about an ancestor, a brave young rider who enjoys a night of love before he rides to his death in the war against the Turks.

A trip to Russia with Lou Andreas Salomé and her husband in the spring, 1899, another trip in the summer of 1900 left Rilke with a profound impression of the vastness and spirituality of that country. *The Book of Hours* (1905) in its two parts, "Of the Monastic Life" and "Of Pilgrimage," bears witness to the Russian experi-

287

ence. The God to whom the young Russian artist-monk prays, however, is not the God of Christianity. He is an immanent God, whom the monk addresses directly, expressing their intimate relationship with countless metaphors inspired by the most diverse objects and situations: "You are a deer with dapples on it/and I'm the dark a forest hides."[4] Above all, his God is a God whom man constructs and who is dependent upon man for his existence. "What will you do, God, when I die?" one poem begins. Another expresses the idea that God is only a beginning, just as man is: "You made such a great beginning on yourself/on that day when you began us." The third section, "Of Poverty and Death," records Rilke's impressions of Paris; he asserts that death, like life, is an affair of growth. "For what in dying so alienly shakes us/is that it's not our death, but one that takes us/only because we've not matured our own."[5] The proper end of life is one's "own" death, a death evolving from one's own life and character.

In *The Book of Images* (1902, 1906) Rilke's spiritual quest is focused upon the objects of the world about him. The word "thing" (*Ding*) is all important in the language of this devotion to earthly objects. No longer did Rilke express his yearning, as in the early poetry, to be in the world; he was in it, he was in the things of the world. "The things become more and more related and all the images become more and more intensely observed" ("Progress"). Rilke saw God in all things; God was the "thing of things."

In 1902 Rilke went to Paris to write a monograph on Rodin. The experience was another decisive influence on his development as an artist. Rodin taught him to observe with precision and objectivity and, most importantly, to work. Rilke learned that the artist is a craftsman and must know the material he works with. Great art demands of the artist not merely inspiration but also the most rigorous devotion and sacrifice. In the painting of Cézanne, Rilke found another great model of the plasticity he resolved to achieve in his poetry.

Under the influence of these lessons, Rilke attained the high point of his middle period in the *New Poems* (1907) and *New Poems, Part II* (1908), written mostly in Paris. Now highly conscious of language as the material of his art, Rilke avoided the extravagant virtuosity of his earlier poetry. His mastery of language allowed him to take bold, effective liberties. Inner rhyme and enjambment sometimes eclipse end-rhyme; the traditional sonnet divisions are thus in effect dispensed with in "Archaic Torso of

Apollo." The skill in rhythm, the music of assonance and alliteration are amazing. These are *Dinggedichte* (thing-poems), poems
which attempt nothing more than a graphic description of an object
without explicitly expressing the poet's feelings. Eduard Mörike and
Conrad Ferdinand Meyer had written a very few such poems, but
Rilke was the poet who perfected the genre. There are no limits to
his subject matter: people, animals, flowers, works of art, and
mythical subjects are all portrayed. The metaphors are strikingly
vivid and well chosen: a Spanish dancer is likened to a match
bursting into flame; the legs of the gazelle are "loaded with leaps"
(the word *Lauf* means leg as well as rifle barrel). Among the favorites are the animal portraits from the Jardin des Plantes in Paris:
the gazelle, the panther, flamingoes, and parrots. Rilke tried to
capture not merely the exterior but the very essence of the "thing."
As poet, he usually recedes behind the picture in his *Dinggedicht*,
but there may be a hint of symbolic meaning as in "Carousel" or
explicit commentary as in the abrupt last line of "Archaic Torso of
Apollo," the reaction of the poet to the sight of superb statuary:
"You must change your life."

The novel *The Notebooks of Malte Laurids Brigge* (1904–
1910) sheds much light on Rilke's development as a poet. The
central figure, Malte, is a Danish poet (Rilke greatly admired Jens
Peter Jacobsen) who lives in Paris, poor and unknown, "seeking
among visible things for equivalents for what he has seen within
himself." *The Notebooks* is a novel of decadence; Malte is a
neurasthenic who suffers from the harsh world of reality. He flees
from reality into art, from the bonds of community to the undisputed realm of his inner self. A curious recast of the parable of
the prodigal son ends the book. It is the "legend of one who did not
want to be loved." The son returns home in order to continue the
ripening process of his self begun in childhood. Instead of forgiveness he begs his parents not to love him; love would lay claims upon
his freedom.

In 1912 Rilke wrote two elegies at the Duino Castle where he
stayed as the guest of the Princess of Thurn and Taxis. For ten years
after that he wrote almost no poetry. Then, in a burst of inspiration
while living at the Muzot castle in Switzerland in 1922, he not only
finished the elegies but also composed the cycle of *Sonnets to
Orpheus*. The ten *Duino Elegies* are a complete break with the
celebration of the visible world in the *New Poems*. The rhythms are
free, the long lines unrhymed. The radical departure from the

earlier style reflects Rilke's intention of transcending his earlier impressionism, which in his own words, ended with his tour of Spain 1912–1913: "Spain was the last 'impression.' Since then my nature has been impelled from within, so intensely and constantly that it cannot be merely 'impressed' any more." Rilke felt that he had completed his work of observation; it was now his task to transform the pictures he had gathered.

The elegies are directed to the angels, the "almost deadly birds of the soul" whose perfection is unbearable to humans. The first two elegies emphasize the contrast between lonely, frail man and the perfection of the angels. It occurs to the poet that lovers in their conviction of the eternity of their feelings are perhaps freed from the consciousness of human transitoriness. But then he realizes that this feeling itself is transitory. In the third elegy Rilke treats the other aspect of love, Eros, a brutish but necessary force which links the individual to his forebears, for their culture lives on in his blood and helps determine his choice of mate. In the fourth elegy the poet laments man's increasing alienation from nature. Disharmony characterizes man's life, so that he is blind to the essence of life. Man is a bad actor in the drama of life because he constantly struggles against his role. It is the marionette with no will of its own who, in the hands of the angels, can perform the perfect drama, for through the marionette the angels' will is expressed without impediment. In the fifth elegy Rilke describes a troupe of circus acrobats whose efforts fall short of success and yet with a smile they always try again. In contrast to their imperfection stands the hero, described in the sixth elegy. Like the fig tree which sets fruit without visible blossoming, the hero is destined to early fulfillment. In the seventh elegy Rilke's praise is extended to all the earth: "Being here's glorious!" Here he develops his idea of the inward transformation of the external world:

Nowhere, beloved, can world exist but within.
Life passes in transformation. And, ever diminishing,
outwardness dwindles.[6]

The elegiac tone is struck again in the eighth elegy which laments man's limitations. Man cannot, like animals and, at times, children lead an unreflective existence, free from all yearning. In the ninth elegy, however, Rilke affirms this existence and defines man's earthly task: he is to immortalize the things of earth by transforming them within himself: "Earth, is it not just this that you want:

to arise invisibly in us?" The tenth elegy affirms sorrow and ends with the legend of the Land of Lamentations, where the dead become acquainted with their new condition before they pass on to the realm of death.

The fifty-five *Sonnets to Orpheus*, jubilant complement to the somber elegies, celebrate the triumph of the artist over life and death. The insights of the elegies are translated into practise. The poet endeavors to save the world from the machine age by his praise which transforms it into an inner world beyond the reach of time. And Orpheus, the poet-singer who has visited the realm of death, is well qualified to reveal the relationship of this world to the world of death.

III

The group of writers born between 1880 and 1890 which followed upon the heels of Hofmannsthal, George, and Rilke rebelled against the world about themselves first of all as a means of asserting their own individuality. Gottfried Benn, looking back on the epoch, commented that the youth of today accepts it as a matter of fact that the expressionist generation burst traditional language asunder, but that "they know nothing any more of Heinrich Mann, d'Annunzio, Oscar Wilde, Huysmans, Maeterlinck—all those who influenced us, charmed us, but whom we also had to overcome in order to arrive at ourselves." Thus the rebellion was not always fair. Georg Heym criticized the "marionette theater" of the "weak cadaver" of Stefan George and spoke contemptuously of that "overly made-up female Maria Rilke." Ernst Stadler, in repudiating his early poetry, remarked that Hofmannsthal had been poison for him.

The clash between generations which the naturalists wrote of—usually a confrontation between traditional and modern views —became much more intense in the literature of the expressionists.[7] The father-son conflict became one of the most popular expressionist motifs. Aside from its shock value it symbolized the struggle for recognition as well as the need to overthrow an establishment which had become impersonal, materialistic, and tyrannical. The threat of industrialization had been seen by Naturalism largely as economic and social; it was not a specific concern of the impressionists. Rilke, long after the onset of Expressionism, did refer obliquely to the increasingly unfeeling, mechanical quality of

291

modern life: "More than ever/Things we can experience are falling away, for/that which is taking their place is imageless activity." In several of the *Sonnets to Orpheus* he gives gentle warning that man must remain master of the machine: "Long will machinery menace the whole of our treasure/while it, unmindful of us, dares to a mind of its own."[8] However for the early expressionist lyric poets the horrors of existence in an urban and industrial society loom with particular urgency. Their work does not register the personal agony of over-sensitive nerves, as Rilke's Malte suffers in Paris, but objectively records the drab life of the soulless city dwellers, whose faces are "alien like animals" (Alfred Wolfenstein, "Verdammte Jugend" ["Accursed Youth"]), and who are dehumanized by the daily routine of factory life: "No prison cell freezes thinking/as does this walking between walls, which see only each other" (Paul Zech, "Fabrikstraße Tags" ["Factory Street by Day"]). At home, despite the overcrowded living conditions, they are desperately lonely:

> Our walls are as thin as membrane,
> So that everyone participates when I weep,
> Whispering penetrates like bawling:
>
> And yet, as if dumb in a secluded cavern
> Untouched and unseen,
> Each is far away and feels alone.
> From: Wolfenstein, "Städter" ("City Dwellers")

Loneliness and isolation were basic conditions in the world as the expressionists experienced it.

It is such a world which the expressionists wanted to *rehumanize*. They saw the urgent need for regeneration and urged their public to overcome isolation by recognizing that all men are brothers. They envisioned an era to come when such communal feeling would be reality instead of mere dream. For some, the possibility of realizing this goal seemed to lie in Communism. Ernst Toller actually participated in the Munich *Räterepublik*, a short-lived Communist secessionist state, but quickly became disillusioned. He was by no means the only expressionist to find the edge of his idealism dulled by the harsh reality of human nature. But some eventually found the community they sought: Hanns Johst, Arnolt Bronnen, Wilhelm Klemm in National Socialism and Johannes R. Becher and Bertolt Brecht in Communist East Germany.

The attacks on middle-class self-righteousness, complacency, and false values which the naturalists had launched were continued with fervor by the expressionists, especially in prose and in drama. One particular target was the school system. Feeling was mounting against the oppressive demands of an educational system which produced a rash of student suicides each year. One of the purposes of the Youth Movement (*Jugendbewegung*), a kind of Scouting organization founded at the turn of the century, was to battle the tyranny of adults in school and at home. Two works predating Expressionism which contain savagely satirical pictures of school life are Frank Wedekind's *The Awakening of Spring* (1891) and Heinrich Mann's *Small Town Tyrant* (*Professor Unrat*, 1905). Mann's novel was filmed twice with great success as "The Blue Angel."

The cult of youth and vitality at the turn of the century continued into the second decade as an important element in expressionistic literature. This vitalism was accompanied by a growing anti-intellectualism which was already palpable in the 1890's. The aestheticist reaction to Naturalism was in part a rebellion against intellectual materialism. In their stress on *l'art pour l'art* the impressionists sought to banish practical reason from the sphere of art; they found image and symbol so important to their art because these communicate directly with the emotions, instead of via reason. Finally, the *fin de siècle* decadents suffered under the burden of their over-refinement and longed for the innocence of an unreflective, instinctive life.

The most important force behind the rising tide of anti-intellectualism was the poet-philosopher Friedrich Nietzsche. In his essay "*Of the Use and Abuse of History for Life*" (*Thoughts out of Season* II, 5. 1873) he argued that excessive knowledge lames and finally destroys the life forces, and that this was one of the serious defects of the German people. Nietzsche was virtually unknown in Germany until 1890, a year after his mental collapse, when the Danish critic Georg Brandes published a lengthy article on his philosophy in *Die neue Rundschau*. The impact was immediate. Nietzsche's distinction between the apollonic (serene, harmonious) and the dionysian (bacchanalian) aspects of art in *The Birth of Tragedy* (1872) found eager acceptance with Richard Dehmel. The members of the George circle saw in their Master the embodiment of the new man whom Nietzsche's Zarathustra (*Thus Spake Zarathustra*, 1883) proclaimed. Thomas Mann's early novellas and his novel *Buddenbrooks* have as a central theme the dichotomy mind-

293

life; Nietzsche's psychology of decadence receives its illustration in these early works. By 1910 Nietzsche's ideas were common currency; his influence on the expressionist writers can hardly be overstated. His vision of a superman to supplant the decadent race of present men, his exhortation to destroy false traditional values and replace them with new, soundly based values, his affirmation of the body and castigation of hollow cultural piety became basic themes for the expressionists. The curious combination of narcissism and expansive love for all humanity which characterizes Zarathustra and his author is encountered repeatedly in expressionistic works. Finally, his ecstatic style undoubtedly exercised a strong influence on the style of many expressionists.[9]

Though the expressionists advocated destruction of traditional literary forms and the creation of new ones, the revolution in practise did not carry so far. In the poem "Form ist Wollust" ("Form is Voluptuousness," 1914), Stadler rejects the "pleasures" of traditional literary form because he finds form too limiting. With characteristic expressionist expansiveness he wishes to "extend his being infinitely." The poem, however, is in a most restrictive form: metrically perfect end-stopped couplets! He did adopt a long, free line for his later poetry but a large portion of expressionist verse was written in traditional form. This can readily be seen by paging through the best known anthology of expressionist poetry, Kurt Pinthus' *Menschheitsdämmerung* (*Twilight of Mankind*, 1920, 1959), which contains representative work of twenty-three poets. Stanzaic verse, sonnets, even *terza rima* mingle with other poems whose authors felt the traditional meters could not contain their flood of feeling; they chose long lines, free rhythms, and an ecstatic tone which reveal their debt to Walt Whitman's *Leaves of Grass* (1855–1880). In drama the break with tradition was more widespread. Expressionists were not usually concerned with external reality but with an inner vision. Hence, the mimetic principle, psychological motivation, the trappings of the theater of illusion were largely discarded. A play was divided into "pictures" rather than acts; drama came to present loosely connected scenes rather than unified action. Narrative prose, not a favored medium for such an emotionally charged era, underwent similar changes: psychological motivation and realism yielded to a predilection for parable.

The range of writing included under the rubric Expressionism is so wide that no simple definition of expressionistic style is possible. The language of Expressionism is usually emotionally intense. Syntax is distorted for the sake of impact, verbs are favored over nouns because they are dynamic, and there is a fondness for superlatives, repetition, and parataxis. One finds on the one hand a verbose, lyrical rhetoric reminiscent of the Baroque, on the other hand the precise opposite: ellipses and sentence fragments, the concentration of language into the fewest possible words, resulting in a kind of explosive stuttering. Neologisms, a difficult problem for the translator, are common. Behind all these stylistic characteristics lay not only a search for a language adequate for conveying the urgency of the expressionist message, but also a conscious attack on the middle class: "A-logical bombs undermine traditional sentence structure, the bourgeois architecture of language" (Johannes R. Becher). We should not, however, overlook the expressionists who did not write in the expressionistic style: the early poets, for example, whose style is often nearer to Impressionism, and Franz Kafka, whose meticulously sober prose is quite traditional in its syntax.

Alfred Mombert (1872–1942), a poet of cosmic perspective and maker of myths, is a forerunner of the religious expressionists. He considered himself a "composer of symphonies" rather than a lyric poet and insisted that his poetry, like music, was to be heard, not read. Mombert's language, though not always successful, is on the whole a powerful vehicle. With its fullness of feeling, its visionary quality, it anticipates ecstatic expressionistic diction already in such an early epic as *Die Schöpfung* (*The Creation*, 1897). His grandiose *Aeon* trilogy (1907–1911) is a vision in dialogues.

Theodor Däubler (1876–1934) was likewise a fashioner of cosmic myth. In his gigantic verse epic *Das Nordlicht* (*Northern Lights*, 1910), the *aurora borealis* symbolizes man's urge to return to the sun, the origin of life. The epic optimistically proclaims eternal existence for the earth, in a rhapsodic language rich in imagery. Däubler's epic, in contrast to Mombert's works, is explicitly Christian.

Gottfried Benn, in his lecture "Probleme der Lyrik" ("Problems of Lyric Poetry," 1951) dates the beginning of expressionistic poetry in Germany from the publication of Alfred Lichtenstein's "Dämmerung" ("Twilight," 1911) and Jakob van Hoddis's "Weltende" ("End of the World," 1911). Whether the birth of expressionistic poetry can be so neatly pinpointed is a moot question; van Hoddis's poem, the earlier of the two, did strike a responsive chord among contemporaries. It consisted of a mere eight lines:

295

The hat flies from the pointed head of the citizen,
In all the air there is a resounding as from shouting,
Roofers fall and break in two
And on the coasts—you read—the flood-tide is rising.

The storm is here, the wild seas hop
To shore in order to crush fat dams
Most people have a headcold.
The railroads fall from the bridges.

The apocalyptic scene and the attack on the middle class were favorite expressionist themes; the poem became an immediate hit with the rebellious avant-garde. More significant from an aesthetic standpoint is the form: within conventional rhymed stanzas a grotesque juxtaposition of incongruities: wild seas hopping, fat dams, roofers who break like dolls. It is a dynamic scene of world destruction about which mankind only reads in the newspapers. The irony of the poem is underlined by its imperturbable singsong rhythm. The poem had a decisive effect on Lichtenstein, who adopted its "simultaneity," i.e., the enumeration of images devoid of spatial or temporal relationships. But a stanza of Lichtenstein's poem "Twilight" shows how closely this technique approaches impressionism:

A fat man is sticking to a window.
A youth is about to visit a soft woman.
A gray clown is putting on his boots.
A baby-carriage cries and dogs curse.

Nor does "Twilight" contain an expressionist program. Lichtenstein displays here, as in his other poems, a striking new way of looking at the world. Filling out each line with a separate and unrelated image enhances the effect of simultaneity and heightens the mood of sadness. There is about the poem an implication of menacing world disintegration which is explicit in other poems of his; indeed, it is characteristic of early expressionistic poetry.

Ernst Stadler's (1883–1914) early poetry is impressionistic: dreaminess and dream imagery, twilight, melancholy, even sultry perversity are characteristic. His models were George and Hofmannsthal. In his collection *Aufbruch* (*Revolt*, 1914) he abruptly abandoned his early tone and the *Jugendstil* landscapes and mannerisms. Much of his mature poetry is written in long lines—thirty syllables are not unusual—which come close to being prose despite their end rhyme. These poems are also frequently impressionistic, but the picture presented is not blurred and static, it is dynamic and original as a few lines from "Bahnhöfe" ("Train Stations") will show:

Like oases of light the curved halls rest in the steel protection
And wait. And then all at once they are overtaken by adventure,
And all brazen power is stowed into their giant body,
And the wild breath of the machine which stands still and looks
    around like an animal in flight,
And it is as if the fate of many hundred men had been poured into
    its trembling bed.

In strange incongruity with his exuberant love of life, the work of Georg Heym (1887–1912) is filled with apprehension of imminent evil and haunted by death. His poetry, unlike Stadler's, is in strict form. His pictures of the modern city go beyond Stadler's dynamic impressionism; he conjures up nightmare visions in such poems as "Dämonen der Großstadt" ("Demons of the Metropolis," 1910), "Der Gott der Stadt" ("The God of the City," 1911), and "Der Krieg" ("War," 1912). In his preference for ugliness, his perception of a demonic world, and his tendency to see in reality mere appearance or empty mask, Heym rejected, even attempted to destroy the reality he knew.

Georg Trakl's (1887–1914) poetry also presents melancholy landscapes, but the mood is restrained and elegaic, and the imagery is a private symbolism which can best be understood with reference to the entire corpus of his poetry. The symbolic use of color, reminiscent of Franz Marc's paintings, is particularly striking. The preference is for blue, black, red in all variations, yellow, and gold. Melancholy and apprehension of decline are the dominant mood of Trakl's poetry, a mood born of loneliness and guilt.

The poem "Ruh und Schweigen" ("Peace and Silence") consists, not unlike the typical impressionist poem, of a series of unconnected images, but the landscape is not a stylization of external reality. It is a construct of objects and figures which have become symbols of the poet's sufferings and yearning, ciphers of an inner landscape which defy precise interpretation:

Shepherds buried the sun in the barren forest.
A fisher drew
The moon out of the chill pond in a net of hair.

297

In blue crystal
Dwells the pale person, his cheek leaned against his stars;
Or he bows his head in crimson sleep.

But the black flight of the birds always touches
The watcher, the sacredness of blue flowers,
Thinks the close quiet something forgotten, extinguished angels.

Again the forehead nights in moon stone;
A radiant youth
The sister appears in autumn and black decay.

The first stanza sets the poem in Trakl's favorite time of day, evening and night. The words "barren" and "chill" set the tone. The "pale person" and "watcher" is the poet himself, who seldom used the first person in his mature poems. The figure of the sister, who frequently appears in Trakl's poetry as a source of comfort, here appears as a "radiant youth," merging perhaps with Trakl's longing for innocence, which is often symbolized in the figure of a youth (the boy Elis in a number of poems). The use of "night" as a verb, "moon" as an adjective ("monden") seem natural liberties; otherwise Trakl's syntax and form are conventional, his language simple, his content primarily personal confession.

The poetry of August Stramm (1874–1915) presents an extreme contrast to the bulk of expressionist poetry, both in effect and in creative originality. Through Herwarth Walden, Stramm became acquainted with the lyric theory of Arno Holz and the writings of F. T. Marinetti, the founder of Futurism in Italy. Walden was the leader of a group of expressionists, *Der Sturm* (storm), and had introduced Futurism to Germany with an exhibition of Futurist art in his Sturm Gallery in 1912. Marinetti's manifestoes were published in Walden's periodical *Der Sturm* (1910–1932) that same year. Marinetti called for radical stylistic changes in order to achieve the "modern" tempo. Nouns and verbs, the most important elements of language, were no longer to be modified by adjectives and adverbs (they slow down the sentence) but were to be set down in a natural order of importance without regard for the rules of syntax. Verbs were to be in the infinitive form because infinitives express continuity and are the most objective form of the verb.

Stramm was so overwhelmed by his new insight into the expressive possibilities of language that in 1914 he discarded all the poetry he had written earlier. The poetry we have from him was written during the less than two years left to him before he died on the battlefield. Stramm concentrated his content into lines of few words, frequently a single word. He achieved startling impact by transforming nouns into verbs, by omitting articles, conjunctions, and punctuation:

"Patrol"

The stones foe
Window grins treachery
Branches strangle
Mountains bushes scale off rustly
Shrill
Death.

Stramm approaches more closely than any other expressionist poet the abstract poem. His love poetry, collected under the title *Du* (*You*, 1915), examines the relationship between the poet ("I") and his beloved ("you"). Stramm's marked tendency toward transcendentalism suggests a broader interpretation of the poetry; his love is directed toward man, the universe, and God. His last collection, *Tropfblut* (*Dripblood*, 1915), records his experience of the war, not only as horrible slaughter, but also, in cosmic perspective, as an awesome natural phenomenon.

In an article for Franz Pfemfert's activist periodical *Die Aktion* (*Action*, 1911–1932), Franz Werfel (1890–1945) foresaw an era of artistic creation when reality would no longer reside in nouns but in verbs. He pointed out that verbs are the vehicle of passion and action. In his own poetry Werfel did not venture far from the conventional. The power of his verse lies in its rhetorical qualities. The mainspring of Werfel's expressionist poetry was his desire to promulgate the brotherhood of man. "My only wish, O Man, is to be related to you!" The first line of "An den Leser" ("To the Reader"), is the basic thought in his collections *Weltfreund* (*The World's Friend*, 1911), *Wir sind* (*We are*, 1913), *Einander* (*Each other*, 1915), *Gerichtstag* (*Day of Judgment*, 1919). Werfel was highly regarded as a poet in his day; for us, even if we do not doubt his sincerity, the poetry seems excessive. In his late expressionistic novels and dramas he takes a critical stance toward ecstatic Expressionism. From 1911–1914 Werfel worked as editor for the Kurt Wolff Verlag, the most important publisher of expressionist literature. Here he performed invaluable service by recognizing and promoting young writers, among them Georg Trakl.

The Alsatian Yvan Goll (1891–1950) began his career with poetry related in tone and content to Werfel's. The Panama Canal, which was opened August 5, 1914, is celebrated in his poem-cycle *Der Panama Kanal* (1914) as a step towards the unification of nations and a symbol of brotherly love: "Everything which is yours, earth, will call itself brother." The experience of World War I was disillusioning; the 1918 version of the poem is more sober. A final version appeared in *Der Eiffel-Turm* (*Eiffel Tower*, 1924). In 1921 Goll declared Expressionism dead; his way as poet led from imagistic, rhapsodic expressionism to a surrealism of cosmic symbols. He did not experiment with language but scrupulously sought the appropriate image. He went to Paris in 1919 where he joined the surrealists and published in French from 1925 on.

Of all the expressionist poets undoubtedly the most important in Gottfried Benn (1886–1956). He began his career with poetry which, in the spirit of early Expressionism, rejects reality. From 1912, when *Morgue und andere Gedichte* (*Morgue and Other Poems*) appeared, until 1922 his poems are cynical, concerned with death of the flesh but deliberately shocking in their indifference to it. Their language is cruelly matter-of-fact and replete with medical and technical terminology, student jargon, and dialect forms:

"Cycle"

The solitary molar of a whore
who had died incognito
wore a gold filling.
(The rest had decamped
as if by silent agreement.)
That filling was swiped by the mortician's mate
and pawned, so he could go to a dive
and dance, for, as he put it:
"Earth alone should return to earth."[10]

Benn's poetry from 1927 until 1938, when the Nazis forbade him to publish, is cast in more conventional form: musical qualities, which are notably absent from the earlier poetry, are now characteristic; indeed, music sometimes dominates. In these poems, Benn turns back to a reality of myth and dreams, a reality which precedes the intellectualism he, like other expressionists, felt to be oppressive. His postwar poetry tends to be prosaic again, and presents contemporary reality in a montage of modern slang and jargon.

Benn spoke out in 1921 in favor of a substantive style; he saw the task of the poet as evocative. The poet is not to make definitive statements but to evoke associations, and for this the noun, not the verb, is best suited. Benn reminds us of the French symbolists when he speaks of the associative power of words: "We will have to resign ourselves to the fact that words possess a latent power which affects those properly attuned like magic and enables them to reproduce this magic. This seems to me to be the ultimate mystery." Closely related to this view is his reaction against the nineteenth-century concept of history as progress. This has given him the reputation of being a nihilist but he is not a complete nihilist: he posits a static realm in which "nothing happens and everything stands still"—the spiritual realm of art. The artist in constructing works of art engages in the highest metaphysical activity of man.

Benn's *Statische Gedichte* (*Static Poems*, 1948) may have been influenced by his inner emigration but they are also a consistent step in his artistic development. The title poem of the volume begins with the lines: "Being foreign to development/is the depth of the wise man." The static principle focuses on a reality deeper and more permanent than development. Benn is perhaps the most consistent of the expressionists, not in his early rejection of reality, but in his belief, adhered to throughout his life, that content must be extinguished in favor of expression, and expression, or artistic form, is the highest value.

IV

One of the most important precursors of expressionist drama was Frank Wedekind (1864–1918), who, despite his proximity to the naturalist circle in Munich, rejected the aims and aesthetic of Naturalism from the first. The rift between Wedekind and the naturalists was widened by an unfortunate personal experience. Hauptmann used details from Wedekind's family life in his play *Das Friedensfest*. Wedekind retaliated with his play *Children and Fools* (1891) in which he satirized both Naturalism and the movement for the emancipation of women. He considered the goals of both movements contrary to nature. The central figure of the play, the poet Meier, is a caricature of Hauptmann; like the naturalists, Meier scrupulously collects data—the confidences of friends!—in notebooks to use later as material for his art.

Wedekind's *The Awakening of Spring* directed its satire at the hypocrisy, false values, and unnatural prudery with which adults tyrannize the world of youth. A group of adolescents is portrayed, who are beset by the anxieties of puberty. Melchior, somewhat more enlightened than the others, tries to help Moritz by giving him a booklet he has written and illustrated. But Moritz does badly in school and despair drives him to suicide. When Melchior's booklet is discovered among the dead boy's things, he is brought to trial before the school administration. But his guilt extends further. Wendla, whose mother had told her that babies come only to people in love, had allowed Moritz to go too far; without even knowing she was pregnant, she dies from the abortion her mother has arranged. In the final scene the moral of the play is specified. As Melchior wanders in the cemetery contemplating suicide, he is greeted by Moritz, who is carrying his head under his arm. As Moritz tries to persuade Melchior to escape the problems of life as he had, a masked man appears (the dramatist himself) and vigorously affirms the value of life, despite its problems.

That the play was seen as pornography is readily understandable—the variety and explicitness of sex scenes were certainly new to the contemporary stage. The mixture of comedy and tragedy was also novel. Büchner, whom Wedekind revered, had presented the same admixture in *Danton's Death* and *Woyzeck*. Wedekind's humor is more pronounced and more pervasive. The schoolmaster scene is downright caricature: the schoolmasters' names are humorous, their language is pompous almost to the point of unintelligibility. Thus, the subtitle, "A Tragedy of Children" is misleading. When Max Reinhardt was preparing the play for its premiere performance in 1906, Wedekind, who played the part of the masked man, had to urge him not to interpret the play as unrelieved tragedy, but to bring out the humor of the play.

An important point in *The Awakening of Spring* is that the sexual urge is natural and can be repressed only at great cost to individual and society. Only one of the characters in that play is completely free and happy: Ilse, who has broken away from the restraints of home. She gives herself freely to all the boys because she loves them all, and she lives in complete harmony with herself. In *Earth Spirit* (1895), Wedekind's Lulu, like Ilse, embodies the sexual drive. In a prologue, Wedekind makes it clear that he intends to show the animal aspect of man in a more flattering light than the naturalists had done. He speaks through a circus ring-master:

> The true animal, the wild, beautiful animal,
> That—my ladies!—you will see only with me.

The naturalists, it is true, revealed man to be quite a different sort of animal; one need only think of Hauptmann's signalman Thiel. Lulu is the true, wild, beautiful animal. She is all instinct, the "primal form of woman" for whom modern intellectualized man is no match. A doctor, a painter, an editor are destroyed in turn. The second part of *Earth Spirit, Pandora's Box*, brings Lulu's degradation and death. Penniless, she is forced to become a prostitute, but in so doing she compromises her nature and surrenders her freedom. Her death comes at the hands of Jack the Ripper, a figure diametrically her opposite, a man whose instincts are perverted; he is a symbol of the extreme alienation from nature produced by civilization.

Wedekind anticipated Expressionism in his language, in his renunciation of realistic, psychological motivation, in his grotesque mixture of humor with tragedy. More than three quarters of a century after Wedekind's first plays, the grotesque, so important in Expressionism (Kaiser, Barlach, Brecht) and Dada, is still very much the mode in the theater of the absurd.

Experimentation in theater directing and staging, which had begun with impressionist drama, continued with even greater zeal during the phase of Expressionism.[11] The expressionist aesthetic lent impetus to such experiments, for, despite the wide differences between expressionists, they were in general agreement about the aim of their art: not form, but content, not beauty, but effectiveness were the primary considerations. They recognized that theater is a political force; some indeed considered theater the most effective form of artistic expression and sought to utilize it to carry out their program.

Early indications of a definitive break with theater tradition were given in Paul Scheerbart's series of dramas, *Revolutionäre Theater-Bibliothek* (*Revolutionary Theater Library*, 1904), whose grotesque satire goes beyond Wedekind. His plays reject ordinary reality and, in staging, attempt to concentrate the spectators' attention on the protagonists. A rebellion against traditional theater actually takes place on stage in Alfred Döblin's (1878–1957) first published play, *Lydia und Mäxchen* (*Lydia and Maxie*, 1906). The protagonists rebel against their "tame" roles and incite others to rebellion, finally driving director and author from the stage.

Oskar Kokoschka (1886–   ) also rebelled against conventional theater as well as against all superficial ornamentation and façade. He was trained as an illustrator in Vienna's industrial school of art, and his first exhibition showed his indebtedness to Gustav Klimt and *Jugendstil*. But his art also presented a keen analysis of the morbidity of the period. His dramas are concerned with essential human problems, not with everyday realism. The early plays deal with the battle between man and woman, but not just in the sphere of Eros as with Strindberg and Wedekind. Kokoschka sees innate disharmony arising from the essential and irreconcilable difference between men and women. His dramas are myths in which parody and nonsense mix with seriousness and profound symbolism. Cabaret techniques jar the spectator and destroy any theatrical illusion of reality. Although Kokoschka opposed abstract theater, his own plays approach abstractness in their compactness and symbolism. The language is outcry, condensed and epigrammatic. The imaginative use of lights and color, as well as pantomime and gesture replace stage sets. Two one-act plays *Murderer, Hope of Women* (1907) and *Sphinx and Strawman* (1907) scandalized the solid middle class but were hailed by the avant-garde and had a lasting influence on later theater. They may be considered the first expressionist dramas. Kokoschka's visual imagination was an important ingredient in his dramatic art. In his view of the function of art, he is clearly expressionist. His work was the direct expression of his inner vision and vision for him is not merely the nucleus of art, it is an experience during which man's self-serving ego is momentarily eclipsed so that the essential nature of man's existence is revealed.

Wassily Kandinsky (1896–1944) was, like Kokoschka, a gifted artist, indeed, one of the founders of abstract art. He turned from impressionistic experiments to abstract art in 1910, producing a watercolor which is perhaps the earliest example of non-objective art. His great theoretical work, *On the Spiritual in Art* (1912) explains art as arising from an inner necessity to communicate feelings in objective form. Art is a construction or composition making use of all possibilities of form and color to harmonize the eternal disparity between the artist's inner consciousness and the unfeeling external world. Thus, Kandinsky's poetry *Klänge* (*Sounds*, 1912) "composes" words and syllables; his drama *Der gelbe Klang* (*The Yellow Sound*, 1912), which he calls a "stage composition," synthesizes words, gestures, color, light, and music in a series of pictures. That element traditionally basic to drama—action, plot—is all but replaced by the pictorial element. In comments on the technique of the Belgian symbolist playwright Maeterlinck, Kandinsky indicated that the repetition of key words leads to their revelation as pure sound. His suggestion that this principle holds vast possibilities for the art of the future seems unlikely to be followed. It is interesting to note, however, the similarity to Benn's associative technique.

Kandinsky's art was related to the interests and experiments of Herwarth Walden and his Sturm group; he exhibited in the Sturm Gallery in 1912. For the Sturm writers, drama was a unity of words, sound, form, color, rhythm, and movement. Lothar Schreyer, who, together with Walden, founded the Sturm-Stage (1918–1921), declared that theater itself was passé; the traditional stage play, a work consisting of words, had been replaced by a new concept of theater as a total work of art. But the dramatic attempts of the Sturm group had no great impact even in their time.

Walden's Sturm-Verlag published August Stramm's dramas, but even though they form the bulk of his literary work, they have remained little known; none was performed before 1919. The first dramas were naturalistic attempts in the *Sekundenstil* of Holz and Schlaf. Two prose sketches show skillful use of Schnitzler's inner monologue. The play *Sancta Susanna* (1914) set to music by Paul Hindemith (1922) portrays a nun whose spiritual love for Christ turns sensual under the influence of a sultry spring evening and her own inner drives. Like Kaiser's "new man" she makes the breakthrough to a more meaningful existence: she shakes off the unnatural religious fetters to become a martyr to her own nature. The shock of what must have seemed to many spectators an obscene travesty was increased when the climactic scene was played in the nude. Stramm's maturer dramas show the same language characteristics as his last poetry: severe reduction of the language to virtually only personal pronouns. The play becomes almost pantomime. *Kräfte* (*Powers*, 1915) portrays a woman whose insane jealousy unleashes a destructiveness which makes the drama seem an intensified version of Strindberg. *Geschehen* (*Happening*, 1916) follows a man through life in his relationship to women. It is a kind of *Everyman*: the five women symbolize the various stages in the man's development from immature relationships to enduring uxorial love.

It is possible that Stramm was influenced by Marinetti's futuristic ideas on theater. Though the vaudeville, the shock effects, slapstick, and parody recommended by Marinetti in his first manifesto, October 1, 1913, do not have a place in Stramm's drama, his idea of synthetic theater does seem to be realized in Stramm's concentration upon the high points of the plot, his reduction of acts to a few sentences, his total renunciation of logical relationships and psychological development.

The first of the religious expressionists was Reinhard Johannes Sorge (1892–1916). He was conscious at an early age of his mission as a poet; significantly Stefan George and Nietzsche were among his early models. But George's stress on artistic individuality (style) is greatly intensified with Sorge; his art is less an impression of external nature than an expression of internal subjectivity: "All art is personal idiom and never like the things [of reality]." Sorge's early work drew ethical energy from Nietzsche; his later rejection of Nietzsche and conversion to Catholicism are a realization of the ideal of transformation which became so important a theme in expressionist literature. Sorge's poem "Drama" (1910) has been termed his expressionist manifesto. The scene is *Jugendstil*: a man lies naked upon a seashore amid rocky cliffs. He is called to life by the poet's (dramatist's) electrifying cry "Man, become man" (*Mensch zum Menschen*). Sorge's manuscript shows the line in capital letters though without the expressionists' favorite mark of punctuation, the exclamation point. This life-giving cry of the dramatist to his characters is essentially the cry of all the ethical expressionists, although for them, to be sure, it is an admonition to regeneration.

Sorge's one-act play, *Der Jüngling* (*The Youth*, 1910), is an allegory set in a Zarathustra landscape. The youth—Sorge himself—rebels against the words of the Wanderer: "The life of the high ones is yearning. Yearning to free themselves from their life for a more fervent life." In an encounter with an Old Man who wishes to initiate him into the ranks of all the others who could not overcome themselves, he performs the self-liberating deed: he kills the Old Man. The symbolic murder is the first appearance of the patricide theme which became so popular in expressionist literature.

The protagonist of Sorge's *Der Bettler* (*The Beggar*, 1912), "a dramatic mission," is a beggar-poet who writes experimental drama which is not to entertain but to offer humanity religious sustenance. It is no closet drama for individual readers but must be staged before masses in order to be effective. The beggar-poet's ideal is never realized. A sponsor recognizes his talent, but sees his theater only as a financially impractical venture. *The Beggar,* despite the ideal of communal theater, is concerned with the spiritual development of the protagonist. Each act brings a higher stage of self-conquest. In the last act the beggar-poet's refusal to compromise his ideals costs him a deep friendship and at the end of the play, the love of his sweetheart.

For this strikingly unconventional drama Sorge conceived an appropriately unconventional form. The play is a series of often highly realistic tableaux with little logical connection. Sorge prescribed that changes of setting be accomplished by directing lights from one part of the stage to another. Sorge's play itself is an attempt to realize the beggar-poet's ideal theater and when the beggar-poet speaks at length to the audience directly, the illusion of theater is momentarily suspended.

The Nietzschean fanaticism of *The Beggar* belies the protagonist's professed goal of communal love. However, the play is a work of transition. Sorge had already glimpsed the dangerous implications of Nietzsche's doctrines (cf. *Zarathustra,* 1911, in which a student under the influence of Zarathustra commits murder), and in *Gericht über Zarathustra* (*Judgment on Zarathustra,* 1912) he broke completely with Nietzsche. His conversion to Catholicism in Rome in 1913 did not alter the essential character of his further work. It remained esoteric expression of self-conquest. In his zeal to serve God, he planned to enter the priesthood but World War I intervened. Sorge did not live to see any of his plays staged; Reinhardt produced *The Beggar* in 1917.

In his comedies and novellas Carl Sternheim (1878–1942), social critic and satirist, followed Wedekind's lead in attacking the middle-class morality and urging freedom for the individual. Even in his earliest work the motif of the individual nuance (*eigene Nuance*) appears: each man must live according to his own individuality or sacrifice happiness in the attempt to adapt to the scheme of values imposed by society. For later refinements of this basic view Sternheim owes a debt to the philosophers Heinrich Rickert, who saw the task of history as the neutral description of the individual, and Wilhelm Windelband, who stressed the value of the individual and unique, and the obligation of each man to develop his individuality.

The artist according to Sternheim must discover what is unique and necessary in the object he depicts and must do this without permitting preconceived notions or personal dreams to distort reality. Sternheim saw in Van Gogh the ideal of the artist who lives his own nature; Gauguin, on the other hand, in the story *Gauguin und Van Gogh* (1924) is a dangerous seducer of men, who conjures up an alluring dream world which entices the onlooker to flee from reality. Another equally dangerous art, in Sternheim's opinion, is that which depicts men in their dependence upon the prescriptions and traditions of middle-class society instead of showing men in their independence from such restraints. He cited Goethe's *Tasso* and Kleist's *Prince of Homburg* as examples of literature which, by demonstrating that any attempt to live beyond the established code is wrong, threatens to rob the spectator of his vitality and his potential for developing as an individual. On the other hand, he praised Hölderlin, Büchner, Heine, and Nietzsche as poets who wrote for the liberation of men rather than the perpetuation of middle-class morality.

Sternheim saw the role of the artist as that of the chronicler who reports reality without impinging his own personality upon it. His short stories have the collective title (*Chronik von des zwanzigsten Jahrhunderts Beginn*) (*Chronicle of the Beginning of the Twentieth Century*). He believed the world could be understood as a clearly defined order; the bourgeois order, however, was in his opinion outmoded and hampered individual development. In particular he considered the use of metaphor an obstacle to unbiased recognition of reality. "The need to use metaphor bespeaks the belief that imperfect man must be raised to a higher level, but the use of metaphor actually degrades him by overlooking his real worth. Furthermore it prevents him from realizing his potential by impressing upon him the idea of his own inferiority." This device of poets is comparable to the bourgeois cliché which persuades parents to develop their child's alleged possibilities by comparing others' achievements instead of looking to the child's own inner necessity.

Sternheim's language is almost telegrammatic in its compactness and in revising his manuscripts he sought to heighten even this density. His use of metaphor, of course, scrupulously avoids comparisons with loftier spheres but he uses image effectively as well as alliteration, assonance, and rhythm. Even though he championed characters who are filled with enthusiasm for life, many people find his characters cold. The criticism is justified insofar as they tend to speak a stylized language, they have a tendency to preach, and they are ruthless in practising what they preach.

Sternheim produced a series of comedies under the collective title *The Heroic Life of the Bourgeoisie*. The first and probably best known of these, *The Underpants* (1911) is typical in its apparent ambivalence: it satirizes the middle class, yet portrays its strengths as well. An untoward incident triggers the action of the comedy. While watching a parade, Mrs. Theobald Maske's panties had dropped to her ankles. When the curtain rises, her husband is fuming at her, but all works out to his advantage. Two men who saw the incident rush to rent rooms at the Maske home with the intention of seducing her. The one, a neurotic barber, sees the world in terms of Wagnerian opera, the other, Scarron, is a Nietzschean and a fanatic worshipper of intellect. Thus neither can cope directly with reality. In the crucial moment with Mrs. Maske, Scarron rushes off to immortalize his feelings in a poem. The barber, Mandelstam, in his turn—faints. It is Maske who knows how to live: in an opportune moment he quietly seduces the spinster neighbor and with the same self-satisfaction announces to his wife that with the rent money from the tenants they can now afford to have a baby.

Theobald Maske, then, is the middle-class hero. Sternheim does not mean the title ironically. Maske's motto is "What is comfortable is right," an ethical standard very different from that of the Princess in Goethe's *Tasso*: "Only what is proper is permitted." Maske believes firmly in the lack of individuality, indeed he takes delighted refuge in his middle-class anonymity because it allows him to live uninhibitedly according to his innermost nature. He has no interest in ideas other than his own, or in problems outside his own small sphere of existence. He is the Philistine so despised by the expressionists, but he is also the man who lives his own "nuance," stubbornly refusing to be lured away from reality by ideals. That is the secret of his strength.

Georg Kaiser (1878–1945) was one of the most productive expressionist dramatists and one of the most radical innovators. Kaiser described drama writing as "thinking a thought through to the end"; for him the idea embodied in art was of supreme importance. He rejected contemporary theater, which, with its lavish spectacle, distracts the audience from the idea of the play, and praised the "theater" of Plato's dialogues. The dialogues do not present *Schauspiel*, drama for the eye, but *Denkspiel*, drama of thought. His own plays accordingly dispense with customary realism. Kaiser, anticipating Brecht, is concerned to prevent the spectator from identifying with the characters and does so by presenting a play which has little of ordinary reality in it. The form is often carefully symmetrical, even mathematical (or dependent upon mathematical relationships), the language abbreviated to its essentials, the characters typically nameless (since they are abstractions rather than individuals), and stage settings are reduced to a stark minimum.

The early plays, *The Jewish Widow* (1911) and *King Cuckold* (1913), under the influence of Wedekind, treat sexual themes. *From Morning till Midnight* (written 1912, published 1916) is a mystery play in the manner of Strindberg's *To Damascus* (1898). Strindberg's monodrama is a modern mystery play which grew out of his own soul torture. It presents the stations along the way to the salvation of the protagonist, and provided the model for the expressionists' *Stationendrama* (station drama). Kaiser's play is a *Stationendrama* in modern dress and seasoned with wry humor. In the first part, a bank cashier, whose existence has become colorless monotony, is awakened to life one day at his bank window when a beautiful woman in distress accidentally touches his wrist. He fills his pockets with money from the cash drawer, hoping to start a new life with her, but he has mistaken her motives. Nevertheless, the break has been made; in a grotesque confrontation with a skeleton he declares he has a number of obligations before evening; Death should telephone again "about midnight." The second part of the play depicts the stations along his way. At home his family is startled at his deviation from routine. When his wife asks where he has come from, he answers "From the grave. I have bored my forehead through clods. There is still ice clinging here. It has cost great effort to get out. I got my fingers a little dirty." The family, of course, can understand neither the symbolic nor the real import of what he is saying. When he leaves again before eating lunch, the unheard-of breach of routine kills his mother. His search for life takes him to the race track next, where he fans the spectators' enthusiasm to the utmost by offering extravagant prizes. But their passion proves hollow: the entrance of the Kaiser abruptly hushes the throng. The women in the dancehall he visits are equally disappointing. The final station in his search is the Salvation Army, but he does not find the answer here either. When he casts his money disdainfully upon the floor, a mad scramble ensues and a Salvation Army girl betrays him to the police in order to get the reward. At last the cashier understands that he will not find life and shoots himself. As he falls against a cross on the backdrop, the sounds "Ecce homo" issue from his lips.

Kaiser's central idea, his vision of man's regeneration, is first given form in an historical play, *The Burghers of Calais* (1914). The city of Calais in the year 1347 is under siege by the King of England, who demands the lives of six citizens in return for protection of the city. The citizens favor defending the city to the end, even though it means certain destruction of their town and harbor. Eustache de St.-Pierre persuades them that honor is less important than preserving the great achievement of their people, the harbor. His opponent is a young man whose values belong to the old order; he believes in honor above all else. Eustache, an old man, is Kaiser's "new man" who would prefer to die in "dishonor" to save the harbor than to die honorably amid the destruction of the city. Although Eustache's suicide is an unnecessary self-sacrifice—the king does not kill the hostages after all—it serves as an example of how regenerated man can sacrifice himself in the service of a humane ideal no less nobly than the "old man" could die to preserve honor. Indeed, the new man's deed is braver, for it was born of cool resolve, not impulse or social pressure, as the old heroism often is.

The theme of regenerated man is further developed in Kaiser's trilogy *Coral* (1917), *Gas* I (1918), and *Gas* II (1920). The austerity of the settings, the lack of names for the figures, the turgidity of language give the effect of abstraction. *Coral* portrays a billionaire who has amassed money as a protection against the fears which had plagued his poverty-stricken childhood. But he cannot buy happiness any more than Kaiser's cashier could. Even his children turn against him; they are socially conscious and consider their father a parasite. When an explosion occurs at the gas factory they hold him responsible. The billionaire, in a desperate search for happiness, kills his secretary, his exact double, and hangs the secretary's coral—a symbol of a happy childhood—to his own watch chain.

In *Gas* I capitalism has yielded to socialism, the billionaire's son now directs the factory, but the dream of a better society has not yet been fulfilled. Instead, industrialization has dehumanized the workers. The gas upon which industry is so dependent is danger-ously unstable. When an explosion destroys the factory, the billion-aire's son urges the workers to build a pastoral community in its place. The workers, however, prefer to remain automatons; the billionaire's son cannot even force them to become human. The gas is so vital for the state armaments that the factory is nationalized. The desperate cry of the billionaire's son, "Where is man?" is answered optimistically by his daughter: "I will bear him!"

But the promise with which *Gas* I concludes is not realized in *Gas* II. The "new man" has grown up and works in the gas factory, awaiting the moment to fulfill his mission. The country is at war and gas production is critical. But production collapses because automatization has destroyed the workers' sense of purpose. The billionaire's grandson urges overtures of peace but it is too late. The enemy marches in and the workers must resume production under duress. In the final act the engineer discovers a poison gas with which to destroy the enemy. Once more the grandson urges love and humility, but when the workers' hatred overrules him, he seizes the container and hurls it among his own people.

Kaiser's "new man" was thus not a naively held vision but a dream for whose realization he had little hope. *From Hell to Earth* (1919) does present an optimistic vision of the "new man" but a final treatment during World War II, *The Raft of the Medusa* (1942), is once again pessimistic. In Kaiser's original conception, a group of children floating in a life raft after their ship has been sunk condemn the world of grown-ups who wage wars upon each other. When they are rescued, one commits suicide rather than return to that world. But the drama as Kaiser wrote it is even gloomier. The children themselves are evil. They kill one of their number to save their own skins. The boy who refuses to be saved—he was not involved in the murder—is rejecting much more than just the adult world: "The children will be like the adults—because already as children they are like adults!"

Kaiser and Sternheim stood apart from the expressionist group even though they were regarded as fellow expressionists. Kaiser's attitude toward the expressionist program was skeptical, Sternheim was actually espousing an anti-expressionist view of man, since he did not urge regeneration but self-recognition. But the expressionists could easily overlook Kaiser's pessimistic treatment of the theme of regeneration, and Sternheim's battle against the middle class made him an ally.

Fritz von Unruh (1885-   ) was one of the most popular dramatists of the expressionist generation. His play *Officers* (1911), aside from ecstatic language, is conventional in form, and, in Reinhardt's production that same year, won him immediate acclaim. The dramatic conflict is somewhat reminiscent of Kleist's *Prince of Homburg*: an army officer, Schlichting, after languishing in the inactivity of peacetime, is called to help subdue the Herero rebellion in South Africa. The war loses its intoxicating quality even before he arrives on the battlefield. Then, in order to save his men, he is forced to act contrary to his orders. In so doing, he rebels not only against established order but against a long-standing family tradition, against "blood trained for centuries to obey." This rebellion, though, is not the rejection of tradition typical of later Expressionism; it is really a humane renewal of the tradition. This is true also of *Louis Ferdinand* (1912), which Unruh, spurred by success, rewrote from an earlier version. The play's great popularity was perhaps due to a misunderstanding of it as a military exemplum. Prince Louis Ferdinand tries to stir Frederick William III to action against Napoleon, but the weak king wishes to preserve peace at any cost. The generals are ready to rebel and place the prince on the throne; the only salvation the prince can see is to force the king to action through the revolution, but then—to avoid ascending the throne by violence—to die in battle.

Unruh's own experience of the war in 1914 confirmed his earlier misgivings about militarism. At Verdun he was wounded, robbed, stripped, and left to die; when he regained consciousness he was a confirmed pacifist. A dramatic poem, V*or der Entscheidung* (*Before the Decision*, published 1919), written at the front, records his inner transformation and is at the same time his first expressionist work.

Unruh's play A *Family* (1916) is one of the landmarks of Expressionism. A mother, with the aid of her daughter and youngest son, has just buried her favorite son, who was killed in battle. Two remaining sons are brought in chains by soldiers. Both have been sentenced to death, the eldest son for committing rape, the other for cowardice in battle. Imminent death brings the eldest son to the insight that the law of the state is hypocrisy; violence is condoned, even glorified when it serves the state, but severely suppressed when it serves private ends. He rebels also against his mother who has borne her children for patriotic reasons. He finds not just the military ethic absurd, but life itself: "O Mothers,

Women!/You carry the grave in your moist womb,/what you give birth to is death and nothing but death!" His rebellion and suicide bring about his mother's inner transformation. She too rebels against the militarists and seizes their staff of authority, proclaiming that the power of the world resides in her. She declares a revolution against the patriarchal system which brings only destruction and death; only the matriarchal principle, continuing creativity, can prevail over death. The soldiers are attracted to her side, but their leaders, seeing their system threatened by mass revolt, execute her. Her vision lives on in the youngest son. The soldiers choose him leader and together they storm the seat of power.

Plaza (1920) is the second part of Unruh's trilogy (the third never appeared). Here the earlier view of *A Family* is revised and a critique of Expressionism itself is presented, for Unruh saw the style of his earlier work becoming a fashionable mannerism. Schleich, pacifist and preacher of brotherly love, speaks a language which consciously parodies Sternheim's telegrammatic and distorted diction, so much so that Dietrich, the youngest son, in their first encounter asks in surprise, "What language is being spoken here?" On the threshold of accomplishing the goals of the revolution, Dietrich suddenly realizes as he looks at the monuments on the Plaza, that revolution will not resolve the problem of power. When Dietrich falls in love with Irene, he sees that the answer to the problem lies not in a society based on abstract love for all mankind, but in a society growing out of the harmony of spiritual and sensuous love between individuals. Dietrich does not succeed in convincing his companions. His defection from the cause brings condemnation and separation from Irene. Schleich becomes the leader and proves as ruthlessly tyrannical as the regime which has just been overthrown. Schleich is the victor, but Dietrich's sister foresees ultimate victory for Dietrich: "I look deep into the heart of the world where your power creates new men from new love."

Like Unruh, Ernst Toller (1893–1939) immediately volunteered for duty when war was declared in 1914. After a year at the front he had to return home, sick in body and spirit. He immediately engaged in activist attempts to stop the war, particularly the Munich demonstrations in early 1918 and the revolution which led to the end of the war. Toller's first play, *Die Wandlung* (*The Conversion*, 1919) is a *Stationendrama*. The protagonist, Friedrich, oppressed by loneliness as a Jew among Christians, welcomes the war as an opportunity to find acceptance. The horrors of war dispel his illusions; he begins to sculpt a statue symbolizing the victory of the fatherland as justification for all the suffering, but the actual sight of the human cost of the victory overwhelms him and he searches for community by living and working among the poor. He seeks a union of humanity which transcends national boundaries; the niche he finally discovers is a role which provides this: he teaches the people to recover their human dignity—taken from them by the machine—through a bloodless revolution.

Toller's involvement in the revolutions which flared up against the early Weimar Republic cost him five years' imprisonment. It was during these years that the works for which he is remembered were published. *Masses and Man* (1921) treats problems facing Toller as a revolutionary leader and is consequently less naively idealistic. Sonia must try to maintain the ideals of non-violent revolution against the ardor of fanatics. Her loneliness is intensified when her husband disowns her. When her own faction captures him, she pleads for his life but her plea is interpreted as evidence that her insistence on non-violence was really an attempt to undermine the revolution. When she is captured, her escape is guaranteed if she will agree to the killing of the guard; she accepts death rather than compromise her ideal of non-violence.

The Machine-Wreckers (1922), based on the Luddite riots in England (1815), poses a dramatic problem similar to that of *Masses and Man*. Jimmy Cobbett, the leader of the weavers, realizes that they can express their demands effectively only if they organize with other weavers. Moreover he sees the wisdom of accepting the machines since they can actually raise the workers' standard of living. But the weavers listen to the voice of violence, rise up, murder their leaders and destroy their machines.

In general, Toller's plays have been unable to survive the era for which they were written; they are too filled with unrelieved emotion and idea to be suitable for later generations. *Brokenbow* (*Hinkemann*, 1922) is something of an exception. It is the tragedy of a soldier, maimed in the war, unable to take up life again, even with incredible self-sacrifice, when he returns home from the war. The play invites comparison with Büchner's *Woyzeck*; Brokenbow's plight is firmly rooted in the postwar era but his human situation is very similar to Woyzeck's.

The critical attitude toward Expressionism which marks the later works of Toller, Kaiser, and Unruh was also shared by Werfel. In the novella *Not the Murderer* (1919) the familiar father-son

conflict is significantly not resolved by murder as in early expressionist plays such as Walter Hasenclever's *Der Sohn* (*The Son*, 1914)
or Arnolt Bronnen's *Vatermord* (*Parricide*, written 1915). Karl
Duschek's father, an army general, has tyrannized over his childhood and reduced him to an emotional wreck. Just as Karl is about
to kill his father, he suddenly sees him for what he is: a pitiable old
man. He understands that he cannot save himself by destroying his
father, but only by starting anew. His emigration to America is
rebirth for him into a free, healthy life.

The criticism of Expressionism is more pointed in Werfel's
play *Mirror-Man* (1920). It is patterned after Strindberg's *To
Damascus*, utilizing a double, as Strindberg does, to represent the
protagonist's other self. Thamal goes to a monastery to escape life
but is told he is not mature enough to renounce the world. A monk
explains that there are three visions of existence: the first in which
one sees in the world only himself, the second in which one is aware
that one sees himself and is consequently torn within and unhappy.
Only if one can succeed in overcoming his egocentrism is he capable
of genuine love. The third vision is not for ordinary men but for the
chosen savior; he sees the world rather than himself, and redeems it.
Thamal is convinced he was born with the second vision. When he
smashes his mirror in order to destroy his mirror image—it reminds
him of his imperfection—he succeeds only in liberating the Mirror-
Man, his alter ego. So filled is he with vitalistic exuberance, that
the Mirror-Man has little difficulty persuading him he is a god. His
career of evil begins with the murder of his father and culminates in
his allowing himself to be publicly declared a god. He believes he is
doing it for the good of the people; actually, as with Unruh's
Schleich, leadership is only a form of self-aggrandizement. His
moment of glory is brief; his following deserts him with comments
which are a direct criticism of activist Expressionism: "Even yesterday that ethical Communistic hooch was a stagnant bluff." In the
end, Thamal hands down his own sentence at his trial. By drinking
the hemlock he defeats the Mirror-Man; he awakens in the cloister,
liberated from his egoism.

The plays of Ernst Barlach (1870–1938) treat some expressionist themes—the father-son relationship, the idea of transformation—but Barlach did not consider himself a member of the group
and even wrote diatribes against expressionist theater. Directors of
his plays at that time overlooked their originality and produced
them in the same style as the expressionist medieval mysteries

instead of as sheer entertainment. Barlach's relationship to the people of the theater was full of misunderstandings on both sides; his plays have never really been successful on the stage. This was, in part at least, his own fault for making no attempt to aid directors in their interpretation of his plays. He attended only one performance—*The Genuine Sedemunds* (1920)—and the experience of seeing his own work "stylized," as he put it, so that it was no longer his work, was so traumatic that he had no desire to see another performance. What directors generally overlooked was the down-to-earth realism of the characters and the genuine comedy of the plays. The sentimentality and emotional intensity of the expressionist stagings were completely alien to Barlach's conception of theater.

It is true that some of Barlach's plays are mystery plays, though not in the sense of Karl Vollmoeller's extravaganza, *The Miracle* (1912), nor even modernizations like Hofmannsthal's *Everyman* (1911) and *The Salzburg Great Theater of the World* (1922). Barlach's *The Poor Relation* (1918) is a modern parody of the Easter theme; *The Flood* (1924) a revision of the Noah story which Barlach considered absurd in its traditional form; *The Foundling* (1922) is reminiscent of a Christmas play; *The Good Time* (1929) is a Passion play. What Barlach was doing with Biblical themes and motifs may be illustrated by *The Flood*. The play presents a contest between God-fearing Noah and Calan, a God-seeker who finds Noah's God a master rather than a father, and Noah more a servant than a son. In a cruel effort to put Noah's God to the test, Calan orders an innocent shepherd's hands severed. Neither Noah nor his God intervene. At another point Noah meets God who appears in the form of a beggar. Noah nearly fails to recognize Him: "I'm confused. You were once my father, weren't you?" To which the beggar replies: "You were once my son." Calan rejects the God who is master rather than father. In the end Calan is reduced to the state of beggar by the rising flood. This is the revenge of Noah's God but it brings revelation of the God he has been seeking; now physically blind he gains spiritual sight. Triumphantly he announces his reunion through death with a formless, voiceless God. Noah will remain alive but remain a servant.

Barlach was acutely aware, like Hofmannsthal's Chandos, that language is hopelessly inadequate, especially for formulating religious realities; yet he fashioned language into a tool as effective, for those who understand it, as that of any other dramatist of the time, except Bertolt Brecht. Barlach's alliteration, assonance, and word play are not mere embellishment as with typical expressionist rhetoric, but are extremely effective expressions of character. The simplicity of his vocabulary is illusory. In reality he repeats his simple words until "they are gradually isolated and stripped of their usual connotations. Eventually they become exhausted of meaning and dissolve, or, as Barlach says of the word *Gott*, 'if one takes it repeatedly on the tongue, one makes a mess of stewed prunes out of it.' "[12] Barlach practises the kind of grotesque one finds in the poetry of Christian Morgenstern (1871–1914), but his aim is serious: to demonstrate the meaninglessness of the language we take for granted, to irritate his audience into seeing beyond words to actual relationships.

V

The expressionists had shown originality and boldness in their search for a valid language and new forms with which to express themselves, but the revolution had not proceeded as far in literature as in art. The experiments of the Sturm group pointed in the direction of, but did not actually produce abstract art, as did some of the painters who contributed to their periodical—Kandinsky, Paul Klee, August Macke, and Franz Marc. The final step to abstractionism was taken by the Dadaists.

On February 1, 1916 in Zurich, where numerous artists of various nationalities had gathered during the war, the German Hugo Ball founded the Cabaret Voltaire, a literary café where readings of avant-garde as well as more conventional literature were held. Half in fun and half in earnest, Ball, Hans Arp, Richard Huelsenbeck, and the Rumanians Tristan Tzara and Marcel Janco formed the movement. It was a loosely knit group not in complete agreement about their aims or even the origin of the name Dada; perhaps, as Huelsenbeck reports, they stumbled upon it in a French dictionary.[13] It was the childlike sound rather than its meaning of "hobby horse" which was felt to be appropriate to the new movement. While humor is a much larger ingredient of Dadaism than of Expressionism, Dada was a serious protest against the war and an intensified attack against the materialistic middle class. The dadaists also rejected the futurists, who affirmed the war, and the expressionists, "tired people, alienated from nature, who do not dare to look the cruelty of the epoch in its face." Dada had no definite program except to give expression to the "mechanization, the sterility, rigidity, and the tempo of the times." It intended both to shock and to provoke the middle class as well as to express the chaos of modernity. In its destructive fervor, Dada quickly acquired notoriety as a completely anarchistic, anti-art movement; a fact which should not obscure the achievement of the movement.

One innovation, the *poème simultan*, in which various speakers simultaneously chant different texts in different languages, had nonsense for content, but both content and delivery were intended symbolically. According to Ball, the simultaneous poem showed "the conflict of the *vox humana* with a world which threatened, ensnared, and destroyed it, a world whose tempo and noise are inescapable." Ball also wrote "sound poems" which consisted of rationally meaningless sounds, "verses without words." A mimetic element might be vaguely perceptible as in "Karawane" ("Caravan"), which seems to reproduce the sounds of a passing caravan. Another innovation, "optophonetic poetry," achieved visual effects through the use, under futurist influence, of widely varying type faces and sizes.

The Dada movement spread rapidly to other cities—Berlin, Hannover, Cologne, Paris—but on the whole it was a short-lived development; its fervor subsided in the early twenties. Understandably, the dadaists' achievement in art was more durable than in poetry (some of which existed only in performance). The Berlin dadaist illustrator George Grosz scandalized many an honest citizen with his blasphemous caricatures. He has been called the Daumier of the twentieth century but he was more vicious than the French satirist. He was fined on several occasions for attacking the army, for religious blasphemy, and for obscenity. Hans Arp and Kurt Schwitters, of the Hannover group, were accomplished artists as well as lyric poets: their collages, montages, and assemblages stand at the beginning of an art genre which is still viable.

VI

Developments in theater directing and staging fully kept pace with the change from realistic to impressionistic and expressionistic theater. The genius of a few men laid the groundwork for modern stage design and theater techniques. As early as 1895, a Swiss, Adolphe Appia, appalled by the unconvincing realistically painted backdrops used for Wagnerian sets, proposed replacing the fixed lighting with mobile lighting in order to heighten the plasticity of the set and suggest mood. He demanded massive proportions and utmost simplicity. His rhythmic organization of space—combinations of columns, cubes, steps, and drapery—had a far-reaching effect on European theater though he did not design for the plays of Expressionism.

Like Appia, the English stage set designer and producer Edward Gordon Craig advocated massiveness and simplicity of stage sets. Thwarted in his mission at home, Craig came to Germany where he designed the stage set for Otto Brahm's production of Hofmannsthal's *Venice Preserved* in the Lessing Theater (1905). Brahm's insistence on realistic detail clashed with Craig's desire for suggestiveness rather than realism, however, and his attempt to work with Reinhardt was also abortive since he would not agree to changes Reinhardt desired. Nevertheless, his views were decidedly influential on German stagecraft.

The great director of the period, Max Reinhardt, left Otto Brahm's *Freie Bühne* in 1903 to take over the *Kleines Theater* (Little Theater) which had been formed from a Berlin cabaret. His stagings of Hofmannsthal's *Electra* and Maeterlinck's *Pelléas et Mélisande* that same year were a breakthrough for impressionistic theater and for his impressionistic style of production. Reinhardt was the first to fully utilize the revolving stage, which had been introduced to Germany in 1896. Like Appia, he insisted that scenery be plastic rather than flat painting. With his use of lights he sought to capture the mood of each play: in *Electra* a daring symbolism of blood-red light, in *Pelléas* the ominously mysterious twilight.

Reinhardt's style was less well suited to expressionist plays. He staged Sternheim's *Citizen Schippel* in 1913, successfully supplementing the text with the pantomime of Philistinism, but he produced more typical expressionist dramas only near the end of the war when it had become evident that his position of leadership was being challenged. In Berlin *Das junge Deutschland* (Young Germany, 1917–1920) was established under his direction for the purpose of presenting the work of the young dramatists. In three seasons plays by twelve expressionists were staged. Reinhardt's production of Sorge's *Beggar* (1917) was only a partial success; the staging of other expressionist plays he entrusted to helpers or to the playwrights themselves (Kokoschka, Kaiser). His efforts helped to bring such dramatists as Wedekind, Sorge, and Unruh to deserved recognition. Reinhardt also had a leading role, along with the critic Hermann Bahr, Hugo von Hofmannsthal, and Richard Strauss, in the founding of the Salzburg Festivals (1920), which each year present a superb selection of dramas and operas.

The period from the 1890's to 1930 is one of such ferment and experimentation, reactions and counter-reactions that it seems difficult to discern any unity in the confusion. Each movement seeks to differentiate itself from other movements, often rather aggressively, yet most of them also were careful to point to ties with tradition and, consciously or unconsciously, they built upon the gains of their predecessors. Faced with a welter of short-lived -isms, the present-day reader is all too inclined to find them somewhat ridiculous. It is a mistake, however, to dismiss them lightly, as the reexamination of Expressionism and Dada presently going on, indicates.[14] They are, rather, phases in a single broad development.

Both the impressionistic reaction and the expressionistic revolt were responses to increasing materialism in all areas of life. Like Naturalism, the impressionistic view was relativistic and in its emphasis on man's dependence on the material world, it was even materialistic. Impressionism contained the seeds for transcending its materialism and relativism, however. In its emphasis on form and symbol it prepared the way for the development of art beyond the ordering of impressions of the external world to an art which is expression of self. It is thus not surprising that the artistic development of Hofmannsthal or Rilke parallels the general shift from the impressionistic to the expressionistic temper. Hofmannsthal's conservatism and Rilke's principle of inner transformation grew out of the conviction that spirit is the ultimate reality, the same conviction held by the expressionists. Benn has pointed out that Stefan George's "will to form" is not empty aestheticism but the expression of faith in a spiritual order; thus his art is akin to Benn's expressionism: both were engaged in creating autonomous artistic form. The relationship of Impressionism to Expressionism is evidence that the two movements are phases of the development of modern literature, which has led, since the French Parnassians in the second half of the nineteenth century, more or less steadily away from the mimetic principle codified by Aristotle. And that trend is a consonant part of the international development of modernism in all the arts.

9. The Twentieth-Century Novel ✍

Edward Diller

With somewhat startling suddenness the German novel burst fullgrown and brazen into the twentieth century.[1] In fewer than ten years there appeared on the scene novels of such national and international significance as *Buddenbrooks* by Thomas Mann (1901); *The Street of Triumph* (*Aus der Triumphgasse*, 1902) by Ricarda Huch; *Peter Camenzind* by Hermann Hesse (1904); *Small Town Tyrant* (*Professor Unrat*, 1905) by Heinrich Mann; *Young Törless* (*Die Verwirrungen des Zöglings Törleß*, 1906) by Robert Musil; *The Little Town* (*Die kleine Stadt*, 1909) by Heinrich Mann; *The Road to the Open* (*Der Weg ins Freie*, 1908) by Arthur Schnitzler; *Royal Highness* (1909) by Thomas Mann; *The Fool in Christ Emanuel Quint* (1910) by Gerhart Hauptmann, and *The Notebooks of Malte Laurids Brigge* (1910) by Rainer Maria Rilke; while at the same time but in less public circumstance, Franz Kafka was already beginning to write some extraordinary literature that would be published posthumously two decades later and gain world-wide acclaim after World War II. Even after such vigorous beginnings the number of significant novels in Germany continued to proliferate at an astounding rate, gaining quickly in popularity but losing rapidly the literary critics who unsuccessfully tried to find order in the flood of publications.

Examined from our present perspective in time, however, it would seem that the novels of twentieth-century Germany now center for the most part around the works and influence of three indisputably great novelists, each of whom in turn appears to follow a distinctive literary tradition: Thomas Mann reflecting on cultural history and on the psychological problems of the artist in society; Hermann Hesse exploring the soul and the greater destiny of man (Neo-Romanticism) and Franz Kafka groping frantically for acceptance, understanding and purpose in a bizarre universe. One is tempted, therefore, to line up the German novelists of our century into three groups of a general nature with Thomas Mann, Hermann Hesse, and Franz Kafka as their major representatives; for without the help of the great men who somehow embody and reflect the

322

substance of an age, few periods of as much as fifty or sixty years can be labeled convincingly, and certainly not the twentieth century, which has been marked by more than its share of innovations, destruction, and upheaval. In a half century we have seen a dramatic transmogrification of politics, technology, economy, culture, and mores. Our century has witnessed the death of Old Germany, the miscarriage of the Weimar Republic and, since 1945, the abandonment of narrow nationalism in favor of participation in world affairs. The German postwar literati like to pinpoint the change of attitude at the year 1945, the year "zero," the start of a new emerging reality which automatically and arbitrarily rejected the high style, the flowing rhetoric, and the elusive abstractions of the idealism that once clouded the literary scene. The giants of prewar German literature, the Nobel prize winners, Thomas Mann, Hermann Hesse, and Gerhart Hauptmann, were summarily discarded by younger writers for being too obtuse, too immersed in abstract and irrelevant rationality, too absorbed in the profound awe of German culture and soul, and too much lost in the noise of endless metaphysical discourses. Golo Mann, Thomas Mann's son, comments in retrospect that his father's novel *The Magic Mountain* (1924) presented "a stage on which everything was discussed and nothing decided" and that his elaborate and lengthy tome *Reflections of a Nonpolitical Man* (1918) was a "noble, highly intelligent, honest muddle"; but though such comments may sound convincing in substance, they carry with them the prejudicial overtones of one generation rejecting another in tacit support of its own superiority. Our times and values may be changing, but for all that there is no way in which lesser critics can dislodge or even weaken, for example, the position of Thomas Mann as the grand monarch of German novelists.

He ushered in the twentieth-century German novel with a work that continues to be read and regarded as one of the significant novels of world literature. Though *Buddenbrooks* may not be Mann's most famous novel, it certainly is one of his best. Its sweeping force, its striking characterizations, and its subtle grasp of human *faiblesse* and spiritual degeneration speak for the author's inherent greatness as a man of letters. The novel was a tour de force for a young writer of twenty-five who had only a few, but nevertheless excellent, short stories in print. Mann's profound gift of observation, his erudition and mastery of language are readily apparent as he embarks upon an exploratory investigation of the genealogy of a family, the Buddenbrooks, which, it turns out, has striking similarities to his own. He traces the family line of a wealthy bourgeois family in Lübeck through four generations and relates its history as a decline of vitality from generation to generation, as a deterioration of strength and determination into physical illness, cultural debility, and aesthetic escapism. The final heir apparent of the Buddenbrook tradition is characterized as a kind of sickly, ineffective exotic; one too frail to stay alive for long but capable, nevertheless, of appreciating for the moment the painful beauty of music and the delicate tragedy of human existence.

Woven into the entire fabric of the novel are those elements which soon come to characterize the nucleus of Mann's novels as dichotomous or ambivalent. The Mannian hero (an artist figure, a gifted pariah) is repeatedly prevented from feeling at home or finding satisfaction in a world seemingly divided between society and art, between the bourgeois and bohemian, and between full participation in life and conscious commitment to death. Though structures of society and the middle-class routines of life seem solid enough at a glance, Mann consistently reminds the reader with an ironic smile that the forces of sickness, decomposition, and death are gnawing away at the foundations of society and at the souls of men. And if that is the case, then health itself must be a temporary, perhaps even an unnatural condition which, soon and in spite of efforts to preserve itself, will sink pathetically and perhaps ludicrously back into a lifeless sea of oblivion.

Royal Highness (1909) is Mann's avowed contribution to the forces of altruism and humanism, although here again the novel ultimately centers on the problem of man's loneliness in the midst of society, with the hero presented this time in the role of a monarch. The plot remains secondary to the careful description of Prince Klaus Heinrich, whom Mann describes elsewhere as "unsubstantial, vague, or with one word, artistic." The fate of Klaus Heinrich is supposedly a hard one, one imposing a kind of "love and nobility" that distances him from life in a manner of fate not unlike that confronting the artist. Indeed, Thomas Mann himself characterizes Klaus Heinrich's isolation with a quote from Schiller: "The poet should accompany the king, for both dwell on the heights of mankind."

After *Royal Highness* Mann wrote some short stories which are now recognized among the best in German literature, some critical essays on men of letters, and a lengthy tome in defense of

Germany's position in World War I. He also became singularly concerned with the "meaning and image" of Germany, and with time succeeded in becoming the spokesman and interpreter of German cultural values for the rest of the world.

Some of Mann's conclusions to the problems of responsibility to his country and to European civilization as a whole may be examined in detail in the now world-renowned novel, *The Magic Mountain* (1924). The work, like most of Mann's, contains more reflection and characterization than it does active plot. The protagonist, Hans Castorp, a young engineer from Hamburg, travels from the northern flatlands of Germany to the mountains of Switzerland to visit his cousin who is taking a cure for tuberculosis. Once there, Hans Castorp becomes intrigued by the unreal qualities of the place, and then, upon discovering that he himself has traces of tuberculosis, he remains there for seven years until World War I. Only then does he decide to leave, to go to war and probably to his death.

The plot of this novel is only a thin string holding together a huge canvas on which the qualities of nations and the concerns of a host of individuals are painted. People of all nationalities and levels of society are thrown together in a health sanatorium, an international microcosm isolated from the concrete demands of society by geography and disease. In the rarified atmosphere of this high Alpine resort, Hans Castorp embarks upon an exploration of the elusive physical and metaphysical elements that comprise the greater meaning of life and society. In a consciously perceived framework of time and space, Thomas Mann composes a "symphony, a work of counterpoint, a fabric of themes in which ideas play the role of musical motifs." And as the symphony develops, Hans Castorp experiences and learns, somewhat passively, a good deal about astronomy, biology, politics, religion, art, superstition, love, psychology, his own lassitude, and lack of commitment.

The conclusion of the novel (Hans Castorp's decision to leave the Magic Mountain and go to war) has been interpreted in one of two different ways: as his recognition of a responsibility to the outer world and to his homeland, a commitment that can be defined as "humanistic"; or as his final defeat in a persistent attempt to find real value in life, for he returns not to the world of men but rather to the field of battle where death awaits him. But regardless of interpretation, this adventure of mind and spirit has been acclaimed by public and critics alike as one of the great novels of development of all time. Hans Castorp, like Odysseus in his time, travels through regions which are not entirely of this world but lead him nevertheless back to the unfinished tasks of life.

With the arrival of Hitler and National Socialism in the early 1930's, Mann was forced to flee from Germany to the United States with his family. As a writer of world-wide fame (he had received the Nobel prize for literature in 1929), he was invited in 1939 to teach at the Institute for Advanced Study at Princeton, but several years later found him settled in southern California as the nominal head of a colony of German expatriates. The rest of Mann's life, an extremely productive time, was spent in exile. The majority of the Joseph novels, for example, were written outside of Germany proper. When he returned to Europe after the war he chose to remain in Switzerland until his death in August, 1955.

The Joseph novels, Mann's Biblical tetralogy, took more than sixteen years to write. They (*The Stories of Jacob*, 1933; *Young Joseph*, 1934; *Joseph in Egypt*, 1936; *Joseph the Provider*, 1942) may be considered along with *The Beloved Returns* (*Lotte in Weimar*, 1939) and *The Holy Sinner* (*Der Erwählte*, 1951) as studies in demythologization. At the center of each of these novels stands one great historical person surrounded by an aura of legend and mystery; and with one figure as a focus—Joseph, Goethe, and Gregorius—Mann undertakes an impressive project of introgesis: the practice of expanding, modernizing, and humanizing historical texts without necessary loss of original significance. It should go without saying that a good deal of sensitivity and thorough scholarship are necessary to complete such projects successfully. Mann skillfully interweaves the words and the original stories of Goethe, Jacob, Joseph, Gregorius, and others into these novels, but so smoothly that it is seldom obvious where Mann's writing ends and interpolation begins.

The Joseph tetralogy begins with a long and interesting survey of information which Thomas Mann accumulated from the fields of theology, anthropology, archeology, history, mythology, and psychology. Then slowly out of this mass of scholarly information, the person of Jacob, the father of Joseph, begins to emerge, life-size and with dramatic impact. The groundwork is laid for the appearance of Joseph, who develops slowly and convincingly into a young man and a dreamer, a prophet, and finally a monarch, a leader of nations. Mann regarded this lengthy historical project as his search for man's "origin, his essence, his goal." But contrary to expectations and countless allusions, Joseph falls less into the pattern of a divine prophet than into the pattern of a clever, subtle, and separated Mannian artist. Once the active plot begins, one finds more revelry than revelation and more cunningness than contrition. And Mann himself regarded his rendering of the Joseph stories as "humorous and lyrical," meaning perhaps that these episodes of human interaction and historical concern are little more than a playful, archetypal scenario upon God's vast stage, for the tenor of the Joseph stories is certainly lighter than in Mann's preceding works and stands in extreme contrast to Mann's next novel, *Doctor Faustus* (1947).

From 1943 to 1945, during the last two years of World War II, Serenus Zeitblom, a schoolteacher in *Doctor Faustus*, sits serenely amid the final holocaust of Germany's defeat, writing the story of his intimate, lifelong friend, Adrian Leverkühn. Leverkühn has studied theology at the seminary in Halle, which, in Mann's hands, is enveloped in a heavy, foreboding atmosphere. But Leverkühn then rejects theology in favor of music; he becomes enamoured with a prostitute from whom, after conscious deliberation, he contracts a venereal disease that leads him both to madness and artistic greatness. Leverkühn accepts the Satanic imposition of physical suffering and madness which he deems necessary in order to reach the heights of artistic greatness. Disease, therefore, becomes his binding commitment to hell, and the terms of his subsequent pact with the Devil are that he shall have twenty-four years in which to create inspired masterpieces, for the sake of which during that time he agrees to renounce love.

Doctor Faustus has been interpreted as Mann's commentary on the political fanaticism of the Third Reich (symbolized by the Nietzschean-like figure of Leverkühn) and again as an example of the artist-burgher dichotomy. As he relates the story, Serenus Zeitblom, the philologist, the bourgeois schoolteacher and moralist, becomes a kind of alter ego for Leverkühn, the black theologian, the desperate artist, and fanatic aesthete. But out of this polarity arises a most interesting paradox: whereas some critics have stated that Leverkühn is Germany damned in greatness and destruction, he is also nonetheless an artist figure of the same unique order as Mann's earlier gifted pariahs. Mann's pathetic, lonely, sensitive artist figure of earlier works is transformed into a magnificent demon here, a glorification of evil, a Faustian *diabolus!* The question of how Mann, writing in exile and in opposition to the Third

Reich, can allow creative greatness to reside at the heart of a nation presently dedicated to villainy of a sub-human order is an interesting one, for it suggests that Satanic malevolence and artistic greatness are inseparable (for Thomas Mann at least), but destined to end like Leverkühn and Germany itself in the euphoric pleasure of their own death, laughing madly at their own monstrous creations, collapsing finally in discord, illness, and impotence. It is therefore not without significance that the titles of Leverkühn's two great compositions are "Apocalypsis cum figuris" and "The Lamentations of Dr. Faustus;" nor should it be overlooked now that Mann's artist figures have from the outset been a strange admixture of beauty and blackness, inspiration and evil, creation and destruction, all rooted inextricably in the soil and soul of Germany, just as Leverkühn's diabolical music is. For all its sweeping pleasure and aesthetic grandeur, music is for Thomas Mann the "demonic realm," a demonism that was the starting point of a long path leading to greatness, judgment, and death.

If in retrospect one cares to regard Mann's Joseph novels as a journey into divine realms and his *Doctor Faustus* as a descent into hell, then Mann's last novel, *The Confessions of Confidence Man Felix Krull* (1954), may be taken as a literary excursion into the realm between, Earth itself. The protagonist, Felix Krull, is a soldier of fortune, a confidence man, a rogue who is capable of deceptively acting out the part which any situation demands of him. This novel, and the preceding one, *The Holy Sinner*, present a light touch that is unique in Mann's works. But these works are not without the usual long scholarly treatises, pedantic elaborations, and the philosophical polemics that characterize the Mannian novel. Mann is an indefatigable synthesizer of European intellectual and cultural history, often at the expense of the fundamental literary power of his novels. As a result, his short stories, where he restricts himself to a single event and a unified plot, often exceed the novels in dramatic impact.

In spite of all his forays and digressions into cultural problematica and intellectual history, Thomas Mann remains essentially a psychological realist whose writing rings truest when exploring the "soul" of the artist, the bohemian, the outcast. From Mann's earliest short stories to his last novel it is the artist figure who remains the vital epicentrum of humanity counterpoised against the massive, ponderous structures of society. In him reside penetrating perceptiveness, painful but stimulating solitude, and the fertility of mind which are akin to Mann's own. He alone among all the figures of German society is capable of transforming subjective disturbances into aesthetic configurations of universal format, of transforming the basest of psychic concerns, symbolically altered, into the most noble and majestic realms of literature. Hanno Buddenbrook, Tonio Kröger, Hans Castorp, Adrian Leverkühn, Gregorius, Felix Krull, and the countless other Mannian heroes are striking studies of alienated genius, surviving necessarily in guilty withdrawal, separated from a society that may well deserve little more than disdain for its boorish obtuseness.

Social novels of the Mannian order, with society as the antagonist apparently set against the hero, have a long and complicated history in nineteenth-century German literature. From the forays into society of Goethe's *Wilhelm Meister* through the journalistic examination of the social structure by writers of Young Germany, through the glorification of the middle-class routines and possessions of the Biedermeier period, through the various periods of German realism regarding society as the theater of life, down to the late nineteenth century, there occurs a slow but steady conceptual transformation of the individual's position in society. In the novels of Classicism and Romanticism the individual could still assert his will and sustain inner freedom, declaring by example man's independence and ability to control his life and destiny. But as the nineteenth century progressed, greater restrictions were imposed on man's freedom by the onslaught of technology, industry, urbanized masses of people, and the expanding mechanism of a growing society.

Offering a threshold at the end of nineteenth-century German literature for twentieth-century novelists to cross, Theodor Fontane stands as a master observer of society and an appropriate predecessor to Thomas Mann. Concentrating his attention on the upper classes of the Prussianized society of Berlin, Fontane was able to describe the fixed and formal atmosphere with a degree of precision that forced the natural shortcomings of society to reveal themselves. Fontane set the tone and suggested the appropriate style for the contemporary social novel in several works from *L'Adultera* to *Effi Briest*. In keeping with the earlier trends toward Realism in France and partly in Germany and Switzerland (Gottfried Keller, Jeremias Gotthelf, Wilhelm Raabe, Conrad Ferdinand Meyer, Theodor Storm, and others), Fontane demonstrated a keen sense of observation in recording the objects, conversations, events, that reduced his world to a composition of fixed parts that lacked nothing but human freedom and understanding.

The influence of Theodor Fontane on Thomas Mann is also made apparent by their mutual concern for the problems of individuals in an impersonal, historically conditioned community. In regard to time also, we should not forget that Fontane was completing his last historical novel, *The Stechlin* (1899), as Thomas Mann began to work on his first great novel of social decadence, *Buddenbrooks*.

Thus, the predominant trend of novelization in Germany was established. A trend, a literary climate or movement got underway with Theodor Fontane and Thomas Mann that lasted almost half a century and eventually embraced such important authors as Arthur Schnitzler, Stefan Zweig, Robert Walser, Otto Flake, Hermann Broch, Robert Musil, and many others. But before taking a closer look at these men of letters, we must examine some of the foreign trends in literature that prepared the way for the thinking and writing of the new century.

Our purpose in having begun this chapter on the twentieth-century German novel with a step-by-step commentary on Thomas Mann's works should be rather obvious by now. Thomas Mann, as much as anyone in modern literature, exemplifies the historical schism of our times; and whereas on the one hand he reaches into almost every era of history from recent European to Biblical times, he tries on the other hand to find a genuine place for contemporary men who have inherited a history so vast that its past totality and present significance elude one's grasp. This is the dilemma of a good number of twentieth-century German novelists who have gone in search of history and culture in order to find themselves. The German historian Wilhelm Dilthey (1833–1911) defines the problem as a failure to integrate the facts and influences of the past into our present processes of development. He asseverates the necessity of genuine historical knowledge as an inward experience in addition to history as objective knowledge, as a kind of scientific penchant for understanding phenomena that leave the human being at a distance, untouched so to speak, by meaning of a personal nature.

Almost without exception the great novelists of this period—Robert Walser, Otto Flake, Hermann Broch, Robert Musil, and even those who chose Romanticism or Expressionism as their mode of expression, Hermann Hesse and Franz Kafka—undertake a search for a meaningful present, one that should somehow become integrated with all of history and embrace modern man within the spectrum of a universal harmony. The problem may be restated as an extension of Herder's organic concept of history, that men should stand in harmonic unity with their world and not be isolated from real knowledge by their own intellects, that they should not be separated from reality by objective analysis nor divided from nature or mankind through well structured but impersonal learning. Herder feared that the feeling of completeness which primitive men once possessed might be lost eternally. His hope for changing the direction of civilization from alienation toward unity lay in the integrating efficacy of literature and poetry; but unfortunately, and especially in the twentieth century, literature set out on the same path as science toward objective analytical knowledge gained at the expense of human concern and subjective experience.

The primary, though not exclusive, impetus to the German scientific novel came from France, where Hippolyte Taine popularized a theory of literature based on Auguste Comte's philosophy of Positivism. Anticipating the field of applied sociology to some degree, Comte asserted that people behave according to the principle of cause and effect, in a logically predictable manner. Physical and moral behavior is subject therefore to scientific explanation, and unobservable concepts such as freedom, mind, and spirit, are illusory and must be excluded from any factual theory or clear conception of man. Taine then goes on to establish Positivism as a basic standard for art in his book *Philosophie de l'art* by positing the formula of *heredity, environment*, and the *moment* as the necessary observable ingredients to explain human behavior. He and others, going back to Darwin in England for authority, regarded mankind then as just another species of life that has happened to survive through natural selection and one that must be studied therefore in terms of biological history, present environment, and social challenge.

But theory alone probably would not have influenced German literature much if Emile Zola had not appeared on the scene. His powerful novels, a total of twenty volumes, *Les Rougon-Macquart*, put into practice what others were advocating in principle. In keeping with the scientific propositions of the times, he observed and studied life with uncompromising precision, formulating his results finally in what he labeled a *roman expérimental*, a novel that was a "slice of life." But this movement was not restricted to France, where the brothers Goncourt and Guy de

Maupassant added strength to the literary trend. The Danish author Jens Peter Jacobsen (1847–1885), another proponent of Darwinism and a novelist of some stature, made his influence felt along with that of the Russians Tolstoy and Dostoyevsky. The eventual synthesis of these forces on German soil came to be known by the term of "Naturalism," a harsh style of realism imbued with Taine's scientific pretensions concentrating exclusively on the sordid side of life. Although this powerful literary movement rapidly succeeded in adding a new dimension to German theater, the novelists of some importance compromised the doctrine by insisting on the free use of general impressions and shifting focus while recognizing at the same time the demand for precise narration, portrayal of cultural negativism and decay, passive victims rather than heroes, social coercion, and psychological understanding. And only by listing such general characteristics as these does it become possible to characterize some of the vast number of authors of a general nature, such as Hermann Sudermann (1857–1928), Hermann Löns (1866–1914), Jakob Wassermann (1873–1934), Gustav Frenssen (1863–1945), Clara Viebig (1860–1952), Eduard von Keyserling (1855–1918), Emil Strauss (1866–1960), and Arnold Zweig (1887–1968); but still, in the wide panorama of this time, Thomas Mann stands above an ocean of novelists, who, were it not for his overwhelming presence, would undoubtedly be receiving more attention today by critics and public. Many, perhaps too many to mention here, are worthy of attention or serious study. Thomas Mann's brother for example, Heinrich Mann (1871–1950), examined intensely, even violently, a restricted area of his brother's concerns. The bourgeois culture which is ironically illuminated by Thomas Mann is satirically devastated in the hands of his brother. Heinrich, rabidly antagonistic toward the hypocrisy, the evil, and vileness of so-called good German society, exposed its unsavoriness with satire and invective in a number of novels, the most readable of which are *Small Town Tyrant* (*Professor Unrat*, 1905), *The Little Town* (*Die kleine Stadt*, 1909), *The Patrioteer* (*Der Untertan*, 1918), and *Young Henry of Navarre* (*Die Jugend des Königs Henri Quatre*, 1935). His criticism of Germany is uncompromising and harsh, unrelenting in fact as only that of a native might be against his own country, from which he perhaps expects the best of social values expressed. Others, writing outside of Germany proper, were in many respects more tolerant with its mistakes and weaknesses.

Foreign readers frequently overlook the fact that there is a difference between literature of Germany and German literature. The former is restricted to works written by authors of Germany proper, while German literature may be written anywhere in the world, an important concept to keep in mind when considering the twentieth-century novel, which is dominated by authors residing outside of Germany—Austria, Switzerland, Czechoslovakia, and the United States. Arthur Schnitzler, for example, although primarily a dramatist and an Austrian by birth, must be regarded as an important German novelist. Drifting between a kind of philosophical realism and psychological naturalism, Schnitzler wrote a number of fascinating short novels, in addition to the full-length novels *The Road to the Open* (1908) and *Theresa* (1928). Schnitzler's novels have, however, a subtle Austrian character and quality all their own that lifts them out of the common and facile classifications of literature. The number of writers active in Vienna around the turn of the century, approximate contemporaries of Schnitzler, is impressive (Ludwig Anzengruber, Peter Rosegger, Marie von Ebner-Eschenbach, Hermann Bahr, J. J. David, Peter Altenberg, Richard Beer-Hofmann, Hugo von Hofmannsthal, Karl Kraus, and others); and although the vast majority of their writings center on variegated styles of drama, poetry, and criticism, some did contribute novels of consequence as well as a singularly strong literary tradition for other Austrian novelists, the most well known of which are probably Stefan Zweig, Robert Musil, Joseph Roth, Heimito von Doderer, and Hermann Broch.

In a most readable book about the disposition of pre-World War I Vienna, *The World of Yesterday* (1942), Stefan Zweig (1881–1942) succeeds in recapturing the unique attitudes and concerns of this period of time that did much to determine the thinking of twentieth-century Austrian writers. As is so often the case with a writer of great human sympathies, Zweig, writing about a period of history, manages to grasp the magic of the times while implicitly reflecting the nostalgia, resignation, self-doubt, and melancholy of his own soul. The political security and the underlying psychological confusion of the era, an era that gave rise to Sigmund Freud (1856–1939) and psychoanalysis, is reflected in the titles of Stefan Zweig's stories, novels, and biographies: *Amok* (1922), *Conflicts* (1926), *Fantastic Night* (1929), *The Struggle with the Demon* (1925), *The Ride of Fortune* (*Sternstunden der Menschheit*, 1927), *The Triumph and Tragedy of Erasmus of Rotterdam* (1935), *The Right to Heresy: Castellio against Calvin*

(1936). Throughout his career Zweig continues the attempt to find the "Worlds of Yesterday" by writing historical biographies that search out the roots and reasons for man's actions; and tracing them from inception to conclusion, he creates suspense and intrigue comparable to the best of novels.

Zweig, like so many of his contemporaries, goes on an unsuccessful search of a cultural past and a meaningful present, a search whose final desperation is symbolized by his suicide in South America in 1942. And though his fate was unfortunate and more pathetic than that of many coeval writers, it varied from theirs in intensity rather than in pattern. Nazidom and the Third Reich turned the great writers of German literature, almost without exception, into expatriates, exiles in search of some satisfactory place to spend their last years, an impossible task considering the deep investment of vitality each had in the German language and in the cultural life of Europe.

But prior to and during exile, with a sense of deep regret, epic greatness, and tragic resignation, the Austrian novelists continued to examine and formulate a vanishing mode of life in the moribund Austro-Hungarian monarchy. Joseph Roth's (1894–1939) thirteen novels deal for the most part with the decline of the monarchy, but they are often too sentimentalized or impassioned (with the possible exception of *Radetzkymarsch*, 1932) to be considered seriously nowadays. Heimito von Doderer (1896–1966) is also concerned with the historical and cultural past and even regards the role of the novelist as "a harbinger of returning history with an eye that perceives the worthwhile which is slipping into the distant past." This, essentially, is the theme he pursues from beginning to end, from his well known novel *Every Man a Murderer* (1938) to *The Demons* (1956).

Though the general topic remains the same in the novels of Hermann Broch (1886–1951), his understanding of the agonies of society, his formulations of the decline of tradition, and his penetration into the externally formal but inwardly confused people of the old Austrian monarchy, lifts his novels above those of his contemporaries and imbues them with lasting literary value. His lengthy (three-volume) and subtle study of the moral, spiritual decline of society prior to and during World War I, *The Sleepwalkers* (1931), displays with precision the semi-conscious stages which men suffer in the degeneration process of an established order. *The Death of Virgil* (1945) removes Broch from the established tradition of cultural histories almost into the camp of James Joyce, as Broch renders a final struggle of the Roman poet as a feverish phantasmagoria of inner monologues, impressions, images, events, emotions, and dreams. *The Innocent Ones* (1950), Broch's last novel, again experiments with technique to some degree while analyzing man's intricate psychological investment in reality during the period of history leading up to the Third Reich. Techniques and styles interested Broch, but the late history and last misfortunes of Europe fascinated him; so if Hermann Broch seemed a great writer on the one hand, he was no less the social commentator or political critic on the other. With him the best of literary sensitivity and historical perceptiveness combined to create lasting works of quality.

Robert Musil (1880–1942), like Broch, was an Austrian, an author of novels describing the decline of the Austro-Hungarian Empire, a subtle observer of human psychology, a master of style, a creator of a lengthy novel of lasting value. When Musil's greatest work, *The Man Without Qualities* (1952), appeared, a literary critic reviewing for *The New York Times'* literary supplement, called Musil the greatest German author of the twentieth century. Other critics compared him (to his advantage) to James Joyce and Marcel Proust as a result of this voluminous socio-psychological novel that runs well over 2,000 pages and offers a biography of a talented, well-educated young man of thirty whose life unravels parallel to a surrounding world that is saturated with human beings who people events in an extremely graphic but yet unreal tableau. Ulrich, the protagonist, observes, analyzes, and inspects the substance of life to the point of a fine metaphorical gossamer that ultimately eludes him, just as the world around him does. It is interesting indeed to compare Ulrich as a person with his earlier "psychological" counterpart in the novel *Young Törless* (1906), where Musil describes the anxieties, challenges, and doubts of adolescence that lead a young lad to discover the manifold possibilities beyond the surface configurations of life.

Before examining the Neo-Romantic[2] novel of twentieth-century Germany, we must briefly name two additional novelists for their growing significance and new-found popularity: Robert Walser (1878–1956), the Swiss author whose major novel, *The Assistant* (*Der Gehülfe*, 1907), concentrates (like Thomas Mann's *Buddenbrooks*) on the decline of a bourgeois family (presented in an unusual fashion bordering at times on surrealism); and Otto

Flake (1880–1963), the Alsatian writer of socio-philosophical novels. Especially his *Fortunat* cycle (1947) makes a serious attempt at finding answers to the contradictions and conflicts which have plagued and still torment the men and nations of Europe.

The difference between these somewhat realistic and diverse romantic novels of twentieth-century Germany does not reside so much in distinction of style as it does in the author's decision to emphasize either the elusive inner nature of man or simply the physical, exterior one. Whereas the latter propounds an historical, cultural, biological, "scientific" determination of man, the former assumes the primordial importance of deeply felt but abstract concerns such as freedom, individual fulfillment, spiritual growth, and the dignity of self; and yet, as contradictory as these two positions may seem, it often becomes difficult to separate them and simply label a novel "realistic" or "romantic." Part of the confusion of overlapping categories even turns to irony occasionally when the most representative writers of consistent naturalism or scientific realism, for example, become the first to drift away from their own "scientific" principles. In Zola's later novels, objects and events begin to acquire obvious metaphorical and even symbolic significance; and Gerhart Hauptmann, often considered the proto-author of Naturalism, switches abruptly to extreme lyrical mythos in drama and to religious symbolism in the novel. *The Fool in Christ Emanuel Quint* (1910), for example, presents the poignant story of a Christ figure in the twentieth century, who seems to possess all the tender qualities of divinely inspired human goodness and must, it seems, be rejected from the purposes of society and considered mad. Hauptmann's later novels *Atlantis* (1912), *The Heretic of Soana* (1918), and *The Island of the Great Mother* (1924), though still presented in a realistic fashion, rest ultimately in a symbolic realm somewhere beyond the outer threshold of realism.

Viewed chronologically, Naturalism barely had an opportunity to develop in Germany before writers like Hesse, Rilke, Mombert, Ricarda Huch, Clara Viebig, and even Gerhart Hauptmann himself launched a kind of informal counter-naturalistic movement, a new literary trend that endeavored to capture those very realities which Naturalism chose to ignore. The efforts took an aesthetic, existential direction, searching for and simultaneously glorifying life's personal meaning in an emotional, a sensual, or often mystical way. If one were to choose a single work here to designate the "official" arrival of this new trend, then Ricarda

Huch's (1864–1947) book *The Golden Age of Romanticism* (1899) would undoubtedly be the best choice. In this lengthy study—a second volume on the spread and decline of Romanticism appears in 1902—she opposes the creative power, the Olympian figures, and the inspiring spirit of the romantic movement to the dehumanization, the impersonality, the mechanical apparatus of society and the current trends of science. And Ricarda Huch also supports her position in no uncertain terms by contributing a number of studies and novels to German literature that add to its richness and establish, at the same time, Ricarda Huch as one of the foremost women of the twentieth century.

But if Huch and others introduce a new kind of romanticism in the novel, it is still Hermann Hesse (1877–1962) who contributes the novels of international importance to the movement. At the turn of the century Hesse conceived a moving first novel, *Peter Camenzind* (1904) that has continued up to the present day to be read and studied with great interest. The hero, like Hesse himself, finds it impossible to locate a fixed place for himself in society and it is only when wandering in Italy, lost to the world and alienated from mankind, that he discovers spiritual nourishment in the "dark but beautiful language of nature" and in the concept of passionate love (as exemplified by Francis of Assisi) for all life. Freed consequently from his most disquieting concerns, he is able to return to his home town in Switzerland to actively fulfill on a modest level his obligations to his fellow men.

The other novels of Hesse's early period of writing, similar to *Peter Camenzind*, are novels of development dealing with self-discovery, with one's responsibility to other men and to some higher realm of nature or spirit. *Under the Wheel* (1906) depicts another confrontation of a young lad with a callous world, this time in the form of a brutal school system whose teachers destroy the sensitive nature and even lives of young men whom they cannot understand or appreciate. In the novels *Gertrude* (1910) and *Rosshalde* (1914) the hero, again without compromising his poetic sensitivity or integrity, tries rather unsuccessfully to find a place as a husband and an artist in a restrictive society. With *Knulp* (1915) the expansiveness of Hesse's spirit returns as he relates the free-flowing story of a gypsy-like wanderer in the kingdom of nature. Years come and go, and Knulp roams through the countryside with a restless heart, open eyes, and an alert mind. One learns later that a disappointing love affair is the reason for this wandering, but that point seems to be of less importance to the total work than is the final recognition of a kind of natural grace and greatness in this wanderer whose steps and direction were so subtly guided by providence.

The abrupt catastrophe of World War I seemed to shock Hesse and a number of his colleagues in *belles lettres* out of their idyllic dreams, and forced them to do a good deal of observing, questioning, and soul-searching. Though Hesse was forced to conclude finally that he had little to offer in the arena of politics, he contributed wherever he could to help alleviate the suffering of men and nations. But World War I still marked a turning point in Hesse's writing. The autobiographic, nostalgic, romantically idealized writing of his younger years is replaced by extensively symbolic explorations in the realm of emotion, mind, and spirit. From here almost to the conclusion of his career Hesse becomes actively concerned with the process of individuation as he pursues a goal of inner unity and fulfillment. "I only wanted to try to live what was inside me and wanted to come out," concludes the protagonist of *Demian* (1919) after learning that one must also come to terms with the dark side of one's soul by liberating the demonic forces within oneself if one wishes to realize his own unique destiny.

What may be called "psychological" in one context may well be recognized as religious or mystic in another; so the step from the psychiatry of Europe to the mysticism of India—the setting for Hesse's next novel, *Siddhartha* (1922)—is not necessarily dramatic. Beginning with a middle-class Brahman youth, Hesse traces his development as an expression of spiritual ascendancy until he finally attains a state of mind or order of consciousness comparable to Gautama Buddha's. However, Siddhartha's view that every object, person, or event in society is a possible barrier or restricting limitation to his growth, blocking individual development, compares in principle rather than intensity to the opposing hidden, dark side of one's own soul in Hesse's next novel, *Steppenwolf* (1927). Breaking the limits of his own style, Hesse cuts a wide swath of expressionistic hyperboles and grotesque distortions to underscore the seething conflicts in a modern man who is simultaneously a vicious beast and a docile citizen. In highly symbolic forms Hesse relates the forced and uncomfortable state of man's repressed condition, but he does so not without showing that some hope does ultimately exist, that in the "magic theater" of man's mind some freedom is still possible, that certain aesthetic pleasures (though distorted) may yet be enjoyed, and that humor (black though it may be) can still liberate one from the stress of living in bitter and impersonal times.

Steppenwolf seems to have been a necessary storm to clear the air for Hesse and allow him to attain some measure of tranquillity, for his remaining novels reveal a degree of the unity and harmony reminiscent of earlier works while adding, at the same time, a dimension of philosophical understanding that was lacking before. In Death and the Lover (Narziß und Goldmund, 1930) Hesse chooses a medieval setting to portray the story of two friends, one a monk and the other a troubled, worldly traveler. Though their inherent natures force them to part, they meet again at the end of a perplexing but rich life and reestablish a bond of friendship so profound that it borders on revelation. The deep fraternal relationship can be compared with those of earlier works, especially if one regards the two men here as personifications of a single psyche's related but yet opposing elements, each of which must experience and satisfy its own needs before a degree of harmony can be established. Speaking in terms of psychology and the psyche, one must again compare this process of growing integrity to the Jungian concept of "individuation," or in religious terms of spiritual union and providential fulfillment; but yet, though accurate, these terms serve only as a meager "explanation" of a novel! A novel, especially one of Hesse's, is not merely a tractatus philosophicus that can be summed up with a terse conclusion: it is an emotional and intellectual progression that must be experienced fully in the reading before it can be comprehended.

This admonition applies with double force to The Journey to the East (1932), which defies summarizing and critical interpretation alike, unless it be as a prelude or five-finger exercise that prepares the way for Hesse's last and most ambitious novel (dedicated to the Eastern Wayfarers) Magister Ludi: The Bead Game (1943), which in large part seems to represent and synthesize the purposes of all the earlier works. The plot hinges on an elaborate metaphor, a glass bead game, that symbolizes man's urge to intellectual engrossment in hope of finding ultimately some kind of "unified field theory" for all knowledge and experience of an aesthetic, intellectual, and spiritual nature. The game is cultivated within a rigid and rigorous monastic order of which Joseph Knecht, the protagonist, becomes the master. Meanwhile, his close friend Plinio Designori leaves the order to make his way in the outside

339

world where he succeeds, by external standards, superbly; but yet both men fail to find real satisfaction or peaceful fulfillment for themselves even in the highest offices within or outside the order. Their lives represent in fact the journey of the Eastern Wayfarers, and confirm the remoteness or unattainability of spiritual completeness, of Nirvana, the Vedic concept that neither inspired individuality nor social function constitute the ultimate purpose in life. After spending the major part of his life becoming the Magister Ludi, Knecht decides finally to leave the order to return to the world of common men and become the tutor of Designori's son, but his enterprise hardly begins before it is brought to an end with his death by drowning in a cold Alpine lake. It seems that Knecht had not, as a member of the Castalian order, been able to cement a bond between his art and his life. As a bead player, Knecht was concerned with the abstract universal, with "the cult of truth closely bound up with the cult of the beautiful and, in addition to this, with the contemplative care of the spirit"; and though he had surpassed all others in finding an overriding harmony between the principles of "science, reverence of the beautiful, and meditation," he also desired to experience life concretely, in the particular, to be gathered up by individual entities and immediate events. Knecht, like his many closely related antecedent protagonists, discovers that the unreflective life may not be worth living, but the reflective life may finally be no life at all. The abstract "parlor game," the glass bead game "has only been an endless repetition, an empty exercise and a meaningless formula. . . . It was high time to make an end of it;" so Knecht returns finally to the world of man and nature which Hesse created in his earliest novels, in order to find the fulfillment, perhaps even the tangible completeness between self, men, and nature, which he found wanting in his abstract endeavors as Magister Ludi.

It is Joseph Knecht, therefore, who though a creation of Hesse, becomes one of the best commentators on the author's life, for it is he who formulates the guiding principle which Hesse seems to have regarded as his own, "that coincidental with the experience of awakening, there actually were such steps and realms, and that each time a life stage was coming to an end it was fraught with decay and a desire for death before leading to a new realm, and awakening and to a new beginning." Thus, as this novel and Hesse's life suggest, one's acceptance of progressive stages of personal growth outstrips the value of man's other most striven for accomplishments, and (as *Siddhartha* showed so clearly) inner fullness is somehow related to external simplicity, to modesty, and effortlessness of conduct, ultimately the highest of virtues and in our time the most difficult to achieve and retain.

Unlike other novelists of the twentieth century, Hesse wrote a good deal of lyric poetry which can be classified along with the romantic poems of Stefan George, Rainer Maria Rilke, and Hugo von Hofmannsthal as a growing expression of the need of art for its own sake. The vast stream of Neo-Romantic writing enveloped all genres of literature, but in the field of the novel it is Hesse who stands above all others as herald and carrier of the Romantic tradition. In his writings one finds all the characteristics of the movement: *symbolism* that employs objects and events metaphorically to extend thought beyond the surface of things to a basic or higher reality which in itself is indescribable; *aestheticism* that confirms beauty as a primary value of life, irrespective of any moral or materialistic consideration; and *Weltschmerz*, resignation, heroic weakness, or exhausted efforts that characterize a person's hunger and failure to satisfy the appetite for spiritual completeness. This inner frustrated longing for fullness of life is most often described with a style deeply imbued with lyrical refinement and abstract, artful devices that best serve to glorify the deep loneliness, the alienation, and the subtle inadequacies of the romantic soul.

Neo-Romanticism found its widest public in the areas of poetry and drama, but specific works of other authors besides Hermann Hesse and Ricarda Huch are deserving of mention here. *The Notebooks of Malte Laurids Brigge* by Rainer Maria Rilke is a rather unusual kind of autobiographical novel centered on the dilemmas of a young artist whose inclination towards morbid reflection and passionate feelings reduce him to a state of apathy. Rilke casts his hero in the form of a young Danish lad (very similar to the one in *Niels Lyhne* by Jens Peter Jacobsen) who confronts the inner monsters of doom and loneliness, defeating them finally with strong resolution and submission to the providence of God. The theme of the Prodigal Son, the search for God, illumination and salvation is preserved also in the novels of Hermann Stehr (1864–1940), especially in *Heiligenhof Farm* (1917) and *Peter Brindeisner* (1924), where he traces man's path to God through one's own soul. Stehr's later novel, *Nathanael Maechler* (1929), repeats the message of the primacy of religious submission, this time in relationship to the welfare of the community.

341

A different kind of religious theme is developed in the two-volume novel of Gertrud von le Fort (1876–   ), *Veronica's Handkerchief* (1927 and 1946), which relates the story of insistent Catholic faith and final grace for a young girl who grows up in Rome and is exposed to the conflicting forces of the heathen behavior and the Christian values of that cosmopolitan city. The second volume takes place in Germany after World War I and follows the course of a woman's conflict between love of God and of a man who is not compatible with her beliefs. Religious novels, such as these similar in tone and intention but of lesser quality, constitute a separate category of novel writing, and certainly other novelists of a religious or romantic inclination could be listed here, and though some do have literary merit, they are probably of less significance than are even the secondary representatives of a third mainstream in twentieth-century German literature—Expressionism.

Now, almost a half century after his death, Franz Kafka (1883–1924) continues to be regarded as one of the most intriguing and enigmatic authors of our century. Few of his countless readers agree upon the central meaning of his writings, but all are unanimous in proclaiming his brilliance. Like most great authors, Kafka is more of an individual than a proponent of a specific school or a general set of principles, but still critics of consequence have classified his writing in turn as metaphysical, existential, Judaic, social, theological, nihilistic, psychoanalytic, Zionistic, surrealistic, *ad infinitum;* and whereas these rubrics bespeak the confusion of ideas surrounding Kafka scholarship, they reveal the multi-level vastness of his writing.

Generally speaking, Kafka's writing is part of the expressionistic movement which prevailed on the German stage and in lyric poetry between the two world wars, a movement which was plagued by concepts such as man's solitariness in the midst of others, the indifference of fate and nature, the remoteness of God, and the injustices of society; but above all (and especially in Kafka's writings) the movement emphasized the concept of *self* as the proper and primary concern of the writer. Implicit in the word Expressionism is the image of "pressing out" of one's heart and soul the dark anxieties, the distorting fears, and even the secret hopes of reconciliations or salvation. Subjective visions predominated over reality in a dreamlike manner which denied the usual rules of objective logic, cause and effect, sequential time, logical proximity, and

342

conceptual unity. Unlike Realism, Expressionism did not manifest faithfulness to actual appearances or events but examined man as one might through a penetrating magnifying glass that dramatically enlarged objects while distorting them into accurate but yet unreal forms.

The three novels and many of the short stories upon which Kafka's fame rests were found as fragments after his death. Although actually unfinished, the novels *America* (begun ca. 1912), *The Trial* (begun ca. 1914), and *The Castle* (begun ca. 1920) can be regarded as a coherent expression of expanding human experience. In *America* a sixteen-year-old boy, Karl Rossmann, is sent by his parents to America where he finds, despite his earnest diligence, little more than rejection, frustration, and increasing degradation. A threefold fate unfolds for him with a stoker aboard ship, then in his wandering, and finally in the Oklahoma Nature Theater, all of which seem to represent man's Fall, Life, and mechanical Salvation in the present-day technological world. In *The Trial* a bank official Joseph K. is arrested on his thirtieth birthday, subdued by court officials whose authority is uncertain, condemned by forces one cannot comprehend, and executed one year later for a crime that is never defined. In *The Castle,* a surveyor (again identified with the initial K.) travels to a strange town where he has evidently been commissioned to do a job for some unidentified authority residing in a castle which is situated just above the town and dominates its existence. Throughout the novel, K. struggles in every conceivable way to establish contact with the higher authorities of the castle but without significant success. His existence, at best precarious, achieves meaning only in the search for recognition and acceptance.

In an effort to find some unity in Kafka's works, one might consider the three novels as psychological thresholds of growth from youth to manhood or even as a modern myth, a related trilogy in which the hero departs at first to explore the material realm of man; at the second stage he is jolted out of the work-a-day structure of the business world into the moral sphere of guilt, judgment, and punishment; and at the last level he travels through a highly unreal realm in visible proximity of the highest authorities who, without revealing themselves, at least remotely acknowledge the hero's presence.

Ultimately, Kafka's novels deal with nothing less than man's search for his place in the cosmos. And if there is confusion in his

343

novels, then it is no less the confusion of the world at large which at one time or another would be grasped by men in terms of psychology, philosophy, theology, sociology, etc., according to one's own needs and predilections. For Kafka such systems of thought seem to offer little hope for comprehending a world of parables and paradoxes, though each system may reveal a particular facet of the overall problem. The questions of man's existential anxieties, alienation, loss of faith, remoteness, guilt, doubt, loneliness, and so forth, are experiential for Kafka, not conceptual. Driven by a measure of curiosity and concern, Kafka's heroes reject the intellectualized, mechanistic answers and invest their energies in a search for individual purpose and fulfillment in an otherwise impersonal age. The final result is one of frustration of course, because Kafka simply cannot abandon his sense of compelling logic for the wishes of his soul. His protagonists live, therefore, between two worlds, in a state of "fear and trembling," with a feeling of pathetic loneliness, morbid guilt, restlessness, longing, and self-estrangement; in the style of surrealism, these inner conditions are projected as grotesque objects, broken events, or distorted people among which modern man must make his way. Kafka therefore also represents a literary movement that relates and combines the internal sense phenomena with the factuality of objective experience rather than accept the world of the senses only and declare the inner world of dreams, fantasy, and faith worthless or even void.

Writers who have experienced how insubstantial the pageant of external reality can be, how ephemeral and artificial it may seem, realize a positive sense of purpose in presenting a fantastic event as a concrete occurrence, as Hermann Kasack (1896–1966) does in his novel, *The City beyond the River* (1947), a chronicle of a city peopled by visions and voices, ghosts, strange shapes, and apparitions, a city that is at one and the same time the realm of death and the ghostly state of Germany after World War II. The structures of sanity and sense have been broken by history, turning people into walking corpses with mechanical movements, distorted gestures, empty language, and hollow spirit. People are presented as grotesque and dehumanized figures, but Kasack finds a hopeful aspect in this place where the traditional foundation of society and life have been lost. Old purposes are no longer viable, old meanings of words and society are senseless, and the power of the external has been broken. So the city beyond the river is really an in-between realm from which many depart into final death but one that may provide others with a terrifying experience that will simultaneously shock and then liberate them from falsity and self-deception.

Alfred Döblin (1878–1957), in his excellent book *Alexander Square, Berlin* (1929), also chose to examine the inhuman aspects of a city, but in this case through the eyes of a helpless and victimized ex-convict. This epic novel, still accepted as the foremost example of expressionistic prose, reveals Berlin as a twentieth-century Babylon complete with corruption, fears, thievery, prostitution, hunger, and despair. A chaotic mass of impersonal, unscrupulous forces rob men of their last bit of hope and dignity, reducing them finally to an animal existence of hunt and survival. Döblin claimed, however, that his basic position was one of a humanist who wanted to remove the repressive layers of evil and indignity which forced people of the lower classes to become something less than human. In about a dozen novels, which were popular when published but are largely disregarded now, Döblin assailed again and again the distorting, oppressive, smug forces of society that obstructed the expression and growth of human spirit; or in the words of one of his characters in *The Three Leaps of Wang-lun* (1915): "The attempt to master the world through human behavior fails; it is of a spiritual nature."

Franz Werfel (1890–1945) is best known to the American public for his best selling novel, *The Song of Bernadette* (1941), a work he wrote in fulfillment of an oath made at Lourdes, while he was trying to escape the Nazis in France, that should he escape his pursuers, he would write a novel about the miracle of Lourdes, about this sacred meeting ground where a young, French farm girl once encountered Mary, the mother of God, and where suffering human beings still continue to experience Divine grace in the form of miraculous cures. But though this novel may have been Werfel's most popular one, it is not necessarily his best. The book that continues to be read as serious literature of our times is *The Forty Days of Musa Dagh* (1933). It is a powerful story of Turkish persecution of the Armenians during World War I told with sweeping force and human concern. In his last novel, *Star of the Unborn* (1946), Werfel projects another conflict of mankind 10,000 years into the future and examines the development of human hopes and values in an era of absolute technology. Werfel's fame now rests primarily on these two major novels and one play, *Mirror-Man* (1920), although other of his works such as *Class Reunion* (*Der Abituriententag*, 1928), and *Embezzled Heaven* (1939) are still

345

valuable as an examination of the outcropping and final escape of repressed guilt in the first work, and a mother's sacrifices for a worthless son in the second.

Along with other expressionist novelists who lived in Prague (Kafka, Werfel, Max Brod) Gustav Meyrink (1868–1932) remains established among notable authors of the twentieth century primarily for one long and curious book, *The Golem* (1915). This story, which straddles the supernatural and yet plays in the ghetto of Prague, anticipates to some degree the grotesque devices and figures of Kafka; but whereas Meyrink reduces his characters to mechanical, dehumanized automatons, Kafka moves in the opposite direction to search out the humanizing character of man. Max Brod (1884–1968) is probably best known nowadays as Franz Kafka's friend, mentor, and editor of his manuscripts. Kafka requested in his will that Brod destroy what he, Kafka, had written, but recognizing the value of Kafka's works, Brod decided instead to organize and publish them. As a result, one tends to forget that Brod is also an essayist, short story writer, and novelist in his own right. *Nornepygge Castle* (1908) is regarded as one of the earliest attempts at an expressionistic novel. Later, however, Brod drifted into a more realistic style as evidenced by his major work, *Tycho Brahe's Road to God* (1916).

Readers of American literature tend to compare German expressionistic prose with the bizarre tales of Edgar Allen Poe and there certainly is ample evidence to make a case for Poe's influence on the German expressionists. Rilke in his *Letters to a Young Poet* (1903–1908) sees the horror which Poe's characters confront as a provocative challenge to search out and bear the truth of one's dungeon, of one's world. Gustav Meyrink considered himself a disciple of Poe, and in spirit and style at least, one senses a degree of this influence on Kafka. There is also some indication that the loose rhythms and open rhyme of Walt Whitman presented fresh and exciting possibilities to the expressionist poets, but his influence on the German novelists was minimal if at all.

By and large, few American writers influenced the German novel of the first half of the twentieth century; if anything, the reverse is true. Until the United States and Germany had one big, common experience together, namely World War I, the German view of American literature consisted primarily of semi-journalistic detective cowboy-Indian frontier kind of story. Occasionally, some of the better stories and novels of writers like Bret Harte and Mark

Twain were also read, with Mark Twain far and away the most popular, having had more than 100 translations of his works on record in Germany before 1913. Norris, Mencken, Dreiser, et al., or the American schools of Realism and Naturalism, well into what Robert E. Spiller calls the "Second American Renaissance," were strongly affected, even determined, by European literary theory and production. Of course, after being influenced by literary movements from abroad, U.S. writers did produce some novels which were then translated into German and helped reinforce those stylistic trends which directly or indirectly gave birth to them in the first place. Upton Sinclair's books, for example, especially *The Jungle*, *Jimmie Higgins*, and *Oil*, criticized the social, monetary, and military establishment in a way that was singularly realistic and refreshing for the Germans; and as a result Sinclair's books remained on the best seller list in Germany until they were finally banned by the leaders of the Third Reich. In fact, Upton Sinclair, Jack London, Dos Passos, and some minor writers enjoyed greater sales in Germany for a while before 1933 than they did in the U.S. It would seem that novels of "real" Americana such as *Babbitt* and *Main Street* by Sinclair Lewis would find rapid acceptance in Germany, but that response was slow in coming (perhaps due to poor early translations) and it was not until Lewis received the Nobel prize in 1930 (and fresh translations were made of his works) that he gained some fame. But in 1938 his early works were also added to the black list of the *Reichsschrifttumskammer* as degenerate and undesirable in Germany. But all in all the rising wave of American literature was withstood by the censorship of the Third Reich, and only after the defeat of Germany in 1945 did the dike really break and allow the works of novelists like John Dos Passos, Thomas Wolfe, Ernest Hemingway, William Faulkner, the lost generation writers of the late 1920's and the social commentators of the 1930's, to inundate the country.

In the vast range of books published in this century, a small group of German novelists dealing primarily though not exclusively with the First World War, succeeded in producing a number of novels that were written rather simply and clearly. As the name of the movement indicates, "The New Matter-of-Factness" committed itself to a precise, uncompromising examination of man's world. An attempt is made through these novels to let the facts, undistorted by theory, speak for themselves. Of these novels, *All Quiet on the Western Front* (1929) by Erich Maria Remarque (1898–1970) is the best known. Characterized by a soft style and understatement rather than by drama, the book follows the experiences of a young soldier leading up to his death. In *The Road Back* (1931) and *Three Comrades* (1937) Remarque outlines the hardships confronting former soldiers as they return to a society in a state of disruption, a state of political and economic war in which the enemy is elusive and the adversary formless, but where the victims, the artless people, remain the same.

Other authors of the "Matter-of-Factness" movement, such as Ludwig Renn (*War*, 1928), Paul Alverdes (*The Whistler's Room*, 1929), Georg von der Vring (*Soldier Suren*, 1927), are worthy of mention here; but along with Remarque it is Arnold Zweig who must be separated from the others for his eight-volume fiction of the First World War, and especially one novel of this group, *The Case of Sergeant Grischa* (1927), has won a permanent place among anti-war novels of moving, literary quality.

World War II marked the end of a certain implicit agreement on the value of *Kultur* in Germany, and along with that demise came the end of the monumental and essentially idealistic German novel; although even with all their abstraction, obscurity, and dislocations, the German novels written prior to the Second World War were novels of hope rather than despair; and even where they were engendered with evil and destruction, they were still meant to be uplifting: "Out of this universal feast of death, out of this extremity of fever, kindling the rain-washed evening sky to a fiery glow, may it be that Love one day shall mount?"

This conclusion to Thomas Mann's *Magic Mountain* is only an indication of the fantastic extremes between some envisaged heaven and hell which these authors explored before the real inferno of Hitler's Germany flamed up. Then the German novelists were, as a result of the war, scattered into the wind; and as fortune would have it, the majority of them took up residence in the U.S., enriching the country with an abundance of literary genius the equal of which has seldom been found anywhere. At one time this country could count among its fold such German authors as Thomas Mann, Heinrich Mann, Franz Werfel, Lion Feuchtwanger, Bertolt Brecht, Stefan Zweig, Fritz von Unruh, Carl Zuckmayer, Leonhard Frank, Ernst Toller, and Hermann Broch. And it was not only their vital presence that enriched American thought and culture. Their works were rapidly translated into English. Many became professors at universities; a number worked with publishers, with theater groups, or lectured. Then, when some of the grand old men of German letters eventually died in America, they left their libraries to universities and their personal papers to scholars whom they had learned to call their friends. As a result, the American repositories and archives of literature of twentieth-century German letters are often more fertile ground for scholarship than those that are located in Germany. This mutual sharing of cultural materials then served, when the time came, to rejoin and cement that schism caused by war. Scholars and artists of Germany and America have learned to exchange materials and ideas now as never before; and even among the American lay public names such as Thomas Mann, Franz Kafka, Hermann Hesse, and others have become moving and meaningful.

It would certainly not be an exaggeration to refer to the twentieth century as the "Golden Age of the German Novel," for in both quantity and quality this genre surpassed in five decades what had previously been done in five centuries. From all the previous novels of German literature, one can select only Grimmelshausen's *Simplizissimus,* Goethe's *Wilhelm Meister,* and Keller's *Der Grüne Heinrich* to place with confidence in the same category with the best novels of this century. And the period of great novelists is, fortunately, still with us! History, as we have seen, was less than kind to the great artists and intellectuals of the 1900's, restricting and ending the productivity of some and the lives of others. But what was already written could not be erased, what was thought could not be withdrawn, and what had been contributed to national and world literature could not vanish. The novelists of German literature continue to live and affect others as long as their books are read, their thoughts examined, their experiences relived and cherished by so many readers. And even if their grandiose purposes and eloquent styles were prevented by political upheaval from flowing uninterrupted into the second half of the century, the quality and scope of their works set examples for the postwar writers to measure themselves by—but that, as we shall see, is a worthy topic for another chapter in German literature.

10. Literature Since 1933 ✌

Diether H. Haenicke

From an historical viewpoint, German literature of the last forty years defies being ordered into a meaningful continuum. Literary historians have been unable to coin an all-encompassing name for this period; recurrent themes, similarities in style, and common tendencies reveal themselves only slowly under the scrutiny of the most recent research. Political events—the rise of fascism, the subsequent apocalyptic Second World War, and the irreparable division of Germany into eastern and western political camps—have disrupted all continuity in the development of the intellectual and literary life.[1]

At the end of the twenties and beginning of the thirties, German literature had undeniably attained world-wide significance. In the works of Thomas Mann, who was awarded the Nobel prize for literature in 1929, and in the novels of Robert Musil, Alfred Döblin, Franz Kafka, and Hermann Broch, the German narrative art found its place in modern world literature. Brecht's plays, along with his new theory of the epic theater, began to spread with significant effect. The poetry of Rainer Maria Rilke and Hugo von Hofmannsthal withstood critical comparison with the works of the most notable poets of the time. Heinrich Mann, Walter Benjamin (1892–1940), Kurt Tucholsky (1890–1935), and Carl von Ossietzky (1889–1938) mastered the art of the essay and the brilliant *feuilleton*. Many great talents were silenced in the early stages of their development as the fascists' seizure of power jeopardized the lives of numerous German intellectuals. The outstanding feature of National Socialism, the German variant of fascism, was its marked opposition to intellectualism. Like all totalitarian regimes, National Socialism recognized in the artist a natural and most dangerous enemy. To take effective measures against him was from the start one of the most urgent tasks of the Nazis' cultural apparatus. In addition, according to the fascist *Weltanschauung*, any comparison of German cultural achievements with those of other nations, and thus with world literature, was undesirable and meaningless. All art,

350

in order to be recognized as such by the rulers, had to be, above all else, national and had to rest on imaginary millenniums of Germanic tradition. From the viewpoint of such a narrow concept of art, the greatest accomplishments in German literature appeared decadent (Thomas Mann, Alfred Döblin), degenerate, that is, Jewish (Else Lasker-Schüler, Lion Feuchtwanger and numerous others), or anti-German and Bolshevist (Brecht, Ossietzky). For many years, a steady flow of artists emigrated and for twelve years mediocrity prevailed inside Germany.

The literature that arose in tyrannized Germany under the benevolent eye of party officials deserves little attention because of its inferior artistic quality. A literature did develop in Germany, however, which because of its pointed opposition to the Nazis' violent system is popularly called the literature of the "inner emigration." The large number of writers who fled Germany developed a literature of exile or "outer emigration." It is typical of the literature of the inner as well as the outer emigration that artistic considerations and questions of form become secondary to the main concern: open or concealed expression of opposition to the regime.

The writers who remained in Germany found themselves in an almost unique situation. Aside from the fact that all their works were subject to the strictest censorship, the authors themselves lived in almost complete intellectual isolation. The many works of the banned German authors were as inaccessible as the rest of the literature written in the world outside Nazi control. Intellectual and artistic relationships with neighboring lands had to be given up as a result of the regime's favoring a self-satisfied nationalism.

After the defeat of the Third Reich a vast literary vacuum appeared. Literary historians are fond of speaking of a "literary zero point" out of which the new postwar literature developed, free from the bonds of tradition. This viewpoint, however, overlooks the fact that the authors returning from the inner and outer emigration played an important role in the intellectual life of postwar Germany. Kafka was rediscovered; Thomas Mann, Bertolt Brecht, and Gottfried Benn dominated the literary arena well into the mid-fifties. The first years after the war were marked by great controversies about guilt or complicity in the criminal, inexplicable events of the Nazi era. Postwar literature has provided no satisfactory answer, no clarifying, decisive explanation. In view of the atrocity of the events this may indeed be impossible. Even twenty-five years after the end of the Third Reich, the theme of guilt and the portrayal of human failure under tyranny are still fashionable in German literature.

Along with the continuing tradition of Thomas Mann, Brecht, and Benn, a new literature arose which in the late fifties attained a place in world literature. In its earlier stages the younger literary generation which gathered shortly after the war, mainly in the "Group 47," was strongly oriented toward politics and social criticism. They underscored their truly literary-political program with a sober, matter-of-fact language, eschewing all emotionalism and sentimentality.

Another literary theme related to the war experience which began to develop was the authors' search to comprehend the immediate past; to their keen disappointment the rapidly developing prosperous society refused to do the same. It was not until ten years after the war that problems of form, of identity, and of the creative process entered literature again as a main theme. In Günter Grass, Heinrich Böll, and Uwe Johnson, German postwar literature found novelists of importance. The poetry of Paul Celan, Ingeborg Bachmann, Nelly Sachs, and Karl Krolow also represents a significant artistic accomplishment. The Swiss playwrights Max Frisch and Friedrich Dürrenmatt supplied the postwar stage with provocative dramas, while Günter Eich and Wolfgang Hildesheimer introduced to Germany a new genre, the radio play.

A final phase has become clearly recognizable in the last few years. Literature is again becoming strongly relevant and is oriented above all toward current political problems. Hans Magnus Enzensberger and Peter Weiss, among others, have been the leaders in this tendency. Günter Grass's intense involvement in the West German election campaigns of 1965 and 1969 is another clear sign of the political commitment of the most recent literature. Here a distinct relationship to the early postwar literature seems to present itself. Once again political teachings and socially critical protest stand on a level above the problems of artistic expression.

I

Hitler's rise to power in January, 1933, caused an unprecedented exodus of German artists and intellectuals. The new regime declared in no uncertain terms that it intended to promote only art of the Germanic people (*"völkisch-germanisch"*). In establishing this basis for evaluating the various art forms, the regime arbitrarily and methodically began to extirpate from public life all Jewish, communistic, and other "decadent" artists. The new ideology forced the artists to direct all forms of creative expression toward the Nazi *Weltanschauung.*[2] Writers who had publicly opposed the party soon disappeared into concentration camps. The most prominent among them, Carl von Ossietzky, a courageous and outspoken editor and writer, received the Nobel Peace Prize in 1935 while in a concentration camp. Subsequently, the German government forbade the future acceptance of this prize by any German citizen.

This decree was only the first of many steps leading to the dreadful provincialism which characterized the arts in Germany under the Nazis. The party cleared all public galleries of works created by those artists whom the regime found displeasing. This group included the painters Otto Dix, Lyonel Feininger, Paul Klee, Oskar Kokoschka, Emil Nolde, Franz Marc, and Ernst Barlach. In May of 1933, the Nazis purged the highly distinguished Prussian Academy of Writers in Berlin. An extensive "reorganization" resulted in Heinrich Mann's removal from the presidency and the dismissals of fourteen other members. Among those dismissed were the novelists Thomas Mann and Alfred Döblin, the poets Alfred Mombert and Franz Werfel, and the dramatists Fritz von Unruh and Georg Kaiser. The novelist Ricarda Huch, named "the First Lady of Germany" by Thomas Mann, declared her withdrawal from the Academy in an act of noble indignation against this decree. She adamantly refused to remain a member of any institution which selected its members by other than artistic criteria. In a letter she denounced the violence, the defamation of dissenters, and the ostentatious self-conceit of the new rulers of Germany as both un-German and extremely dangerous. Repeated efforts by the Nazis failed to persuade her to reconsider the withdrawal. Richarda Huch was not the only artist who had become disgusted and deeply disturbed by the activities of the government. The novelists Hans Carossa (1878–1956) and Ernst Jünger (1895–   ) declined their appointments to the now Nazi-oriented Academy.

A symbolic auto-da-fé consisting of a book burning of all dissenting and non-conforming German writers took place in all parts of Germany on May 10, 1933. The works of many great writers, including Sigmund Freud, Karl Marx, Heinrich Mann, Emil Ludwig, Lion Feuchtwanger, Kurt Tucholsky, and Arnold

Zweig were burned. The book burners' slogans echoed the rallying cries of the anti-intellectual petty bourgeoisie of all times and all countries. They staunchly opposed decadence, moral decay, and internationalism and with equal strength supported decency, morality, order, and patriotism. Oskar Maria Graf (1894–1967), a Bavarian realistic writer, became highly incensed upon learning that his books were not among those burned. His protest caused a great sensation. "Burn my books, too!" he wrote and asserted that he did not deserve the disgrace of being acceptable to Nazi literary standards.

Soon afterwards the party compiled lists naming the authors and the books that were henceforth to be banned from publication and distribution. These lists enumerated the works of Brecht, Max Brod, Lion Feuchtwanger, Alfred Döblin, Heinrich Mann, Klaus Mann, Theodor Plievier, Erich Maria Remarque, Arthur Schnitzler, Kurt Tucholsky, Arnold Zweig, Stefan Zweig, and many others. New cultural organizations, such as the *Reichskulturkammer*, headed by Joseph Goebbels, Nazi minister of propaganda, completely controlled the realms of literature, music, the visual arts, the theater, the press, the radio, and the movie industry. Any artist who did not conform faced at least financial ruin and often more serious repercussions. More than a thousand writers chose to flee the Third Reich. This stream of emigrants never stopped as the intellectual elite abandoned their country. Almost no name of international reputation was left behind.

The Third Reich never developed a clear-cut program for the arts. For the Nazis, the primary value of literature lay in its usefulness as a means of spreading propaganda and thus as a tool for attaining their particular political goals. Literature had the task of preparing the citizens for the heroic deeds expected of them. Few recognized the hollowness behind the irrational call for heroism and national pride. The National Socialists sought to destroy the progressive literature of the first decades of the twentieth century, and labeled the linguistic and structural experiments in modern writing *Verhunzung* (disfiguration). The objective approach to history and to the realities of the twentieth century was denounced as misrepresentation and degradation of heroic historical figures; the cosmopolitan became a traitor to the nation. In opposition to the ideas presented by modern writers, National Socialist authors stressed the cult of race, *Volksgemeinschaft* (spiritual community of the people), and allegiance to the leader. Man's greatness had been envisaged by the expressionists in their proclamation of the "new man." The Nazis made use of this same vision, but their "new man" was solely a representative of the Germanic race, not of all mankind. The Nazis' lack of perception was revealed in their acceptance of the eclectic and elite attitude of Stefan George as compatible with their own. They were incapable of differentiating between their own biologically based theory of selection and the poet's criteria based on similarity of spirit. The aging George left Germany and in his will expressly refused the state funeral the Nazis offered to him.

In place of the literature of the twentieth century which they violently rejected, the fascists tried to bring about a revitalization of nineteenth-century regional literature. Under the impact of expanding industrialization and the consequent pauperism of the city masses, a strong tendency to re-examine the value of rural life had evolved. The novels of Peter Rosegger (1843–1918), Ludwig Anzengruber, Hermann Stehr (1864–1940), and many others depict individualistic people from rural areas whose roots are firmly established in their native soil. Often these heroes are contrasted with the decadent inhabitants of the city whose way of life seldom results in the establishment of strong ties with their particular locality. The rural life of simplicity and peace, regulated by the natural cycle of the seasons, offered a feeling of security to the protagonists. Many twentieth-century authors revived this quest for the true values of the simple life. Good examples are to be found in the novels of Ernst Wiechert (1887–1950): *The Girl and the Ferryman* (*Die Magd des Jürgen Doskocil*, 1932), *Wälder und Menschen* (*Woods and People*, 1936), *The Simple Life* (*Das einfache Leben*, 1939), and *Die Jerominkinder* (*The Jeromin Children*, 1946). Wiechert was raised in the woodlands of East Prussia as the son of a forester. A secondary school teacher by profession, he was typical of a segment of German academicians: the religious humanists who were sceptical both of the so-called scientific progress and of the sociological innovations of their time. They often combined their strong resentment of the modern technical world with a romantic concept of nature, a strong desire for independence, and an insatiable love for hiking. The dominant theme in Wiechert's works is nostalgia for the life of a hunter, a fisherman, or a shepherd, with its innocence, peace, and abundance of time for contemplation.

However, because of his strong religious convictions, Wiechert was an ardent foe of Nazism and fearlessly raised his voice against it in public.

Other writers turned away from the present and wrote of their national or Germanic past. Hans Friedrich Blunck (1888–1961) attempted to revitalize Germanic history in his trilogy *Die Urvätersage* (*The Saga of the Forefathers*, 1925–1928), for which he was highly honored by the Nazis. Paul Ernst (1866–1933), in one of the most voluminous epics in world literature, *Das Kaiserbuch* (*The Book of Emperors*, 1923–1928), portrayed the time of the medieval German emperors. Just as the Romanticists after the Napoleonic Wars, some German writers after World War I turned to the past for reassurance of the greatness and national unity of their country. Such themes were welcomed warmly by the fascists who promised the return of those heroic times in the form of the Third Reich.

In the midst of this trend toward escapism, the only concrete references to the immediate realities of war were to be found in the novels of Erich Maria Remarque and Arnold Zweig. Remarque's novel *All Quiet on the Western Front* emphasized the senseless death in the trenches and the deplorable waste of human potential in war. This book did away with the misconception of heroism and has remained one of the most effective anti-war novels ever written. Zweig's *The Case of Sergeant Grischa* (1927), another realistic war novel, describes the judicial murder of a Russian prisoner of war, Grischa, by the German army command. Grischa's innocence is proved and several people of various social classes attempt to save him. However, the High Command senses the threatening influence of the Russian revolution on its soldiers and deems it necessary to execute Grischa in order to re-establish discipline. Both novels forced the reading public to re-evaluate the official propaganda about the glory of the war. Unacceptable to the Nazis, both Remarque and Zweig emigrated.

Despite all Nazi efforts, the renaissance of German literature scheduled to take place after the exodus of all "decadent" writers never occurred. But, as the literature entered a period of decline and apparent decay within the boundaries of the *Reich*, German literature outside the country flourished.[3] Between 1933 and the beginning of the war in 1939, the emigrants published several hundred books in other European countries. They claimed to represent German literature and to continue the traditional values of humanism. Alfred Kantorowicz (1899–   ) substantiated this claim in his book of essays, *In unserem Lager ist Deutschland* (*On Our Side Is Germany*, 1936). Vienna, Prague, Paris, Amsterdam, and Stockholm became the centers of German literary life. The Malik, Bermann-Fischer, Querido, and Allert de Lange publishing houses printed the books of the emigrants. Some authors, whose books were translated and printed in large editions (Thomas Mann, Franz Werfel, Stefan Zweig, Lion Feuchtwanger), captured a new literary audience. The emigrants in New York founded a weekly newspaper, *Der Aufbau*, which militantly attacked Nazi politics and tried to ease the emigrants' way into the new culture of their host country. The major figures of exile literature regularly contributed articles and editorials. *Der Aufbau* is an important source of information for the student of intellectual life among German exiles in the United States.

Exile did not promote uniformity in style, genres, or themes. Most writers continued to write along the same lines they had established in their homeland. However, in a great number of their works either a new or stronger socio-political commitment becomes observable. Exile literature thus became largely *littérature engagée*. Although exile literature was written almost exclusively in German, translations sometimes appeared even before the German original text became available. Almost no writer gave up his native German; the majority strove to preserve the German language which, as they claimed, was being prostituted by the Nazis. The duration of the exile sometimes offset efforts to keep the language pure, but in most cases the exile intensified the writer's closeness to and familiarity with the language, the major bond with his native land. The exiled philosopher Ernst Bloch (1885–   ) even contended that anyone who abandons his mother tongue destroys his cultural heritage within himself.

The hospitality extended by the host countries to the exiled German writers varied greatly. The Soviet Union provided strong financial support for two excellent literary journals, *Das Wort* and *Internationale Literatur*. To a large extent, the fascination which Russia held for many exiled writers stemmed from the communist regime's outspoken hostility toward fascism at a time when western powers still practised the politics of appeasement. The most desired haven, Switzerland, was, at the same time, the least hospitable. The Swiss government barely tolerated many of the literary emigrants and forbade them to publish in Switzerland.

Often the immigration laws of other countries deterred many

would-be emigrants from escaping the Nazis. With the beginning of World War II and the initial success of the German armies, the situation became even more dangerous. France was the first major European nation to collapse militarily. After the armistice with Hitler, the Pétain regime imprisoned many German writers who had sought refuge in southern France and turned many aliens over to the *Gestapo*. In this desperate situation the talented essayist Walter Benjamin, whose works have experienced an overwhelming renaissance with the German youth of today, and the expressionist dramatist Walter Hasenclever (1890–1940) committed suicide. For many others fleeing France (Anna Seghers, Heinrich Mann, Lion Feuchtwanger, Fritz von Unruh, Franz Werfel), the escape was narrow.

One of the best novels about the exile situation, Anna Seghers's (1900–   ) *Transit* (1943), mirrors the chaos incited in Marseilles by the approaching German troops. The mortal terror of the emigrants lining up in the consulates for the certificates and visas which hold the power of life and death over the applicants dominates the picture. In most of her novels, Anna Seghers attempts to depict an historical situation by adding individual fates and numerous characters to a total picture of the epoch. Although there is often an outstanding protagonist, he is always embedded in the background of his social class. Before the Nazis took power, Anna Seghers had become a member of the Communist party. Her commitment to the revolutionary cause is strongly felt in all her works.

She first earned recognition with the narration *The Revolt of the Fishermen of Santa Barbara* (1928), which exemplifies her best prose writing and immediately won her the coveted Kleist Prize. The story describes the uprising of exploited fishermen against the capitalistic ship owners and the suppression of their revolt by the army. Anna Seghers achieved her greatest success with her novel *The Seventh Cross* (1942), which recounts the escape of seven men from a concentration camp. The commander of the camp orders seven crosses erected in the courtyard to which the recaptured men are affixed as a deterrent to the other prisoners. One of them, however, a young Communist, succeeds in fleeing with the help of party comrades who work against the fascist regime in the underground. The seventh cross thus remains vacant and becomes the symbol of hope for the inmates of the camp since, day by day, the vacant cross exemplifies the impotence of the regime.

Anna Seghers took up residence in Mexico; after the war she returned to East Germany where she is recognized as one of the most representative writers of the Communist state. The novels written after her return, however, do not compare with the vigor and the intensity of artistic expression which characterize those written in exile.

Stefan Zweig completed a comprehensive book of memoirs *The World of Yesterday*, shortly before he committed suicide in Brazil. He was one of the most widely read authors of his time, and his books were translated into all European languages. He possessed the refined qualities of an educated gentleman of the old Austrian empire and represented the best traditions of European humanism. Expelled from his native Austria and separated from his cultural bonds in Europe, he saw no sense in beginning a new life in a foreign culture at the age of sixty. The elegant style of his memoirs mirrors an enlightening portrait of the world of European intellectual life before the rise of Fascism.

As might be expected, a large portion of this literature centers around exile as a form of human existence. The books of Feuchtwanger, Döblin, Seghers, and Hasenclever illustrate the writers' attempts to cope with the unusual situation or to give meaning to it. For the older authors like Zweig, exile lends itself to a review of one's life and to disclosure of the historical trends that lead to the catastrophe. Heinrich Mann's memoirs, *Ein Zeitalter wird besichtigt* (*An Epoch Is Reviewed*, 1946), and Klaus Mann's *The Turning Point* (1942) belong here, too.

Upon examining exile literature one notices the exiled writers' predilection for history. There are some basic reasons for this. History contributed many exemplary figures and situations to which the reader could compare himself or in which he could identify his own predicament. Novels about Napoleon could thus demonstrate a dictator's rise to power but at the same time show his final doom and the suffering brought to an entire continent. History also supplied these writers with heroes who had successfully resisted suppression and preserved their dignity as human beings. On the other hand, an author could use history to detach himself completely from the persecution and the politics of his nation and thus move away from the historical present into the relief of the historical past.

In his plays *Mother Courage and Her Children* (1938–1939), *Galileo* (1937–1938), and in his novel *Die Geschäfte des Herrn Julius Caesar* (*The Business Dealings of Mr. Julius Caesar*, 1938–

1939) Brecht creates parables involving historical figures and events which relate to the present. In exile, Thomas Mann completed his Joseph novels *Joseph in Egypt*, *Joseph the Provider*, and published his ingenious Goethe novel *The Beloved Returns*. Heinrich Mann achieved a new sophistication of his narrative work in his novels *Young Henry of Navarre* (1935) and *Die Vollendung des Königs Henri Quatre* (*The Perfection of Henry of Navarre*, 1938). His nephew Klaus Mann (1906–1949) completed a novel on Tchaikovsky called *Pathetic Symphony* (1935). Other works deserving mention include Hermann Broch's *The Death of Virgil*, Stefan Zweig's *Erasmus of Rotterdam* (1935) and *The Right to Heresy* (*Castellio gegen Calvin*, 1936), Bruno Frank's (1887–1945) *Cervantes* (1934), Hermann Kesten's *Ferdinand and Isabella* (1936) and *König Philipp der Zweite* (*King Philip II*, 1938), Franz Werfel's *The Song of Bernadette*, Robert Neumann's (1897–) *Struensee* (1935), Ludwig Marcuse's *Ignatius von Loyola* (1937), and finally Lion Feuchtwanger's *Der falsche Nero* (*The Wrong Nero*, 1936), a biting satire on Adolf Hitler.

The novel, as the most translatable genre, dominated exile literature. Lyric poetry found it more difficult to establish itself in foreign countries. Max Herrmann-Neisse (1886–1941) wrote one of the first collections of exile poetry, *Um uns die Fremde* (*Strangeness around Us*, 1936). Karl Wolfskehl (1869–1948) also wrote a small volume of poems, *Sang aus dem Exil* (*Song out of Exile*, 1950, posthumously), in New Zealand "from the last island reef on the earth." Wolfskehl, a former member of the circle surrounding Stefan George, expressed the sufferings of his exile in formally perfect stanzas. The Jewish poet considered himself the representative of German culture and tradition whom the eternal foes of the spirit had banned to the opposite end of the world.

Johannes R. Becher (1891–1958), an expressionist poet and early follower of communism, emigrated to Russia where he wrote several books of poetry. He authored the national anthem for communist Germany upon his return to East Germany after the war, where he served as the minister of culture from 1954 until his death. His collection *Deutschland ruft* (*Germany Calls*, 1942) displays a stronger militant character than Wolfskehl's poems. Becher's poems are documents of politically committed literature in accordance with his conviction that the problem of art is not one of form but rather one of ideology.

By far the most powerful and aggressive poetry in resistance to the Nazi movement came from Brecht (1898–1956). His fame as a playwright has always overshadowed his great achievements as a poet. Brecht's political poetry continues the tradition of Heinrich Heine, who also lived in political exile a century before Brecht. Brecht's poetry of these years combines the fervor of political commitment with a genuinely strong artistic talent for form and a keen, biting, and witty intellect. The poet left Germany a few days after the Nazis seized power and then made his home-in-exile in Svendborg, Denmark, where he remained for the next six years. He later escaped the advancing German armies in an adventurous and risky flight to California via Sweden, Finland, and Russia. From there he continued the long battle against fascism. He wrote his best plays while outside of Germany. Some of his works did, however, find their way into Germany. Many were smuggled into the country between book covers bearing the inconspicuous title *Practical Guide for First Aid*. Other exile literature entered Germany camouflaged as travel brochures or as packages of Lipton's Tea. With the outbreak of the war, Brecht's *Svendborg Poems* (1939) were published. They attacked the Nazis' war preparations and encouraged the working class to resist the Nazi regime. Brecht's admiration for the Soviet Union and her outspoken opposition to Fascism became obvious in poems such as "The Carpet Weavers of Kujan-Bulak Honor Lenin," "The Great October," and "The Moscow Workers Take Possession of the Great Metro on April 27, 1935." Almost all of Brecht's poems written between 1933 and 1947 are concerned with the various aspects of life in exile: flight, hunger, humiliation, nostalgia, and impatience. The feelings of the exiled poets found lasting expression in his work.

Brecht's *Flüchtlingsgespräche* (*Discussions among Refugees*, written in 1940–1941, published 1961) comprises one of the most interesting pieces of exile literature. Two German refugees, a physicist and a worker, meet regularly at the Helsingfors railroad station restaurant to philosophize about their lives in Germany, the political changes taking place in their homeland, Marxism, and the experiences of their exile. In these talks Brecht, in the guise of wise humor, sharply attacks the present political and economic condition of the world. The worker proves to be an intelligent and adequate partner for the physicist. The dialogue between the two men is one of the wittiest and most perceptively critical exchanges of dialectical aphorisms in Brecht's work.

Brecht's exile lasted fifteen years. In spite of this obstacle as far as his artistic work is concerned these years were the most satisfying of his entire life. The plays which later established his world fame are practically without exception products of the years of exile: *The Life of Galileo* (1938–1939), *Mother Courage and Her Children* (1938–1939), *The Good Woman of Setzuan* (1938–1939), *Mr. Puntila and His Servant Matti* (1940–1941), and *The Caucasian Chalk Circle* (1943–1945). However, Brecht was already well known as a playwright in Germany before he left the country. He had won the Kleist Prize for his play *Drums in the Night* (1923). His *Three Penny Opera* (1928), modelled after John Gay's *Beggar's Opera* and with music by Kurt Weill, was an international success. After the war, the "opera" played in New York for five consecutive years.

Brecht's insights into the inequity of the social conditions of his country had led him, beginning in 1926, to study Marxism intensively. He considered capitalism the sole cause of all of society's ills, and regarded Communism as the only functional weapon in the fight against capitalism and Fascism. Since 1927 most of his plays served the purpose of teaching the need for transformation of the social system. His dramas became didactic pieces, the stage his podium. The most significant play of this early period, *St. Joan of the Stockyards* (written 1929–1930), takes place in the slaughter yards and meat markets of Chicago. It shows the merciless, inhuman battle of the capitalists who attempt to ruin each other through fraud and unscrupulous stockmarket dealings while outside their closed-down factories, workers are starving and freezing to death. Religion is in league with money. The clergy, paid by the capitalists, constantly alludes to the joys of the world beyond, thus diverting the workers' attention from the misery from which revolution could free them. The heroine comes to the realization that only through the solidarity of the working class and the use of force can the exploitative system be destroyed. However, in a crucial moment she remains trapped by her bourgeois thinking and cannot concede to the use of force. Because of her refusal, the strike fails. As she dies she bewails her unpardonable error. Her punishment is that she must helplessly watch as she is canonized by the capitalists. As in most of his plays, Brecht does not open the eyes of his audience solely through the message of the play. The classic blank verse in which the capitalists talk over their base dealings and the ingenious parodies of passages of Goethe's *Faust* and Schiller's *The Maid of Orleans* are intended to unmask the "cultured" bourgeois world as hollow and deceptive. The irreconcilability of the classes, the necessity of the use of force and of absolute obedience to the party are again the themes of the didactic pieces *The Exception and the Rule* (written 1930) and *The Measures Taken* (1930). Both make Brecht's close association with Communism plain.

Since 1930 numerous theoretical texts have accompanied the production of Brecht's works. They deal with widely varied aspects of the theater: the play itself, the manner of presentation, the actors, the stage backdrop, the movable scenes, the music, the lighting, the curtains, and all technical details. The sole purpose of these theoretical endeavors is to emphasize the intent of Brecht's plays: to convince the viewer that the world can be changed and that there is an urgent need for this change. Brecht attempts to prove, not merely to persuade. He presents the viewer with some exemplary human behavior on which to pass judgment. The viewer is to follow and to evaluate the development of the play, thinking critically, and should never become emotionally involved in the action. All emotional involvement impairs the capability of impartial and relevant reflection. For this reason, Brecht calls his new theater "non-Aristotelian," that is, a theater which does not aim at arousing empathy, at creating illusions, and at catharsis. On the contrary, Brecht's theater demands scrupulous observation, destruction of illusions, and decisions in place of emotions. Brecht tries to alter the habits of the traditional audience which passively observes the events on the stage by, for example, having a poster bearing the inscription "Don't stare so romantically" mounted in the theater. The impression that the action on stage is taking place in the present should never arise. It must always be obvious that a past event (thus "epic" theater) is being portrayed. In *The Exception and the Rule* the actors turn to the onlookers and demand that they follow the behavior of the characters scrupulously:

> Follow the conduct of these people closely:
>
> .   .   .
>
> Even the most petty action, on the surface simple
> Watch it with mistrust! Probe, if it is necessary
> Above all into the ordinary!
> We ask you expressly, don't
> Take what always comes, as natural![4]

In *The Measures Taken* the Communist agitators must make the difficult decision whether to kill a comrade or to risk the failure of the revolution. In this situation they interrupt the action and turn to the audience with the words:

Five minutes, with the pursuers close behind,
We thought about a
Better possibility.
Now you, too, think about
A better possibility.

Epic theater is theater which relates historic events. Just as the Greeks listened calmly to the narrator of an epic, so the onlooker, relaxed and when possible even smoking, should follow the events on the stage with critical distance. The action on the stage is never the account of suspense-filled incidents, but rather the portrayal of human behavior. Often in Brecht's theater the content of a coming scene is made known beforehand, either by means of a narrator or a projected scene title. From the outset a title such as "On June 22, 1663 in the face of the Inquisition Galileo Galilei disavows his theory of the earth's movement," robs the subsequent scene of all the suspense generally directed at its end. In this way the onlooker is not diverted from his primary task, which is to observe the events on stage keenly and reflect on them simultaneously. Familiar with the "what" of the event, he can then concentrate on its "how." There are numerous supplementary epic devices which demand and facilitate the viewer's reflection: charts, statistics, maps, and instructive facts can be projected on screens during the presentation. Thus the onlooker may always compare the event on stage with relevant facts of a similar nature.

An essential component of Brecht's theory is the *Verfremdungseffekt* (alienation effect or V-effect). For Brecht this involves presenting a familiar state of affairs or object in such a manner that it appears in a totally new or unusual light. "A V-effect is necessary in order for a man to be able to recognize his mother as the lover of another man. This occurs, for instance, when a stepfather enters the picture. A V-effect is generated if a man sees one of his teachers under pressure of the law; the teacher is snatched out of a context in which he appeared great and is put into one where he appears small." (Brecht) The possibility of alienation was recognized long before Brecht's time. Hegel maintained: "That which is well known is not understood for the very reason that it is well known," and Shelley remarked: "Poetry lifts the veil from the hidden beauty of the world, and makes familiar objects be as if they were not familiar."

The V-effect functions solely by intensifying the onlooker's perception. V-effects create distance between the onlooker and the action on the stage; they show a subject in a remote impartial light. These effects may be of various sorts. Simply to set the action back into an historical era or to transfer it to another part of the world is to alienate it. Brecht makes plentiful use of both of these possibilities: his plays take place in Chicago, Setzuan, India, in the Caucasus, on the Mississippi, during the Thirty Years' War; but only seldom in Germany or in the present. And alienation penetrates even into the language. In this realm the V-effects, through surprising verbal transformations of clichés, often lend unexpected insight into evidence which unmasks the speaker or the social conditions. Mother Courage's honesty becomes questionable when she protests, "I don't take war booty," and adds, "not at that price." The poverty of the clergy is proved a falsehood in the lines: "In the trial of the Barefoot Beggar Monks of San Stefano against the Needy Nuns of San Barabas the damages demanded by the Barefoot Beggar Monks are set at seven million." Even through a seemingly trivial alteration, such as the changing of a punctuation mark, Brecht sometimes produces a significant alienation effect.

The third vital point of Brecht's theory involves his views about dramatic art, which he sets down in the essays "The Street Scene" and "New Technique of Dramatic Art" (both written in 1940). His reforms were revolutionary in the field, yet at the same time had a limited effect. Brecht turned sharply away from method acting, espoused by the Russian director Konstantin Stanislavsky (1863–1938), which had as its ideal the complete identification of the actor with his role. For Stanislavsky the best theater is that which lets the onlooker forget that he is sitting in a theater, and whose effect is such that the viewer is overcome by the illusion that a real event is taking place before his eyes which he experiences as an unnoticed witness. In his poem "About Everyday Theater" (written 1930) Brecht pokes fun at the mysterious transformation of an actor into a king which supposedly takes place between the dressing room and the stage. Nevertheless, today Stanislavsky's method is still generally considered binding for most commercial productions.

Good theater according to Brecht never lets the spectator forget for one instant that he is in a theater. The hypnotic effect which the *Einfühlungstheater* can have on the onlooker is for Brecht a disaster since it eliminates critical observation. Using the model of a street scene Brecht makes plain what the actor should accomplish. A traffic accident has occurred; and an eye-witness "demonstrates to a crowd of people how the misfortune happened. The bystanders may not have seen the event, they may not be of his opinion, they may have 'seen it differently'—the essential point is that the demonstrator present the behavior of the driver or the person who has been run over or of both persons in such a way that the bystanders can pass judgment on the accident." Realism is unimportant for this type of presentation. A rapid action which cannot be precisely repeated may be intimated and accompanied by an oral explication. Under no circumstances should the illusion be created that the accident is happening for the second time. "The presentation of the street demonstration has the character of repetition. The event has taken place; here the repetition takes place." The demonstrator points out ways of behavior, actions of the parties concerned, and thus makes it possible for the audience to draw conclusions about the characters of the protagonists. In so doing Brecht reverses the practice of the traditional theater which explains the actions of the heroes through their characters.

The essential point of the demonstrative theater is, however, that the actor's demonstration "has practical social meaning. Whether our street demonstrator means to show that in the case of this or that action of a pedestrian or driver an accident was inevitable whereas in another it was avoidable, or whether he demonstrates in order to clarify the question of guilt—his demonstration aims at a practical goal, it is socially engaged."

Ideally not only the onlooker but also the actor gains a critical distance from the action on stage. The actor who plays a role in a certain way also either hints at or actually indicates the possible alternative to what he is doing. When Brecht was offered the opportunity to manage his own theater with almost unlimited resources in East Berlin after the war, he tried in a few exemplary performances to practice his theories. The results of his work are summarized in the volume *Theater Work* (1952).

Above all, Brecht's theater was a protest against the dusty cultured theater of his time, which staged emotion-packed, hollow classical productions for a middle-class audience. Brecht tried to replace these plays with dramas relevant to and critical of his time. These new plays could not be performed with the conventional apparatus and outdated concepts of the theater. Thus Brecht set himself a threefold task: to write new, relevant plays, to call upon socially conscious actors, and to educate an audience to seek in the theater not epicurean pleasures but insight and understanding.

Among the plays written in exile, *The Private Life of the Master Race* (*Furcht und Elend des Dritten Reiches*, 1938) refers directly to the actuality of Nazi Germany. The realistic scenes, which are based on eye-witness reports and newspaper articles, and which may also be played individually as they describe different circles of people, tell of the growing distrust between the closest relatives, of the increasing brutality of the party's agencies, and of the cowardice and greatness of men. *Life of Galileo* deals with the life of the physicist who furnished the proof of the Copernican theory of the universe. Against its better judgment, the church condemns Galileo's teachings, for the shock of the revised astronomical order would necessarily give rise to social, economic, and religious upheaval. The chance to interest the masses in scientific findings and to free them from the yoke of the oppressor exists for a short while. However, Galileo misjudges the historic hour and disavows his teachings. Progress stands still for an entire century. At the end of his life, which he spends as a prisoner of the Inquisition, Galileo comes to the realization that this act made him a criminal.

In the play *Mother Courage and Her Children*, the camp-following canteen proprietor Anna Fierling, called Mother Courage, trails the Protestant as well as the Catholic troops throughout Europe through the sites of battle operations of the Thirty Years' War with the intent of making money from the war. Whereas her main concern is to make profit and to have her business flourish, the war demands its sacrifice: she loses her two sons and her daughter to the war. At the end of the play, impoverished but no wiser, she continues to follow the troops with her covered wagon.

Galileo and *Courage* are Brecht's most important plays. In them he turns away from the ideological and structural rigidity of his early works. Brecht often calls his later plays parables, and thus indicates that they have retained their didactic character. Both heroes, Galileo and Courage, are negative prototypes. Yet as a result of their vitality they appear likable in spite of all weaknesses. Similarly in *Puntila* the proletarian Matti seems decidedly colorless in contrast to the squire Puntila.

Brecht continues his series of important female characters in the parable *The Good Woman of Setzuan*. Having descended from heaven, the gods find only one good person: the prostitute Shen Te. However, her own goodness is the basis for Shen Te's exploitation by others. In *The Caucasian Chalk Circle* two women fight over a child. The judge does not award the child to its natural mother, but rather to the mother who is better for the child—in this case the servant girl Grusha, who rescued and brought up the baby after it had been abandoned by its wealthy mother. Here Brecht preaches a legal pragmatism which awards all goods and property to the one who can use them to a better end.

In 1947, while a resident of the United States, Brecht was summoned before the House Un-American Activities Committee to defend himself against the suspicion of Communist activity. The minutes of the hearing, of which a tape recording exists, prove Brecht to be a careful and intelligent man who knew precisely how to conduct himself before the jury with such cleverness and apparent naiveté that at the end of the hearing he was actually praised for his exemplary cooperation! Brecht left the U.S.A. immediately after the hearing and arranged his return to Germany by way of Switzerland. In the end he decided to take up Austrian citizenship, to run a theater in East Germany, and to find a West German publisher. Brecht died in East Berlin in 1956 during the rehearsals of *Life of Galileo*. Galileo's cunning, his pragmatism, and the delight he took in thinking are also characteristics of Brecht himself.

Emigration hindered the development of drama. Only in Switzerland could the exiled German playwrights find an adequately large German-speaking public. In the U.S. during the war, Brecht himself had no opportunity to present his plays.

Among the dramatic works written in exile, two in particular, besides Brecht's, deserve mention: Franz Werfel's comedy *Jacobowsky and the Colonel* (1944) and Carl Zuckmayer's play *The Devil's General* (1946). *Jacobowsky and the Colonel* centers around a colonel of the Polish army and a Polish Jew, who are hunted by the ever-advancing German troops as they flee together through France. Necessity rather than desire brings the two together. The highly reserved and almost anti-Semitic attitude of the colonel is transformed little by little into unwilling admiration for the ingenuity of the Jews, whose presence of mind continually pulls them through seemingly hopeless situations. The comical effects of the play lie not only in the situations but also in the witty dialogue and the contrasting characters of the two men: the cheerful and humorous modesty of the basically superior Jew as compared to the pompous boastfulness of the aristocratic officer. The film version with Danny Kaye as Jacobowsky was equally successful.

Carl Zuckmayer (1896–   ) ironically was dismissed from his post as dramatic producer of the theater at Kiel because of his "complete incompetence as an artist." Following his dismissal, he wrote a comedy in the dialect of his home district on the Rhine entitled *Der fröhliche Weinberg* (*The Gay Vineyards*, 1925) for which he received the highly esteemed Kleist prize. He has since published numerous plays including the well known *The Captain of Köpenick* (1930). Zuckmayer's immediate success hinged heavily on his realistic and down-to-earth characters. He thus broke with the tradition of the extremely stylized characters often found on the stage of late Expressionism. Although not a renovator of the theater, Zuckmayer surely stands among the most effective creators of stage drama.

He left Berlin in 1936 and fled to the United States of America. There, during the final years of the war, he wrote *The Devil's General*. Zuckmayer's sensitivity and insight enabled him to create a genuine and convincing picture of the mood reigning within Germany without having lived there himself during the last Nazi years. The play centers around a strong character, General Harras of the German air force. He openly despises the Nazi regime and continually scoffs at their twisted *Weltanschauung*. The play presents the last days of the hero, who is constantly observed by the SS. A feeling of threat and dread, caused by the eternal presence, secret or actual, of the all-powerful authorities of the state pervades the play. In the midst of a group of fascinating personalities Zuckmayer places Harras, a person in conflict. His human qualities make him the ideal of many younger officers who serve the regime only because Harras remains their general. Thus, in his desire to exclude politics from his life Harras serves the purpose of the "devil" through his non-commitment. Despite the power of his engaging personality Harras remains as controversial a character as the sabotaging engineer-officer who purposely disables the planes which the pilots, often his personal friends, take into the air. At the end of the drama, the two men are placed in irreconcilable opposition. The saboteur battles against the all-consuming violence of the criminal regime but must employ violence himself and become the murderer of his comrades. The general, bound by his oath, fulfills the duties of the soldier, and his example involuntarily lends support to the ruling powers.

After the war, the play caused heated discussion about the attitude of the military during the war. Zuckmayer did not make accusations, as did many of the returning emigrants. Instead he tried to present the very difficult and frustrating situation of those who remained in the Reich.

The hopes of the emigrants that Hitler's rule would only be a short, insane period of history were not realized. After 1940, the United States became the major haven of emigration and only a small number among them, Thomas Mann, Feuchtwanger, and Werfel, continued to be successful. A great number of exiles found Mexico a hospitable nation. For most of the emigrants the exile lasted until several years after the war. Some returned to Germany immediately following its defeat, others had established roots in their new environments and had little desire to return and many writers died before they could see Germany again. Some of the best, overcome by fear or sorrow, took their own lives. Stefan Zweig, a world-famous author both before and during his exile, wrote in his farewell note: "Having seen the land of my own language decline and my spiritual homeland, Europe, destroy herself, I no longer, at the age of sixty, have the strength for the tremendous effort of building up my life again. My energies have been exhausted by the long years of wandering spent as a man without a homeland. I therefore think it is time to end a life that was devoted entirely to intellectual work and in which my own personal freedom and that of mankind was always considered the world's greatest gift."

II

Among the numerous emigrants, Thomas Mann, the Nobel laureate of 1929, became Germany's most prominent literary representative. In 1933, Mann took up temporary residence in Switzerland, although at that time he did not yet consider himself in exile. He carefully avoided the clubs formed by the emigrants and never attended any of their meetings. His condemnation of Nazi Germany, long awaited by the less famous emigrants, did not come until 1936. Then, in a letter to the editor of the *Neue Zürcher Zeitung* (February 3, 1936) Mann joined the emigrant writers and denounced the Nazis. A few months later the Nazis revoked Mann's citizenship, and the University of Bonn informed him that his honorary doctorate had also been revoked. Mann took this opportunity to write an impassioned letter (New Year's Day, 1937) to the Dean of the School of Liberal Arts in Bonn which circulated secretly throughout Germany under the title "Ein Briefwechsel" ("An Exchange of Letters"). Today this letter ranks among the most clairvoyant documents of resistance against Nazi Germany. In it Mann urged the civilized elements of the "other Germany" to rise up, to withstand the brutal suppression of freedom and to fight the forces of anti-intellectualism and destruction. With this appeal to his countrymen, Mann's status as an emigrant became irreversible. He left Europe, becoming an American citizen in 1944. The man who, in 1918, wrote the conservative *Betrachtungen eines Unpolitischen (Reflections of a Non-Political Man)* now became the champion of freedom and political commitment. Frequently throughout the years of Nazi rule, Mann attacked the political developments in Germany. His numerous essays, his voluminous correspondence, and especially his radio speeches broadcast during the war years distinguish him as the most acid and bitter foe of Fascism and, at the same time, as a staunch supporter and protector of German intellectualism and humanism.

For this reason, the men and women who hoped to establish a new democracy in Germany after World War II looked to Thomas Mann for leadership and support during the period of reconstruction. Walter von Molo (1880–1958), a historical novelist, who had retired from public life during the Nazi rule, wrote an open letter to Mann (August 13, 1945) asking him to return and assist his countrymen. Molo's letter, which claimed that the majority of Germans had stood in silent opposition to the atrocities of the past decade, stirred considerable sensation in Germany. Several days later (August 18, 1945) a Munich paper published an article by Frank Thiess (1890–   ), a novelist who had remained in Germany throughout the war as a mute opponent of the Fascist rule. The article, entitled "Die Innere Emigration" ("The Inner Emigration"), enthusiastically invited those who had left their country to return home. Thiess pointed out that the two groups of emigrants— those who had remained in Germany without collaborating ("inner emigration"), and those who actually left the country ("outer emigration")—should unite in the enormous task of reconstruction. He also made it clear that he considered it more difficult to have stayed within Germany opposing the regime than to have cursed the Nazis in radio messages from the safe shores of America. In October of that same year, Mann's cutting reply, an open letter entitled

"Warum ich nicht zurückkehre" ("Why I do not return"), revealed the emigrant writer's extreme bitterness. Mann contended that the entire German intelligentsia should have emigrated in 1933 and expressed his disagreement and disgust with artists who continued to work under Hitler. The letter contains Mann's controversial statement: "It may be superstition, but books that could be printed in Germany between 1933 and 1945 are, in my eyes, less than worthless and not good to touch. The odor of blood and shame adheres to them. They should all be reduced to pulp."

This unfair observation as well as Thomas Mann's insistence that in his eyes there was no "inner emigration," heightened the tension between those who had remained in the homeland and the emigrants. Frank Thiess' reply appeared in the form of a sharp polemic, "Abschied von Thomas Mann" ("Farewell to Thomas Mann"), in which he accused Mann of self-righteousness and ruthless ignorance. It is not surprising that the debate over the guilt of the German people under National Socialism was carried out with such rigor. An impartial article by Wilhelm Hausenstein (1882–1957) "Bücher ohne Schande" ("Books without Shame"), appeared in many journals. Hausenstein, an art historian and journalist, had remained in Germany but had been forbidden to publish any of his works. In this piece he comments on the many veiled anti-Nazi novels, articles, scholarly works, and translations of foreign literature which were published during the war years at great personal risk to both authors and publishers.

Shortly after the Nazis seized power all literature became subject to an official censor. To take a stand against the party publicly, expected by many emigrants of those authors who had remained in Germany, was totally impossible. Criticism of the system could only be found between the lines, or under the mask of historical allegory. The party did not hesitate to nip any courageous expression of resistance and opposition in the bud. In two important speeches to university students in Munich (1933 and 1935), Ernst Wiechert warned against anti-Semitism, the mad ambitions of the Führer, and implored the academic youth to stand bravely against the despot. As late as 1937 he publicly read his short story Der weiße Büffel oder Von der großen Gerechtigkeit (The White Buffalo or On Great Justice) which remained unpublished under the Nazis. The story, set in the legendary past of India, relates the struggle of truth and spirit against falsehood and force, and is an admirable piece of literary camouflage. In 1938 Wiechert was arrested by the *Gestapo* and sent to the notorious concentration camp Buchenwald. Following his release, Wiechert wrote a shocking description of his days in the camp, *Der Totenwald* (*The Forest of the Dead*), which he buried in his garden and published in 1946. Wiechert's rank as an author is widely disputed today. The desire of most of his heroes to flee from the active world into the tranquillity of nature seems, to the modern audience, a strange and illusory flight from reality. In addition, Wiechert's language appears far too lofty and overdone to the essentially realistic and clear-thinking postwar generation. Nevertheless, his high moral rank remains undisputed. Embittered by criticism of his work and by the development of the postwar era, Wiechert emigrated to Switzerland where he lived until his death.

The novelist and philosopher Reinhold Schneider (1903–1958), banned in 1942 from further writing, had previously written a large number of historical novels. Schneider circumvented this restriction and produced smaller and usually religiously toned works which were printed in secret. He camouflaged his clearest accusations against the persecution of his fellow citizens in historical fiction. *Las Casas vor Karl V* (*Las Casas Appears before Charles V*, 1938) relates the story of Las Casas, the Catholic priest and "Father of the Indians" who travels to Spain to bring charges to the emperor against the slavery and extirpation brought upon the American Indians by the conquistadors' feelings of superiority towards the "lower" race. We witness the fight of an individual who dares to resist a powerful apparatus of the government and a dangerous military organization. The book was generally recognized as a protest against the mass murder of the Jews.

The Baltic author Werner Bergengruen (1892–1964), a close friend of Schneider, also fought against National Socialism. The belief in a healthy, intact world, the confidence in man's salvation from fear and guilt, and the assurance of God's grace stand as main themes in his many works. His characters "are born, fall into guilt, and finally surrender themselves to God's mercy." In 1937 Bergengruen was banned from the *Reichsschrifttumskammer* because his publications were "not suited to help build German culture." Until then the author had concentrated mainly on historical novels. During the Third Reich he continued writing in this genre and authored two impressive novels which reflected aspects of National Socialism. *A Matter of Conscience* (*Der Großtyrann und das Gericht*, 1935) takes place during the Italian renaissance. The story centers around "the temptation of the powerful and the easy seduction of the weak and threatened." A dictator orders his secret police to investigate a murder he himself has committed. He also demands that the murderer be found within three days. Suspicion and distrust fall over the city. The fear of the dictator and the ever-present secret police demoralize the people. They spy on each other and make insinuations against their neighbors. Finally a person who is not guilty tries to free the city from the growing feeling of guilt by confessing the crime. A lengthy judgment scene at the end of the novel leads to the conclusion that everyone in the city bears part of the guilt, but the city tyrant bears the largest part "because you tried to raise yourself above humanity and to be an equal to God." This novel, expressing opposition to dictatorship, is still suppressed in Spain today.

A second novel, Am Himmel wie auf Erden (In Heaven as on Earth, 1940) deals with the theme of man's fear of death. When a flood is predicted for the year 1524 an uncontrollable fear of the end of the world overcomes the people of the neighboring cities of Berlin-Kölln in Brandenburg. The elector Joachim I tries to quell the rising terror by forbidding further circulation of the prophecy as well as all precautionary measures. His measures fail to subdue the panic and in a crucial moment he as well as his subjects fall victim to fear. Eventually each character recognizes that nothing can dispel his fear, and that only he who recognizes his fate as the will of God and who unquestioningly yields to God's mercy can conquer fear. The mood of an entire population on the eve of a great catastrophe is convincingly portrayed in this novel, which had frightening relevance in the war years.

After the war Bergengruen's The Last Captain of Horse (1952) was a huge success. It is a book full of anecdotes, told in a cheerfully philosophical tone, which many readers consider his most beautiful work because of its serene wisdom and deep humor. Bergengruen's novellas Die Feuerprobe (The Test of Fire, 1933), Die drei Falken (The Three Falcons, 1937), Der spanische Rosenstock (The Spanish Rosebush, 1940), Das Tempelchen (The Small Temple, 1950), and many others are among the most popular prose of the twentieth century. The author has collected his best poems in the volume Die heile Welt (The World Intact, 1950), a title which expresses Bergengruen's attitude toward the world.

Jochen Klepper (1903–1942), a Protestant theologian, also stood in opposition to the political system. Married to a Jewish woman, Klepper and his family committed suicide during the war. His most important achievement consists of hymns, collected in the volume *Kyrie* (1938). His greatest success was the historical novel *Der Vater* (*The Father*, 1937) which portrays the Prussian soldier-king Frederick William I, founder of the Prussian military power, bowing humbly before the will of God. The novel contains direct criticism of the Third Reich; it constantly mentions the old Prussian principles of justice, propriety, faith, and honor, to which, to be sure, the Nazis also liked to refer, but which they totally perverted. Klepper's diary from the years 1932–1942, published posthumously under the title *Unter dem Schatten Deiner Flügel* (*Under the Shadow of Your Wings*, 1956), reveals his oppressive inner doubts and the agonizing daily misery of a politically persecuted man.

Albrecht Haushofer (1903–1945), professor of politics in Berlin, joined the Resistance which had as its goal the assassination of Hitler. After the unsuccessful attempt at a takeover, Haushofer was arrested and murdered by the SS shortly before the allied troops marched in. A notebook containing the *Moabiter Sonette* (*Moabit Sonnets*, 1946), written during his imprisonment, was found on his body. The sonnets, a poetic documentation of the German Resistance, deal with the difficulties of life in prison, the forces of conscience, and the development of guilt. The consciousness of a doomed existence is recognizable in all of the poems.

While a soldier in Italy, Rudolf Hagelstange (1912–   ) wrote a group of sonnets *Venezianisches Credo* (*Venetian Credo*, 1945) which were printed illegally in Verona. The poems contain sharp accusation of the inhumanity of the dictatorship, and at the same time, the consolation that a new spirit is reawakening in the nation. The sonnet, with its strict format, was a literary form often used by the Resistance. To Haushofer as well as to Hagelstange, it seemed in its very strictness to be the form which could most effectively contrast the chaotic forces of the time.

The hymns of Rudolf Alexander Schröder (1878–1962) were, for the most part, circulated illegally. Schröder, an architect from Bremen, was one of the most productive lyricists of the century and possessed a masterful command of many poetic forms including the ode, the sonnet, the elegy, the ballad, and the hymn. His poems, in content as well as in form, are not specifically modern but rather consciously set in the context of Western tradition. His numerous translations of Homer, Virgil, and Horace, as well as Racine and Shakespeare, earned Schröder a reputation as a classicist. The work of the second half of his life is characterized by a return to the Christian faith. *Ein Lobgesang* (A *Song of Praise*, 1937, expanded 1939) adds to the wealth of Protestant hymns. *Die Ballade vom Wandersmann* (*The Ballad of the Wanderer*, 1937) is a frank renunciation of the unspeakable horrors of Nazism. In a totally deformed world the wanderer of the poem finds only hate, cruelty, and baseness. Well into the war years R. A. Schröder dared to recite his poems in public. When the Nazis forbade him to appear publicly, he still managed, as a lecturer of the Lutheran church, to speak during church services, mostly to students.

Today we possess two extensive anthologies which grew out of resistance to National Socialism: *De Profundis* (1946), edited by Gunter Groll, and *An den Wind geschrieben: Lyrik der Freiheit 1933-1945* (*Written to the Wind: Poetry of Freedom 1933-1945*, 1960), edited by Manfred Schlösser. In both volumes the intensity of the spiritual resistance is visible as well as the broad social spectrum of the Resistance itself.

National Socialism was also bravely defied in several literary periodicals. By far the most candid assaults on those in power were carried out by the renowned *Deutsche Rundschau* under its publisher Rudolf Pechel, who had an early opportunity to become acquainted with the leaders of National Socialism. An encounter with Adolf Hitler and the first murders of political opponents drove Pechel into an inner emigration. The men of the political Resistance frequented his home and his office. Pechel turned down an opportunity to emigrate, as he was convinced that he would be able to fight National Socialism more effectively from within Germany. The sharpest attacks on the Fascists are found in his periodical after 1937. The criticism was mostly clothed in the form of criticism of the political and social conditions in Russia, for example in the articles "Sibirien" ("Siberia," Sept. 1937), "Bei Dr. Leete" ("With Dr. Leete," Aug. 1941), and "Stalins Ende" ("The End of Stalin," Nov. 1941). The readers of the magazine knew well they had only to substitute the name *Gestapo* for *GPU* and Hitler for Stalin in order to find the precise description of the terror and horrifying oppression in Germany. Articles about dictators of other countries, especially "Francisco Solano Lopez" (April, 1941), were also direct criticism of Hitler. In 1942 the *Deutsche Rundschau* was forced to cease publication and Pechel himself was dragged through prisons and concentration camps until the end of the war. Pechel has made the most important articles from his periodical available again in the collection *Deutsche Rundschau: Acht Jahrzehnte deutschen Geisteslebens* (*Deutsche Rundschau: Eight Centuries of German Intellectual Life*, 1961).

Gottfried Benn's position in the course of the political events is a great deal more difficult to judge. He has repeatedly maintained that his position is completely non-political. Yet the opinions he expressed with regard to the daily political events at the beginning of the Nazi era have led to Benn's incurring displeasure on all sides. When, in 1948, he was asked by the publisher of the highly respected periodical *Merkur* to present himself once again to the literary public, Benn replied: "When one has been, as I have been, publicly labeled a swine by the Nazis, an imbecile by the Communists, an intellectual prostitute by the democrats, a renegade by the emigrants, and a pathological nihilist by the religious, one is not so keen on breaking back into this public." ("Letter from Berlin, July 1948").

When the National Socialists came to power, Benn did not recognize their danger immediately but expected a revival of his nation. He did not even withdraw from the Prussian Academy of Writers, to which he had been elected in 1932, when the Jewish members were expelled. For almost a year he glorified the new National Socialist state which held him up as a shining example before the foreign literary world. The extent to which Benn fell prey to the fatal irrationality is shown by his famous essay "Züchtung I" ("Biological Selection I," 1933) in which he hailed the totalitarian state. Benn understood the Nazis' questionable *Führer*-theory as a spiritual principle, as the embodiment of a fundamental creative power. He accused the German intellectuals of failing to recognize the world's historical hour and of failing to be part of it. In his delusion, Benn did not recognize the very primitiveness of the Nazis' racial theory. He believed in a universal, historic turning point, which would be brought about by an anthropological transformation of his people. In this context, man is no longer to be interpreted as a rational being; irrationality is regarded as his most unique characteristic, and man is placed within a racial and mythical continuum. Benn felt he was witnessing the birth of the Expressionists' visionary "new man" brought about by biological selection. He declared racial purity to be the unavoidable precondition for great cultural achievement. Without the strict laws against mixed

377

marriage laid down by Moses, the "greatest eugenicist of all peoples," the development of Christian monotheism would not have been conceivable.

In an April, 1933, radio broadcast Benn read his essay "The New State and the Intellectuals." In it he maintained that history always proceeds violently at its turning points. A new biological type appears which forcefully reshapes the world, in the process destroying many of the antiquated structures. It would be wrong to see in Benn's statements the questionable attempt to justify the violent acts of the Nazis. His picture of history is substantially more complex. He erred by placing the daily political events of the early years of National Socialism within a context of world history into which they do not fit. A study of Benn's position makes it especially clear why a number of expressionist poets turned to totalitarian systems— Fascism and also Marxism-Communism—either for their entire lives or temporarily. The totalitarian systems seemed to do away with the isolation of the individual which was especially strongly felt by the poets. They placed the isolated man into the longed-for community of the nation as a whole (*Volksgemeinschaft*) or of the commune (*Kollektiv*).

Here the way seemed to be paved for a solution to several central problems which had stood in the foreground since the turn of the century. The feeling had generally spread that the powerful Western cultural tradition, to which the poets considered themselves heir, was no longer a blessed wealth, but a tormenting burden under the weight of which fresh creative power could hardly unfold. Expressionism had made an attempt to loosen the bonds of this tradition linguistically as well as formally. But added to the burden of tradition was that of the intellect. Only since Schiller, and at the very latest, since Kleist, had it been clear what devastating consequences consciousness, that is, reflection, can have for the natural grace of man. Intellect seen as an "incurable wound" (Georg Kaiser), as the "anti-luck" ("Gegenglück"; Benn), became a leading literary theme. The artist, bearer of the intellect and thus disabled in a special sense, felt ever more pushed out of the community of the unintellectual bourgeois world into a painful isolation from which he longed for the "pleasures of an ordinary life," a feeling reflected in Thomas Mann's novellas *Tonio Kröger*, *The Hungry*, and Kafka's *The Hunger Artist*. In Heinrich Mann's novella *Pippo Spano* true natural experience is no longer possible for the artist. The ever-present reflection transforms all normal emotions into the material for artistic creation. Clearly, the writer longs for the original vitality and the ecstatic sensuality and brutality of the Renaissance man Pippo Spano.

Different routes have been taken to break out of this isolation imposed by the intellect. They include the attempt to leave the Western world of tradition in order to find instinctive happiness close to nature on far continents or on islands (for example, the poems "Alaska" and "Palau" by Benn, and "Nightwatch Red" by Ernst Wilhelm Lotz). Another escape route is to search for release from this isolation in sensual and sexual spheres. One can read Brecht's play *Baal* from this viewpoint. All the routes end in the area of longing, all regress to the pre-intellectual first stages of human existence—water, swamp, spermatozoa. This mood is prominent in Brecht's early "water-poetry," especially in his poem "On Swimming in Rivers and Lakes," and in Benn's "Gesänge I" ("Songs I") and "Am Brückenwehr II" ("On the Bridge II").

Since the intellect was regarded as the essential dilemma, it appeared completely correct to Benn in his radio speech, to hail the very loss of intellectual freedom which others deplored. Overcoming isolation through negation of the intellect and through integration into the mythically conceived national community seemed a fortunate possibility to Benn. He interpreted the outbreak of the new generation into the irrational, into the instinctive, into the uncontemplated act, as a positive and necessary revolution in the struggle against the worn-out European intellect, whose crisis, according to Benn, seemed to have reached its climax. It is Benn's personal tragedy that he sensed the Expressionists' new man in the so-called new biological type, and that he saw a heroism in the Nazis which they did not possess.

To the emigrant authors, Benn's behavior was completely incomprehensible. From his exile in France in May, 1933, Klaus Mann wrote Benn a letter which Benn subsequently printed in his autobiographical account *Doppelleben* (*Double Life*, 1950). In retrospect Benn recognized that the younger man had judged the situation more clearly and comprehensively than he himself had. In his "Answer to a Literary Emigrant" (1933) Benn offered as a reason for not having emigrated, aside from his agreement with the new state, his strong attachment to his nation. His words once again reflect the longing of a lonely man for the security of the community. Benn replied that it would have been impossible for him to close himself off from this nation. "I can try to guide it, as far as lies in my power, in the direction I should like to see followed; but if I failed, it would still be my people. People means much! My intellectual and economic existence, my language, my life, my human relations, the sum total of my brain—all this I owe to my people."[5]

During the first two years of Nazi rule, which he experienced in Berlin, Benn became conscious of his monumental error. Not prepared to leave Germany, Benn coined the phrase: "The army is the aristocratic form of emigration." In 1935 he joined the army in which he had previously served as a doctor. The National Socialists too had a change of heart. They accused him in various publications of being a decadent Expressionist and a slanderer of his race because of his love-affair with the Jewish poetess Else Lasker-Schüler. Although he had not published anything since 1936, the *Reichsschrifttumskammer* formally removed his name from the list of acceptable writers and forbade him to publish.

During these years Benn continued his "double life" as doctor and poet. In his creative work during the war his rejection of the new power appears even sharper after his earlier affirmation of it. His notes and poetry from the years 1940–1944 are the plainest and most outspoken exposés of the Nazis that were written during the Third Reich. They appeared after 1948, as Benn's reputation began to spread over Europe. The poem "Monolog" (1943), printed privately and sent to his friends, and his essay "Kunst und Drittes Reich," ("Art and the Third Reich," 1941) reflect the disgust which seized Benn in the face of the events in Germany. The essay "Block II, Zimmer 66" ("Block II, Room 66," 1943–44) describes his life in the military and reveals Benn as a critical, clear-sighted analyst of the decadence of the National Socialist power which surrounded him.

In the first years after the war Benn's works were barred from publication in Germany. After 1948, when he came back into public life, his significant rank as a poet was recognized. Benn's high intelligence, his elegaic bearing, and his artistic command of form made him the most dominant poet of the first decade after the war. The essay "Probleme der Lyrik" ("Problems of Poetry," 1951) summarizes Benn's concept of the essence of modern poetry. In his numerous volumes of verse—*Statische Gedichte* (*Static Poems,* 1948), *Fragmente* (*Fragments,* 1951), *Destillationen* (*Distillations,* 1953), *Aprèslude* (1955), and *Primäre Tage* (*Primary Days,* 1958) —Benn's pessimism turns increasingly into mourning, suffering, and lamentation of loneliness. At the same time, the form of his poems becomes more lucid, as Benn is guided by the desire to replace the German penchant for mythical depth and romantic obscurity with Latin stability and clarity. Benn can without doubt be named, along with Rilke, the most important German poet of the century.

Today Thomas Mann's observation that there was no inner emigration stands refuted. A multitude of writings bears witness to the courageous opposition of German intellectuals against National Socialism.

III

The military, social, and economic collapse of Germany in 1945 may well have been the most complete and devastating of its long history. After the unconditional surrender, Germany was faced with the demoralization resulting from twelve years of Nazi rule: fifty million people killed, seven million of them Germans; the major cities in ruin; a 25 percent loss of state territories in the east of the country; the expulsion of about ten million Germans from the eastern provinces; the political division of the country; and the military occupation. Even more hopeless, however, was the enormous guilt the nation felt for the rise of the Nazi regime and its atrocious crimes against humanity.

Postwar literature must be seen against this background.[6] Among the young men and women returning from the battlefields, the penitentiaries, and prisoner-of-war camps were the writers who would climb to literary fame several years later. Their hopelessness and disillusionment found exemplary expression in Wolfgang Borchert's (1921–1947) play *The Man Outside* (1947). It was staged a day after Borchert's death and subsequently became the most successful play immediately following the war. The younger generation could easily identify with Beckmann, the hero of the play, who returns from war and finds himself incapable of readjusting to civilian life and of finding any meaning in what happened during and after the war. Borchert, also the author of a number of impressive short stories, was court-martialed twice and threatened with the death sentence. He left the penitentiary at the end of the war reduced to a physical wreck and died two years later.

Critics have often called these poets members of a new "lost generation." Their lives and ideas had been misguided and abused. They were physically worn out and psychologically battered; their education proved to be worthless. Particularly their concept of history had been distorted. Works of Thomas Mann, Franz Kafka, Heinrich Heine, Bertolt Brecht and dozens of other leading authors were not available to them. Foreign literature, if permitted entrance at all, was admitted only after a highly selective screening. In fact, as the war continued books became increasingly scarce due to the paper shortage. By the end of the war Germany was an intellectual vacuum.

It is not surprising then that writers and literary historians have labeled 1945 the "literary zero point." However, the widespread use of this term has led to much misunderstanding. The term seems to suggest that the year 1945 marks the beginning of a new German literature created from scratch by the young "lost generation." On the contrary, it was some time before new voices became discernible. The main action on the literary scene immediately after the war was centered around the books of foreign writers. These served to familiarize the German literary audience with the developments which had taken place in the world of literature during the German cultural eclipse.

Among the foreign writers, the work of Ernest Hemingway had by far the strongest and most immediate impact on the younger generation. The American writer's vigorous individualism, his zest for independence, and his portrayal of true and simple heroism evoked the admiration of a generation which had been trained to follow orders or to subordinate themselves to the mystical *Volksgemeinschaft*. In addition, Hemingway's matter-of-fact diction provided a striking and refreshing contrast to the emotional and bombastic style prevalent in the years following the Nazi takeover. His influence can be seen chiefly in the genre of the short story, which soon became the preferred form of expression of the postwar writers of prose. This genre lent itself well to the literary beginnings of the young writers not yet certain enough of their artistic talent to tackle the more difficult and complex genre of the novel, which became more widespread in Germany a decade after the war. The most productive novelist of the young generation, Heinrich Böll (1917–), made his start with short stories of high literary caliber. The modern short story became the heir apparent to the more rigorously structured novella which had flourished in German literature throughout the nineteenth century and in the twentieth century until World War II. The short story reflects the most obvious and most powerful foreign influence on postwar German literature.

It is very difficult to trace any direct personal influence on the young writers aside from that of Hemingway. The impact of foreign literature was of a more general nature. The young writers were gradually exposed to various literary techniques and learned a great deal about themes and ideas in contemporary world literature. Similarly, they were also introduced to previously unknown aesthetic concepts and, most importantly, became acquainted with the high standards of literature outside of Germany.

The strong interest in literary criticism after the close of the war partly arose from the scepticism of the young generation and its need for factual critical analysis. Yet this interest can also be attributed to several outside influences. German professors had always considered themselves literary historians and had been reluctant to function as critics of contemporary literature. But after the war, exposure to the example of the Anglo-American scholar, who usually combines the study of literary history with criticism, began to have an effect in Germany. Today many competent and sensitive critics comment on contemporary literature in leading newspapers such as *Die Zeit, Frankfurter Allgemeine Zeitung, Süddeutsche Zeitung,* and *Die Welt*. Following the example of T. S. Eliot, Ezra Pound, Paul Valéry, Vladimir Majakovskij and many others, the poet-critic combination has become very common among younger German writers. The *poeta doctus* is a widespread phenomenon. Many of the postwar writers hold doctorates or are professors of literature, e.g., Ingeborg Bachmann (1926–), Hans Magnus Enzensberger (1929–), Walter Höllerer (1922–), Walter Jens (1923–), Gerd Gaiser (1908–), Hans Egon Holthusen (1913–), Curt Hohoff (1913–), and Martin Walser (1927–). The poetess Hilde Domin (1912–) has published two books in the field of criticism. In 1959, the Johann Wolfgang Goethe University in Frankfurt established the first chair for poetics in Germany; it has since been held by some of the most outstanding young writers.

Aside from foreign literature, for a number of years literary discussion in Germany centered around the works of the older generation. Thomas Mann's *Doctor Faustus,* Hesse's *Magister Ludi,* Kasack's *The City beyond the River,* Broch's *The Death of Virgil,* Ernst Jünger's *On the Marble Cliffs* (1939), and the religiously toned novels such as Elisabeth Langgässer's (1899–1950) *The Indelible Seal* (1946) and the poetry of the inner emigration dominated the literary scene. The works of the emigrants appeared in Germany. Writers like Kafka were rediscovered by the literary

383

audience, and Brecht began to stage his plays in his East Berlin *Theater am Schiffbauerdamm*. Gottfried Benn was a revered poet. Only later did the young generation decide that it was not willing to adhere to literary traditions and that it needed a fresh start complete with new forms, new themes, and, above all, a new language.

The first rallying point of the young literary generation after the war was Group 47, which received its name from its founding year, 1947. Its beginning was of a political-journalistic nature. The writers Hans Werner Richter (1908–) and Alfred Andersch (1914–), both of the socialist camp, had founded the periodical *Der Ruf* in 1946, in which a lively discussion of all urgent daily problems was carried on. Since both had resisted National Socialism they refused to adhere to the concept of collective guilt. Now they fought against the spirit of obedience which was fostered this time by the occupying powers. The editors expressed open criticism of the numerous administrative measures taken by the military authorities. When in April, 1947, the American military government forbade publication of the magazine, the editors and contributors decided to meet at regular intervals for critical discussions and the presentation of manuscripts.

The circle limited itself to writers who were politically engaged and whose works had been introduced after the war. These writers broke with the traditions before 1933 since they felt that the only possible way to spiritual rebirth lay in an absolute and radical new beginning. Group 47 possessed from the start a program of engagement, which Hans Werner Richter outlined in the following manner: "They wanted under all circumstances to prevent a repetition of that which had happened, and at the same time they wanted to lay the cornerstone of a new democratic Germany, of a better future, and of a new literature which would be conscious of its responsibility in regard to political and social development. They did not consider German journalism and literature without guilt for what had happened. Thus they believed it imperative to begin completely anew with fresh methods, under different conditions, and with better goals."

It was thought necessary at that time to completely weed out the language in order to be able to make a fresh start with those meager resources left unspoiled by the Nazis. Much of the literature of the inner emigration was rejected by Group 47 as mere "calligraphic literature." Wolfgang Weyrauch (1907–) coined the term "literarischer Kahlschlag" ("literary deforestation"), the linguistic renewal of literature. The best example of this language is Günter Eich's (1907–) well-known poem "Inventory," in which the speaker counts his few remaining possessions in the most simple manner, renames them, so to speak, and thus reassures himself of his ownership.

Postwar German literature brought forth a number of talented prose writers. It is mainly in the genre of the novel that the younger generation achieved international recognition. Heinrich Böll, a prizewinner of Group 47, became the most productive author of the postwar era. The central theme of his early work is the senselessness and absurdity of the war, and the chaos which he himself experienced for six years as a soldier on the eastern front. He first published short stories, which had as their content practically without exception episodes from the war and the time immediately following. The first collection of these short stories, *Traveller, If You Come to Spa* (1950), expressed perfectly the mood of the generation of returning soldiers. Even today Böll names the short story as his favorite genre though he has won world-wide recognition as a novelist.

His first novel, *Adam, Where Art Thou?* (1951), depicts in nine sections the experiences of the soldier Feinhals during the last months of the war. In the center of the novel is his encounter with the Jewish teacher Ilona, whom he loves but cannot rescue from execution. He meets death in the moment of his return home at the close of the war. The characters in the novel are shoved about by the horrible forces of the war which they face devoid of understanding. Their passivity is the child of hopelessness. Böll's heroes are mostly simple, average men, not active heroes who take a firm stand against their fate. They are good, but weak and are not able to make their way through this world of violence, cruelty, and deception.

In his next novel, *Acquainted with the Night* (*Und sagte kein einziges Wort*, 1953), Böll portrays the effects of the war on the life of a small family. The marriage of Käte and Fred Bogner breaks up under the pressures of insufficient living space and the absence of love for others. Here Böll uses for the first time a narrative technique which he intensifies in later works. The action of the novel takes place during one weekend—later Böll often concentrates the action into one day or even into a few hours. Numerous flashbacks occurring during this narrow span of time portray a past which turns out to be the second and unquestionably the more important level of the narrative. Husband and wife describe their experiences in alternate chapters, thus two different perspectives are presented. Here, by giving up the one-sided perspective of the narrator, Böll attempts to strengthen the objectivity of his portrayal.

The Unguarded House (1954) describes the situation of two boys whose father died in the war, and who are helplessly now handed over to the "immoral" adult world. Visible for the first time in this novel is Böll's strong criticism of those who, guilty in the war, nevertheless survived, and now continue in the postwar era to rise once again to respected positions.

Billiards at Half Past Nine (1959) takes place in the span of one day in 1958 when three generations of the Fähmel family gather to celebrate the grandfather's birthday. His son, on the occasion of the retreat of the German armies, had blown up the St. Anton Abbey which his father had built, thus destroying the latter's life work. His action was to create a "monument of dust and ruins" to the nameless dead of the senseless war. After the war, however, the abbey is rebuilt precisely according to the old model and thus the symbolic monument is destroyed. Fähmel cannot become reconciled to the shocking guilt of the older generation, whose hypocrisy and opportunism disgust him. In this novel Böll blatantly contrasts the two opposing human prototypes which are characteristic of his work: the buffaloes and the lambs. The former are the powerful, the wealthy, the ruthless, the hypocrites; the latter are the weak, the poor, the helpless, who painfully endure the conditions of present-day Germany. They have not come to terms with the guilt of the Nazi era, but merely look on despairingly as those guilty of all the evils of the Third Reich again seize power in the new state of the postwar era.

Böll's social criticism is substantially stronger in his novel The Clown (1963). The novel's hero experienced the war as a child and the recollection of events is told from a child's point of view. The transformation of his National Socialist mother into a convinced democrat, that of a fanatical leader of the Hitler Youth into a distinguished representative of Catholicism, and the opportune fusion of politics and the Catholic Church set the hero in opposition to his bourgeois family. He takes up the profession of a clown. In this way Böll demonstrates the complete isolation of his hero from a society which only laughs at him and brushes off his critical reproaches as jokes. Again the focus is on Böll's central themes: the National Socialist past of the new authorities, and the political influence of the Catholic Church on the development of postwar

Germany. Once more matters revolve around Böll's typical hero: weak, vulnerable, sensitive, and incapable of repressing his memories or of adjusting to the changed circumstances.

Böll is often criticized for the monotony of his themes. This can, however, be explained by the intensity of his commitment to his helpless contemporaries, lost in the confusion of the economic miracle (*Wirtschaftswunder*). The critical picture of today's society, which Böll portrays in his latest novel *End of a Mission* (1966), is often presented in his numerous short stories in an even more ironic and satirical tone than in the novels. Nevertheless, Böll's weakness lies in his polarization of rich and poor which often appears overly simplified. He portrays the poor as fundamentally better, nobler, and worthier of imitation than the rich. Furthermore, his criticism is too seldom directed at the actual institutions and phenomena which he is attacking—the church, the Bonn Republic, Neo-fascism—but rather at their representatives. Nevertheless, the high moral rank of his commitment remains undisputed.

Böll's language makes his books easily readable. They have been translated into all major languages and because of the author's critical stance towards West Germany are also widely read in Russia and East Germany.

As a young man, Alfred Andersch was a member of the Communist Party and was deported by the Nazis to the Dachau concentration camp. After his release Andersch became a soldier. In *Die Kirschen der Freiheit* (*The Cherries of Freedom*, 1952), he tells the story of his life up until his desertion from the German army in 1944 in Italy. The escape to freedom remained the dominant theme of his works. *Flight to Afar* (*Sansibar oder Der letzte Grund*, 1957) takes place in 1937 in a harbor city where five refugees meet who, for various reasons, want to reach Zanzibar, the symbol of a distant freedom. The novel, with its exceptionally modern structure and treatment of situations and human destinies under the Third Reich, is recognized as Andersch's major work. *The Redhead* (1960) deals with the wife of a West German capitalist who suddenly deserts her husband because she can no longer bear the empty and meaningless life at his side. In his latest novel *Efraim* (1967), Andersch portrays the life crisis of the emigrant Jew, Efraim, who has returned to his home city of Berlin where he searches for missing relatives and friends. At the end of the novel Efraim, too, breaks out of his old sphere into the freedom of a new life. Alfred Andersch's novels deal critically with the Nazi era and the prosperous society of the postwar times. He is especially interested in the fate of the Jews and the conduct of the Communist Party in the Third Reich.

The novels of Wolfgang Koeppen (1906–   ) appeared in rapid succession in the early fifties. His work stood in sharp contrast to the "deforestation" literature. Koeppen had published several novels before World War II, then was silent for twelve years. *Tauben im Gras* (*Doves in the Grass*, 1951), his first novel after the war, takes place in an American-occupied large city and portrays the chaos of the early postwar years. In his novel *Das Treibhaus* (*The Greenhouse*, 1953), Koeppen deals with the fate of a Bonn politician between 1945 and 1953. The idealism of the representative Keetenheuve is slowly transformed into bitter resignation as he is forced to see that the forces of reaction and restoration are in motion again in West Germany. He recognizes that although the form of government has changed after the war, the men themselves have not. In the face of this realization he commits suicide. The novel *Death in Rome* (1954) takes up the same theme of the basic unchangeability of men, and pictures several former Nazis from West Germany who are still dominated by their old prejudices, on vacation in Rome. Since 1954 Koeppen has written no additional novels, rather several excellent travel books, of which *Amerikafahrt* (*Trip to America*, 1959) deserves special mention.

The East Prussian Siegfried Lenz (1926–   ) has published a large number of short stories and several novels, all of which prove him to be an extremely talented narrator. In their structure and language his short stories show the influence of Ernest Hemingway. In his novels Lenz avoids formal experiments, but his themes are nevertheless modern. Generally the novels portray a hero in a crisis situation where his lack of freedom or his personal failure is made evident. One of Lenz's heroes formulates the author's intent: "One ought not to judge men according to what is possible but rather according to what is impossible for them. Only then does one obtain a relevant picture."

In Lenz's first novel, which was enthusiastically received by the critics, *Es waren Habichte in der Luft* (*There were Hawks in the Air*, 1951), the freedom-loving teacher Stenka tries in vain to escape the authority of a totalitarian state. Lenz's subsequent novels, *Duell mit dem Schatten* (*Duel with the Shadow*, 1953), *Der Mann im Strom* (*The Man in the Stream*, 1957), and *Brot und Spiele* (*Bread and Games*, 1959), show aging men in crisis situations. All three novels are critical of the postwar conditions in West Germany. When Lenz deals with the experiences of the war, he attempts to disengage man's failure from its specific historical context and to give the event general and universally applicable meaning. In *Stadtgespräch* (*Talk of the Town*, 1963) a member of the Resistance survives the war and persecution, but dies in peace time when his actions, which were regarded as heroic during the war, are branded by public opinion as cowardly and utilitarian. In his best-known drama, *Zeit der Schuldlosen* (*Time of the Innocent*, 1962), Lenz deals with nine men living under a dictatorship who face the critical decision of whether to sacrifice their own lives or to become guilty of the death of a man. Lenz's latest novel to date, *Deutschstunde* (*German Lesson*, 1968), depicts the happenings in a small village during the last years of the Nazi dictatorship. It is one of the best portrayals of human behavior during the Third Reich and also, in comparison with Lenz's earlier novels, has a decidedly more interesting and modern narrative structure.

Gerd Gaiser (1908–   ), a former air force officer, cannot be classified as belonging to one particular literary school. Basically Gaiser is a conventional narrator in the best sense of the word. For him the story itself is of primary importance. The author's self-depiction and the description of the creative process, which occur frequently in German novels in place of the story, are unknown in Gaiser's works. His first novel *Eine Stimme hebt an* (*A Voice Is Raised*, 1950) is the story of a war veteran who returns home and is unable to pick up the pieces of his prewar life. Gaiser's *The Falling Leaf* (*Die sterbende Jagd*, also translated as: *The Last Squadron*, 1953) is one of the best German war novels next to Peter Bamm's (1897–   ) *Die Unsichtbare Flagge* (*The Invisible Flag*, 1952). Here Gaiser describes how, in the course of one week on a German air base in Scandinavia, a group of pilots sense the turning point of the war. The collection *Einmal und Oft* (*Once and Often*, 1956) includes the brilliantly written stories *Gianna aus dem Schatten* (*Gianna out of the Shadows*) and *Aniela*, which rank among the best examples of postwar German prose. However, the climax of Gaiser's work is *The Last Dance of the Season* (also translated as: *Final Ball*, 1958). This novel is the most all-encompassing, critical portrayal of the economic miracle and its effects on the postwar society. Gaiser depicts the way prosperity attacks the residents of a small industrial city like a disease. Unpleasant memories of hunger, cold, and want lead many citizens to hoard as much property and money as they can to insure that they never again will have to face such deprivation. Thoughts of guilt for the war and recollections of the ghastly past are consciously avoided during the rapid economic success. A man's value comes to be measured only by his material possessions. Past and present are fused in thirty monologues spoken by both the living and the dead. The action culminates on the evening of a farewell ball of a dancing class. In his last novel, *Am Paß Nascondo* (*At the Nascondo Pass*, 1960), Gaiser seems to renounce his earlier narrative style and places his story in an imaginary country whose establishments in certain ways appear patterned after those of both present-day German states.

Danzig's Günter Grass (1927–   ) received the Group 47 prize for his first novel, *The Tin Drum* (1959), which earned him a place among the German literary elite. He had made his debut with the collection of verse, *Die Vorzüge der Windhühner* (*The Advantages of the Wind Chickens*, 1956). In the controversial play *The Plebeians Rehearse the Uprising* (1966), Grass tries to revive German tragedy. The hero of the drama, named the Boss, has certain characteristics which are unmistakably reminiscent of Bertolt Brecht. The background of this play is the Berlin workers' revolution in 1963. A delegation of workers appears in the theater where the play *Coriolanus* is being rehearsed and tries to convince the Boss to support their cause. He, however, betrays the workers' revolt by integrating them into his rehearsals as plebeians in a revolution scene of *Coriolanus*. Thus, he uses the revolutionary reality only as a model for his theater instead of making his theater a model for the revolution. This play, as well as Grass's newest novel (*Local Anesthetic*, 1969), gains in liveliness from the author's self-acknowledged political commitment which he demonstrated again in 1969 by his many campaign speeches in support of the Social Democratic Party.

Grass's novels form his most substantial contribution to postwar literature. *The Tin Drum*, the most discussed novel of the early sixties, was especially well received in France and the United States of America. It consists of the recollections of an inmate of an insane asylum; the memoirs of the thirty-year-old Oskar Matzerath begin in the twenties and end in the postwar period. He possesses all kinds of magical powers. He can break glass with his voice and express his feelings on a tin drum. Even at birth he was in full possession of his special powers of understanding, and at the age of three decides not to grow any more. This hideous gnome experiences and describes

390

the world with a distorted perspective. From his lower level of observation he can see things which are hidden from the normal observer. Not surprisingly the sexual sphere in particular forces its way into Oskar's field of vision.

The Tin Drum along with the short novel *Cat and Mouse* (1961) and the novel *Dog Years* (1963) form a trilogy. It is unified by its common background, by the appearance of the same line of characters in each work, and by scenery from Grass's German-Polish hometown. Danzig for Grass fulfills the same function as Dublin did for Joyce: it is the center of his literary universe.

In *Dog Years* Grass abandons the unusual narrative perspective of the gnome and has a team of authors relate the story. Three men, one after the other, describe their common past and their present situation. The first, Eduard Amsel, is a half-Jew, artist, ballet master, and manufacturer of scarecrows. He tells of his blood brother, the actor Walter Matern, a former stormtrooper and anti-Fascist. The second part of the novel contains letters of another author in which Grass characterizes three generations of Germans living through the Hitler regime. The third part consists of a report of Walter Matern's wanderings through West Germany. As in his first novel, Grass reveals a fascination for detail which swells the novel to oversize proportions. The shifting of the narrator enables Grass to practice his inclination for grotesque perspectives and situations. Grass proves himself an accomplished story teller although he regularly interrupts the flow of the story to make room for his ludicrous notions and his linguistic gags.

The technique of changing narrators and Grass's absurd humor continue the traditions of the German novel established by Jean Paul and E. T. A. Hoffmann. A second look at Grass's novels shows them to be formally quite traditional. Although critics label *The Tin Drum* a modern novel of development, it must be recognized as a parody, a metamorphosis of this particular genre. *Cat and Mouse* is developed along the traditional patterns of the German novella; even the *leitmotif* can be plainly identified. Certain passages in his novels, especially the description of the attack on the Polish post office in *The Tin Drum*, compare favorably to the best classical prose.

Grass has found few followers among the youngest novelists; they find his novels too conventional. Indeed, Grass does not experiment with structural problems of the narrative forms. However, his tremendous public success and his convincing narrative talent refute all modern theories about "the death of the novel" in modern literature.

Divided Germany of the 1950's is the novelist Uwe Johnson's (1934–   ) primary concern. Johnson grew up and studied in East Germany, moving to the West in 1959. His thorough familiarity with East Germany makes possible his expressive descriptions of everyday life in the German Democratic Republic. Johnson's first novel, *Speculations about Jacob* (1959), focuses on speculations about the mysterious death of Jacob Abs, a railway official, who is killed while crossing a train track in thick fog. Jacob leaves the East Zone after the Hungarian revolution, following his girl friend, Gesine, to the West, where he does not feel at home. He eventually returns to the East, but is unable to readjust to life there. After his return Jacob is constantly watched. Is his death an accident, suicide, or liquidation? The novel seems to reveal the truth of the matter through fragments of conversation, reports, monologues, and reminiscences, none of which, however, manage to go beyond superficial evidence. All the remarks about the hero remain pure conjecture, and the reader finally realizes that he has been exposed to the hideous atmosphere of everyday life in a totalitarian state, one in which everyone is suspected and no one knows what really happened.

In Johnson's *The Third Book about Achim* (1961) the West German journalist Karsch tries to show the true personality of the East German sports idol, Achim T., about whom two other books had been written. But Karsch's intent remains unfulfilled. The discrepancies between the star's image, built up by political propaganda, and the actual man Karsch meets make it impossible to supply a complete and unified picture of the star: the third book about Achim cannot be written. The differences between the two Germanies are even more evident here than in Johnson's first novel. Various linguistic means make their alienation particularly visible: for instance, when two speakers using the same word have two different conceptions of its meaning. Once again everything remains shrouded in vagueness and speculation. For this reason, Johnson clings intensively to detailed descriptions of tangible objects, thereby pointing to that realm alone in which clear assertions are possible.

Two Viewpoints (1965) indicates even in the title the author's intention to present East and West from varied perspectives. The building of the Berlin wall separates the West German photographer-journalist, B., and the East German nurse, D., who had been brought together by a superficial love affair. In this clearly structured book B. and D. are presented in alternate chapters. Their separation does not particularly affect either of them. In spite of their physical intimacy B. and D., abbreviations for *Bundesrepublik* (West Germany) and *Deutsche Demokratische Republik* (East Germany), can find no meaningful mutual relationship. It is remarkable that Johnson handles a highly political subject quite unpolitically. Political realities are implied in the fortunes of the characters without polemics or propaganda. In no way does Johnson intend to present the West German nation in more favorable light than the East German. The author's own position on the dividing line where the two Germanies touch as well as diverge is appropriate to the subject of his works.

Martin Walser's (1927–   ) novels mirror German society of the fifties and early sixties. *Marriage in Philippsburg* (1957) is a conventionally narrated novel depicting the social climb of a young man into the "high society" of a small German city. *Half Time* (1960) and *The Unicorn* (1966) are more cutting in their critique of the conditions in prosperous postwar Germany. In style essentially more complicated, they show Walser's obvious effort to pattern his hero, at least to some extent, after himself. Both novels have the same protagonist, Anselm Kristlein, who in *Half Time*, thanks to his gift of articulation, reaches the position of public relations manager for a large concern and obtains entry into the upper echelon of society. Here Walser especially attacks verbal clichés, as well as the hollowness of the roles most people play. In *Unicorn* Kristlein has become a writer commissioned by a woman publisher to write a work of non-fiction on love. Walser's critique of social conditions continues in this novel and focuses, in the form of a parody, on the bureaucratic aspects of literary life. He describes the futile attempt to write a factual book about love. Walser's novels tend to be structurally somewhat weak; his great literary talent is to be found in the realm of detailed description.

The problem of identity is the major theme of Max Frisch's (1911–   ) novels. The Swiss author, who gave up his profession as an architect in 1950 in order to devote his full time to writing, greatly contributed to the drama and the novel after the war. Having published since the early thirties, he gained international repute with his first significant novel *I'm not Stiller* (1954), in which the imprisoned protagonist writes an account of his life. He claims not to be the missing sculptor, Anatol Stiller, who left his wife and country six years ago, but to be one Sam White, an American of German descent. Stiller's diary ends with the verdict of the court that he is, in fact, Stiller. The protagonist accepts this verdict even though he rejects the identity of Stiller. The Stiller whose marriage was a failure, who was only a mediocre sculptor, and who proved his lack of heroism in the Spanish civil war remains foreign to him. The fact that everyone who used to know him has created a different image of him is unacceptable to him: none of these images is the true Stiller. By putting him in jail society forces him into the straitjacket of his old identity. Yet Stiller learns that man cannot escape himself by attempting to acquire a new identity: he had become Mr. White but is nevertheless still Stiller to the world.

Frisch focuses attention again on the question of identity in the novel *Homo Faber* (1957). Its protagonist, the engineer Walter Faber, is a technocrat who believes only in the powers of reason and efficiency. His world view is a completely technical one which negates the forces of spontaneity, enthusiasm, love, and fate. But upon realizing that he has unknowingly had a love affair with his own daughter, Faber suffers a complete breakdown and admits that forces other than technology do exist.

A Wilderness of Mirrors (Mein Name sei Gantenbein, 1964) presents a narrator-protagonist whose real identity is never revealed. The central question is again: does the true identity of a man disclose itself to the people around him? In this loosely structured novel the narrator imagines various situations for the character Gantenbein who plays the role of a blind man although he can see perfectly well. Under the impression that he is indeed blind many people stop playing their everyday roles in his presence. Thus, paradoxically, being blind enables him to see the true character of those around him. At times Gantenbein identifies with his role to such an extent that he is convinced he is blind. The narrator lets Gantenbein try on situations in his imagination like clothes. The variety of imaginary possibilities reveals itself to be the author's search for the true identity of his hero.

Postwar German poetry did not gain the same international reputation as the novel. However, numerous fine poets are publishing in Germany today, and the last Nobel prize won by a German author was awarded in 1966 to the poetess Nelly Sachs (1891–1970). It is noteworthy that the last three German Nobel laureates —Thomas Mann, Hermann Hesse, and Nelly Sachs—all emigrated from Germany. The Jewish poetess had sporadically published conventional poems and stories before the Nazi catastrophe changed the path of her life. Shortly before her scheduled deportation, Nelly Sachs was able to emigrate to Sweden with the help of Selma Lagerlöf and a member of the Swedish royal family. She later revisited Germany and expressed her trust in the younger generation of Germans. The immediate presence of death during the Third Reich gave Nelly Sachs's poetry a completely new dimension. After 1940, when she took up writing again, her previously emancipated attitude towards Judaism changed into a deep submersion in Jewish religion and mysticism. In her poems she mourns the suffering of her people and tries to find an answer for the Jewish martyrdom. Her verses, reminiscent of Biblical psalms, are epitaphs for the unknown graves of her people's dead. The titles of her numerous volumes of poetry reflect the darkness of her world and the endless suffering she experienced: *In den Wohnungen des Todes* (*In the Dwellings of Death*, 1947), *Sternverdunkelung* (*Eclipse of Stars*, 1949), and *Und niemand weiß weiter* (*And Nobody Knows a Way Out*, 1957). Most of her poems are collected in the volume *Fahrt ins Staublose* (*Journey to a Dustless Realm*, 1961). Her last collection is *Glühende Rätsel* (*Glowing Enigmas*, 1964).

The Austrian poetess Ingeborg Bachmann (1926–   ) received the prize of Group 47 and was the first writer to hold the chair for poetics at the University of Frankfurt. Her collections *Die gestundete Zeit* (*Borrowed Time*, 1953) and *Anrufung des Großen Bären* (*Invocation of the Big Dipper*, 1956) are characterized by a sound of deep and rich quality, and in their imagery are heavily based on nature. Ingeborg Bachmann does not believe that modern poetry can exist without social commitment. Her poems are typical for the war generation's acute consciousness of the past. They reflect the existential involvement of the poetess in the problems of her time. She views the future as holding the promise for a new man and a new world. Her ultimate goal is "perfection, the impossible, the unobtainable, be it in love, freedom or in any other pure thing." Ingeborg Bachmann also gained renown as a prose writer in her book *The Thirtieth Year* (1961), as an author of two excellent radio plays, *The Good God of Manhattan* (1958) and *Zikaden* (*Cicadas*, 1954), and especially as a librettist for Hans Werner Henze's operas, *Prince Frederick of Homburg* (1960) and *The Young Lord* (1965).

Günter Eich (1907–   ) wrote the famous poem "Inventory" which became the classical example of *Kahlschlag* literature. He made his debut in literature before the war with rather conventional poems in praise of nature. The experience of the war changed the poet's timbre. His *Ausgewählte Gedichte* (*Collected Poems*, 1960) reveal a continuing closeness to nature, but also show his attempt to look beneath the obscuring surface of things and find their true reality. His poetic language intends to make these hidden realities visible. "The essential language appears to me to be the one in which the word itself and the object it names are in congruence," says Eich, "we have to translate from this language which is all around us but at the same time nonexistent. We are translating without having the original text." Eich is also considered the main representative of the radio play in Germany. This new genre became extremely popular after the war when television was not as prolific as in today's Germany. Eich collected his radio plays in the volumes, *Träume* (*Dreams*, 1953) and *Stimmen* (*Voices*, 1958). The protagonists in his plays usually enter a situation endangering their existence and in this crisis find the truth about themselves. Eich is married to Ilse Aichinger (1921–   ), an accomplished writer of short stories and author of *Herod's Children* (*Die größere Hoffnung*, 1948), a poignant story of Jewish children in Nazi Germany.

One of the most outstanding lyricists, Paul Celan (1920–1970), was born in Rumania, the son of German speaking Jews both of whom died in a concentration camp. Celan emigrated to France in 1948, became a French citizen and taught German at the École Normale Supérieure in Paris. Celan is the author of the most famous poem written after the war, "Fugue of Death," which treats the atrocities of the concentration camps in a remarkable montage technique that seems to transcend the possibilities of linguistic expression. His early volumes, *Mohn und Gedächtnis* (*Poppy and Memory*, 1952) and *Von Schwelle zu Schwelle* (*From Threshold to Threshold*, 1955), capture impressions of his chassidic background and reveal the influence of French surrealism on his poetry. The untranslatable titles of the next volumes, *Sprachgitter* (1959), *Die Niemandsrose* (1963), *Atemwende* (1967), and *Fadensonnen* (1968), show Celan's attempt to dissociate his poetry from conventional imagery. Bold oxymora and daring catachreses characterize his pursuit of new linguistic tools. His images often seem to be ciphers of his complex existence rather than mere visual impressions. Aside from his poetry, Celan was a renowned translator of French and

Russian writers, especially Paul Valéry, Arthur Rimbaud, Jean Cocteau, Aleksandr Blok, and Osip Mandelshtam.

Germany's most "angry young man" is probably Hans Magnus Enzensberger (1929–   ) who grew up in Hitler's Nuremberg. At the age of sixteen, he was inducted into the army. He now makes his home in Norway. In his three volumes of poetry, *verteidigung der wölfe* (*Defense of the Wolves*, 1957), *landessprache* (*Language of the Country*, 1960), and *blindenschrift* (*Braille*, 1964), Enzensberger presents himself as a political lyricist in the tradition of Heine and Brecht. His poems are weapons with which he violently attacks complacency and self-righteousness in his fellow citizens. Enzensberger is a foe of all sentimentality and authoritarianism. The goal of his unmerciful polemics is postwar Germany. He achieves clever shock effects by arranging plays on words, slightly twisted quotations from the German classics, advertising slogans, and the jargon of businessmen in a montage technique. In one of his collections, Enzensberger included "Directions for use" of his poems. He declares them to be products for consumers and not vehicles for aesthetic revelation. He wishes his readers to use them as a basis for discussion, protest, and change of societal conditions. His best poems are now available in English translation accompanied by the German texts in the collection *Poems for People Who Don't Read Poems* (1968).

The aforementioned poets represent the major trends in postwar German poetry. Many others—especially Karl Krolow (1915–   ), Heinz Piontek (1925–   ), and the East German poets Johannes Bobrowski (1917–1965), Peter Huchel (1903–   ), and Stephan Hermlin (1915–   )—have established themselves through an *oeuvre* of high poetic rank.

Two Swiss authors, Max Frisch and Friedrich Dürrenmatt (1921–   ), especially contributed to the reputation of postwar German drama. During the war, Zurich offered the last prominent stage in a German-speaking country; some of Brecht's best plays had their premiere there; later the Zurich Schauspielhaus was the first European stage to perform Thornton Wilder's *Our Town* and *The Skin of Our Teeth*. Both Wilder and Brecht greatly influenced Zurich's Max Frisch, who employs forms typical of Brecht's epic theater and who shares his deep moral commitment. He does not, however, share Brecht's naive faith in Marxism. Frisch called one of his plays a *"Lehrstück ohne Lehre"* (a didactic play without a lesson) and critics have accordingly dubbed Frisch a Brecht without

397

Marxism. Frisch constantly warns against man's inclination to create false images of a person, a race, or a nation. He maintains that the attempt to say anything definitive about "the Jews," "the Russians," and others can result only in brutal distortion. This thesis is particularly evident in his novel *Stiller* and in the play *Andorra*.

Frisch's early plays, *Nun singen sie wieder* (*Now They Sing Again*, 1945), *The Chinese Wall* (1947), and *Als der Krieg zu Ende war* (*When the War Was Over*, 1949), deal with problems of the immediate postwar life. His next play, *Count Oederland* (1951), depicting the transformation of a representative of law and order into an anarchist, has generally been understood as a rather inadequate explanation of the events of the Hitler era, which shows that every common man has a certain potential for violence and cruelty. *Don Juan or The Love of Geometry* (1953) is Frisch's first comedy. Here Don Juan possesses none of the qualities usually attributed to him. Instead of seducing women he is constantly seduced by them. He despises love because it implies a realm of vague, indefinable emotion; he longs instead for clear, discernible relations as represented to him by geometry. But his attempt to escape women and to enter a monastery in order to indulge in the study of geometry fails, and he ends up a married man. Frisch's dominant theme is visible even in this comedy: Don Juan realizes that women merely love in him the image they have created of him.

The Firebugs (*Biedermann und die Brandstifter*, 1956) is the parable of a man who thinks he can appease those who want to destroy his world. In a city plagued by arsonists, the rich and hypocritical Biedermann shelters two firebugs in his home. He fails to hinder their preparations for a colossal fire. Unable to accept the idea of imminent catastrophe he simply closes his eyes and refuses to acknowledge any danger. Eventually the arsonists burn down his house and the entire city with it. Thus Biedermann lets his world catch fire because of his unwillingness to resist the forces of violence.

The climax of Frisch's work is his play *Andorra* (1961), a study of prejudice. Here a teacher brings his illegitimate son Andri to his homeland of Andorra, telling his fellow citizens that the boy is a Jewish child whom he rescued from the dangers of the anti-Semitic neighboring state. The boy grows up and gradually experiences the racial prejudice of the entire community. Andri is molded into the stereotype image the people of Andorra have of the Jews. As the armies of the neighboring anti-Semitic state invade Andorra, the teacher reveals his son's true identity. But Andri thinks his foster father is trying to save him and refuses to accept the story. He has been convinced that he is Jewish and that he possesses all the "Jewish" qualities people have observed in him. The enemy executes Andri as a Jew. In the ensuing trial, the people of Andorra declare themselves not guilty of Andri's death. But obviously their latent prejudices have led to Andri's violent death as much as has the open anti-Semitism of the invaders.

Friedrich Dürrenmatt, by far the most significant playwright after Brecht, has written several high caliber detective novels, successful movie scripts, and a whole series of noteworthy radio plays. The author's main interest centers on the stage, however. His plays break away from the theater of illusion and often display characteristics of the literary cabaret for which Dürrenmatt wrote many texts at an earlier stage of his career. His dialogue is often farcical, his protagonists are exaggerated prototypes, and his scenes may exhibit burlesque elements. Yet Dürrenmatt is not an innovator of forms. Rather, he uses forms of the theater introduced by Brecht and Thornton Wilder, both of whom had great impact on German dramatists after the war. Wilder's technique of destroying theatrical illusion by letting actors frequently step out of their roles and his ability to blend farce and metaphysical symbolism made their mark on Dürrenmatt's plays as did the parable character of Brecht's later plays.

In 1955, the Swiss author formulated his dramatic credo in an essay entitled "Problems of the Theater." He declares the traditional laws of drama unacceptable for the modern author, for the modern times are void of tragic heroes. The recent catastrophic events of history appear to him as monstrous disasters caused by madmen. Hitler or Mussolini cannot be seen as tragic heroes like Wallenstein. Dürrenmatt claims tragedy is impossible in our modern world of bureaucracy and overadministration in which the individual has become invisible and "Creon's secretaries handle the case of Antigone." Only in comedy does Dürrenmatt see a chance to depict the complex problems of modern man.

Dürrenmatt's first plays after the war, *Es steht geschrieben* (*It Is Written*, 1947) and *Der Blinde* (*The Blind Man*, written in 1947), concern the theme of religious belief in revolutionary times and do not fully reveal the author's dramatic potential. The protagonist of his first comedy, the Roman emperor *Romulus the Great* (1950), takes a greater interest in chicken farming than in ruling the empire. He confesses to "love people more than the idea of a fatherland" and feels quite relieved to turn Rome over to the barbarian conquerors without bloodshed. *The Marriage of Mr. Mississippi* (also translated as: *Fools Are Passing By*, 1952) scored the first international success for Dürrenmatt. He puts four main characters on the stage, each of whom, in the manner of a morality play, personifies an abstraction: absolute justice in the person of Mr. Mississippi, a public prosecutor; absolute equality in the person of Saint-Claude, a Communist world revolutionary; Christian love in the person of Count Übelohe-Zabernsee, an alcoholic doctor; and absolute amorality in the character of Anastasia, a theatrical sister of Wedekind's infamous Lulu. The stage becomes the battlefield of different world views. Only the alcoholic who refrains from any foolish attempt to change the world with absolute ideas survives.

The historical comedy *An Angel Comes to Babylon* (1954) is a parable showing how greed for power corrupts people. The tragicomedy *The Visit* (1956) ranks among the best plays of the century. The multibillionaire Claire Zachanassian returns to her decrepit hometown of Güllen in order to "buy justice." Decades before, she had had a child by a Güllen citizen, who instead of admitting his fatherhood bribed witnesses to testify that they, too, had relations with Claire. Driven out of town she later inherits the wealth of her first husband, an oil billionaire, and thus gains the means for her macabre revenge. She had the two false witnesses castrated and now arrives in Güllen with a coffin for Ill, her former lover. She promises the citizens of Güllen one billion upon his death. The prospect of incredible wealth soon so perverts the minds of the people of Güllen that they believe they are acting in the name of justice when they execute him under the pretext that he has to pay for the injustice he did to Claire.

The Physicists (1962) are inmates of an insane asylum who believe themselves to be Einstein and Newton. A third one, Möbius, claims to be guided in his experiments and insights by King Solomon. Actually, none of them is insane. Möbius tries to save mankind from the results of his scientific discoveries which could destroy the universe. Fifteen years earlier, he had assumed the guise of a mentally disturbed man in order to be committed to this clinic directed by Dr. Mathilde von Zahnd, a hunchbacked woman psychiatrist. Einstein and Newton are themselves famous physicists, who are in the clinic as secret agents of their nations trying to get hold of Möbius's "world formula." The scholars eventually reveal their true identities to each other and, after discussing the precariousness of science, decide to stay where they are and hide their dangerous knowledge. Only then do they discover that they are prisoners of their mad psychiatrist who has stolen Möbius' formula so she can rule the world and the universe. Together with Brecht's *Galileo*, Frisch's *Chinese Wall*, and Kipphardt's *Oppenheimer*, *The Physicists* reflects the moral conflict of the modern scientist whose discoveries can either ease or terminate human existence.

Dürrenmatt's love for the grotesque culminates in his last comedy, *The Meteor* (1966). The protagonist, the Nobel laureate Schwitters, dies and experiences an immediate resurrection. In biting scenes Dürrenmatt displays the reactions of the "survivors."

Dürrenmatt's comedies do not echo the bitter laughter of a despairing and disillusioned author. They often show the perversion of man through power, greed, and money, and mirror the wretched situation of the world. But Dürrenmatt also presents heroes who, often masked as fools, encounter this world with courage and firmness. His comedies are an attempt to regard the world from a critical distance. "Seeing the senselessness, the hopelessness of this world, one might despair," says Dürrenmatt, "yet despair is not the result of this world. It is an answer one gives to this world. A different answer might be: not to despair, but to decide to accept the world in which we often live like Gulliver among the giants. But he who wants to evaluate his opponent, who prepares himself to fight or to escape his enemy, has to step back a little in order to create distance. It is still possible to present the courageous man."

Rolf Hochhuth (1931–   ) is recognized as the founder of the documentary theater. His first work, *The Deputy* (1963) has drawn world-wide attention. The play centers around the question: did the persistent refusal of Pope Pius XII to condemn publicly the persecution of Jews make him party to the death of millions of human beings? Hochhuth adopts the view that the Pope's powerful moral force could have brought the murder of the Jews to an end. Further, he believes that the Pope abdicated his responsibility as head of the Catholic Church and as Christ's earth representative, in the interest of political expediency. Filled with doubt over the Pope's dogmatic obstinacy, the Italian priest in Hochhuth's play, Riccardo Fontana, follows the path of suffering of the persecuted. He pins the yellow star of David, the obligatory badge of Judaism in Nazi-occupied countries, to his frock and steps into the Auschwitz gas chamber as the Pope's self-appointed deputy.

The heated discussion aroused by *The Deputy* focused on

the controversial theme, overlooking the play's relatively weak dramatic form. Many German theaters refused to perform the play. Catholic critics attacked the piece, claiming that the author had distorted the actual character of the Pope. Hochhuth does indeed attempt to document his theory and, thanks to intensive research, tries to present the historical facts as accurately as possible. He departs from the tradition of the German historical drama in that he draws his material from the immediate past and that he documents the central thesis of his play with comprehensive appendices which include transcripts, letters, and eyewitness accounts. Unlike Schiller, Hochhuth does not freely transform historical fact. Nor does he attempt to formulate universal axioms from the concrete situation, or point out the historical repetition of man's failure. He believes that the moral responsibility and the individual decision of a prominent contemporary figure can alter the course of history, a theme, which recurs in his second play, *Soldiers* (1967). It accuses the British Prime Minister, Winston Churchill, of mass murder in the bombing of defenseless cities during the Second World War, as well as of the murder of Sikorski, the premier of the Polish government exiled in London. Understandably, because of its content, this play also stimulated enormous reaction and counter-reaction. Thus, in addition to "historical evidence," each play contains pointed criticism of an actual situation.

Heinar Kipphardt (1922–   ) turned his attention to the theater in 1950. After spending nine years as a theater producer in East Berlin, he returned to West Germany where he introduced successfully three of his plays. Kipphardt's drama clearly follows the tradition of Brecht in that it employs the technique of successive individual epic scenes. The author demonstrates a strong political commitment and intends his plays to stimulate social criticism rather than to entertain.

Kipphardt's two most important plays are *In the Matter of J. Robert Oppenheimer* (1964) and *Joel Brand* (1965). Each is based on an intensive study of its historical source, which at times forms an integral part of the play. The setting for *Oppenheimer* is the hearing at which the long-time head of the United States Atomic Research Program was interrogated. The hearing questions whether the physicist's hesitance to continue work on the development of nuclear weapons casts doubt on his loyalty to the United States. The outcome of the hearing is the removal of his security clearance. Oppenheimer realizes that in remaining loyal to his country by placing the results of his work in the hands of the military, he has betrayed the ethics of science. In this context Brecht's physicist Galileo comes to mind. At the end of his life, Galileo held to the belief that the only goal of science should be to lighten the hardships of human existence. Oppenheimer himself accused Kipphardt of misrepresentation and threatened to sue. However, nothing came of the charge and the play enjoys a continuing success. *Joel Brand* relates the story of a frustrated business deal in which the SS man Eichmann wants to trade one million Jews for ten thousand trucks, but the Jewish go-between, Brand, cannot come up with the trucks because the Western Powers do not want to give the Nazis any important war materials.

Recently Peter Weiss (1916–   ) has become the major representative of documentary theater. Because of his Jewish extraction, Weiss left Germany in 1933 and presently resides in Sweden. He became world famous with his play *The Persecution and Assassination of Jean Marat as Performed by the Inmates of the Asylum of Charenton under the Direction of the Marquis de Sade* (1964) in which he skillfully draws on all modern dramatic techniques in the tradition of Büchner, Brecht, and Beckett. The play is an example of theater within theater. The Marquis de Sade, himself an inmate at Charenton, dramatizes the life of the French revolutionary Jean Marat and his assassination. The play is performed in the asylum by the mentally ill patients for their fellow inmates. The inability of the patients to stage a theatrical performance produces a grotesque alienation.

Documentary plays followed this drama in rapid succession. *Die Ermittlung (The Investigation,* 1965) brings testimonies and events from the Frankfurt Auschwitz Trials (1963–1965) to the stage. Weiss does not attempt to depict the horror of the extermination camps in realistic scenes, but rather clothes his play in the form of an oratorio. *Gesang vom lusitanischen Popanz (Song of the Portuguese Bogy,* 1966) protests the colonial politics of Portugal in her African possessions, and further, the reprehensibility of every imperialistic political power. The content of Weiss's latest play is summarized in its long title: *Discourse about the Antecedents and the Development of the Long-Lasting Fight for Freedom in Vietnam as an Example for the Necessity of the Armed Battle of the Suppressed against Their Suppressors as well as for the Attempts of the United States of America to Destroy the Basis of Revolution* (1968). Weiss bases his plays on a strong political engagement.

In 1949 the division of Germany into two adverse political camps was manifested in the foundation of the Federal Republic of Germany and the German Democratic Republic. From this time on, two different trends in German literature became discernible. The emigrants who chose to return to the Communist German state —among them the outstanding authors Anna Seghers, Brecht, Johannes R. Becher, and Arnold Zweig—demonstrated with this decision their particular political beliefs. East German literature was from the start committed to the ideas of Socialism. The Communists fostered literature as long as it followed the party's official cultural program. Thus, the two major themes of West German postwar literature—the digestion of the Nazi past and the unsparing criticism of social, economic, and political conditions—never appeared in the East. East Germany denied any part in the guilt of the past, and writings critical of or in opposition to the Communist Party were suppressed or denounced as destructive and bourgeois. Foreign literature, especially that from the West, was never freely available. The official cultural program promoted the style of socialist realism which allowed only for the realistic depiction of positive heroes who are conscious of their obligations towards their socialist state. Since it is almost impossible to judge today the merits of such a literature, special attention was devoted in this chapter to the postwar literature of West Germany. The artistic freedom which writers enjoy in this part of the country certainly accounts for the much greater diversification of their literature.

Today German literature has undisputedly regained international rank. All literary genres are well represented by an array of highly talented authors who direct their artistic attention to problems confronting not only their own country but the entire world. The concern of the writers is man's situation and role in a technical and often dehumanized environment, his attempts to change and improve societal conditions, and the vision of a peaceful future world. The multitude of highly interesting structural artistic experiments is often overshadowed by the artists' clear commitment to the improvement of society. He no longer wants to present a reflection of society in his work, instead he wants his work to reflect upon and thus influence society.

Notes ✌

The contributors have referred to works by their English titles whenever translations are readily available. The German title follows when German and English titles differ. The German title precedes the English when works have not been translated or are inaccessible to the general reader.

Chapter 1

1. Now, after nearly a half century, the most useful handbook on Middle High German Literature is still G. Ehrismann, *Geschichte der deutschen Literatur bis zum Ausgang des Mittelalters,* 2 parts, 4 vols. (München, 1918–1935, reprint 1959). More modern in interpretation and bibliography, but less easy to read, are H. de Boor, *Die höfische Literatur. Vorbereitung, Blüte, Ausklang* (1170–1250) (München, 1953), and *Die deutsche Literatur im späten Mittelalter. Zerfall und Neubeginn* (1250–1400), Part 1 (1250–1350) (München, 1962). Brief but excellent are H. Kuhn, *Die Klassik des Rittertums in der Stauferzeit* (1170–1230); F. Ranke, *Von der ritterlichen zur bürgerlichen Dichtung* (1230–1430), and S. Beyschlag, *Städte, Höfe, Gelehrte* (1430–1490), all in F. Genzmer et al., *Geschichte der deutschen Literatur von den Anfängen bis zum Ende des Spätmittelalters* (1490) (*Annalen der deutschen Literatur* 2, Stuttgart, 1962).

   The best histories in English are M. O'C. Walshe, *Medieval Literature* (Cambridge, 1962), and Paul B. Salmon, *Literature in Medieval Germany* (New York, 1967).

   The most thorough reference work for both biography and author bibliography is W. Stammler, *Die deutsche Literatur des Mittelalters. Verfasserlexikon,* 5 Vols. (Berlin, 1933–55); supplements by G. Eis and G. Keil in *Studia Neophilologica* 30 (1958), 232–250; *ibid.* 31 (1959), 219–242, *Beiträge* 83 (Tübingen, 1961), 167–226. The standard reference work for subject matter is P. Merker and W. Stammler, *Reallexikon der deutschen Literaturgeschichte* (Berlin, 1958).

   For many works in this chapter the most recent and concise study and bibliography are to be found in the series *Realienbücher für Germanisten* of the *Sammlung Metzler,* J. B. Metzler Verlag, Stuttgart, hereafter abbreviated as (SM). Editions of many works are found in the series *Altdeutsche Textbibliothek,* Max Niemeyer Verlag, Tübingen (ATB) and *Deutsche Klassiker des Mittelalters,* F. A. Brockhaus, Leipzig, later Wiesbaden (DKM). Translations of several works are found in Penguin Classics, Penguin Books, Baltimore, Md., and in *University of North Carolina Studies in the Germanic Languages and Literatures* (U. of North Carolina Press, Chapel Hill, N.C., hereafter abbreviated as UNCS).

2. *Tristan,* ed. Ranke, vv. 4621–4820. No dates are known for Gottfried, but most scholars agree that he stopped writing his *Tristan* about 1210.
3. Gottfried mentions Henric as previously—and Reinmar of Hagenau as recently-deceased, whereas he mentions Hartman, Wolfram, and Walther as still living.

4. See E. Steinmeyer and E. Sievers, *Die althochdeutschen Glossen.* 5 Vols. (Berlin, 1879–1922). "High German" (*Hochdeutsch*) designates the dialects of southern and central Germany that underwent the second sound shift; and "Old" designates their stage of development from roughly 750 to 1100 A.D., while "Middle" designates the period from 1100 to 1500.
5. Tacitus, *Germania. Cornelii Taciti de Origine et Situ Germanorum,* ed. J. G. C. Anderson (Oxford, 1938) Eng. trans. H. Mattingly, *Tacitus on Britain and Germany* (Baltimore, 1948; Penguin Classics L 5).
6. This ballad seems to have been composed in the Bavarian dialect and then clumsily adapted for a North German audience. It survived only because the two sheets of parchment on which it had been recorded were later used to bind a religious work. These sheets disappeared during World War II, but one was recovered in New York. *Hildebrandslied, Wessobrunner Gebet, Muspilli, Georgslied, Christus und die Samariterin, Ludwigslied,* and excerpts from Otfried in Wilhelm Braune, *Althochdeutsches Lesebuch,* 15th ed. (Tübingen, 1969). Eng. trans. of *Hildebrandslied* and part of *Muspilli* in L. Foster, *The Penguin Book of German Verse* (Baltimore, 1959). The most detailed history of OHG literature in English is J. K. Bostock. *A Handbook on OHG Literature* (Oxford, 1955).
7. *Heiland,* ed. O. Behagel, 7th ed. rev. by W. Mitzka (Tübingen, 1958, ADT 4). NHG prose trans. by Wilhelm Stapel (München, 1953); verse by Karl Simrock (Insel Verlag, 1959). Eng. trans. Mariana Scott, *Heiland* (Chapel Hill, 1966; UNCS 52).
8. *Waltharius,* ed. K. Strecker (Berlin, 1947). NHG verse trans. with text in Karl Langosch, *Waltharius, Ruodieb, Märchenepen* (Berlin, 1956). NHG prose trans. Peter Vossen in Strecker edition, above. Eng. prose trans. F. P. Magoun and H. M. Smyser, *Walter of Acquitaine* (New London, Conn., 1950; *Connecticut Monographs* 4).
   Ruodlieb, ed. and trans. in E. H. Zeydel, *Ruodlieb, the Earliest Courtly Novel* (Chapel Hill, 1959; UNCS 23). Trans. Gordon B. Ford, Jr. (Leiden, 1966).
   Ecbasis cuisdam captivi, ed. Karl Strecker (Berlin, 1935). Edition with Eng. trans. E. H. Zeydel, *Ecbasis Cuisdam Captivi: Escape of a Certain Captive* (Chapel Hill, 1964; UNCS 46).
   Hrothswitha, 2nd ed. Karl Strecker (Leipzig, 1930). Bert Nagel, *Hrotsvit von Gandersheim* (Stuttgart, 1965; SM 44).
9. W. J. Schröder: *Spielmannsepik* (Stuttgart, 1962; SM 19). *König Rother,* 2nd ed. by Theodor Frings and J. Kuhnt (Halle, 1961). NHG trans. Günter Kramer (Berlin, 1961). Eng. trans. Robert Lichtenstein (Chapel Hill, 1962; UNCS 36).
10. The "Hohenstaufen Era" includes not only the reigns of Frederick Barbarossa (1152–1190), Henry VI (1190–1197), Philip II (1198–1208), and Frederick II (1211–1250), but also the overlapping and interim reign of Otto of Brunswick (1198–1210).
11. Lyrics of Kürenberger, Frederick of Hausen, Henric of Veldeken, Henry of Morungen, Reinmar of Hagenau, and Hartman of Aue in *Des Minnesangs Frühling,* ed. Karl Lachmann, 34th ed. rev. Carl von Kraus (Stuttgart, 1967). All these and also Walther of the Vogelweide, Gottfried of Strassburg, Wolfram of Eschenbach, Neidhart of Reuental, and many others are found, with Eng. notes and glossary, in *Poets of the Minnesang,* ed. Olive Sayce (Oxford, 1967). Limited selection of English trans. in J. W. Thomas, *German Verse from the 12th to the 20th Century* (Chapel Hill, 1963; UNCS 44), and in *Penguin Book of German Verse* (Baltimore, 1957).

12. Veldeke: *Eneide*, ed. T. Frings and G. Schieb (Berlin 1964–1965; DTM 58, 59). See Gabriele Schieb, *Heinrich von Veldeke* (Stuttgart, 1965; SM 42).

13. The term "courtly love" may have been furthered by its appearance in the title of John Jay Parry's translation of Andreas Capellanus's *Ars honeste amandi* (*The Art of Courtly Love*, New York, 1941). The term is used in Herman J. Weigand's *Three Chapters on Courtly Love* (Chapel Hill, 1956) to designate adulterous love as practiced by Lancelot and praised by Andreas. Such love had no binding validity for Wolfram, who championed passionate sentiment leading to monogamous fidelity.

14. *Die Lieder Reimars des Alten* (München, 1919). Friedrich Mauer, *Die Pseudo-Reimare* (Heidelberg, 1966) argues convincingly that von Kraus rejected many genuine songs because of his "cycle-theory," which caused him to reject as spurious any songs that did not fit comfortably into a sentimental Reinmar biography.

15. See Peter Wapnewski, *Hartmann von Aue*, 3rd ed. (Stuttgart, 1967; SM 17). Hartmann von Aue, *Die Klage, Das* (*zweite*) *Büchlein*, ed. Herta Zutt (Berlin, 1968). *Erec*, ed. A. Leitzmann, 3rd ed. rev. L. Wolff (Tübingen, 1963; ATB 39). *Iwein*, edited G. F. Benecke and K. Lachmann, 7th ed. rev. L. Wolff (Berlin, 1968); ed. with literal NHG trans. Thomas Cramer (Berlin, 1968).

16. *Gregorius*, ed. Hermann Paul, 9th ed. rev. L. Wolff (Tübingen, 1959; ATB 2). Eng. trans. E. H. Zeydel and B. Q. Morgan, *Gregorius* (Chapel Hill, 1955; UNCS 14). *Der arme Heinrich*, ed. Hermann Paul, 12th ed. rev. L. Wolff (Tübingen, 1961; ATB 3). Eng. trans. in C. H. Bell, *Peasant Life in Old German Epics* (New York, 1931).

17. See Gottfried Weber, *Gottfried von Strassburg* (Stuttgart, 1962; SM 15). *Tristan und Isold*, ed. Friedrich Ranke (Berlin, 1958). Abridged Eng. trans. E. H. Zeydel (Princeton, 1948). Eng. prose trans. A. T. Hatto, *Tristan* (Baltimore, 1960; Penguin Classics L 98).

18. See J. Bumke, *Wolfram von Eschenbach* (Stuttgart, 1964; SM 36). *Willehalm*, in *Wolfram von Eschenbach*, ed. A. Leitzmann, Heft 4, 5; (Tübingen, 1963; ATB 12–16); with NHG trans. in *Willehalm*, ed. Dieter Kartschoke (Berlin, 1968). J. Bumke, *Wolframs Willehalm*, (Heidelberg, 1959).
      Parzival and *Titurel* in Wolfram von Eschenbach, Vol. I: *Lieder, Parzival und Titurel*, ed. Karl Lachmann, 7th ed. rev. Eduard Hartl (Berlin, 1952). Text with *Nacherzählung* in Wolfram von Eschenbach, *Parzival*, ed. G. Weber (Darmstadt, 1963). Abridged Eng. verse trans. E. H. Zeydel and B. Q. Morgan (Chapel Hill, 1951; UNCS 5). Eng. prose trans. Helen M. Mustard and Charles E. Passage (New York, 1961; Vintage Book V–188).

19. This "dangling nominative" construction, which is now considered substandard, was still acceptable in both Middle High German and Middle English literature.

20. See George F. Jones, *Walther von der Vogelweide* (New York, 1968). Walther von der Vogelweide, *Die Gedichte*, ed. Karl Lachmann, 13th ed. rev. Carl von Kraus (Berlin, 1965). *Die Lieder Walthers von der Vogelweide; I Die religiösen und politischen Lieder, II Die Liebeslieder*, ed. Friedrich Maurer, 2nd ed. (Tübingen, 1960–61; ATB 43, 47). NHG trans. *Minne, Reich, Gott*, ed. Hans Böhm, 2nd ed. (Stuttgart, 1949); *Sprüche, Lieder, der Leich*, ed. Paul Stapf, 2nd ed. (Frankfurt, 1963). Eng. selections E. H. Zeydel, *Poems of Walther von der Vogelweide* (Ithaca, N.Y., 1952).

21. *Das Nibelungenlied,* nach der Ausgabe von Karl Bartsch, 12th ed. rev. Helmut de Boor (Leipzig, 1949; DKM 3). Text and NHG trans. (strophe by strophe, but not verse by verse) Helmut de Boor (Hamburg, 1949). Eng. verse trans. *The Song of Nibelungs,* Frank Ryder (Detroit, 1962). Eng. prose trans. *The Nibelungenlied,* trans. D. G. Mowatt (New York, 1962); with excellent commentary, A. T. Hatto, *The Nibelungenlied* (Baltimore, 1965; Penguin Classics L 137). See also G. Weber and W. Hoffman, *Nibelungenlied,* 3rd ed. (Stuttgart, 1968; SM 7).
22. *Die Märe von Helmbrecht,* ed. F. Panzer (Tübingen, 1960; ATB 11). Eng. trans. in C. L. Bell, *Peasant Life in Old German Epics* (New York, 1931).
23. See Gerhard Eis, *Fachsprache* (Stuttgart, 1967; SM 14).
24. Typical Easter play: *Das Redentiner Osterspiel,* ed. Willy Krogmann (Leipzig, 1937; *Altdeutsche Quellen* 3), reprint 1964. Eng. trans. A. E. Zucker, *The Redentin Easter Play* (New York, 1941).
25. Johannes von Tepl, *Der Ackermann,* ed. Willy Krogmann (Wiesbaden, 1954). Text with Eng. notes and glossary: J. v. T., *Der Ackermann aus Böhmen,* ed. M. O'C. Walshe, *Duckworth's German Texts* (London, 1951); ed. K. Spalding, *Blackwell's German Texts* (Oxford, 1950). Eng. trans. from a NHG edition: Ernest N. Kirmann, *Death and the Plowman* (Chapel Hill, 1958; UNCS 22). Also *Death and the Plowman,* trans. K. W. Maurer (London, 1947).
26. *Die Lieder Oswalds von Wolkenstein,* ed. Karl Kurt Klein (Tübingen, 1962; ATB 55). NHG selections trans. Hubert Witt, *Um dieser Welten Lust, Leib-und Lebenslieder des O. von W.* (Berlin, 1968).
27. *Heinrich Wittenwilers Ring,* ed. Edmund Wiesner (Leipzig, 1931). Eng. trans. with commentary, George F. Jones, *Wittenwiler's "Ring" and the Anonymous Scots Poem "Colkelbie Sow"* (Chapel Hill, 1956; UNCS 18).
28. *Sebastian Brant, Das Narrenschiff,* ed. F. Zarncke (Leipzig, 1854, reprint Darmstadt, 1964); ed. M. Lemmer (Tübingen, 1962; *Neudrucke Deutscher Literatur Werke,* N.F. 5); Eng. trans. with notes and commentary, E. H. Zeydel, *The Ship of Fools* (New York, 1944), reprint of New York, 1926.

Chapter 2

1. The term Renaissance was coined by Voltaire in *Essai sur les moeurs et l'esprit des nations* (1756). Giorgio Vasari spoke of *Rinascità* in *Lives of the Painters* (1550). Numerous meanings have been given to both terms. Some recent opinions in: J. Trier, "Zur Vorgeschichte des Renaissance-Begriffs," *Archiv für Kulturgeschichte* XXXIII (1950), 45–63; H. Lucas, "The Renaissance: A Review of Some Views," *Catholic Historical Review* XXXV (1950), 377–407; H. Baeyens, *Begrip en Probleem von de Renaissance* (Louvain, 1952); T. Kardos, "Zusammenhänge der Begriffe Renaissance und Humanismus," in *La Littérature comparée en Europe orientale* (Budapest, 1963), pp. 257–270. Of further interest to the reader should be R. Alewyn, ed. *Deutsche Barockforschung* (Köln, 1965); W. Andreas, *Deutschland vor der Reformation: eine Zeitwende* (Stuttgart, 1959); H. Blum, *Martin Luther: Creative Translator* (St. Louis, 1965); H. Bornkamm, *Das Jahrhundert der Reformation. Gestalten und Kräfte* (Göttingen, 1966); J. Burckhardt, *The Civilization of the Renaissance in Italy* (London, 1951); R. Froning, *Das Drama der Reformationszeit* (Darmstadt, 1964); G. Müller, *Deutsche Dichtung von der Renaissance bis zum Ausgang des Barock* (Darmstadt, 1957); F. W. Wentzlaff-Eggebert, *Deutsche Mystik zwischen Mittelalter und Neuzeit* (Berlin, 1947); Heinrich Wölfflin, *Renaissance and Baroque* (Ithaca, 1966).

2. See P. Hofmann, "Der Humanismus in der abendländischen Geschichte," *DVjs*, XXV (1951), 137–158; and A. Chastel and R. Klein, *L'Age de l'humanisme* (Brussels, 1963).
3. See F. Bäuml, *Rhetorical Devices and Structure in the Ackermann aus Böhmen* (Berkeley, 1960).
4. *Devotio moderna* was a school and trend of spirituality that originated in the Netherlands at the end of the fourteenth century and spread during the fifteenth century through that region and through the Rhineland, Northern France, and Spain. Gerald Groote (1340–84) was its father and founder. It was called "modern" in opposition to the "old" spirituality of the thirteenth and fourteenth century which was highly speculative and scholastic in character. See M. Ditsche, "Zur Herkunft und Bedeutung des Begriffes 'devotio moderna,'" *Historisches Jahrbuch* LXXIX (1960), 124–45; A. Hyma, *The Christian Renaissance. A History of the "Devotio moderna"* (Hamden, Conn., 1965).
5. On the ambiguous attitude of Erasmus towards the Reformation, see H. Bornkamm, "Erasmus und Luther," *Luther-Jahrbuch* XXV (1958), 3–22; and K. Oelrich, *Der späte Erasmus und die Reformation* (Münster, 1961).
6. Quoted and translated by myself from G. Müller, *Deutsche Dichtung der Renaissance und des Barocks*, p. 116.
7. See R. Minder, *Kultur und Literatur in Deutschland und Frankreich* (Frankfurt, 1962).
8. For investigations of the Baroque problem (concept, style, epoch, mannerism) see: R. Wellek, *Concepts of Criticism* (New Haven, 1963); the special issues on Baroque of the *Journal of Aesthetics and Art Criticism*, XIV (1955) and *Colloquia Germanica* I (1967); A. Buker, "The Baroque S-T-O-R-M: A Study in the Limits of the Culture–Epoch Theory," *JAAC*, XXII (1964), 303–313. Suggested further readings: H. Cysarz, *Deutsche Barockdichtung* (Leipzig, 1924); W. Flemming, *Deutsche Kultur im Zeitalter des Barock*, ed. Thurnher (Konstanz, 1960); Carl J. Friedrich, *The Age of the Baroque 1610–1660* (New York, 1952); Paul Hankamer, *Deutsche Gegenreformation und deutsches Barock* (Stuttgart, 1935); B. L. Spahr, "Protean Stability in the Baroque Novel," *Germanic Review*, XL (1965), 253–60; Fritz Strich, "Der Barock," in *Deutsche Literaturgeschichte in Grundzügen*, ed. B. Boesch (Bern, 1946), 155–181; Werner Weisbach, *Der Barock als Kunst der Gegenreformation* (Berlin, 1921); Karl Viëtor, *Geist und Form* (Bern, 1952).
9. B. L. Spahr, "Baroque and Mannerism: Epoch and Style," *Colloquia Germanica* I (1967), 78–100, argues convincingly that "Mannerism is a style; Baroque is an Era," and "mannerism is the *maniera* of the Baroque."
10. R. Alewyn, *Vorbarocker Klassizismus und griechische Tragödie. Analyse der Antigone-Übersetzung des M. Opitz* (Darmstadt, 1962).
11. Also known, according to country, as *Marinism* after Giambattista Marino (1569–1625), *Gongorism* after Luis de Gongora (1561–1627), *Euphuism* after John Lyly's (1554–1606) novel *Euphues*. See on Mannerism in literature: G. R. Hocke, *Manierismus in der Literatur, Sprachalchemie und esoterische Kombinationskunst* (Hamburg, 1959).
12. See Wentzlaff-Eggebert, *Deutsche Mystik*; W. E. Peuckert, *Pansophie. Ein Versuch zur Geschichte der weißen und schwarzen Magie* (Berlin, 1956²).

Chapter 3

The American reader will find the most useful information in: Eric A. Blackall, *The Emergence of German as a Literary Language, 1700–1775* (Cambridge, 1959); W. B. Lockwood, *An Informal History of the German Language* (Cambridge, 1965); Robert Priebsch and William E. Collinson, *The German Language* (London, 1962, 5th edition; older and less readable but still valuable for special topics); John T. Waterman, *A History of the German Language* (Seattle, 1966), with excellent selected vocabulary; George O. Curme, *A Grammar of the German Language* (New York, 1922).

1. For a discussion of the various Continental South Germanic dialects and languages, see W. B. Lockwood, *An Informal History of the German Language* (Cambridge, 1965).
2. See Uriel Weinreich, *Languages in Contact* (New York, 1953, reprinted, The Hague, 1963).
3. Stanley N. Werbow, "Die 'gemeine teutsch' Ausdruck und Begriff," *Zeitschrift für deutsche Philologie*, LXXXII (1963), 44–63, esp. p. 47.
4. See George O. Curme, *A Grammar of the German Language* (New York, 1922, reprint 1952), paragraph 70.3.
5. Ivar Ljungerud, *Zur Nominalflexion in der deutschen Literatursprache nach 1900* (Lund, 1955). This work provided the basis for the treatment of noun inflection in the *Duden Grammatik* in the 1959 and 1966 editions.
6. Adolf Bach, *Geschichte der deutschen Sprache* (Heidelberg, 1965), p. 108.
7. Cf. M. M. Guchmann, *Der Weg zur deutschen Nationalsprache (Bausteine zur Sprachgeschichte des Neuhochdeutschen*, Bd. I) (Berlin, 1964), p. 54, p. 77.
8. Gerhard Eis, "Mittelalterliche Fachprosa der Artes" in: Wolfgang Stammler, *Deutsche Philologie im Aufriß*, II, col. 1112 f.
9. Cf. Bach, *Geschichte*, p. 249 but also the contrary view of Arno Schirokauer, "Frühneuhochdeutsch," in Wolfgang Stammler, *Deutsche Philologie im Aufriß* (Berlin, 1957²), col. 883. A full discussion of the share of the settlers' language would exceed the goal of this chapter and lead to a complex sociolinguistic and dialectological discussion. The interested reader will find ample bibliography in Bach's *History of the German Language*; especially, however, in Theodor Frings, *Mitteldeutsche Studien* (Halle 1956) in which important contributions of the 20's and 30's are reprinted, on which Bach's treatment rests substantially.
10. See Glenn Gilbert, "The Linguistic Geography of the Colonial and Immigrant Languages in the United States" (unpublished paper read at Linguistic Society of America meeting, December, 1969).
11. V. M. Schirmunski, *Deutsche Mundartkunde* (Berlin 1962), p. 418 f.
12. Johann Christoph Adelung, *Versuch eines vollständigen grammatisch-kritischen Wörterbuchs der Hochdeutschen Mundart*. 5 vols. (Leipzig, 1774–86, second edition, 1793–1801).
13. Werner Besch, *Sprachlandschaften und Sprachausgleich im 15. Jahrhundert, Studien zur Erforschung der spätmittelalterlichen Schreibdialekte und zur Entstehung der neuhochdeutschen Schriftsprache* (Munich, 1967); Johannes Erben expresses important reservations to Besch's theses in his review, *Beiträge zur Geschichte der deutschen Sprache und Literatur*, LIV (1968), 404–411.
14. For a brief comparison of a sample passage see Bach, *Geschichte*, p. 292; see also John T. Waterman, *A History of the German Language* (Seattle, 1966), p. 130 and Hans Eggers, *Deutsche Sprachgeschichte*, III. *Das Frühneuhochdeutsche* (Hamburg, 1969), pp. 152–172.
15. August Langen, "Deutsche Sprachgeschichte vom Barock bis zur Gegenwart," in Wolfgang Stammler, *Deutsche Philologie im Aufriß*, I. col. 1028.
16. Cf. Max Hermann Jellinek, *Geschichte der neuhochdeutschen Grammatik*, (Heidelberg, 1913), I, 76.

17. C. M. Wieland, "Über die Frage Was ist Hochdeutsch? und einige damit verwandte Gegenstände." *Sämmtliche Werke*, XLII, Suppl. VI (Leipzig, 1798), 293.
18. For a recent scholarly treatment of this subject from a dialectological point of view see H. Henne, "Das Problem des 'Meissnischen Deutsch' oder 'Was ist Hochdeutsch' im 18. Jahrhundert," *Zeitschrift für Mundartforschung,* XXXV (1968), 109–29.
19. Quoted from Paul Kretschmer, *Wortgeographie der hochdeutschen Umgangssprache* (Göttingen, 1916), p. 1.
20. Martin Luther, *Werke. Kritische Gesamtausgabe.* Zweite Abteilung: *Tischreden* (Weimar, 1912), I, 524 f, No. 1040.

Chapter 4

1. Conversations of Goethe with Eckermann, March 27, 1831.
2. H. B. Garland, *Lessing: The Founder of Modern German Literature*, 2nd. ed. (New York, 1962), p. 120.
3. J. G. Robertson, A *History of German Literature* (New York, 1902), p. 271.
4. These poets belonged mainly to the Second Silesian School, which owes much of its style to Spanish Gongorism (*estilo culto*) and Italian Marinism. Common to these movements, to which English Euphuism and the French *précieuses* should be reckoned, is an artistic affectation which generally takes the form of elaborate antithesis and depends upon heavy ornamentation and other stylistic luxuriances. In the hands of the Germans this European mannerism reached such excesses that Gottsched felt it necessary to fight this bombast, verbal virtuosity, and frivolity that had led German literature more and more towards stagnation.
5. *Die vernünftigen Tadlerinnen*, I, no. 11.
6. Gottsched himself lists the main sources of his *Critical Poetics*. In the preface to the second edition (1737) he writes: "I have no hesitation on the occasion of this new edition to confess that I did not think up all my critical rules and judgments of old and new poetry myself but learned them from the greatest masters and experts of poetry: Aristotle, Horace, Longinus, Scaliger, Boileau, Bossu, Dacier, Perrault, Bouhours, Fénelon, St. Évremond, La Motte, Corneille, Racine, Des Caliéres and Furetiére; and finally also Shaftsbury, Addison, Steele, Castelvetro, Muralt, and Voltaire."
7. Robertson, p. 248.
8. Gianvicenzo Gravina's (1664–1718) *Della Ragion Poetica*, published in 1716, deals with the real and the invented in poetry. His "novelty is the mother of the marvelous" expresses an attitude widely held in European criticism in Bodmer's day. Gravina's well known poetics was probably one of the basic sources for this change of critical thought in the eighteenth century.
9. *Conversations*, November 9, 1824.
10. A few other eighteenth-century Germans should be mentioned in this connection also. Christian Günther (1695–1723) did not succumb to the bombastic fashion of his time but wrote intensely personal lyrics about the pain and happiness of love. Barthold Heinrich Brockes (1680–1747) also freed himself from the prevailing mannerism and created poetry with a genuine feeling for nature. His *Irdisches Vergnügen in Gott*, a three-volume collection, owes much to Alexander Pope's pastoral poems and to James Thomson's *Seasons*. Ewald von Kleist (1715–1759) shared in this revival

of nature poetry; his *Der Frühling* (*Spring*), modeled also on Thomson's *Seasons*, represents a sentimental turn to nature with a pronounced tendency to *Schwärmerei*, the rapture that Klopstock was to make respectable.

11. George Saintsbury, *A History of Criticism and Literary Taste in Europe from the Earliest Texts to the Present Day*. III: *Modern Criticism* (London & Edinburgh, 1904), p. 34. René Wellek also quotes this harsh judgment in his *History of Modern Criticism*, I (New Haven, 1955) and admits to understanding Saintsbury's disappointment while offering generally a more balanced view of Schiller's critical achievement.

12. Numbers 101–104 (written together as one number) of the *Hamburg Dramaturgy*. All quotes are from the Helen Zimmern translation, reprinted by Dover (New York, 1962) and edited by Victor Lange.

13. "When I observe order I have a sense of pleasure; and so, when I observe a similarity of imitation to original, I react in the same way." Johann Elias Schlegel, *Abhandlung von der Nachahmung* (*On Imitation*, 1742), Sect. 15. This important contemporary of Lessing was virtually without influence as critic during his lifetime. He was praised as a dramatist, but his essay *On Imitation* must also be regarded as one of German criticism's most significant treatments of the problem in the eighteenth century. Cf. my introduction to the English edition of this work, *Schlegel: On Imitation and Other Essays* (New York, 1965), pp. xix–xxv. For a recent account of *mimesis* covering principally the older criticism, see John D. Boyd, *The Function of Mimesis and Its Decline* (Cambridge, 1968).

14. For a full discussion of the aesthetic implications of the *ut pictura poesis* theory, see Jean Hagstrum, *The Sister Arts* (Chicago, 1958).

15. *Laocoön*, chapter 4. This and subsequent quotations are from *Laocoön: Gotthold Ephraim Lessing*. Trans., intro. Edward Allen McCormick (Indianapolis & New York, 1962).

16. As quoted in the Cotta edition of Lessing's collected works, *Sämtliche Werke*, ed. H. Göring, 20 vols. (Stuttgart, 1883–1885), V, 56.

17. *ibid.*, V, 50.

18. Cf. Garland, p. 122: "The tragic ending of man's struggle for knowledge was unacceptable to an age which believed so firmly in moral progress."

19. *Hamburg Dramaturgy*, no. 12.

20. *Vorrede zu Thomsons Trauerspielen* (*Preface to Thomson's Tragedies*, 1756).

21. *Hamburg Dramaturgy*, no. 14.

22. *Conversations*, October 12, 1825.

23. *A History of Modern Criticism*. I: *The Later Eighteenth Century*, p. 197.

24. James Boyd, *Goethe's Knowledge of English Literature* (Oxford, 1932), p. 29.

25. Cf. Goethe's essay of 1799, *Über Wahrheit und Wahrscheinlichkeit der Kunstwerke*: "A perfect work of art is a work of the human spirit, and in this sense a work of nature also. But by uniting the disparate objects into a whole and including even the most common by virtue of their importance and dignity, it is above nature."

Chapter 5

1. German scholarship distinguishes between *Klassik* and *Klassizismus*. The style and world view of *Klassizismus* are characterized not only by the unoriginal imitation of existing forms but also by the acceptance of values which may appear alien or meaningless since they are superimposed by one age on another. The literature of the *Klassik*, in contrast, born of a crisis

in man's self-knowledge, tries to formulate a new view of man's relationship to the world and ultimately to the universe.

Presently there are no complete modern translations available of either Goethe's or Schiller's works. Recent editions of Goethe's works in German are the *Hamburger Ausgabe*, ed. Erich Trunz, 14 vols. (Hamburg: Wegener, 1948–1960) plus 4 vols. of letters, ed. K. R. Mandelknow (Hamburg: Wegener, 1962–1967) and the *Gedenkausgabe der Werke, Briefe und Gespräche*, ed. Ernst Beutler, 24 vols. (Zürich: Artemis, 1948–1964). Current editions of Schiller's works are the *Sämtliche Werke*, ed. Gerhard Fricke, 5 vols. (München: Hanser, 1958–1959) and *Sämtliche Werke*, 5 vols. (München: Winkler, 1968).

Suggested further readings: *The Permanent Goethe*, ed., selected, intr. Thomas Mann (New York: Dial, 1948); *Goethe: Wisdom and Experience*, selected by L. Curtius, trans., ed. H. Weigand (New York: Pantheon, 1949); *Goethe's Literary Essays*, selected by J. E. Spingarn (New York: Ungar, 1964); W. H. Bruford, *Culture and Society in Classical Weimar* (Cambridge: Cambridge University Press, 1962); R. B. Farrell, "Classicism," in J. M. Ritchie, *Periods in German Literature* (London: Wolff, 1966), pp. 99–120; Arnold Bergstraesser, *Goethe's Image of Man and Society* (Freiburg: Herder, 1962); Barker Fairley, *A Study of Goethe* (Oxford: Clarendon, 1947); Richard Friedenthal, *Goethe: His Life and Times* (Cleveland: World Publishing Co., 1965); Ronald Gray, *Goethe. A Critical Introduction* (Cambridge: Harvard University Press, 1967); Henry Hatfield, *Goethe. A Critical Introduction* (Cambridge: Harvard University Press, 1964); Erich Heller, *The Disinherited Mind* (Cambridge: Cambridge University Press, 1952); Victor Lange, ed., *Goethe. A Collection of Critical Essays* (Englewood Cliffs: Prentice Hall, 1968); George Henry Lewis, *The Life of Goethe* (1855, new ed., New York: Ungar, 1965); Fritz Strich, *Goethe and World Literature* (London: Routledge & Paul, 1949); Karl Viëtor, *Goethe, the Poet* (Cambridge: Harvard University Press, 1949); Karl Viëtor, *Goethe, the Thinker* (Cambridge: Harvard University Press, 1950).

Thomas Carlyle, *The Life of Schiller* (London, 1872); John R. Frey, "American Schiller Literature. A Bibliography," in John R. Frey, ed., *Schiller 1759/1959. Commemorative American Studies* (Urbana: University of Illinois, 1959), pp. 203–213; Frederick Norman, ed., *Schiller. Bicentenary Lectures* (London: Institute of Germanic Languages & Literature, 1960); *Schiller in England. A Bibliography*. Compiled under the direction of R. Pick (London: University of London, 1961); Ernst Ludwig Stahl, *Friedrich Schiller's Drama. Theory and Practice* (Oxford: Clarendon, 1954); Elizabeth M. Wilkinson, *Schiller. Poet or Philosopher?* (Oxford: Clarendon, 1961); William Witte, *Schiller* (Oxford: Blackwell, 1949); A. Leslie Willson, ed., *A Schiller Symposium in Observance of the Bicentenary of Schiller's Birth* (Austin: University of Texas, 1960).

2. See Goethe's letters to Buchholtz (February 14, 1814), to Schubarth (July 8, 1818), to Boisserée (August 19, 1825), to Zelter (June 6, 1825 and November 13, 1829), and the important letter to Carlyle (July 20, 1827), also his remarks to Riemer (November 18, 1806), to Müller (April 7, 1830), and to Eckermann (March 11, 1832).

3. See Goethe's letter to Humboldt (March 17, 1832), and his observation to Odyniec (August 25, 1829).

4. A similar sentiment was expressed in 1869 by Matthew Arnold, who greatly admired Goethe: ". . . culture being a pursuit of our total perfection by means of getting to know, on all matters which most concern us, the best

which has been thought and said in the world; and through this knowledge, turning a stream of fresh and free thought upon our stock notions and habits, which we now follow staunchly but mechanically. . . ." *Culture and Anarchy* (Cambridge, 1935), p. 6; see also pp. 27 f., 44 f.

5. This view provides for unintentional change in the pattern of a culture. Any action undertaken for an immediate end may bring about in the future some unforeseen pattern. See Schiller, "Why Study World History?" ("Was heißt und zu welchem Ende studiert man Universalgeschichte?").

6. See "The Legislation of Lycurgus and Solon."

7. See "World History."

8. The reader is urged to consult *On the Aesthetic Education of Man*, ed. and trans. Elizabeth M. Wilkinson and L. A. Willoughby (Oxford: Clarendon Press, 1967). The editors' stimulating introduction should prove most rewarding.

9. Letter to Augustenburg, July 13, 1793.

10. The translations of poems are adapted from the English versions of Bowring, Longfellow, et al. The reader should consult the recent translations by either Barker Fairley, *Selected Poems* (New York: Rinehart, 1955) or Edwin H. Zeydel, *Goethe, The Lyrist* (Chapel Hill: University of North Carolina Press, 1955) and *Poems of Goethe* (Chapel Hill: University of North Carolina Press, 1957).

11. All Egmont quotations are from: *Egmont*, English version by Michael Hamburger in Eric Bentley, ed., *The Classic Theatre* II: *Five German Plays* (Anchor Books, 1959), pp. 1–91.

12. Readily available in the recent translation by Charles E. Passage (New York: Ungar, 1963). See also James Boyd, *Goethe's "Iphigenie of Tauris,"* *An Interpretation and Critical Analysis* (Oxford: Blackwell, 1942) and J. M. Browning, "The Humanity of Goethe's Iphigenie," *German Quarterly*, XXX (1957), 98–113.

13. Many excellent translations are available. Among them: *Faust*, trans. Bayard Taylor, intro. Victor Lange (New York: Modern Library, 1950); the Bayard Taylor ed. rev. and ed. Stuart Atkins (New York: Collier Book, 1962); *Faust*, trans. and intro. Philip Wayne (Penguin Book, 1959); *Goethe's Faust*, trans. and intro. Walter Kaufmann (Anchor Book, 1963); *Faust*, trans. Charles E. Passage (Indianapolis: Bobbs Merrill, 1965).

Suggested further readings: Stuart Atkins, *Goethe's Faust. A Literary Analysis* (Cambridge: Harvard University Press, 1958); Erich Heller, *The Artist's Journey into the Interior* (New York: Random House, 1965); Harold Jantz, *Faust as a Renaissance Man* (Philadelphia: University of Pennsylvania Press, 1951); Eudo C. Mason, *Goethe's Faust. Its Genesis and Purport* (Berkeley: University of California Press, 1967); George Santayana, *Three Philosophical Poets* (New York: Doubleday, 1953).

14. Kenneth Rexroth, "Classics Revisited—LXXXIV: Goethe," *Saturday Review*, April 19, 1969.

15. English version by James Kirkup, available in Bentley, *The Classic Theatre*, pp. 93–206.

16. All *Wallenstein* quotations are from the translation by Charles E. Passage (New York: Ungar, 1958). Reprinted by permission of Frederick Ungar Publishing Co., Inc.

17. Translated by Joseph Mellish and adapted by Eric Bentley in *The Classic Theatre*, pp. 207–311; also *Mary Stuart. The Maid of Orleans*, trans. Charles E. Passage (New York: Ungar, 1961).

18. All quotations are from *The Bride of Messina. William Tell. Demetrius*, trans. Charles E. Passage (New York: Ungar, 1962).

Chapter 6

1. Throughout this chapter, the word "romantic" and its derivatives will be capitalized when applied to the German Romanticists and their program. It will be uncapitalized when used of general aesthetic qualities (even by the Romanticists) or applied to medieval and Renaissance literature. The reader should find the following works on German Romanticism and Romanticists useful: Ernst Behler, *Friedrich Schlegel* (Hamburg, 1966); Hans Eichner, "Friedrich Schlegel's Theory of Romantic Poetry," *PMLA*, LXXI (1956), 1018–1041; John Gearey, *Heinrich von Kleist* (Philadelphia, 1968); Michael Hamburger, *Reason and Energy* (New York, 1957); Rudolf Haym, *Die romantische Schule* (Hildesheim, 1961); Frederick Hiebel, *Novalis* (Chapel Hill, 1954); H. A. Korff, *Geist der Goethezeit: III. Frühromantik, IV. Hochromantik* (Leipzig, 1958–1959); S. S. Prawer, ed., *The Romantic Period in Germany* (London, 1970); Lawrence Ryan, *Friedrich Hölderlin* (Stuttgart, 1962); Oskar Seidlin, *Versuche über Eichendorff* (Göttingen, 1965); Emil Staiger, "Die reissende Zeit: Clemens Brentano: Auf dem Rhein," *Die Zeit als Einbildungskraft des Dichters*, 2. Auflage (Zürich, 1953), pp. 21–106; Marianne Thalmann, *The Romantic Fairy Tale* (Ann Arbor, 1964); Ralph Tymms, *German Romantic Literature* (London, 1955), René Wellek, "The Concept of Romanticism in Literary History," *Concepts of Criticism* (New Haven, 1963), pp. 128–198; and *A History of Modern Criticism: II. The Romantic Age* (New Haven, 1955); E. H. Zeydel, *Ludwig Tieck* (Princeton, 1935).
2. Cf. E. R. Curtius, "European Literature and the Latin Middle Ages," Bollingen Series, XXXVI (New York, 1953), 30 ff.
3. Cf. R. Immerwahr, "The First Romantic Aesthetics," *Modern Language Quarterly*, XXI (1960), 3–26.
4. Cf. Hans-Joachim Mähl, *Die Idee des goldenen Zeitalters im Werk des Novalis* (Heidelberg, 1965), and Hans Wolfgang Kuhn, *Der Apokalyptiker und die Politik* (Freiburg i. Br., 1961), pp. 17 ff.
5. A strikingly similar cyclical view of cultural history is found in the twentieth-century poet William Butler Yeats.
6. "Youth" in *Some Poems of Friedrich Hölderlin*, trans. Frederic Prokosch, "The Poets of the Year" (Norfolk, Conn., 1943), unnumbered pages. Other translations of interest to the reader are: *Selected Poems of Friedrich Hölderlin*, trans. J. B. Leishman, 2nd ed. (London, 1954), and *Hölderlin: His Poems*, trans. Michael Hamburger, 2nd ed. (New York, 1952). Critical prose cannot convey even a dim impression of the depth and grandeur of these poems, the breathtaking beauty of their imagery, the vast scope of their symbols. But their difficulty has been a challenge to translators, and at times Prokosch, Leishman, or Hamburger recapture their meaning and something of their beauty. For a summary of their ideas, the student is referred to the introduction of Hamburger's edition.
7. *Hyperion or The Hermit in Greece*, trans. Willard R. Trask (London, 1959).
8. Translation of Prokosch; the last word of the poem (*Fahnen*) is more correctly rendered "weathercocks" (Hamburger) or "weather-vanes" (Leishman).
9. The original titles of the three essays mentioned are "Raffaels Erscheinung," "Einige Worte über Allgemeinheit, Toleranz und Menschenliebe in der Kunst," and "Von zwei wunderbaren Sprachen und deren geheimnisvoller Kraft." The most useful edition of Wackenroder's writings is *Herzensergie-*

415

βungen eines kunstliebenden Klosterbruders together with Wackenroder's contributions to the *Phantasien über die Kunst für Freunde der Kunst*, ed. A. Gillies (Oxford, 1948).

10. Translations from Wackenroder are my own. Original text on p. 42 of the Gillies edition.
11. *Ibid.*, p. 55.
12. Translations of works by Tieck, F. Schlegel, A. W. Schlegel, Novalis, Brentano, Arnim, Hoffmann, Eichendorff, Fouqué, and Chamisso can be found in *The German Classics*, ed. Kuno Francke (New York, 1913). All quotations, unless otherwise indicated, are from this edition.
13. Cf. Raymond Immerwahr, "Der blonde Eckbert as a Poetic Confession," *Germanic Quarterly*, XXXIV (1961), Marianne Thalmann, "The Tieck Fairy Tale," *The Romantic Fairy Tale* (Ann Arbor, 1964), and Victoria L. Rippere, "Ludwig Tieck's 'Der blonde Eckbert': A Psychological Reading," *PMLA*, LXXXV (1970).
14. *The Runenberg* and *The Fair-Haired Eckbert*, trans. Thomas Carlyle, *German Romance* (New York, 1898).
15. Friedrich Schlegel, *Dialogue on Poetry and Literary Aphorisms*, translated, introduced, and annotated Ernest Behler and Roman Struc (University Park, Pa., and London, 1968), p. 101. This translation is referred to below as "Behler-Struc."
16. Cf. Ernst Behler, "The Origins of the Romantic Literary Theory," *Colloquia Germanica* (1968).
17. See "Behler-Struc."
18. "Vom ästhetischen Werthe der griechischen Komödie" ("On the Aesthetic Value of Greek Comedy"), 1794, in Friedrich Schlegel, *Seine prosaischen Jugendschriften*, ed. J. Minor (Wien, 1882), I, 11–20. For a discussion of this essay, cf. R. Immerwahr, *The Esthetic Intent of Tieck's Fantastic Comedy* (Washington University Studies, New Series, No. 22, St. Louis, 1958), pp. 22–29.
19. The word "form" does not occur in the original. It reads here "im Äußern, in der Ausführung" (more literally: "externally, in their style"). Cf. *Kritische Friedrich-Schlegel-Ausgabe*, ed. Ernst Behler et al., II: *Charakteristiken und Kritiken I (1796–1801)*, ed. Hans Eichner (München, Paderborn, Wien, Zürich, 1967), 152. Quoted from Behler-Struc, pp. 131, 126.
20. This pseudonym, the Latin word for "new land," had been used by some of Hardenberg's medieval ancestors who literally cleared new land; Hardenberg revived it with symbolic reference to the new land of the spirit which he was clearing.
21. Novalis, *Hymns to the Night and Other Selected Writings*, trans. and intro. Charles E. Passage (New York, 1960), p. 5.
22. Novalis, *The Novices of Sais*, tr. by Ralph Manheim (New York, 1949). This attractive little volume is illustrated with 60 drawings by Paul Klee, which were not, however, intended for this purpose and do not seem to be arranged so as to bear on the text.
23. Translated by Passage in *Hymns*.
24. Translation is my own from Novalis, *Schriften*, ed. Paul Kluckhohn and Richard Samuel, 2nd ed., III (Stuttgart, 1968), 302.
25. Translation in *Tales from Hoffmann*, ed. J. M. Cohen (London, 1951). Contains also *Mlle. de Scudéry*.
26. The tragic dimensions of these narrations are emphasized by Horst S. Daemmrich, "E. T. A. Hoffmann's Tragic Heroes," *Germanic Review* (1970), and René Wellek, "Why Read E. T. A. Hoffmann?" *Midway* (1967).

27. The scholar who has done most to illuminate Eichendorff's symbolism is Oskar Seidlin. One of his essays, "Eichendorff's Symbolic Landscape," is in his *Essays in German and Comparative Literature* (Chapel Hill, 1961), pp. 141–160.
28. Heinrich von Kleist, *The Prince of Homburg*, trans. and intro. Charles E. Passage (New York, 1956).
29. Trans. John T. Krumpelmann (New York, 1962).
30. A translation of this story is included in *The Marquise of O. and Other Stories*, trans. and intro. M. Greenberg (New York, 1960).

Chapter 7

1. Suggested further readings for the period are: Ernst Alker, *Die deutsche Literatur im 19 Jahrhundert (1832–1914)*, 2nd rev. ed. (Stuttgart, 1962); George J. Becker, ed., *Documents of Modern Literary Realism*, (Princeton, 1963); Edwin K. Bennett, A *History of the German Novelle*, 2nd rev. ed. (Cambridge, 1961); Hugo Bieber, *Der Kampf um die Tradition: Die deutsche Dichtung im europäischen Geistesleben 1830–1880* (Stuttgart, 1928); Hermann Boeschenstein, *German Literature of the Nineteenth Century* (London, 1969); Ernest Bramsted, *Aristocracy and the Middle Classes in Germany: Social Types in German Literature 1830–1900* (Chicago, 1964); Richard Brinkmann, *Wirklichkeit und Illusion* (Tübingen, 1957); Heinz Otto Burger, "Der Realismus des neunzehnten Jahrhunderts," in *Annalen der deutschen Literatur*, ed. H. O. Burger *Symbolismus 1820–1885* (Gütersloh, 1966); Peter Demetz, *Marx, Engels, and the Poets*, rev. and enl. ed. (Chicago, 1967); Norbert Fuerst, *The Victorian Age of German Literature* (University Park and London, 1966); Martin Greiner, *Zwischen Biedermeier und Bourgeoisie* (Leipzig, 1953); Richard Hamann and Jost Hermand, *Naturalismus* (Berlin, 1959); Arnold Hauser, *Social History of Art*, 2 vols. (New York, 1951); Sigfrid Hoefert, *Das Drama des Naturalismus* (Stuttgart, 1968); F. W. Kaufmann, *German Dramatists of the 19th Century* (Los Angeles, 1940); Franz Koch, *Idee und Wirklichkeit: Deutsche Dichtung zwischen Romantik und Wirklichkeit*, 2 vols. (Düsseldorf, 1956); Georg Lukács, *Deutsche Realisten des 19. Jahrhunderts* (Berlin, 1951); Bruno Markwardt, *Geschichte der deutschen Poetik*, IV: *Das 19. Jahrhundert* (Berlin, 1959); Fritz Martini, *Forschungsbericht zur deutschen Literatur in der Zeit des Realismus* (Stuttgart, 1962); Fritz Martini, *Deutsche Literatur im bürgerlichen Realismus 1848–1898* (Stuttgart, 1962); Roy Pascal, *The German Novel* (Toronto, 1956); Friedrich Sengle, *Arbeiten zur deutschen Literatur 1750–1850* (Stuttgart, 1965); Walter Silz, *Realism and Reality: Studies in the German Novelle of Poetic Realism* (Chapel Hill, 1954); "Skizze zur Geschichte der deutschen Nationalliteratur von den Anfängen der deutschen Arbeiterbewegung bis zur Gegenwart," *Weimarer Beiträge*, V (1964), 643–816; J. P. Stern, *Re-interpretations: Seven Studies in Nineteenth-Century German Literature* (New York, 1964); René Wellek, "The Concept of Realism in Literary Scholarship," *Neophilologus*, XLIV (1960), 1–20; Benno von Wiese, *Deutsche Dichter des 19. Jahrhunderts* (Berlin, 1969); Alfred Zäch, "Der Realismus," in *Deutsche Literaturgeschichte in Grundzügen*, ed. Bruno Boesch, 2nd ed. (Bern, 1961), pp. 348–372.
2. M. J. Norst, in a discussion of the term "Biedermeier" (*Periods in German Literature*, ed. J. M. Ritchie, London, 1966, pp. 147–168), has traced the emergence, history, and use of this category. He has pointed out that many

literary historians ignore it, that it has not been generally accepted, and that, at present, its value as a literary term is doubtful.

3. Raimund's first literary achievement was *Der Barometermacher auf der Zauberinsel* (*The Barometer Maker on the Magic Island*, 1823); it left the efforts of the other authors of Viennese popular drama far behind and established Raimund's reputation as a dramatic poet. Of his later plays, *Der Alpenkönig und der Menschenfeind* (*The King of the Alps and the Misanthrope*, 1828) and *Der Verschwender* (*The Spendthrift*, 1833) have become well known.

4. The outstanding representative of this group was Cecilia Böhl von Faber (1796–1877). Her *novelas de costumbres* established the regional novel in Spain.

5. This designation for a trend in the literary activity of the nineteenth century has become more firmly entrenched in the history of German literature than the term *Biedermeier*, though its validity has also been questioned. Of the recent literature on the Young German movement, the following are particularly useful: C. P. Magill, "Young Germany: A Revaluation," *German Studies Presented to L. A. Willoughby* (Oxford, 1952), pp. 108–119; Martin Greiner, *Zwischen Biedermeier und Bourgeoisie* (Leipzig, 1953); and F. Kainz and W. Kohlschmidt, "Junges Deutschland," *Reallexikon der deutschen Literaturgeschichte*, I (Berlin, 1958), 781–797.

6. Eugène Sue (1804–1857) had used a similar technique in some of his novels. For further information on Gutzkow's endeavors, see Fritz Martini, *Deutsche Literatur im bürgerlichen Realismus 1848–1898* (Stuttgart, 1962), pp. 412–419.

7. On the echo which the weaver riots in 1844 found in German letters, see Sol Liptzin, *The Weavers in German Literature* (Göttingen, 1926).

8. Ranke was the most prominent German historian of the time (*The History of the Papacy in the Sixteenth and Seventeenth Centuries*, 1834–36; *History of Germany during the Reformation*, 1839–47; and others). His emphasis on the scientific, rather than abstract approach to the study of historical phenomena exerted a positive influence on the activities of his colleagues and disciples.

9. Pestalozzi's writings reflect his pedagogical ideas and educational endeavors; his story *Lienhard und Gertrud* (1781–87 and 1791–92) as well as the series of letters, entitled *Wie Gertrud ihre Kinder lehrt* (*How Gertrud Teaches Her Children*, 1801), have enjoyed a wide popularity.

10. Hebel had published a collection of popular stories and anecdotes in the *Schatzkästlein des rheinischen Hausfreundes* (*Treasure Box of the Rhenish Family Friend*, 1811); they had a didactive purpose and were mainly written for the humble reader.

11. Although Friedrich Wilhelm von Schelling had used the term "poetic realism" in a philosophical context already in 1802, it was Otto Ludwig who first employed it as a literary concept. See his *Gesammelte Schriften*, V (Leipzig, 1891), 458–462. As far as the term Realism is concerned, numerous studies have appeared which seek to clarify its meaning. Among the recent attempts, the following are particularly useful: Richard Brinkmann, *Wirklichkeit und Illusion* (Tübingen, 1957); René Wellek, "The Concept of Realism in Literary Scholarship," *Neophilologus*, XLIV (1960), 1–20; *Documents of Modern Literary Realism*, ed. George J. Becker (Princeton, 1963); J. M. Ritchie, "Realism," *Periods in German Literature*, ed. J. M. Ritchie (London, 1966), pp. 170–195; "Realism: A Symposium," *Monatshefte*, XLIX (1967), 97–130.

12. Much of Hebbel's deliberation can be traced to the thought of Hegel, who had emphasized the unity of all reality by proclaiming that continually

merging opposites are constantly bringing forth new phenomena. Hebbel coupled Hegel's dialectic with Schopenhauer's doctrine of an all-powerful world will, and was also attracted by the latter's emphasis on contemplation and art.

13. *Gottfried Keller im Spiegel seiner Werke*, ed. Alfred Zäch (Zürich, 1952), p. 154.

14. Hermann Boeschenstein, *German Literature of the Nineteenth Century* (London, 1969), p. 122.

15. In this connection it should be noted that the teachings of Heinrich von Treitschke (1834–1896) had already left their imprint on German thought and gave rise to a school of historical thinking which glorified the ascent of Prussia and roused nationalistic sentiments.

16. Groth's best-known work is his *Quickborn* (1853–54); it became the most noted collection of verse in Low German and assured the author's high reputation in Northern Germany. On the development of Low German literature, see Gerhard Cordes, "Niederdeutsche Mundartdichtung," *Deutsche Philologie im Aufriß*, ed. W. Stammler, II (Berlin, 1960), 2405–2443.

17. See H. Henel, *The Poetry of Conrad Ferdinand Meyer* (Madison, 1954).

18. For further information on Heyse's theory, see Kenneth Negus, "Paul Heyse's Novellentheorie: A Revaluation," *The Germanic Review*, XL (1965), 173–191.

19. Haeckel, Bölsche, and others spread and popularized the theories of Darwin in Germany and Austria. Haeckel, a professor of Zoology at the University of Jena, gave lectures on the principles of evolution and brought before the public works such as *Die natürliche Schöpfungsgeschichte* (*Natural History of Creation*, 1868); Bölsche applied the new views to the theory of literature in his *Die naturwissenschaftlichen Grundlagen der Poesie* (*Scientific Foundations of Poesy*, 1887).

20. Theodor Fontane, "Die Familie Selicke," *Schriften und Glossen zur europäischen Literatur*, II (Zürich, 1967), 442–445.

Chapter 8

1. See William Eickhorst, *Decadence in German Fiction* (Denver, 1953). For a comprehensive study of Impressionism in art and literature, see R. Hamann and J. Hermand, *Impressionismus. Deutsche Kunst und Kultur von der Gründerzeit bis zum Expressionismus*, III (Berlin, 1960).

2. For an excellent study of the Renaissance fad, see Walther Rehm, "Der Renaissancekult um 1900 und seine Überwindung," *Zeitschrift für deutsche Philologie* LIV (1929), 296–328.

3. Stefan George, *The Works of Stefan George*, rendered into English by Olga Marx and Ernst Morwitz. "University of North Carolina Studies in the Germanic Languages and Literatures," No. 2 (Chapel Hill, 1949), p. 115.

4. Rainer Maria Rilke, *Selected Works*. Vol. II: *Poetry*. Trans. J. B. Leishman (New York, 1967), p. 48, poem 45. Copyright © Hogarth Press, Ltd., 1960. Reprinted by permission of New Directions Publishing Corp. Where literal accuracy is important, I have elsewhere cited lines in my own translation.

5. *Ibid.*, p. 91, poem 8.

6. *Ibid.*, p. 240.

7. A few comprehensive treatments of Expressionism: Richard Samuel and Hinton R. Thomas, *Expressionism in German Life, Literature and the Theatre (1910–1924)* (Cambridge, England, 1939); Walter H. Sokel, *The*

Writer in Extremis. Expressionism in Twentieth-Century German Literature (Stanford, 1959) (contains a very useful bibliography); Wolfgang Rothe, ed., *Expressionismus als Literatur, Gesammelte Studien* (Bern, München, 1969).

8. Rilke, *op. cit.*, p. 273.
9. For an extensive outline of Nietzsche's influence on German literature with copious bibliographical references, see: Peter Pütz, *Friedrich Nietzsche* (Stuttgart, 1967) (Sammlung Metzler, 62).
10. "Kreislauf," trans. Francis Golffing in: E. B. Ashton, ed., *Primal Vision. Selected Writings of Gottfried Benn* (Norfolk, Conn., no date), p. 215. All rights reserved; reprinted by permission of New Directions Publishing Corp.
11. Additional information on expressionist drama may be found in Hugo F. Garten, *Modern German Drama* (London, 1964²). A useful bibliography: Claude Hill and Ralph Ley, *The Drama of German Expressionism: A German-English Bibliography*, Univ. of N. Carolina Studies in Germanic Lang. and Lit., No. 28.
12. Edson M. Chick, *Ernst Barlach.* "Twayne World Authors Series, 26" (New York, 1967), p. 79.
13. For greater detail on Dada see R. Motherwell, ed., *Dada Painters and Poets, An Anthology* (New York, 1951) (with bibliography); L. W. Forster, *Poetry of Significant Nonsense* (Cambridge, England, 1962); Hans Richter, *Dada* (London, 1965); W. Rothe, ed., *Expressionismus als Literatur*. Part 5: "Der Dadaismus," pp. 719–761.
14. Good examples of fruitful revaluation of Dada "nonsense" poetry are L. W. Forster, cited above, and R. W. Last, *Hans Arp, The Poet of Dadaism* (London, 1969).

Chapter 9

1. The following books should prove useful to the reader: Hugo Arntzen, *Der moderne deutsche Roman* (Heidelberg, 1962); Felix Bertaux, *A Panorama of German Literature 1861–1931* (New York, 1935); J. L. Blotner, *The Political Novel* (Garden City, 1955); H. Boeschenstein, *The German Novel, 1939–1944* (Toronto, 1949); H. Friedmann and O. Mann, *Deutsche Literatur im 20. Jahrhundert. Strukturen und Gestalten*, 2 vols. (Heidelberg, 1961); K. A. Horst, *Die deutsche Literatur der Gegenwart* (München, 1957); Walter Jens, *Deutsche Literatur der Gegenwart. Themen, Stile, Tendenzen* (München, 1962); Wolfgang Kayser, *Entstehung und Krise des modernen Romans* (Stuttgart, 1961); Victor Lange, *Modern German Literature, 1870–1940* (Ithaca, N.Y., 1945); F. Martini, *Das Wagnis der Sprache* (Stuttgart, 1964); E. E. Noth, *The Contemporary German Novel* (Milwaukee, 1961); R. Pascal, *The German Novel* (London, 1965); Lawrence M. Price, *The Reception of United States Literature in Germany* (Chapel Hill, 1966); Walter Sokel, *The Writer in Extremis* (Stanford, 1959); H. M. Waidson, *The Modern German Novel. A Mid-twentieth Century Survey* (London, 1959); Werner Welzig, *Der deutsche Roman im 20. Jahrhundert* (Stuttgart, 1967); Theodore Ziolkowski, *Dimensions of the Modern Novel* (Princeton, 1969).
2. Neo-Romanticism, like Realism, is contiguous to Impressionism but professes an opposite intention. The focus of Impressionism rests more on the character of the writer than on the external world which he perceives. When that happens, mood, feeling, and then personalized symbols, subjective concepts, even fantasy become dominant in remaking the outer

images into a desired, idealized world, one that gives the reader a picture of an idyllic or imaginative realm.

Chapter 10

1. Suggested further readings for the period under consideration: Karl August Horst, *Kritischer Führer durch die deutsche Literatur der Gegenwart* (München, 1962); Harry T. Moore, *Twentieth-Century German Literature* (New York/London, 1967); *Handbuch der deutschen Gegenwartsliteratur*, ed. Hermann Kunisch (München, 1965); Franz Lennartz, *Deutsche Dichter und Schriftsteller unserer Zeit* (Stuttgart, 1963).

2. On literature during the Third Reich see Josef Wulf, *Literatur und Dichtung im Dritten Reich: Eine Dokumentation* (Gütersloh, 1963); Dietrich Strothmann, *Nationalsozialistische Literaturpolitik: Ein Beitrag zur Publizistik im Dritten Reich* (Bonn, 1963); Hildegard Brenner, *Die Kunstpolitik des Nationalsozialismus* (Reinbek, 1963).

3. On literature of the inner and outer emigration see also Matthias Wegner, *Exil und Literatur: Deutsche Schriftsteller im Ausland 1933–1945* (Frankfurt/Bonn, 1967); William K. Pfeiler, *German Literature in Exile: The Concern of the Poets* (University of Nebraska Studies, 1957); Walter A. Berendsohn, *Die humanistische Front: Einführung in die deutsche Emigranten-Literatur* (Zürich, 1946); Harald von Koenigswald, *Die Gewaltlosen: Dichtung im Widerstand gegen den Nationalsozialismus* (Herborn, 1962); Charles W. Hoffmann, *Opposition Poetry in Nazi Germany* (Berkeley, 1962).

4. All translations are mine unless otherwise indicated.

5. Translated by E. B. Ashton; G. Benn, *Primal Vision* (New York: New Directions, 1958), p. 51.

6. On post-war literature see *Deutschland: Kulturelle Entwicklungen seit 1945*, ed. Paul Schallück (München, 1969); *Deutsche Literatur seit 1945 in Einzeldarstellungen*, ed. Dietrich Weber (Stuttgart, 1968); Hermann Pongs, *Dichtung im gespaltenen Deutschland* (Stuttgart, 1966); Hans Mayer, *Deutsche Literatur seit Thomas Mann* (Reinbek, 1968); Marcel Reich-Ranicki, *Deutsche Literatur in Ost und West: Prosa seit 1945* (München, 1963); Marcel Reich-Ranicki, *Literatur der kleinen Schritte: Deutsche Schriftsteller heute* (München, 1967); Guy Stern, "Prolegomena zu einer Geschichte der deutschen Nachkriegsprosa," *Colloquia Germanica* (1967).

The Contributors ✍

HORST S. DAEMMRICH is a Phi Beta Kappa graduate of Wayne State University where he received his B.A. and M.A. degrees. At the University of Chicago, where he received his Ph.D., he was a Petersen Kochs and a Goethe Fellow. He has written extensively for leading journals in the field of German literature in the United States and in Germany.

EDWARD DILLER, associate professor of German at the University of Oregon, was granted his D.M.L. at Middlebury College. His B.A. comes from the University of California, Los Angeles and his M.A. from Los Angeles State College. He is the author of two books and many articles in the field of literature and the teaching of foreign languages.

PENRITH GOFF, associate professor of German at Wayne State University, received his B.A. from the University of Kentucky and his M.A. and Ph.D. degrees from the University of California, Los Angeles. In addition to being the author of several reviews and articles on Hugo von Hofmannsthal, he compiled a bibliography on German literature of the Wilhelmian period.

SIGFRID HOEFERT, professor at the University of Waterloo in Canada, received his Ph.D. at the University of Toronto. The author of two books, he is also frequent contributor to German, French and English literary journals.

DIETHER H. HAENICKE studied at the Universities of Marburg and Göttingen and received his Ph.D. degree from the University of Munich. He was a Fulbright scholar in 1963 and 1964. He has edited several volumes of an edition of Ludwig Tieck's writings and has published articles and book reviews both in Germany and the United States. At present he is director of the Wayne State University Junior Year Programs in Munich and Freiburg.

RAYMOND IMMERWAHR is professor and chairman of the German Department at the University of Western Ontario. His

B.A. is from Swarthmore College, his M.A. from Northwestern University, and his Ph.D. from the University of California at Berkeley. His articles on topics ranging from Tieck to Mozart have appeared in leading journals here and in Germany.

GEORGE F. JONES, professor of German at the University of Maryland, received his Ph.D. from Columbia University. A former Rhodes scholar, he is an internationally recognized authority on mediaeval literature. He has published seven books and numerous articles here and abroad.

ALLEN McCORMICK is now at the Graduate Center of the City University of New York where he is professor of German and comparative literature. His B.A. comes from Randolph-Macon College, his Ph.D. from the University of Bern (Switzerland). A recipient of an honorary degree from Dartmouth College, Dr. McCormick has written extensively in literary journals here and in Europe in the field of German literature.

INGRID MERKEL is assistant professor of German at the Catholic University of America where her M.A. and Ph.D. degrees were awarded. She has published a bibliography of German Baroque literature.

STANLEY A. WERBOW received his B.A. from the George Washington University and his Ph.D. from the Johns Hopkins University. Currently professor and chairman of Germanic languages at the University of Texas at Austin, he is the author of two books and innumerable articles in the field of German language.

Index 🌿

429

The manuscript was edited by Leontine Keane. The book was designed by Richard Kinney. Title calligraphy by Gil Hanna. The type face for the text is linotype Electra designed by W. A. Dwiggins in 1935; and the display face is Weiss italic designed by E. R. Weiss about 1926.

The text is printed on Glatfelter RR Antique paper and the book is bound in Columbia Mills' Bayside Vellum and Fictionette cloth over binders' boards. Manufactured in the United States of America.